Give Me
LIBERTY

I believe in the equality of man; and I believe that religious duties consist in doing justice, loving mercy, and endeavoring to make our fellow-creatures happy. —THOMAS PAINE

We are not to expect to be translated from despotism to liberty in a feather bed. —THOMAS JEFFERSON

Men who injure and oppress the people under their administration provoke them to cry out and complain; and then make that very complaint the foundation for new oppressions and prosecutions. —ANDREW HAMILTON

As wolves will appear in sheep's clothing, so superlative knaves and parricides will assume the vesture of virtue and patriotism. —JOSIAH QUINCY

If particular care and attention are not paid to the ladies we are determined to foment a rebellion and will not hold ourselves bound to obey any laws in which we have no voice or representation. —ABIGAIL ADAMS

Liberty cannot be preserved without a general knowledge among the people. —JOHN ADAMS

Give Me LIBERTY

America's Colonial Heritage

By Franklin Folsom

RAND McNALLY & COMPANY Chicago/New York/San Francisco

To Mary Elting, my wife and lifelong collaborator.

Library of Congress Cataloging in Publication Data

Folsom, Franklin, 1907–
  Give me liberty; America's colonial heritage.

  Bibliography: p.
  SUMMARY: A history of the American colonies from
their founding to the adoption of the Declaration of
Independence.
  1. United States—History—Colonial period,
ca. 1600–1775. [1. United States—History—Colonial
period, ca. 1600–1775] I. Title.
E188.F59   973.2   74-16195
ISBN 0-528-81953-4

First printing, 1974

COVER; Liberty Bell, *courtesy Independence National
      Historical Park Collection.*

ENDSHEET; Old State House, *courtesy Historical
      Society of Pennsylvania.*

Preface

As the bicentennial celebration of the Declaration of Independence was drawing near, countless laymen began to glance back at the origins of this country. All these non-historians learned some history—among them the writer of this book. What appears here is the record of my own search for beginnings, and it focuses on the significant tendencies I found, not on the totality of colonial experience, fascinating and obviously important though that is.

The stories I chose to tell, many of them not well known, reflect immensely suggestive aspects of the American past between the time of the establishment of the first real colony in 1564 and the termination of dependence by thirteen colonies in 1776. Connected with these stories there is much of the American past that you can visit in fact as well as in fancy. You can step through actual doors into still-existing rooms where people once did great things. Stand in St. John's Church in Richmond. You are on the exact spot where Patrick Henry stood when he said—and meant—"Give me liberty or give me death." In serene old meeting halls or courthouses or private homes you can, if you will, allow yourself also to enter the turbulent life that once went on there. You may even go further and glance from your new vantage point at the turbulent life of today and perhaps glimpse there a bit of the emerging future.

Most Americans in 1776, headlong in their course, did not dream that their new United States would one day generate new George IIIs. They would not have believed that their great convulsive effort would one day have to be resumed or initiated for important sections of the population —by those who work but do not own, by those who can find no work to do, by women, by Blacks, by Native Americans.

Benjamin Rush, one of the signers of the Declaration of Independence, was more farsighted. Not long after the military conflict with England ended, he said, "The American war is over, but this is far from the case with the American Revolution. Nothing but the first act of the drama is closed."

Even as new freedoms were asserted in 1776, new ways were being invented by which a few could achieve power at the expense of the many. New negatives emerged in answer to the new affirmations. But it is for us to remember that two hundred years ago life was a time of great beginnings. It spoke in a new idiom, strode with a new confidence toward a new dawn. And that dawn should remind us, if it says nothing else, that dawns recur. They break on the world again and again because people need—and dare—to experience them.

FRANKLIN FOLSOM
August 9, 1974

✺ Contents

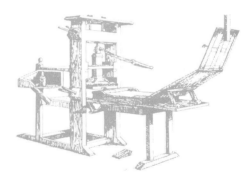

LIST OF FEATURES

Introduction:
The European Background of Colonial North America

In Europe a new type of economic life emerged from feudal society, bringing increased production, commerce, and literacy. A middle class appeared and threatened the landed aristocracy and the clergy who, together, made up the establishment. Feudal lords and the church answered this challenge by opposing the new ideas that appealed to the new class. Dissenters, wanting safety and seeking economic and religious freedom, began to leave Europe.

Patriotism was an invention of the fifteenth and sixteenth centuries in Europe. Like many other inventions it did not seem very impressive at first. Time had to pass before this novelty really began to reshape human lives.

Loyalty on a large national scale was a stranger to the years that stretched back into the Dark Ages. Not that loyalty ran counter to human experience. It certainly did not. But it was not nationalism that called forth this emotion. Local matters prompted men—and men, not women, were usually the recorded actors—to intensities of passionate adherence. And paradoxically, men also felt intense loyalties that were vast and sweeping in scale. These attachments transcended the still-forming state boundary lines, and they provided strong motivations that sometimes drove individuals and groups to violent extremes.

Throughout the Middle Ages, Europe had consisted of very small principalities that were often little more than feudal estates. Each one tended to be self-sufficient, producing little or nothing for export or trade. The princelings who controlled these small units were generally suspicious rivals of their neighbors, although, on occasion, groups of them did unite against a common foe, and all of them supported a common religion, which in turn, supported the feudal system. The medieval Catholic church was an integral part of that system and received great benefits from it.

In Spain, national loyalties began to form when Ferdinand and Isabella, monarchs of two separate kingdoms on the Iberian Peninsula, were married, thus bringing their realms together and forming the nucleus of modern Spain. Using the economic strength which resulted when their countries united, Ferdinand and Isabella were able to fi-

nance the voyages of Columbus, thus expanding the size of the entity to which Spaniards—at least those of the upper class—could feel attachment.

This strong monarchy controlled Spain's international commerce. Consequently, a separate commercial class of Spanish traders and businessmen was slow to develop. In France the situation was different. There a separate commercial class developed, while at the same time French rulers were still trying to subdue petty feudal lords and bring together a nation under a strong central government. The feudal lords, devoted to the status quo, felt threatened by the independent, upstart men of commerce.

The threat was real enough. A revolution was sweeping France and other parts of Europe including England—an upheaval created by traders and businessmen who had developed new markets and were making more and more money, an activity which was not nearly as important in the Middle Ages as it is today. These social innovators needed customers and sources of supply beyond the narrow confines of feudal estates. Inevitably they would look toward America.

As trade expanded, some merchants made so much money that they became bankers, who then supplied capital for a fee to other merchants, thus stimulating the further development of commerce. These early capitalists also lent money to kings, who sought to unite feudal estates under central governments. To unite the principalities it was necessary to abolish the trade barriers that existed between them. Strong kings meant large areas in which commercial capitalists could operate freely—if the kings did not themselves monopolize commerce, as happened in Spain.

The Spanish monarchy, first to explore America, took direct control over colonizing the New World. On the other hand, in France, England, and Holland the colonizing effort came later and was a joint enterprise of commercial capitalists and the monarchy. This expansive effort also interested the craftsmen. They, too, benefited when more cloth and more candles were sold and when more ships were built to make more voyages carrying more cloth and candles and many other products.

In their antagonism toward this growth of commerce, feudal lords had active support from the church. As one element in its anticommercial campaign, the church forbade moneylending by church members. Capitalists who wanted to lend or borrow money found themselves at odds with the clergy, and so did many craftsmen, whose economic lives were hemmed in by the restrictive church.

Nevertheless, commerce and production did increase. At the same time the life of a businessman became more complex. If he was going to conduct expanded operations and keep necessary records, he had to know how to read and write. As a result, literacy, which had been the monopoly of the clergy, began to spread. Increasing numbers of people became not only readers but also searchers after scientific answers to questions that presented themselves as Europeans adventured into new ways of living. Mariners, guiding themselves on earth by their relation to stars in the sky, moved out over the oceans, and the farther they went, the more they needed refined data about celestial bodies. This the astronomers provided, and in order to do so they called improved optical equipment into being. This in turn made possible new advances in fields far removed from astronomy. People could see better with the aid of spectacles. It would be tempting to say that they could now become better readers of the Bible. Certainly they turned increasingly to Holy Writ and found in it much support for their rising opposition to the restrictions imposed on them by church and state. Some of the Scriptures, in fact, appeared to encourage individuals to show initiative and to bypass or ignore existing authority.

A widespread stir of unrest was a direct result of Bible reading. The feudal establishment answered by invoking stern penalties against any layman who was found delving into the sacred book. But the lawbreakers multiplied so rapidly that the law enforcers could not catch up with them. For one thing, the invention of printing had made it relatively easy to obtain Bibles. For another, the threat of death by burning, which began to hang over Bible readers, proved to be much less of a deterrent than the leaders of church and state had hoped for. The Protestants of those days firmly believed that anyone who died for his faith was assured a place in heaven. And what better fate than to be certain of going there?

The literate new class absorbed a great many Bibles recently translated from Latin into their native French or Dutch or German or English. It was necessary to read only a little Scripture to discover that priests were interpreting it to their own advantage. This discovery intensified rebellious attitudes and stimulated political as well as religious disaffection. Bible readers in France and England and other countries began meeting together to read and discuss their findings. In a way, each person assumed some of the functions of priesthood. This, of course, was a direct threat to the professional priesthood. Moreover, the meetings they held— all thoroughly illegal—nurtured organized activity, through which people tried to exercise some of the freedoms denied them by feudal society. In certain of these assemblies were born plans to emigrate to America, where it seemed that pressures against dissenters would be less severe. It is even possible that this habit of gathering for discussion carried over in some degree to the New World, where it reappeared in the form of town meetings. The town meetings, in turn, played a role much later when a new revolution began to

take shape in the colonies on the western shores of the Atlantic.

Feudal leaders of Europe sensed the danger in this new collective behavior, and to find out the names of those who attended the meetings, they resorted to torture. One writer of the period compiled a catalog of more than 600 torture devices used on Huguenots, the religious dissenters in France. Rich Huguenots were often threatened with brutality of one kind or another if they did not pay protection money, and anyone who reneged might be hung upside down between two fighting dogs. Rich Jews received the same treatment unless they paid for the right to remain Jews.

Massive, violent repression went on in France, but the Bible-reading rebels gradually came into possession of weapons, as guerrilla forces often do, by capturing them from the counterinsurgents. In time, they developed an army. A few trained military men and even some feudal leaders began to think that their future might be brighter if they sided with those who were for Protestantism and against small Catholic feudal states.

One French military officer, Admiral Gaspard de Coligny, was especially sympathetic to the Protestant cause. Coligny, who finally became a Huguenot, knew the strength and ferocity of their enemies, and he thought that the dissenters should have a place of refuge from persecution. If that refuge could become a source of strength for the French monarchy, so much the better. Fortunately, from Coligny's point of view, there was a place on earth where both purposes could be served: America. Any increase in French strength there might reduce or cut off the vast quantities of New World gold and silver that were pouring into the royal treasury of Spain. Since authoritarian, Catholic Spain was a great source of strength for the feudal lords in France, a blow at Spain was a blow at them as well. And so Coligny decided to recruit a group of antifeudal Huguenot settlers to build on the coast of Florida a French stronghold close to Spain's vital shipping lanes. Although this first effort by dissenters was not ancestral to the events of 1776, the desire to break free from repression which animated the colony in Florida was part of the same human experience of growth and expansion that later showed itself in English colonies to the north.

PART ONE

The Search for Economic & Religious Freedom

It is by tracing things to their origin that we learn to understand them, and it is by keeping that line and that origin always in view that we never forget them. An inquiry into the origin of rights will demonstrate to us that rights are not gifts from one man to another, nor from one class of men to another.
— THOMAS PAINE

The First Colonies

1564 Fort Caroline and St. Augustine, Florida

Huguenots tried to found in Florida a colony where they could escape restrictions imposed on them in France. The French authorities willingly let them take up a hazardous life in an area of America claimed by Spain. This move by capitalist-minded Frenchmen brought a swift reply from feudal Spanish military forces, which overwhelmed the little Huguenot settlement.

About three hundred men and four women set sail from France in the spring of 1564 bound for Florida. All hoped to find on that distant shore opportunities they did not have in their homeland. All were nominally Huguenots—French religious dissenters who considered themselves followers of John Calvin. But not everyone in the party believed with the same fervor. Some among them looked forward only to extracting silver and gold from the New World as the Spaniards had been doing. Others would be content simply to practice their trades. A very devout minority sought freedom in the New World to worship in the ways of their Protestant faith.

Even the most daring in the party must have felt some relief as they left France behind. There a civil war between Huguenots and Catholics had just ended, and the Catholics had won. Persecution of the losers seemed inevitable, even though a few Huguenots remained in high places. One of these, Admiral Gaspard de Coligny, had persuaded the French rulers to let the three hundred and four colonists depart. Those who financed the venture were more interested in assembling aggressive souls to people a wilderness than

in supporting a deviant form of religion. They did not even provide a Huguenot minister for the expedition.

An aristocratic dissenter was leader of the colonists, René Goulaine de Laudonnière, a nobleman well known at the royal court. Laudonnière had been second-in-command when a previous Huguenot expedition tried to build a settlement on Parris Island off the coast of South Carolina. That effort had failed, in no small part because of hunger. Not a soul among the colonists knew how to grow food. Now Laudonnière had set out again without a single farmer in his party. Perhaps this was not an oversight. The fact was that rural French people responded less eagerly to the new Protestant religion than did craftsmen and tradesmen and sailors who were close to the growing world of commerce. On the other hand Laudonnière had more than enough adventurers in his party—rambunctious young noblemen who had volunteered to serve as soldiers without pay, eager for the treasure they expected to find in America.

The three French vessels reached the coast of Florida on June 22, 1564. Hundreds of local residents, Timucua Indians, gathered along the shore to watch them make their way into the mouth of a river known today as the St. Johns. The vessels dropped anchor about five miles up the river near a knoll on the south bank. This high ground, now called St. Johns Bluff, rose seventy-five feet above the surrounding land, giving a clear view in every direction.

The Frenchmen disembarked, climbed the knoll, and held a council. Every man present was allowed to speak—a touch of democracy that was one of the new trends beginning to develop within, and in spite of, feudal society in Europe. After some discussion, Laudonnière decided to fortify this easily defensible eminence, and the Frenchmen set about piling up earthen walls.

Wary soldiers in the party wore their gilded helmets and corselets as the work went on, for a crowd of Timucua Indians had approached. Although they seemed friendly enough, several of them made it clear to one of the Frenchmen, a captain by the name of La Caille, that the land all about was their home. La Caille could act as interpreter because he had been ashore in this region on an earlier expedition and had learned a little of the Timucua language.

The triangular earthen fort took shape, and now the head chief of the Timucua decided the time had come to have a look at the intruders. His approach was a ceremonious and impressive event. First, armed warriors, resplendent in body paint, appeared. With careful calculation their leader had sent 120 of them—exactly the number of soldiers in the French party. Immediately these warriors set about building a shady arbor that offered a good view of the fort.

Then came a grand procession. At the head walked fifty more warriors. Behind them came twenty youths piping on wind instruments made of reeds. Finally the head chief, Saturiova, arrived, accompanied by two advisers. With great dignity he stationed himself under the arbor and surveyed what was going on. Then, deliberately, Saturiova invited the white men to send representatives to talk with him.

Laudonnière meantime had appointed advisers of his own—Captain La Caille and one M. d'Otigny. The French commander had assumed that it would be he who received

Saturiova

3

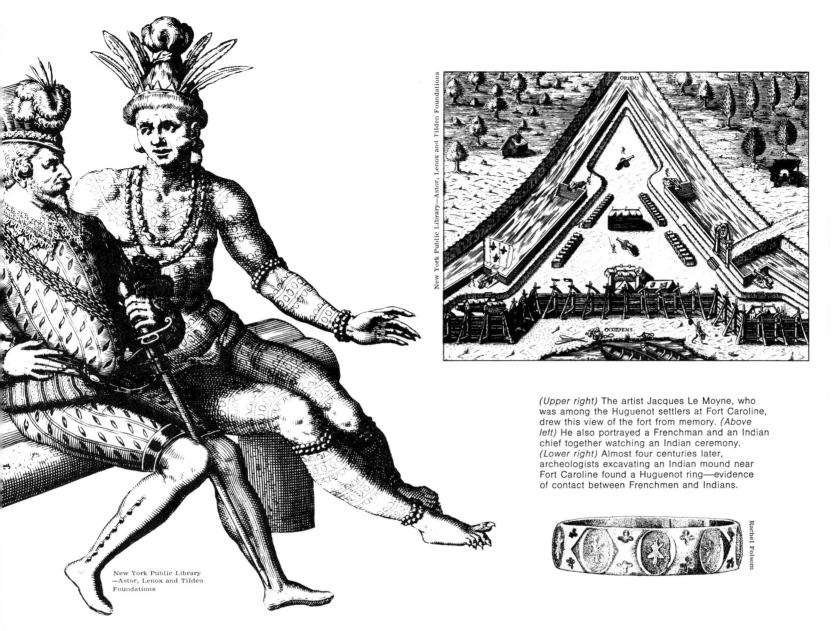

(Upper right) The artist Jacques Le Moyne, who was among the Huguenot settlers at Fort Caroline, drew this view of the fort from memory. *(Above left)* He also portrayed a Frenchman and an Indian chief together watching an Indian ceremony. *(Lower right)* Almost four centuries later, archeologists excavating an Indian mound near Fort Caroline found a Huguenot ring—evidence of contact between Frenchmen and Indians.

the Indian chief, not the chief who would receive him. But now a delicate situation had arisen. Laudonnière decided to swallow his pride and join Saturiova under the arbor.

What, asked the Indian leader, did the Frenchmen intend to do in Timucua territory and why had they chosen to land here rather than elsewhere?

Laudonnière improvised. The king of France, he said, had sent him to befriend Saturiova and offer a treaty promising him support against his enemies. Saturiova had no objection to allies. A bargain between the Timucua and the French was quickly made and sealed with the exchange of gifts. Saturiova then inspected the fort. The advantage of having this structure for the protection of his people seemed obvious, and he assigned eighty of his men to help complete the earthworks.

The lavish show that Saturiova had put on impressed the Frenchmen. Obviously the Indians were not paupers. It might be profitable to trade with them, and some of the Frenchmen wanted to go off immediately to see if they could barter with inland tribes for silver and gold. But Laudonnière vetoed any adventures until they had completed the fort, which was to be called Caroline from the Latin

word for Charles, the name of the French monarch who had allowed their probe into the wilderness. Dwellings also had to be finished, some inside the earthworks, some outside.

In the month it took to build everything, the colonists ate their way through most of the supplies they had brought with them. Since none of them were farmers, they had planted nothing. Although deer and other game could be found in the area, not a man in the party was an experienced hunter. The Indians did trade them some corn and showed them how to catch fish in weirs in the river. Even so the white men had cause for worry.

With food scarce and construction almost done, disagreements started. Some of the more earnest Huguenots, despite the lack of a minister, wanted to spend some time conducting the Protestant religious services that had been outlawed in France. Other members of the party preferred to go off in search of treasure, and go they did. Following the St. Johns River, they made their way upstream into the territory of a people led by a chief named Outina, who was hostile to Saturiova.

The Frenchmen began dreaming of profitable trade with Outina's followers. But Saturiova had other ideas. He re-

4

Le Moyne's drawing of Frenchmen assisting Outina in a battle with his enemies.

minded Laudonnière of the French promise to be an ally against his enemies, and he emphasized his point by bringing 1,500 armed warriors with him to Fort Caroline.

Inside the fort, Laudonnière felt safe and, regardless of promises, did not intend to cut off the possibility of trade with Outina by waging war on him. To impress Saturiova and his followers, Laudonnière put on a great show. Drummers and trumpeters raised a din. Brass cannons were readied. Then to witness the firing of the cannon, Laudonnière let twenty Timucua warriors inside the fort. What they saw and heard terrified them, and their fear spread among the mass of warriors waiting outside the earthworks.

As his men fled from the cannon, Saturiova realized he could not get the French to honor their pledge, and he withdrew. So did all the other Timucua. When they vanished into the woods, hope of getting food from them vanished, too. In a final gesture the Indians removed the fish weirs from the river, and the colonists lacked either the knowledge or the will to build new ones.

A number of Frenchmen equipped with harquebuses, or matchlock guns, were still with Outina. They even fought a battle on his side and helped him win. This did not improve

relations between the colonists and their nearest Indian neighbors, the followers of Saturiova.

Nor were the French able to stay on good terms with the more remote Outina. When he did not offer to trade as much food as they wanted, French soldiers seized him and then offered to exchange him for the desired provisions. Outina's followers gathered the ransom and paid it. But then the Frenchmen found that Indians also could play tricks. Outina's men ambushed them and reclaimed the food—completing the pattern of aggression and counteraction that would scar American history for the next four centuries.

Not only had the French now antagonized the Indians on whose land they wanted to settle, they had antagonized the Indians who might have traded with them, and were about to rouse the ire of Spaniards who had become exceedingly powerful in the nearby West Indies.

Some of the Huguenot colonists at Fort Caroline wanted to seize the food they needed—and with luck some other loot, too—from the hated Spanish Catholics. A number of the Huguenots already thought naturally in terms of raids. They had been pirates. Ever since 1536, claiming to act in the name of their Protestant religion, they had wrought havoc on ships manned by Catholics who in turn were carrying loot stolen from the Indians of Mexico and Peru.

Now when Laudonnière opposed their plan for a raid, some of the men at Fort Caroline showed their flair for independence. They mutinied, seized a ship, and sailed off toward Cuba. Soon they captured a Spanish vessel and then sacked at least one Spanish settlement before they were themselves caught. From the captured Frenchmen, Spaniards learned for the first time that the Protestants had built a fort nearby on the mainland in Florida.

Still no food had arrived at Fort Caroline. More mutineers conspired within the little colony and forced Laudonnière to give them two vessels and permission to raid. This marauding expedition started out, as had the first, with some success. Then it, too, ended in failure. After the Huguenots had seized three ships and had done some looting on shore, they were outwitted and caught. The Spaniards hanged some of the raiders. Others they sold into slavery, but twenty-six escaped. A number of these had been unwilling participants in the whole venture. They contrived to sail back to Fort Caroline, where Laudonnière seized and executed the ringleaders.

The Frenchmen's activity had by now thoroughly alarmed the Spaniards. They rushed reports to the king in Spain, who was in no mood to let Huguenots jeopardize his monopoly in America. He immediately authorized Pedro Menéndez de Avilés, the leading admiral of Spain, to organize (at the admiral's own expense) an expedition that would wipe out the French settlement at Fort Caroline and reaffirm Spain's claim to the continent. The admiral's reward was to be monopolistic control over a vast area on the North American mainland.

Menéndez outfitted a fleet and set sail with 2,600 men. If he had known that the colonists at Fort Caroline were in danger of starving, he might have been satisfied with a smaller expedition. But he did not realize the weakness of his enemy, who had survived only with the aid of supplies recently obtained from the English pirate John Hawkins.

Hawkins, who was soon to be knighted, had piously sailed from England a few months before in a vessel called the *Jesus* with this admonition to his crew: "Serve God daily, love one another, preserve your victuals, beware of fire, and keep good company." After a stop in Africa to kidnap a shipload of black men and women, Hawkins had proceeded to the West Indies, where he forced Spaniards at gunpoint to buy his human cargo. The Spaniards had no moral objection to obtaining slaves, but they were under orders not to buy anything at all from Englishmen. If money was to be made from trade, the Spanish king wanted it all to go into the royal treasury.

The sale of the slaves had netted Hawkins a profit of 60 percent on his investment. But gold didn't satisfy his need for fresh water. So he stopped at the mouth of the St. Johns River to fill his barrels. While he was anchored there the colonists at Fort Caroline learned that he had more food than he needed and also a ship he could spare. The Frenchmen had powder and cannon to offer in exchange. By trading the instruments of death for the stuff of life, the Huguenots hoped to last until the ship they got from Hawkins could

take them back to France. Perhaps in their homeland they might avoid the tortures reserved for religious dissenters. In Florida they could look forward only to sure death.

All this time Laudonnière had no idea that Menéndez was organizing an expedition against Fort Caroline. But Admiral Coligny, back in Europe, had spies who made him well aware of the armada that was gathering in Spain. Promptly he got together an expedition of his own to protect the colony he had sent to Florida. As leader he selected the expert mariner Jean Ribaut, who had already been to America.

SPANISH WORDS IN ENGLISH

In the course of contact between Spaniards and Englishmen in the Southeast and Southwest, many Spanish words had entered English by 1776: alligator, banana (originally West African), banjo, mosquito, quadroon, sarsaparilla, sassafras.

Some words that had entered Spanish from Indian languages, Caribbean and South American as well as North American, went on to enter English before 1776: avocado, barbecue, cannibal, canoe, chicle, chocolate, coyote, hammock, jerky, key (meaning islet), papaw (a variant of papaya), tobacco, tomato.

The French vessels won the race across the Atlantic. Ribaut reached Florida on August 28—St. Augustine's Day —1565, just as the settlers at Fort Caroline were preparing to sail for home in the ship they had got from Hawkins. Close behind the French relief expedition came the Spanish fleet. Menéndez sighted land that same day and ordered an attack on the French vessels in the mouth of the St. Johns River. But adroit sailors among the French took their swift vessels out to the safety of the high seas.

Menéndez decided to prepare a second and more careful attack. He withdrew from the river and on September 8, using the labor of African slaves, started to build fortifications at the place we now know as St. Augustine, about thirty-five miles down the coast.

Now it was the turn of the Frenchmen to take the initiative. Or so thought Ribaut. But his experience, great though it was, did not include knowledge of hurricanes. This was the hurricane season. As Ribaut sailed down the coast looking for Spaniards, a terrible gale carried him much farther than he had planned to go and wrecked all his ships. Most of his men found their way to shore.

Menéndez knew that the French fleet had put to sea and would be no threat as long as the storm lasted. He guessed also that most of the French fighting men from Fort Caroline were aboard the vessels. So Menéndez ordered an overland march to Fort Caroline, despite the foul weather. By the time he reached the fort the storm was so bad that the French officer in charge of sentries had taken pity on the men doing lookout duty. He let them come in out of the rain. This gave Menéndez a perfect chance, and he took it. On September 20, Spanish soldiers poured into the fort through the main gate, which had somehow been left open. Before long, more than 130 French Huguenot men were dead, their bodies stacked up along the riverbank, and the women and children were prisoners, soon to be sold into slavery. According to some historians, Menéndez carved a sign at the fort with this legend:

"I do this not as to Frenchmen but as to Lutherans." All Protestants were Lutherans to Catholics in those days.

Two French ships with some men aboard had remained in the river instead of going off with Ribaut. A handful of survivors from the fort managed to climb aboard these vessels before the Spaniards could capture them, and they quickly sailed off for France. Among those who escaped was Jacques Le Moyne, a mapmaker and artist. Later in England, where he found employment under Sir Walter Raleigh, Le Moyne made drawings from memory of the Indians and Fort Caroline. Thanks to these we have some idea of what life was like on the east coast of Florida in 1564–65. (An example of his work is on page 5.)

Most of the shipwrecked members of the French fleet that had been under Ribaut's command gathered in two parties on the shore. One group of 208 men soon found themselves faced with the alternative of fighting, hungry and without any dry powder, or of surrendering to Spaniards who had discovered them. They chose surrender.

Now Menéndez, on his way back from Fort Caroline, joined his men and their captives. On September 29, he took decisive action. He made a mark—some say it was a cross—

In the upper left-hand corner of this map is St. Augustine as it appeared in 1586, when the Spanish settlement was attacked by Francis Drake, the pirate.

in the sand at a certain place. Then he ordered the prisoners, hands bound, to go in small groups to that mark. With swords and knives Spanish soldiers killed batch after batch of the prisoners until all 208 were dead.

On October 14, Spaniards discovered a second party of shipwrecked Frenchmen—150 in number. These, too, were slaughtered, except for four who said they were Catholics and three others—a drummer, a fifer, and a fiddler. The musicians were spared so that they could play at dances.

One sailor, whom the Spaniards left for dead, managed to survive. Later he returned to Europe and told the details of the massacre. A number of other French stragglers also fell into Spanish hands, and some of these, too, were killed. Others were allowed to live because so few Frenchmen remained in Florida that they presented no threat to the Spaniards. Moreover they were more useful alive than dead: they could be sold as slaves.

Menéndez, aided by the hurricane, had utterly destroyed the French force of about 1,000 men. He had ended one effort of people whom he deemed guilty of deviant behavior to take over territory in which a new way of life could expand. But the outward push of antiestablishment Europeans was to continue to grow in momentum during the years to come.

PLACES TO SEE

FLORIDA

Jacksonville: Fort Caroline National Memorial.

St. Augustine: Fort Matanzas National Monument / St. Augustine Historic District.

For more information, see Gazetteer, page 212.

2

The First Elected Representatives

1607 Jamestown, Virginia

Edwin Sandys, aristocrat, helped to found a colony in Virginia which was designed to bring profit to the investors who financed it. Reflecting new ideas in many ways, Sandys encouraged at Jamestown a measure of representative government, and thus initiated a tradition that would grow in importance. Paradoxically the enslavement of Africans began in the colony at the same time.

Edwin Sandys, the archbishop of York, provided well for his six sons. To each he gave a clerical position with a good salary or an estate carved out of what many people regarded as property of the church. (It was, of course, the Anglican church, which had separated from the Roman Catholic but had never become intensely Protestant.)

To the son named Samuel, the archbishop gave land and a palace at a village called Scrooby, a town later significant in connection with the Pilgrims. Another son, who bore his own name, Edwin, received assets including a well-paid church post that was open to laymen. These assets were destined to be used in a way that had great bearing on events in far-off Virginia.

Young Edwin Sandys was no ordinary rich aristocrat, although he followed some of the patterns that were usual for youths of his position in society. He went to Oxford, then made the grand tour of western Europe, but his travels were very different from those of other young men. He made a point of visiting places where the frowned-on Huguenot religion flourished, particularly Geneva. Here John Calvin, the founder of the Huguenot sect, had exerted an especially strong influence on both religious and community life.

In Geneva Edwin Sandys observed that the industrious Huguenots had moved toward representative government in both church and civil affairs. What he saw did not offend or frighten him as it did the leaders of the Church of England, who felt threatened by the stiff-necked followers of the new religion. Sandys saw evidence that Calvinist beliefs stimulated men to hard work and honesty in business dealings—which seemed to prosper. He could find no reason for persecuting them, as many leaders in western Europe were doing.

At the same time, what he saw in Catholic countries convinced Sandys that Catholics as well as Protestants should be allowed religious liberty in England. Although he came to believe in religious tolerance—a rare idea in his day—he stopped short of joining either the Catholics or the Calvinists. Instead, he hung on, for twenty years, to his well-paid position connected with the cathedral in York. He remained within the Church of England while he spoke out in defense of both the right wing and left wing of Christendom.

When his grand tour was over, Sandys wrote out his thoughts in a manuscript he called *Europae Speculum, the State of Religion in the Western Parte of the World*. Apparently he had no plans to get the manuscript published, but someone who saw it liked its opposition to bigotry and sent the book to a printer. The bishops of the Church of England were outraged when Sandys' attack on their prejudices appeared. The Court of High Commission, which busied itself with censorship, ordered the book burned, and copies of it went up in flames in front of St. Paul's Cathedral. That was in the year 1605.

Young Sandys did not disown the book or retract his statements, but he did turn away from writing and sought a new outlet for his energies. In 1606 he invested some of his patrimony in the Virginia Company. This organization, which he helped to found, was designed to make money from the development of commerce with North America. Among the people of influence and substance who supported the company was the earl of Southampton, who had also given help, as patron, to William Shakespeare.

Before the year 1606 ended, the Virginia Company had obtained three vessels—the *Susan Constant,* the *Godspeed,* and the *Discovery*—and had rounded up more than 140 men of the nonlaboring class, called gentlemen. In the spring of 1607 the little fleet reached Virginia. Leaders of the expedition selected as a townsite a low, marshy peninsula in the river they called the James, in honor of the English king. There the colonists set about building Jamestown. Few in the party knew how to use tools; none had ever grown food. When the gold they had expected to find eluded even the resourceful Captain John Smith, the settlers had to resign themselves to every kind of deprivation.

At the end of the first year, two-thirds of Jamestown's original settlers had died. Year after year Edwin Sandys recruited more settlers, and year after year the same death rate continued. Disease carried off many of the immigrants. Warfare accounted for more losses. Indians very early began to defend their lands from encroachment by the strangers who kept pouring off ships that sailed into Jamestown from across the sea.

Some of the settlers, like those in the first group, were gentlemen adventurers with little talent for life in the wilderness. Others came with special skills. It was their mission to develop industries, which the owners of the Virginia Company hoped would make their increasingly costly venture show a profit. One of the industries was glass-making, and for this craftsmen were transported to the American wilderness from as far away as Poland. But neither glassmaking nor any other activity produced much revenue until a new fad, tobacco smoking, swept western Europe. Indians had discovered the narcotic effect of the tobacco plant, and they valued it for their ceremonies. Englishmen borrowed the habit without the rituals.

The country around Jamestown was ideal for growing tobacco. Suddenly there appeared to be a chance for prosperity after years of hardship and even of starvation. When Sandys considered the future of the colony, it seemed to him that tobacco plantations could be best developed by a new kind of settler. Hard-working, self-reliant individuals, he felt sure, would move to Virginia if they were given some assurance that they could have a voice in controlling their own lives there. The republican sentiments he had encountered among the industrious Huguenots of Geneva might also flourish in Virginia.

Sandys himself had had some experience with challenge to authority in the House of Commons, of which he was a member. The House was a political instrument designed to limit the power of kings, and Sandys had been enthusiastic in trying to develop its uses. For this, King James heartily disliked him, and Sandys was finally thrown into prison, but not before he had translated some of his republican ideas into action. Together with others in the Virginia Company, he drafted for the settlers in America a charter that allowed the participation of elected representatives in the government of the colony.

In the spring of 1619 the new charter arrived in Jamestown. It called for a governor and a number of councillors selected by the Virginia Company, which was financing the venture. It also provided for two burgesses, or representatives, to be chosen by the settlers themselves, from each of ten election districts, called *hundreds*. In all probability the electorate was made up of free, adult, white males. This first step toward democracy certainly did not extend new rights to women, nor is there any likelihood that indentured servants were allowed to vote.

On July 30, 1619, the General Assembly—councillors and elected burgesses—gathered in Jamestown and held their meetings in the church. Members of the Assembly took themselves seriously. Two men who claimed seats as elected burgesses were refused admittance because they represented an area that enjoyed too many special privileges.

For four days the elected representatives, sitting with the appointed councillors, dealt with a variety of questions and adopted a number of regulations. Some of these were against

Thomas Williams

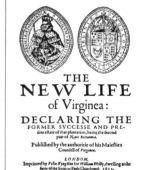

"The New Life of Virginea," from Nova Britannia, London, 1612

THE
NEW LIFE
of Virginea:
DECLARING THE
FORMER SVCCESSE AND PRE-
sent estate of that plantation, being the second
part of *Noua Britannia*.
Published by the authoritie of his Maiesties
Counsell of *Virginea*.

LONDON,
Imprinted by *Felix Kyngston* for *William Welby*, dwelling at the
signe of the Swan in Pauls Churchyard. 1612.

(Above) Sir Edwin Sandys was a leader in the business enterprise which sought to establish a profitable settlement at Jamestown. (Right) Brochures like the one shown here were used to recruit settlers. (Below) A great contribution that Sandys made to Virginia and to America was to encourage the establishment of the first representative legislature among colonists. Here a 19th century artist shows his concept of the first session of that 17th century body.

National Park Service

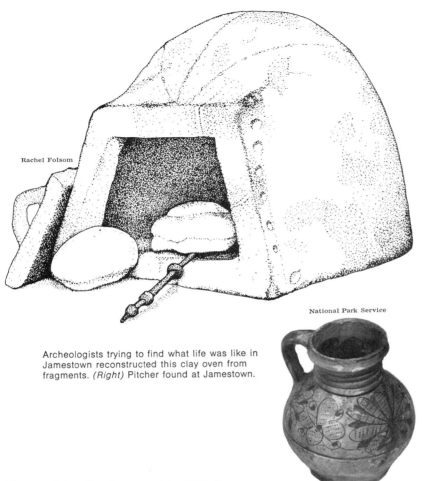

Archeologists trying to find what life was like in Jamestown reconstructed this clay oven from fragments. (Right) Pitcher found at Jamestown.

Three centuries after slavery was introduced at Jamestown an artist recreated this scene.

gambling, drunkenness, idleness, and elaborate clothing. Others concerned the planting of crops and the price of tobacco. Members approved Christianizing the local Indians and discussed how to protect themselves from the Native Americans on whose land they were living.

As the representative body did its work in one of the New World's least healthful spots, several burgesses fell ill and one died. Finally on August 4, after drawing up a petition which asked for greater power, the General Assembly adjourned. The first session of the first organ of representative government was over.

Within a few days another new element entered colonial life—one that was to give increasing numbers of people the strongest motives for wanting to control their own destinies. A pirate vessel, which happened to be Dutch but which had an English captain and crew, appeared off Jamestown and sent word ashore that it had merchandise to sell. The merchandise was stolen, indeed twice stolen. It consisted of men and women who had been kidnapped from Africa. Then either in the West Indies or on the high seas the English pirates on the Dutch vessel had kidnapped them a second time. So it was that the first African immigrants came to the English colonies in North America.

The governor of Virginia and others in Jamestown traded corn and tobacco for eighteen men and two women. Each of these became a bond slave required to work a certain number of years without pay. All twenty seemed to be immune to the diseases that continued to decimate the white population. They survived to the end of their period of servitude and achieved their freedom as all bond slaves were supposed to. Some even became landowners. But servitude for Blacks had been started in North America, and in time it developed into slavery for life, with no rights and no guarantee or even hope for ultimate freedom.

The seeds of republicanism—an attempt to extend the power of free, white males—which had been sown by Edwin Sandys, were to be poorly nourished for a while. King James saw to it that Sandys lost his position in the Virginia Company; then he did away with the company altogether and took over direct control of the colony. But the tobacco planters had liked their taste of representative government, and they began a long process of devising ways to express their dissatisfactions and to right their grievances.

These two events of August 1619 in Jamestown—the first step toward representative government and the first step toward African slavery—foreshadowed developments in the years ahead during which the American Revolution took shape.

PLACES TO SEE ✤

VIRGINIA

Jamestown: Visitor Center / New Towne / Old Church Tower / First State House / Glass House / Jamestown Festival Park.

For more information, see Gazetteer, page 212.

3

"A Civil Body Politic"

1620   Plymouth, Massachusetts

Passengers on the Mayflower, *who established
Plymouth, were for the most part from
England's lower classes. They sought freedom
either for their dissenting religion or for
economic opportunity—or for both. Before
going ashore to start their venture in a strange
land, a majority of those on the little vessel
agreed to support a form of self-government,
launching a vigorous tradition of independence.*

For William Brewster a process of bursting out of
bounds, of entering on new paths, began when he was a
small boy in the little village of Scrooby in Nottinghamshire,
England. For some reason that remains unknown, his
schooling was more extensive than that of the other boys in
that rural neighborhood in the 1570s. He learned Latin, and
he probably learned it from Lyly's *Latin Grammar,* because
teachers were forbidden by law to use any other elementary
key to the ancient language. Certainly orthodoxies of many
kinds surrounded William while he was growing up within
a stone's throw of a great manor house, often called Scrooby
Palace, that belonged to the archbishop of York.

William Brewster's father managed the estate at Scrooby.
He was also employed by the royal court to serve as postmaster. This meant that he was obliged to keep fresh horses
ready for royal messengers to use as they traveled between
London and Edinburgh on the narrow trail grandly known
as the Great North Road. In addition, the postmaster kept
an inn where travelers could put up overnight. And travelers
there were. They brought news from the world beyond

Nottinghamshire, and perhaps this had something to do
with the fact that William took an important step out into
that world when he was about fourteen. In 1580 he entered
Peterhouse College at Cambridge University, quite possibly
with the aid of the elder Edwin Sandys, who was just then
becoming archbishop.

At Cambridge William's mind grew quickly and in a
way that the archbishop had surely not foreseen. Among
the boy's tutors were clergymen determined to reform—to
purify—the Church of England. One aim of these Puritans
was to reduce the power and wealth of such men as the
archbishop of York.

The new religious theories at Cambridge were akin to
the Huguenot teachings that had spread on the Continent.
William responded to their idealism. He had seen at first
hand how much worldly wealth and luxury a church official
could enjoy. Aristocratic guests of the archbishop or of his
son Samuel had come to Scrooby Manor from time to time
to enjoy the good hunting. Scrooby, it happened, was not far
from Sherwood Forest, famed for hunting as well as for the
legends of guerrilla warfare that Robin Hood and his men
had waged there against men of wealth.

Either at Scrooby or at Cambridge, young William
Brewster came to the attention of Sir William Davison, a
man who was quite as powerful in the state as the archbishop
of York was in the church. Davison, a member of the privy
council under Queen Elizabeth, needed a kind of secretary-
messenger and personal servant, and he took William
Brewster out of Cambridge, before he had received his degree, to serve in this capacity. Davison may not have known
or cared about William's heretical religious ideas. It was
enough for him that the boy was intelligent and pleasant and
conscientious.

In the busy city of London, William Brewster's experience of the world grew with exhilarating speed. More than
once, carrying confidential messages for his employer, he
journeyed to the Netherlands, where new ideas were stirring.
He also observed the royal court in London, where great
actions originated—also great intrigues and astonishing corruption. One situation in particular was to affect his whole
future. Recently Queen Elizabeth had begun to fear that
Mary Queen of Scots might somehow seize her throne. Mary
was certainly an inveterate schemer and plotter. The House
of Commons worried because Mary was a Catholic and urged
Elizabeth to have Mary executed. Elizabeth was willing
enough to do away with her rival, but did not want the blame
for ordering the execution. However, order it she did, and
she commanded Brewster's patron, Sir William Davison, to
deliver the order. He did as he was told, and Mary was
beheaded. Then Elizabeth flew into a rage because Sir William had acted too promptly. She imposed a heavy fine on
him and sent him to prison. In due time his secretary-servant,
William Brewster, now about twenty-two years old, returned
to Scrooby.

In 1590 William succeeded to his father's job as postmaster, and over the years he became more and more interested in the movement to end corruption in the Anglican
church. He was a Puritan—that is, he remained within the
church and hoped it could be purified. Others, however, were

losing all hope of reform. They decided that the only road to a pure church lay in setting up a separate religious institution. When William, too, despaired of the Puritan cause he joined the Separatists.

Since church and state were interdependent, any attempt to establish a rival church was considered an attack on the state. Nevertheless, Brewster's heretical views and his official position as postmaster coexisted as long as Queen Elizabeth ruled and even during the first four years of the reign of James I, a religious zealot. By now people who dissented were being intensely persecuted. One college friend of Brewster's had been executed. He had been suspected of working with a printer who published attacks on corruption in the church. In 1607 Brewster had to give up his government job and the income that went with it.

As difficulties mounted, Brewster and his coreligionists in the Scrooby neighborhood decided to seek a safer place to live and worship. It may have been Brewster who suggested that they go to Holland. He, after all, had been there and was in a better position than anyone else in the Scrooby congregation to know that the Dutch allowed maverick

PLYMOUTH, PLIMOTH; PILGRIMS, SAINTS; PURITANS

The immigrants who crossed the Atlantic on the Mayflower *used the name of the last town they saw in old England for the first town they built in New England. Both places were called Plymouth, spelled in various ways. The nonprofit educational corporation that has now reconstructed part of that first New England village chose one of the early spellings and calls itself Plimoth Plantation.*

The settlers in Plymouth had no official title for themselves and never called themselves the Pilgrims. That name came into general use only much later. Because they separated from the Church of England, they were often referred to as Separatists. For a while they were called Brownists, because Brown was the name of one of their early leaders. Brown thought that the members of the Separatist Church should be such dedicated believers that they could be called Saints, and this name was sometimes used for the Separatists—who were actually a minority on the Mayflower. *From the point of view of this minority, the majority of those on board were outsiders or strangers. Because they had not adopted correct religious views, they were also sinners.*

The people known as Puritans in New England did not insist on separating from the Church of England. They only wanted to purify its theology and services. Since no Anglican official was sent to New England for many years, the Puritans there were free to develop their churches in their own way.

Christians more freedom than they had in England. At any rate, members of the Scrooby congregation sold their possessions and started secretly for Holland, hoping to avoid the officers of King James. But the hopes of the refugees were soon dashed. The sea captain they had paid to carry them to Holland betrayed them, and many of the congregation, including Brewster, were hauled off to jail.

Later a second attempt to escape from England was successful. The refugees took up residence in Leiden in 1609. There Brewster began covertly running a press, printing pamphlets that were smuggled into the British Isles. This operation, quite illegal from the point of view of the British authorities, was a cause of embarrassment to the Dutch, upon whom the English authorities put great pressure. Finally it became clear that Holland was no longer safe. For one thing, a truce between that country and Catholic Spain was about to end, and if war resumed, the position of the Protestant refugees might become untenable. So the people from Scrooby, and others who had joined them, once more began to look for a new home.

At this point Brewster seems once again to have played a key role. He was known to members of the family of the archbishop of York, and one of the archbishop's sons, Sir Edwin Sandys, had already helped to finance the Jamestown colonists. Brewster apparently opened negotiations with Sandys, hoping to get financial support for the resettlement of Separatists in America. Sandys, who favored religious tolerance, also wanted profitable colonies. He cooperated with Brewster—or so it seems. At any rate, there is good reason to think that Brewster journeyed secretly to England to arrange passage to America for his coreligionists.

In the end a group of investors, who called themselves adventurers, did put up the money for a new settlement which they supposed would be built in the area controlled by the Virginia Company. The adventurers obtained two vessels to provide transportation for the colonists—the *Mayflower* and the *Speedwell*. After false starts and accidents, and perhaps some chicanery, the *Speedwell* was abandoned. Passengers were reshuffled and reduced in number, and the *Mayflower* alone finally made the voyage.

On board were about 100 passengers, all from England's lower classes, with the exception of one woman who may have been a French Huguenot. Only three passengers had been among the original group of exiles from Scrooby— William Brewster; his wife, Mary; and William Bradford. (Two of Brewster's children who had been born in Holland accompanied him.) All together, the Saints, as the Separatists sometimes called themselves, numbered seventeen men, ten women, and fourteen children. The other passengers were not religious radicals. They were economically motivated individuals, almost all of them at least nominal adherents of the Church of England. One in the party, Miles Standish, a professional soldier, may have been a Catholic.

Besides religious differences, there were other divisions among those aboard the little vessel. For example, five passengers were men who had been hired to work at wages for a year. Eleven men, one woman, and six children were indentured servants—virtual slaves for a specified period of time.

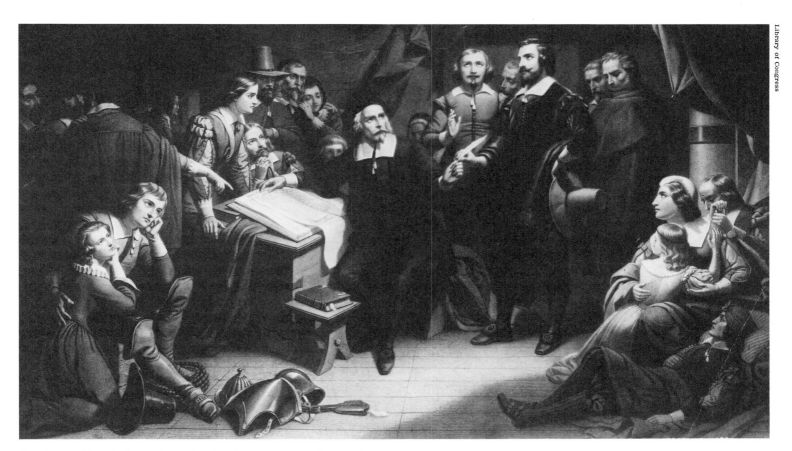

The signing of the Mayflower Compact as imagined by a 19th century artist.

The members of this diverse company had to endure each other in very cramped quarters for sixty-six days after the *Mayflower* finally set sail, following a series of nerve-racking delays. Moreover, they had to cope with a situation which became apparent to all before they set foot on shore. The *Mayflower* had reached America far north of the area where most of the settlers expected to arrive. Why this happened is a matter of speculation among historians, but one possibility certainly is that the tightly knit group of Separatists somehow persuaded the captain of the vessel to land far from their proper destination. They may have thought that their freedom would be much greater if they were beyond the reach of Anglican church officials or the Virginia Company or the king.

Whatever the reason for landing in Massachusetts, instead of farther south, there was going to be a problem of authority once the passengers got ashore. No colonial government of any kind existed in the vicinity of Cape Cod, where they disembarked. It would be every man for himself unless all agreed to a form of government. Indeed, some of the Strangers on the *Mayflower*—that is, all who were not Separatists, or Saints—had threatened to mutiny and to go it alone. Such people would clearly not cooperate in working for the common good unless they were compelled to do so.

To handle mutinous individuals and organize day-to-day life, the Saints—probably led by William Brewster—drew up a plan for a governing body and a pledge to obey the laws that body enacted. Forty-one of the fifty adult males on the vessel signed this agreement, which was modeled on

Separatist church documents and which has come to be known as the Mayflower Compact. Why did nine men not sign? Did they disagree? Were they ill? No one knows. But the great majority of both Saints and Strangers did unite in setting up rules to guide their affairs.

Four indentured servants also signed. Today no one is sure how it happened that this privilege was extended to servants—at least to some of them. Unprecedented though it was, the names of the four are there at the end of the list of signers.

The Mayflower Compact, which Brewster probably drafted in November 1620, followed close on the heels of the charter which Sir Edwin Sandys drew up for the Virginia Colony. In these two documents men took the first but by no means last of many steps toward self-government in America. Each said something eloquent about life before 1776.

PLACES TO SEE

MASSACHUSETTS

Plymouth: Cole's Hill Pilgrim Cemetery / General Society of Mayflower Decendants, Edward Winslow House / Harlow Old Fort House / Jabez Howland House / *Mayflower II* / Pilgrim Museum / Plimoth Plantation / Plymouth Rock / Sparrow House / Spooner House Museum.

For more information, see Gazetteer, page 212.

4

"Wonderful, Searching, Disputing and Dissenting Times"

1631-36   Massachusetts and Rhode Island

Roger Williams enlarged liberty of conscience by denying the right of government to dictate to people in matters of religion. His lifelong insistence on the need for separation of church and state contributed at a later time to that part of the Constitution which reads "Congress shall make no law respecting an establishment of religion or prohibiting the free exercise thereof. . . ."

A date to mark on the calendar of liberty is 1631.

In that year a very gentle, very pleasant, and also very uncompromising young man named Roger Williams came to the small Puritan village of Boston and began a lifetime of agitation. Almost from his first day in the year-old settlement in Massachusetts Bay Colony he talked, argued, split hairs, and suffered for a cause—the separation of church and state—which was finally achieved by the American Revolution.

Williams, twenty-eight years old when he landed, was a qualified clergyman. Although Boston had only about three hundred residents, he was offered a post as a kind of assistant minister in the town's one church. To the chagrin of the elders, the young man turned them down. The Boston Church, he said, was too closely tied to the Church of England, which he thought so corrupt as to be beyond reform. Williams left both employment and the town of Boston behind him and moved on up the coast to Salem, another Puritan village. There he found a congregation more independent in spirit, and he agreed to accept their offer of a post. But he was not allowed to keep it for long. The leaders of the Boston Church, annoyed by his independence, now brought pressure to bear on the Salem congregation. And Williams moved on again. This time he left Massachusetts Bay Colony and went to Plymouth Colony, which was not controlled by Puritan ministers and magistrates. In Plymouth he found a church that he regarded as really independent—that is, separate from the Church of England—and here the energetic young man mixed pastoral duties with activities as a trader and missionary among the Indians on Cape Cod.

This association with Indians produced unexpected results.

In the course of his trading and preaching, Williams learned a good deal of the Algonkian language, spoken by the Wampanoag Indians on Cape Cod and by other tribes elsewhere in Massachusetts. (He had a talent for languages and could already read and speak Latin, Greek, Hebrew, French, and Dutch, in addition to English.) Along with Algonkian words, Williams also learned something of Indian attitudes. The Wampanoag, he discovered, were upset by the increasing number of white men in their midst and by the notions these men had about the fields and forests that Indians had been using for millenia. Almost all Europeans, Protestant and Catholic alike, believed that a Christian sovereign had divine right to claim ownership of any lands they entered, if the people who lived there were not themselves Christian. Royal ownership by what was called "the right of discovery" took precedence over the Indians' ownership by right of possession and use. In 1607 English settlers did not doubt that the king of England had proper title to Virginia and that he could transfer title to them. In Massachusetts, beginning in 1620, householders and farmers felt sure that what was called the King's Patent to the land was legally valid and, accordingly, that they had every right to live there.

Now it happened that Roger Williams knew a surprising amount about the legalities of land titles and about law generally. Before coming to the New World he had served as a court stenographer and was a personal friend of Sir Edward Coke, one of the leading lawyers in London. All this legal experience in England came to Williams' mind when he contemplated the land titles of the Plymouth settlers. One question especially bothered him: Did the English colonists really own this land on which they lived? Did they have any right to it? Although he himself was the most ardent of Christians, Williams began to doubt that the religion of kings should have anything to do with ownership of any portion of this earth. On the contrary, it seemed to him that title to land was a civil matter and should be quite separate from religious beliefs. The proper way for a Christian to get land from non-Christians was to buy it or arrange to get it by treaty. Neither the king of England nor

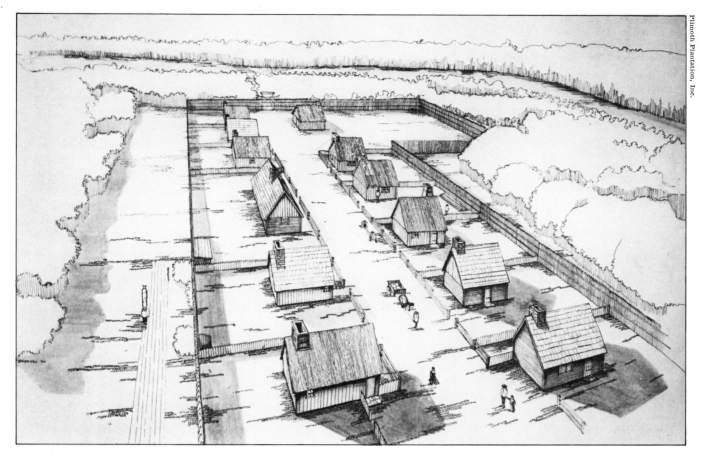

(Above) Based on their studies of old documents and on evidence gathered fom excavations, scholars believe that by 1630 Plymouth houses were lined up as shown here. *(Left)* Roger Williams as shown in an old print of uncertain date and doubtful authenticity.

old, was still a leading spirit in Plymouth. Predictably the younger man's arguments alarmed him. This new doctrine challenged the very right of Plymouth to exist.

Brewster and others now began to pay close attention to what Williams said in his sermons. Some of his religious theories, they found, were extreme, even for the Separatist church, which in turn seemed extreme to the Puritans in Boston and other Puritan towns. Altogether Williams was being a troublesome sort of fellow. Brewster thought that Plymouth and its assistant minister should part company. It is not clear whether Brewster and others now took the initiative and dismissed him or whether Williams asked for release from his pastoral post. At any rate, in 1633 he left Plymouth and returned to Salem.

Soon the same kind of trouble started all over again. No one in Salem—or Boston—could feel secure if Roger Williams was right about the King's Patent. In addition, many people were disturbed by Williams' relentless attacks on what he regarded as survivals among them of doctrines or practices that came from the Church of England. All of the New England settlers had grown up in the Anglican church, which was itself a direct descendant of the Roman Catholic church. It was not surprising that traces of Catholicism persisted in Anglican services, and to Williams any-

the settlers at Plymouth had bought their townsite from the Indians. To Williams this meant that the Pilgrims were guilty of trespass and the same was also true of most Puritans.

As usual, Williams did not keep his ideas to himself, and at the request of Plymouth's Governor William Bradford, he put into writing this disturbing theory about land. At that time William Brewster, now nearing seventy years

Puritans did not encourage artists and
so left no reliable likenesses of Narraganset
Indians or of Roger Williams. More than two
centuries after Williams went into exile,
an artist imagined this scene.

This reconstruction of Aptuxcet Trading
Post in Bourne would look familiar
to Roger Williams.

Rachel Folsom

16

thing that smacked of Catholicism smacked of the Devil.

The Salem authorities now became concerned about Williams. So did the authorities in Boston. The latter insisted that Williams come to Boston to stand trial. In court he spoke out as he did in church, and took back none of his fiery sermonizing. This was bad enough. But underneath the arguments about doctrine, the court magistrates sensed that Williams held an even more threatening belief: that religious and civil affairs should be kept separate. The church should not control civil institutions, and government should not have any control over men's faith.

This alarming idea had never been part of the thinking of either Pilgrims or Puritans. Both groups merely wanted a governmental arrangement—a state—that would protect and support their kind of church. Neither the Pilgrims nor the Puritans, in fact, allowed any churches except their own to operate in their communities.

Standing before the court in Boston, the devout young minister, now aged thirty-three, listened while the following was read to him:

> Whereas Mr. Roger Williams, one of the elders of the church of Salem, hath broached & dyvulged dyvers newe & dangerous opinions, against the aucthoritie of magistrates, as also writt l[ett]res of defamacon, both of the magistrates & churches here, & that before any conviccon, & yet mainetaineth the same without retraccon, it is therefore ordered, that the said Mr. Williams shall dep[ar]te out of this jurisdiccon within six weekes nowe nexte ensueing, wch if he neglect to p[er]forme, it shalbe lawfull for the Govnr & two of the magistrates to send him to some place out of this jurisdiction, not to returne any more without licence from the Court.

This order did not close the dissenter's mouth. When he returned to Salem, he continued to speak his mind, whereupon the court in Boston sent representatives to seize him so they could ship him back to England. But Williams had been warned they were coming. Before they arrived, he escaped into the wilderness, although he was ill and the weather was bitter cold. However he did not go into country that was unknown to him. He had often traveled along the wilderness trails and had dreamed of establishing a trading post and of doing missionary work among the Narraganset Indians in the area now known as Rhode Island. In preparation he had already bought land from the Indians. What he paid for it is not known. It couldn't have been much. Indeed, Williams at one point said he paid mainly in love. But at least he had been consistent and had arranged to get title from the Indians themselves, not from the king.

Now Roger Williams, city bred, college trained, a linguist and theologian, began the precarious existence of a farmer and Indian trader in the wilderness. With him were his children and his wife (who, curiously, remained illiterate while his own knowledge of language continued to increase). Not only she but other women were his devoted followers—in spite of his insistence at one stage that, according to the Bible, all women should wear veils in church.

In the course of time, several English communities grew up near the area where Williams settled. All of the newcomers, he insisted, should buy equal-sized tracts, and of course their land titles had to come ultimately from the Indians. With this egalitarian measure—and in other democratic ways—he had decisive influence in the policies of the newcomers. He continued to believe that church and state should be separate, and he persuaded his neighbors that he was right. Their wilderness settlement, known as Providence Plantations, became a laboratory in which to test the workability of Williams' new theories.

Providence at that time was the only place in the Christian world where real freedom of religion existed, and this freedom led to greater democracy than was known elsewhere. Any adult male could vote, if he owned land and was head of a family. In Massachusetts, by contrast, only adult, male members of the Puritan and Separatist churches could vote, and church members were likely to vote as their ministers directed. A theocracy had developed in Massachusetts, where no church could exist without government approval. Any church at all could exist in Providence. In Massachusetts Bay Colony and in Plymouth Colony the state provided economic support for the ministers of the approved churches. In Providence Plantations, no minister received any state support whatsoever. In Boston and surrounding towns, it was a punishable offense to speak disrespectfully of religious leaders. In Providence, anyone could speak his mind about any minister or about his theories without fear of harsh punishment.

All kinds of dissidents availed themselves of the new freedom offered in Providence. Separatists, of whom Williams was one at the time, were the first to come. Later there were Baptists, whom Williams joined for a while. Antinomians and Seekers came. So did Sephardic Jews and Quakers. Not only did Williams, on principle, insist that the followers of these religious sects be admitted, he also as a matter of principle spoke out vigorously against any of their doctrines with which he disagreed. He attacked the Quakers, for example, with unrestrained language. But he never wavered in his insistence that, wrong though he thought they were, they had full right to live and worship in Providence.

No sooner did the freedom-seeking settlers start to develop their farms than they had knotty political problems to solve. The firstcomers, who were refugees from Massachusetts, had obtained their land directly from the Indians or from Roger Williams, who had it from the Indians. But none of them had any authority from anyone except themselves to establish a government on their land. It may be asked why rebellious souls felt they needed authorization from anyone to organize community life. The reason lay in their weakness. To the north and east of them were Massachusetts Bay and Plymouth colonies, which had no desire to see Providence turn into a successful experiment in freedom of religion. To the west, Puritan settlers were building up Connecticut. They, too, presented a threat to Providence. And Indians were all around, none too pleased at the steady increase of Englishmen who insisted on appropriating the country's resources.

The Providence colonists understandably felt they needed support from a strong center of power. One obvious source of support was the head of the English government, to which all the first settlers had strong emotional ties. Twice Roger Williams journeyed to London to petition for a charter—a document giving official sanction to the colony, which came to be called Rhode Island. Williams did not sense any inconsistency here. Although, to his mind, the land itself belonged originally to the Indians, the right to organize and direct colonies belonged to his mother country. This right could be granted in a charter, but in addition to the usual clauses, the charter Williams sought would guarantee religious freedom in the colony.

Pilgrims had more color in their clothes and less sentimentality in their lives than this 19th century illustration suggests.

In the end he got what he wanted. While England went through a revolution led by Puritans and then a counter-revolution led by anti-Puritans, Williams kept insisting that the Rhode Island colonists must have freedom of conscience. Finally King Charles II agreed.

King Charles II, shown in this miniature by S. Cooper in the Royal Collection at Windsor, too pro-Catholic to please Protestant Englishmen, agreed to grant freedom of conscience to colonists in Rhode Island.

Historical
Pictures Service

Now, alone in America, Rhode Islanders, living on land they had bought from its true owners, could worship—or not worship—in any way they wanted, and for a while they enjoyed this privilege under a government headed by Williams. Nowhere else in the entire Christian world in the seventeenth century was such freedom possible.

But more than a purchase of land was needed to reconcile Indians to the continuing presence of men who held alien views about everything from property to the hereafter. Twice in the lifetime of Roger Williams, Indian resistance to white encroachment took the form of large-scale violence. Although Williams had devoted much time and energy to winning the Narraganset tribe over to accepting peaceful coexistence with the English settlers, the Indians felt the need for a more open way of life than the Europeans allowed them. So they kept shifting to the west. But there they began to encroach on the land inhabited by Pequot Indians. Hostilities developed between the Pequot and Narraganset Indians, and by 1636 war broke out between the Pequot and the English. Williams, although a newly arrived exile in Providence, acted as an expert adviser to the very Englishmen who had driven him out of Massachusetts.

Again, in 1675, when Williams was an old man, he sided with the English settlers against Indians. During the enormously bloody struggle in the Indian war of liberation (sometimes called King Philip's War), he was a captain in the Rhode Island militia. At one time, despite his ideas about Indian rights, he summoned a court which condemned and executed a badly wounded Indian who had come into Providence and surrendered after Indians had burned most of the town.

Williams did not object to the English takeover of North America. He participated in it. He did not oppose colonialism. He was part of it. But he did think in a new way about the relationships between human beings. Kings, he said, were not "invested with Right by virtue of their Christianitie to take and give away the Lands and Countries of other men." The proper way to get land was by treaty or by purchase. Such thoughts were radical, but they had roots in the European tradition that land could be privately owned.

To most Indians, on the other hand, land could no more be bought and sold than air could be. Both were to be used and enjoyed—and, by agreement, shared. Indians usually regarded the sale of land as little more than an agreement that newcomers could join in using a neighborhood where Indians had always hunted and fished and planted corn and where they expected to continue doing so. In the long run, of course, it made no difference whether newcomers got land by purchase or by seizure. The Indians lost either way.

New England Indians are almost all gone now, but a book that Roger Williams wrote about their language survives. It was the first study any European had made of Native American speech. Although this particular gesture of respect for fellow human beings did not contribute to the development of democracy in America, it was consistent with other actions of Williams which did make major contributions. The separation of church and state which he advocated was an attack on tyranny and later became part of the United States Constitution. There is no mention of God or religion in the original text of that document, and the First Amendment to the Constitution specifically began, "Congress shall make no law respecting an establishment of religion, or prohibiting the free exercise thereof. . . ." This amendment—an achievement of the American Revolution—is an enduring monument to the exile who succeeded more than a century earlier in establishing religious freedom in Rhode Island.

A prominent minister in Boston, who may have been embarrassed by the banishment of Roger Williams, called his expulsion an "enlargement." Williams did enlarge liberty, his own and others', when he was forced to live outside Massachusetts, and he became a part of the whole enlarging, expanding process of revolution that would shape a new nation.

Roger Williams himself had different words to describe the years through which he lived. He called them "wonderful, searching, disputing and dissenting times." That they were, and in recognition of the injustice done him in those times, the Commonwealth of Massachusetts, in 1936 revoked the order of 1636 banishing Roger Williams from its territory.

PLACES TO SEE ❦

MASSACHUSETTS

Plymouth: Plimoth Plantation.
Salem: Pioneer Village / Witch House.

RHODE ISLAND

East Providence: Plaque marks site of Roger Williams Home.
North Kensington: Smith's Castle.
Providence: First Baptist Church / Monument of Williams' First Landing / Roger Williams Spring.

For more information, see Gazetteer, page 212.

5

"Ready Wit and Bold Spirit"

1630s   Boston, Massachusetts

Anne Hutchinson, in a world dominated by men, repeatedly defied Boston's theocrats and became an exceedingly popular community leader.

A slight, vigorous woman, mother of fourteen children, was for two years in the 1630s the most important person in New England. Singlehanded she almost succeeded in overthrowing the well-organized and firmly established oligarchy which ruled Puritan society.

Rebel Anne Hutchinson had a "ready wit and bold spirit," according to John Winthrop, who lived across the street from her in Boston. That was considerable praise from a man who actively opposed her radical views and who became governor of Massachusetts Bay Colony in the midst of the crisis she provoked. It was also an understatement. Anne Hutchinson dared to question authority—even to walk out of church when she thought the minister was preaching nonsense. At a time when most women could not read or write, she was not only literate but a scholar. She had a remarkable memory and a fierce ability to detect inconsistencies. By all accounts she was also a sweet and charming person—except when she was doing verbal combat as a skillful, determined enemy of the Puritan establishment.

Long before her marriage to William Hutchinson, in England, she had begun to burst out of the limitations placed around all young English girls of the period. Somehow she

obtained a good education, possibly because her father, the Reverend Marbury, had time to spare when, for many years during Anne's childhood, he was barred from preaching because of his critical attitudes toward the church hierarchy. Whether or not Anne's father was her teacher, she doubtless had access to his books, and she became very learned. Few men who had been trained for careers in the church knew more about the Bible than Anne Hutchinson did.

After her marriage she began seeking out churches in small villages near her home where she could hear the sermons of Puritan-minded ministers. When she could, she rode horseback about thirty miles to hear the Reverend John Cotton preach in the town of Boston, England. Cotton was a fiery rebel at that time. He encouraged Anne Hutchinson's mind to grow in unconventional directions, and when he emigrated to the new Boston in Massachusetts Bay Colony, the Hutchinsons soon followed him. Later, and with great pain, Mrs. Hutchinson saw Cotton return to more conventional and much safer attitudes. She, however, continued to express independence of thought when she differed from the authorities and by so doing brought down upon herself the wrath of ministers and magistrates.

Today it is not easy to follow the intricacies of the path Anne Hutchinson took in her effort to break through the barriers placed around her life first by the Church of England, then by the male leaders of Puritan society in America. Religion in those days encompassed many aspects of life. It took the place of theater, of radio, of television. It was the source of all intellectual excitement in a day when newspapers and magazines and public libraries did not exist. Every kind of experience was expressed in religious terms, and Anne Hutchinson found ways of uttering political revolt in the language of theology. Some of the words she used, some of the ideas she accepted as proven truths are so unfamiliar today that we often find it difficult to understand what she was talking about. But the direction of her thrust was perfectly clear to her contemporaries, both those who loved her as a helpful neighbor and skillful nurse and those who feared her as a relentless opponent of dictatorial authority.

Anne Hutchinson's rebellion was an extension of the great religious movement called the Reformation, which resulted in a shift of authority from the Catholic hierarchy to the Bible. Her logical mind took her even further: If priests were not needed to tell people what God expected of them, then Protestant ministers, too, could be dispensed with. A lay person, she believed, could find out the truth for herself —or himself. Also if the Bible was the result of revelation in the past, why could there not be new revelations—direct from God—in the 1630s?

Anne Hutchinson made no secret of her faith that she had divine guidance. Her accounts of it were persuasive to many. But not to the establishment. Obviously if individuals in Boston in the 1630s could get religious directives straight from heaven without the help of ministers as mediators, the very existence of ministers was threatened.

Anne Hutchinson came only gradually to her final position as a rebel. In 1634 when she and her well-to-do husband

(Left) Seventeenth century women had to master many skills, including spinning, shown in this contemporary print. (Above, center) Governor John Winthrop presided at the court which exiled Anne Hutchinson. (Above) In the 19th century, Augustus Saint-Gaudens sculpted this impression of a Puritan man.

and eleven children arrived in Boston, she was a loyal follower of the Reverend John Cotton. However, she did have some views which disturbed certain clerics. And she soon began a custom which worried many of them. As time went on, it worried them more and more. Every week women met in Mrs. Hutchinson's large foreroom, or living room, to hear her analyze a sermon that had been preached the preceding Sunday. Apparently she could remember almost every word that had been spoken, and her comments were often critical.

So popular were these gatherings that not all the women who wanted to squeeze into the Hutchinson house could do so. She had to hold two meetings a week, and often as many as eighty listeners appeared. Time after time Anne Hutchinson emphasized that women—and men—could bypass church authorities and receive direct guidance from God.

Mrs. Hutchinson's dynamic personality attracted more and more women and, in time, many of their husbands, too. Before long she had won the loyalty of most of the 2,000

people who lived in Boston in the mid-1630s. This was all the more remarkable because of the seventeenth century belief that wives, who were literally owned by their husbands, had no business meddling in affairs of the church. Indeed, women had no business doing anything except taking care of their husbands and their numerous children and their crowded houses. William Hutchinson seems to have been an exceptional husband. Although he did not take a leading part in his wife's subversive activities, he seems to have endorsed her ideas in his own quiet way, and he stood by her when trouble developed.

Trouble was bound to come. A religious dispute in Boston affected every aspect of life, because religion suffused everything. Boston, with the probing, questioning mind of Anne Hutchinson at its center, was seething with contention. Many people now questioned the authority of ministers. This led to questioning the authority of magistrates, who were elected by members of the ministers' congregations. It was only a step further to questioning the wisdom and justice of the shareholders of the Massachusetts Bay Company, among whom John Winthrop was important.

From fear, the officials began to scheme and plot against Anne Hutchinson, and in 1637 they took action against her and her followers. As one step they tried her loyal brother-in-law the Reverend John Wheelwright for sedition and contempt. Soon after that, Wheelwright with many adherents moved to New Hampshire. Another step was more devious. The anti-Hutchinson faction managed to change the voting place of the annual colony election from Boston, where the heretic was exceedingly popular, to Cambridge (then called New Town), where she was little known. In those days it was a long trip from Boston to Cambridge by boat or on horseback. Predictably many Hutchinson supporters would not be able to get there to influence the voting.

The purpose of the election was to choose Massachusetts Bay Colony's governor for the coming year. The incumbent was a young man named Harry Vane, who had become one of Anne Hutchinson's followers. Of course the ministers and magistrates wanted to vote him out of power, and they succeeded. John Winthrop was elected in his place, and Winthrop sought to frustrate Anne Hutchinson's disruptive activities—including her habit of walking out of Boston Church whenever the Reverend John Wilson began to preach.

With power in their hands now, the ministers and magistrates, led by Governor Winthrop, moved against Mrs. Hutchinson herself. On November 3, 1637, they summoned her before the forty-three-man General Court which, like the election, was held in the safe environment of Cambridge.

The charges against her were vague in the extreme and largely religious in nature, although the court was supposedly a civil institution. However, it did not really matter what the charges were. Anne Hutchinson's opponents made up the majority of the court. They could convict her of anything they pleased, and they did not have to show her either mercy or common courtesy. When she appeared in the unheated meeting room on Mount Auburn Street, she had to endure the hardship of standing throughout much of the trial, although she was not well.

All one day and then all the next, confronting the seated men who were both accusers and judges, she matched wits and biblical quotations with them. She was not allowed either an attorney or a jury, and in the end the court found her guilty and sentenced her to banishment from the colony.

"I desire to know wherefor I am banished," Anne Hutchinson demanded.

"Say no more," Governor Winthrop answered. "The Court knows wherefor and is satisfied."

Even so the court had not finished with the rebel. First she had to endure several months of imprisonment outside Boston proper in the home of one of her most bitter enemies. On November 15, while she was separated from her friends, Governor Winthrop directed armed men to enter many homes in Boston and to remove all weapons. Possibly the governor feared armed rebellion in Anne Hutchinson's behalf. Certainly the disarming of her friends would have an intimidating effect.

In this 1640 print a Puritan girl wears a rather unpuritanic fancy ruff.

21

In March 1638, there was a second trial, this one before the members of Boston Church. Many of Anne Hutchinson's friends had by now been forced out of the congregation. Some had fled with Wheelwright to New Hampshire. Others were moving to the colony that Roger Williams had set up in Providence. So when she appeared in Boston Church, there were few sitting on the hard benches who dared to express friendship for her. Although Mrs. Hutchinson was in even worse health than she had been during her first trial, the proceedings went forward.

As shown in this illustration made about two and a half centuries after her trial, Anne Hutchinson was forced to stand throughout the proceedings.

The trial produced the expected result. The Reverend John Wilson, on whose sermons she had often walked out, finally read the following:

Forasmuch as you, Mrs. Huchison, have highly transgressed and offended and forasmuch as you have soe many ways *troubled the Church with your Erors* and have drawen away many a poor soule and have *upheld your Revelations:* and forasmuch as *you have made a Lye,* etc. Therefor in the name of our Lord Jesus Christ and in the name of the Church I doe not only pronounce you worthy to be cast out, but *I doe cast you out* and in the name of Christ *I doe deliver you up to Sathan* that you may learne no more to blaspheme to seduce and to lye. And I doe account you from this time forth to be a Hethen and a Publican and soe to be held of all the Bretheren and Sisters of this Congregation, and of others. Therfor *I command you* in the name of Christ Jesus and of this Church *as a Leper to withdraw your selfe out of the Congregation;* that as formerly you have dispised and contemned the Holy Ordinances of God and turned your Backe one them, soe you may now have no part in them nor benefit by them.

Anne Hutchinson strode out of the church. One young woman in the congregation, a friend from England and a fellow rebel, walked at her side in protest. This brave person was Mary Dyer, about whom there will be more to say.

Now Mrs. Hutchinson had to leave. Against this day her husband had gone ahead to prepare a new home near Providence. With the aid of Roger Williams, he and several other refugees from Boston bought from the Indians the whole of Aquidneck Island (now called the island of Rhode Island) in Narragansett Bay. On April 1, 1638, the Hutchinsons and their friends became the original settlers in the town of Portsmouth on that island.

In Portsmouth Anne Hutchinson had a miscarriage—an event which the authorities in Boston took almost gleefully as proof that God disapproved of her religious views. It soon became clear that even this misfortune, following the others she had suffered, was not enough to satisfy her tormentors. They sent men to Portsmouth to question her and to "reason" with her. They imprisoned two of her sons who visited Boston. Finally they threatened to seize the settlements that were growing up around Providence. If they did that, they would put an end to religious freedom in Rhode Island. And Anne Hutchinson would be once more within the jurisdiction of Massachusetts magistrates. There was very real danger that she might have to endure new harassments. She might even face death.

Early in 1642 Anne Hutchinson's husband died. Now, without the support and protection he had always given his wife, she had to take full responsibility for her children while she was trying to avoid destruction at the hands of her enemies. She decided to make one more move. Soon after her husband's death, she and a number of friends set out for territory controlled by the Dutch, whose record of religious tolerance seemed to be at least somewhat better than that of the Puritans.

With money that still remained of the substantial amount her husband had brought from England, Anne Hutchinson bought land not far from New Amsterdam. So did other members of her refugee party. The exact spot she chose as a site for a home is not known, but it seems to have been somewhere within about a mile, in one direction or another, from the place where 222nd Street and Baychester Avenue meet in the Borough of the Bronx near the northern edge of New York City.

The governor of New Amsterdam, Willem Kieft, who sold the land, said he had bought it from the Indians. Whether he had or not, he was busy at that time persecuting Native Americans. In February 1643, he directed ferocious attacks on them at two different places near New Amsterdam, and many were killed. These slaughters enraged the Indians of the whole area, who were already alarmed by the encroachments of white people. Specifically, they objected to the presence of whites in what is now called the Eastchester section of the Bronx. Governor Kieft, they said, had never paid for this land.

Anne Hutchinson had acted in good faith. She had bought a site which she thought Governor Kieft had the right to sell. But matters had gone too far for her personal innocence to make any difference. Indian warriors appeared one day in August 1643 and killed Anne Hutchinson, five of her children, and all of her friends who had settled in the area. Only her eight-year-old daughter, Susanna, survived, and she was taken prisoner.

Because of the almost universal arrogance of whites toward Native Americans, Anne Hutchinson died. And because of the scorn and intolerance of men toward women—and of ruling men toward anyone who challenged authority—Anne Hutchinson's rebellion came to an end, too. But it was a forerunner of another movement toward freedom that was soon to appear, led by Quakers. Meantime Anne Hutchinson had helped open the way to religious liberty, and because government and church were part of the same tight structure, she had also nudged at the door to political liberty.

PLACES TO SEE

MASSACHUSETTS

Boston: Anne Hutchinson Statue, State House.
Cambridge: Cambridge Common.
Quincy: Anne Hutchinson Square.

RHODE ISLAND

Portsmouth: Site of First Settlement of Portsmouth, Founders' Brook.

For more information, see Gazetteer, page 212.

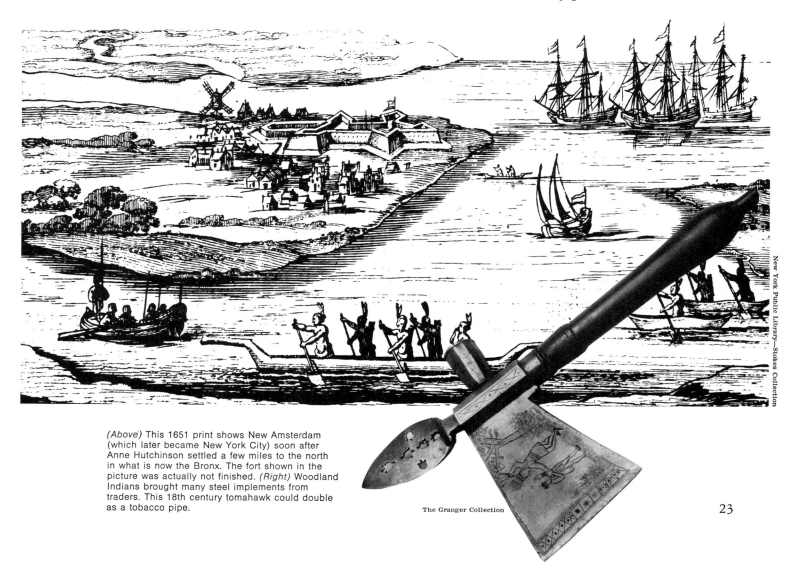

(Above) This 1651 print shows New Amsterdam (which later became New York City) soon after Anne Hutchinson settled a few miles to the north in what is now the Bronx. The fort shown in the picture was actually not finished. *(Right)* Woodland Indians brought many steel implements from traders. This 18th century tomahawk could double as a tobacco pipe.

New York Public Library—Stokes Collection

The Granger Collection

23

"To Bigotry No Sanction"

1650s New Amsterdam and Newport

A group of Jewish refugees were almost enslaved by pirates but managed to reach the Dutch colony of New Netherlands, and some of them later went on to Newport, Rhode Island, where Roger Williams had established religious tolerance. The struggle of these refugees for freedom was not all-inclusive. Some of their descendants were among shipowners of various faiths who later became wealthy in the slave trade.

Fleeing again—fleeing not out of fear but because of necessity—twenty-three Jews boarded a vessel in Brazil on February 24, 1654. They had been forced to sell their homes and leave their businesses when armed and bigoted Portuguese forces took Brazil from the more tolerant Dutch. Because the Dutch had been hospitable to Jews both in Brazil and in Holland, the Twenty-three looked hopefully northward toward the Dutch colony of New Netherlands. In this trading center, which was not yet called New York, they might find a haven.

The refugees could discover no ship bound from Portuguese Brazil to Dutch New Netherlands. These outposts of rival empires were not conducting friendly trade with one another, and so the route had to be indirect, with a stopover in Martinique, a French island in the Caribbean. There the Twenty-three might find a vessel that would take them to their destination.

But their troubles were only beginning. Severe storms almost wrecked their ship. Worse than that, according to

one account, Spanish pirates swarmed aboard the vessel and changed its course toward the island of Jamaica, then owned by Spain. There the Jews were held prisoner, in grave danger of being shipped to the Mediterranean area and sold as slaves.

How did this little band happen to be in the New World, where they were so buffeted about? The Twenty-three were all descended from Jews who had been driven out of feudal Spain by the Catholic Inquisition during the reign of Ferdinand and Isabella. Some, pretending to be Christian converts, had gone to Portugal and from there to the Portuguese colony of Brazil. Others, leaving the feudal orbit, had remained open Jews and had found shelter in Holland, the most capitalistic of countries. When, in 1624, the Dutch expanded their activities and dislodged the Portuguese from Brazil, Jews as well as Christians from Holland settled there. Under the tolerant Dutch regime, Jewish converts returned openly to their own faith, and together with Jews who had come from Holland, made up a large and active religious community.

When the Portuguese returned to Brazil in 1654, so did the Inquisition, and all Jews had to leave. In special danger of punishment were those who had once pretended to be Christians. Some, at least, of the Twenty-three held prisoner on Spanish Catholic Jamaica seem to have been in this category, but others had scarcely more reason to feel safe. While they waited, word of their plight somehow reached Holland, where influential Jews persuaded the Dutch government to protest to the Spanish government. No one knows the details of how matters were arranged, but after this intercession, the Twenty-three, with very little money left, departed from Jamaica, taking along such of their personal and household goods as they still had.

Their journey toward freedom brought them next to Cape St. Anthony on the westernmost tip of Spanish-controlled Cuba. There, five months after they had fled from Brazil they found a French sea captain, Jacques de la Motthe, who agreed to take them to New Amsterdam. All their remaining money went to the captain to pay for their passage on the *Ste. Catherine* (sometimes called the *St. Charles*). To get food on the voyage and transportation for their belongings they had to sign a collective IOU. How they would pay this debt no one knew at that point. Perhaps there would be friendly people in New Amsterdam who would advance the money.

Finally about September 1, 1654, the *Ste. Catherine* found its way into the great harbor at the mouth of the Hudson River. The arrival of any ship was a big event to the 750 people in their red brick homes on the southern tip of Manhattan Island. The arrival of the *Ste. Catherine* stirred up particular interest because controversy began the moment the ship dropped anchor.

Captain de la Motthe demanded payment of the balance the Twenty-three had contracted to pay. They had no money, nor did they find anyone in town who would lend the amount they needed. Indeed Mayor Peter Stuyvesant made it exceedingly clear that he didn't want Jews in New Amsterdam. The Reverend Johannes Megapolensis shared his feelings. These two zealous believers in the Dutch Re-

24

Although England seized New Amsterdam soon after Jews arrived, it still looked Dutch in this 1718 print.

formed church had recently prevented Lutherans from building a church. They did not intend to relax now and let Jews get a foothold in their community. It was bad enough having Jewish traders sent out by the Dutch West India Company. Two of them had appeared within the month—the first two Jews to reach North America.

Unable to get his money in any other way, Captain de la Motthe brought suit against the refugees and arranged to have a public auction of their goods, which he had carefully kept aboard his ship. Fortunately for the Jews, not all Dutchmen shared the inhospitable views of their mayor and their dominie. They seem even to have welcomed a way to show their contempt for both civil and ecclesiastical authority and their sympathy for the friendless strangers. At the auction Dutch citizens saw to it that the bids were all very low. Each piece of furniture went for a small price—and then the buyer immediately gave it back to its original owner.

As soon as de la Motthe found this out he put a stop to the sale. To increase the pressure on the refugees, he arranged to have two of them held in jail as hostages. About this time Solomon Pietersen, one of the two Jewish traders in New Amsterdam, helped to work out an arrangement that solved the problem. He found that the sailors on the *Ste. Catherine* were entitled to half the money the refugees had contracted to pay. Pietersen persuaded the sailors to wait for payment. At this point de la Motthe felt free to sail, and the Twenty-three were free to take up a miserable existence outside the little town, living in makeshift shelters and depending for the moment on the charity of the Dutch Reformed church. This was provided, we can be sure, more through the initiative of

the friendly congregation than that of the hostile dominie.

Both the dominie and Mayor Peter Stuyvesant kept up their campaign against the Jews. Stuyvesant sent off to his superiors in Holland a fierce demand for permission to expel the immigrants, who seemed to have every intention of staying. An answer, of course, would take some months. Meantime Stuyvesant used all his considerable powers to make life so unbearable for the refugees that they would leave voluntarily.

To begin with, Stuyvesant denied them most of the privileges enjoyed by other residents of New Amsterdam. They could not open any retail businesses or work as artisans. Nor could they trade with the Indians. It was impossible for them to get permission to build homes or a place of worship. The Jewish community could not even have a special plot of ground to use as a cemetery, and, given the treatment they were receiving in the winter of 1654, it seemed likely they might need a graveyard in the near future.

But the Twenty-three had not survived so far by accepting defeat, and they did not intend to begin doing so now. As they well knew, they had influential coreligionists in Holland, the most tolerant of European countries at that time. Jews in old Amsterdam had freedom of conscience, and of special importance at this moment, they had economic freedom. They could and did invest heavily in the Dutch West India Company, which had established the settlement of New Amsterdam. And so, shortly after the New Year, word came to Peter Stuyvesant from company headquarters in Holland: Jews had the right to reside and trade in the New Netherlands colony.

25

For the moment the quiet-spoken, self-confident Jewish community had won. But the fanatical and equally confident Calvinist leaders did not give up. Peter Stuyvesant found a new insult and new burden to impose. He forbade Jews to serve in the militia. At the same time he imposed a tax on them for nonservice.

In this matter Stuyvesant reckoned without Asser Levy, a refugee of great spirit. Levy flatly refused to pay the tax. And he insisted on his right to serve in the militia on the same basis as any other male.

Levy won his point and somewhat later was allowed to do military service. Still the running fight went on. Stuyvesant continued to restrict the privileges of Jews; they sent an appeal to headquarters in Holland; Stuyvesant's superiors overruled him, and Stuyvesant obeyed—but only up to a point. The final test came in 1657. In a showdown argument between Stuyvesant and the Jewish community, led by the ever-firm Asser Levy, the Jews came out ahead. They had demanded and won the right to be burghers—full citizens— legally equal to any Dutchman.

All through the fabric of Stuyvesant's bigotry there had run two threads—militant Christian religious orthodoxy and fear of economic encroachment by Jews in business affairs profitable to Christians. In its insistence on orthodoxy, however, Stuyvesant's Dutch Reformed church was by no means alone. The Jewish community in old Amsterdam, at the same moment, was struggling with a doctrinal problem of its own. In 1656, the philosopher Spinoza fought a battle against bigotry within his own synagogue in Amsterdam—and lost. The order expelling him from the congregation read in part: "We order that nobody should communicate with him orally, or show him any favor, or stay with him under the same roof, or within four ells of him, or read anything composed or written by him." What Spinoza wrote, of course, led him to world fame, and who remembers his orthodox opponents?

Meantime in America as in Holland, Jews began to enter the mainstream of economic life. Some of them prospered as traders, others as shopkeepers or butchers or owners of taverns.

Then, ten years after the Twenty-three landed on Manhattan Island, England seized the colony and renamed it New York. Once more, uncertainty hung over the Jewish community. Would English rule be better or worse than Spanish, Portuguese, Dutch? They soon found that King Charles II treated them little better than had Peter Stuyvesant. But most of them clung on and continued to be successful. A few who moved to Newport, Rhode Island, had still more comfortable lives. They had gone to Newport, as had other Jews, because the law of Rhode Island provided that "all men may walk as their consciences persuade them, every one in the name of his God." The spirit of that law prevailed for a good many years, and the Jewish settlement grew along with the busy, expanding seaport. Its members took part in civic affairs, organized the first Masonic lodge in America, and for about a century found few of the obstacles that had been placed in their way in New Amsterdam.

In all that time the Newport congregation conducted religious ceremonies in their homes or in rented halls. But

Peter Stuyvesant, shown in a modern painting by William Henry Powell, tried to keep Jews from settling in Dutch colonial New Amsterdam.

by the 1760s they had become prosperous enough to think of building a synagogue. At this moment, and possibly because of their strong position as competitors of Christian businessmen, the government of once-liberal Rhode Island denied Jews the right of citizenship. A few months later the Jews made their response. They began to build the synagogue they had been dreaming of.

Determined to create the most impressive religious structure in New England, they hired the best architect in America, Peter Harrison. In 1763 they started work on the handsome building which still stands. It is now called Touro Synagogue, after Judah Touro, the first prominent Jewish philanthropist in America, and it is still used for worship.

One of the great candelabras in the rich interior of this outwardly simple building was a gift of a man named Aaron Lopez. The story of Lopez himself reflects a bitter irony in the effort of Jews to break free of persecution. He and some of the other Jewish shipowners in Newport grew wealthy in part out of the slave trade, unmindful that their forebears had narrowly escaped being sold into slavery from Jamaica in 1654. This ambivalence was no special function of the Jewish religion. It was rather a function of the whole ex-

(Left) Descendants of the first Jewish settlers in the colonies were among those in Newport's Congregation Yeshuat Israel who began to build Touro Synagogue in 1763. *(Above)* To Touro Synagogue, Aaron Lopez, known as the Merchant Prince of New England, gave a great brass candelabra, which may still be seen there. Lopez did not like the nonimportation campaign approved by many patriots, but when the Revolution came he supported it.

ploitative economic system from which Christian and Jewish entrepreneurs alike were trying to benefit.

The wealth that slave traders accumulated was immense, and part of it became an element in the driving power behind the Revolution of 1776. At first Aaron Lopez tended to side with those who opposed revolution. But he did not flee to England. He stayed in New England, made his peace with the Revolution, and always kept ties to Newport. He is buried in the Jewish cemetery on Touro Street.

It must have been a stirring moment in the synagogue on that street when, in August 1790, a certain letter came addressed to the congregation, which was known as Yeshuat Israel—Salvation of Israel. The letter, which was no doubt read under the great brass candelabra given by Aaron Lopez, came from George Washington, president of the new United States. It said—a year before the adoption of the first amendment of the Constitution, which guaranteed freedom of religion—that the government of the republic gives "to bigotry no sanction, to persecution no assistance."

Washington remembered well how the Jewish financier Haym Salomon had twice been arrested by the British as a spy—and had then turned his financial genius and his con-

siderable assets over to serve the cause of freedom.

Between 1654 and 1790 Americans had made real advances against bigotry and persecution—although the slaves transported by Lopez and owned by Washington were not among the sections of the population that shared in the benefits of this advance.

PLACES TO SEE ✤

NEW YORK

New York (Manhattan): Flagpole commemorating arrival of first Jewish immigrants in 1654 / Sephardic Jewish Cemetery, established 1682 / Two other colonial Jewish cemeteries.

RHODE ISLAND

Newport: Touro Synagogue.

For more information, see Gazetteer, page 212.

Quaker versus Theocrats

1660   Boston, Massachusetts

Mary Dyer, a Quaker, insisting on freedom of conscience, weakened the control of the theocratic rulers of Massachusetts by the extreme device of forcing them to execute her. Her execution, together with other Puritan excesses, finally prompted King Charles II to order the Massachusetts government to cease persecuting dissidents.

Quakers were new in Boston in 1656. They were new everywhere, and Boston did not yet have laws on the books to deal with this latest form of heresy—this latest threat to authority. However, the town's General Court did not let such a technicality stand in its way. When word came that two Quaker women, Ann Austin and Mary Fisher, were on a ship just in from England, Boston officials ordered them removed and taken to jail. There they were stripped naked so that their bodies could be examined for evidence that they were witches—or had been bewitched. It is not known that this search revealed the sought-for signs of the Devil's handiwork, but the women did have suspect books in their luggage. These were publicly burned the next day, so that no one—apparently not even magistrates of the court—could read them and run the risk of moral infection.

Other Quakers soon arrived. So dangerous were they deemed that the windows of the jail were covered with boards to keep the incarcerated heretics from talking to people in the street and thus polluting them with un-Bostonian ideas. The Quakers, like Anne Hutchinson before them, taught that each individual could commune directly with God, without the mediation of ministers. If this doctrine was generally accepted, where would the Puritan ministers be? Out of work and no longer in control of the society they dominated.

At last the magistrates faced up to what they regarded as the perilous influence of Quakers, several of whom were imprisoned at that time. The General Court adopted its first anti-Quaker law. Men beating drums then went about Boston collecting crowds, and the new regulations against "the cursed heretics" were read aloud. The law placed heavy penalties on sea captains who knowingly brought Quakers to Boston and on local citizens who gave them shelter, once they had arrived. But it was soon clear that the magistrates had not solved their problem. They had merely stimulated resistance among Quakers in England. Many more of them came to Boston.

Now the law-and-order-minded court reasoned that the penalties were not severe enough, so new ones were devised. Henceforth any man found guilty of being a Quaker would lose an ear. For a second offense he would lose the other ear. If he persisted, he would be whipped. Quaker women were to be whipped.

Ear cuttings and whippings were many, but so were converts made by the ever more numerous Quaker missionaries. This meant to members of the General Court only that even sterner measures were needed. They made a third law, this one providing for banishment. And if a banished Quaker returned to Boston, the penalty would be death.

Response to the new measure was as vehement as the law itself. The immigration of missionaries increased, and one day in 1657 a woman named Mary Dyer arrived in Boston.

Certain people in the city remembered Mary Dyer well, although she had not set foot there for nearly twenty years. Now having raised seven children in Rhode Island she was back, one of the many who had been converted to Quakerism. Among the Bostonians with good reason to recall her was the Reverend John Wilson, from whose church she had marched in disdain the day Anne Hutchinson was expelled. Like Anne Hutchinson she was a rebel, and she already had a strong belief that any Christian could be his—or her—own spiritual guide. At that time Governor Winthrop, who found her ideas repulsive, had not been sorry when she left Boston and moved with the troublesome Hutchinsons to Rhode Island. Mary Dyer and her husband settled in Portsmouth, while Anne Hutchinson made one more move—to the Dutch colony of New Netherlands.

After twelve years in Rhode Island, Mary Dyer had returned to England, her original home. No one has discovered the cause of this visit or why it stretched out for seven years. It *is* known that during her long stay she became a Quaker. When she learned of the persecution of Quakers in Boston, she decided to protest—and boarded a ship bound for Massachusetts.

Immediately on her arrival, Mary Dyer was arrested and put in jail. Her husband hastened from Rhode Island, arranged for her release, and took her home with him. But Mary paid no heed to whatever pledge he had been obliged to give for her good behavior. Within a year she was arrested in New Haven, where she had gone to preach Quakerism.

Before many more months had passed she was back in

Boston. This time she accompanied a woman who was bent on engaging in a novel and dramatic form of protest: She had equipped herself with the kind of linen in which the bodies of the dead were wrapped before burial. These shrouds she intended to present to the governor with the suggestion that they be used in burying the innocent people he was executing.

In Boston Mary Dyer and her companion visited some friends in the jail and were arrested. How many prisoners were being held at that time no one has been able to discover, but Mary Dyer was only one of twenty arrested in one day for protesting. She and the others had, she said, come to Boston "to look your bloody laws in the face." And look they did. Boston authorities responded by picking, apparently at random, three Quakers—two young men and Mary Dyer —to be hanged on Boston Common.

The sentence seems not to have been a popular one. To make sure the hangman could carry out his work, the General Court ordered the three Quakers, who hated violence and did not engage in it, to be surrounded by a hundred militiamen "completely armed with pike, and musket, with powder and bullet, to lead them to the place of execution, and there see them hang until they be dead." Certainly it was not Quakers themselves that the court feared.

At the head of the procession, drummers loudy advertised the grisly event. From the crowd the Reverend John Wilson shouted at Mary Dyer, who walked between the two young men, William Robinson and Marmaduke Stevenson.

Each of the three tried to speak before the noose was tied, but fear of their words was so great that the drummers were ordered to drown out their voices and those of any protesters in the crowd. Only the Reverend Wilson, who

(Above) Women rose to prominence among the Quakers and in their distinctive clothes often mingled with the very poor. (Right) Early in this century the famous illustrator Howard Pyle drew this interpretation of a Quaker missionary.

BRITISH AMERICA'S FIRST POET

The words "Compiled with great variety of Wit and Learning: full of delight" were the subtitle of a book of poems published—and much admired—in England in 1650. Contrary to all the traditions of her male-dominated world, the author of this book, which was entitled **The Tenth Muse Lately Sprung Up in America,** *was a woman. She was in fact the first person in British America to publish a volume of verse.*

Born Anne Dudley, in England, she received education and intellectual stimulation at the court of the earl of Lincoln, where her father and her husband-to-be were employed in responsible posts. At the age of eighteen Anne Dudley married Simon Bradstreet, and two years later she sailed in the first of many ships that carried Puritans to New England. A little later Anne Bradstreet and her husband, who later became governor of Massachusetts, settled on a farm in North Andover. There she waited for several years before she began to fulfill the primary role expected of all women. When her biological barrenness ended, she bore eight children, and from then on frail health accompanied her burden of motherhood.

In all her years at North Andover—where she lived until 1672—Anne Bradstreet apparently did everything that her society demanded of her as a mother and a farmer's wife. In addition she somehow found time and energy to explore the world of literature, science, and history. In these probing ways her life paralleled that of the colonial poet and scientist Sor Juana, who added to Spanish literature in the seventeenth century from within the walls of a nunnery in Mexico.

Anne Bradstreet's poems—some lyrical, some reflective, some didactic—all, by their existence, spoke of a woman's determination not to be shut out from one aspect of life that men had always regarded as their own. Some of Anne Bradstreet's verses dealt directly with the sexist attitude of men toward women poets. For example:

> I am obnoxious to each carping tongue
> Who says my hand a needle better fits,
> A poet's pen all scorn I should thus wrong:
> For such despite they cast on female wits,
> If what I do prove well, it won't advance—
> They say it's stolen, or else it was by chance.

Anne Bradstreet also had something to say about men's attitudes toward another woman who had entered territory normally reserved for males. After Queen Elizabeth's death she wrote:

> Nay say, have women worth, or have they none?
> Or had they some, but with our queen it's gone?

Detail from a window in St. Botolph's Church, Boston, Lincolnshire. Reproduced by permission of the Vicar and Churchwardens

Anne Bradstreet, poet, is portrayed in this window in St. Botolph's Church, Boston, England.

> Nay, masculines, you have thus taxed us long,
> But she, though dead, will vindicate our wrong.
> Let such as say our sex is void of reason
> Know 'tis a slander now, but once was treason.

Anne Bradstreet knew she had not written great poetry. When her book appeared, she referred to seeing her "rambling brat in print" and said, modestly, that her "blushing was not small." But she had pushed firmly on a door which men held shut.

had been bellowing at the Devil all his life, managed to be heard. "Hold thy voice. Be silent," he roared. "Thou art going to die with a lie in thy mouth."

First one young man, then the other did die. But while Mary Dyer stood ready with the noose around her neck, Governor John Endecott reprieved her. Who had prevailed upon the governor is not known. One of her sons, a sea captain and an official in the government of Rhode Island, had spoken out in her behalf. Quite likely her husband, who defended her on many occasions, did so now. Or perhaps Governor Endecott listened to the ominous voices in the crowd, which was being held back by a hundred militiamen.

At any rate Mary Dyer was reprieved, and when she got back to jail she protested again. In a letter to the governor she said she chose to die rather than accept life from one who had just killed two innocent young men. She was determined to force Endecott to carry out what was obviously a most unpopular sentence. But the governor decided she would be less dangerous alive than dead. Once more he ordered her out of Massachusetts.

Only by using force could jailers get her onto a horse and keep her there. They conducted her, protesting, for fifteen miles on horseback, then gave up. With strong men ready to bar her way, Mary Dyer could not at that moment return to Boston. Instead she chose to go home, and scorning the horse she had been forced to ride, she traveled the thirty miles to Portsmouth on foot.

Presently, however, Mary Dyer appeared again in Boston and was clapped back into jail. The General Court must have held her in some awe by now, for the magistrates made one more effort to avoid the hazards of executing her. If she would leave Massachusetts and promise to remain away, they said, they would let her go free.

Mary Dyer would not give the magistrates this victory. "I came here before," she told them, "to warn you to repeal your wicked law. I am upon the same mission now."

At this point it could make no difference for ever-faithful William Dyer to send an eloquent appeal to Governor Endecott urging him in effect to ignore Mary's wishes and release her. Endecott had done that before and it had got him nowhere. He refused the appeal.

On June 1, 1660, Mary Dyer was again led to the gallows on Boston Common. The Reverend Wilson was again at the scene. Once more he urged her to recant, and once more she refused. When the final moment came, Mary Dyer herself signaled the hangman to proceed with his work. Her body was hidden in an unmarked grave on the common. Presumably it is still there.

On September 1, 1661, King Charles II, though no friend of Quakerism—or of religious freedom, for that matter—ordered the Puritans of Massachusetts to relent in their persecution of members of the Society of Friends. Prodded by many Quakers in England, among whom women were often the leaders, the king released large numbers of Friends from English jails.

The death of Mary Dyer gave a measure of freedom to the living—a freedom of conscience finally written into the general law of the land only after the success of the American Revolution.

Officials in Puritan Boston answered ideas that frightened them by using force against the dissenters. Puritans executed the Quaker missionary Mary Dyer, who is shown here by a modern artist as she approached the gallows on Boston Common in 1660.

PLACES TO SEE

MASSACHUSETTS

Boston: Boston Common / Statue of Mary Dyer, State House.

North Andover: Governor Simon Bradstreet House.

For more information, see Gazetteer, page 212.

An Inevitable Conflict

Within a five-year period in the late seventeenth century, three widely separated peoples struck three bitter blows for freedom. One was in Virginia—Bacon's Rebellion—of which more later. The other two popular movements are less well known but they involved large numbers of people in actions that were both intense and full of meaning for life in America.

In 1675, Algonkian Indians in New England rose against Protestant English settlers who had gradually taken control of their homeland. In 1680, Pueblo Indians in New Mexico rose against Catholic Spaniards who had enslaved them. Neither of these Indian revolutions fed directly into the American Revolution. Indeed the War of Independence was not a war for the independence of Native Americans. However, as movements for freedom, the widely separated events of 1675 and 1680 had much in common with the events of 1776. They were of the same stuff.

The social explosion of 1675 decided which of two freedoms was to prevail in New England. On the one hand there was the freedom of the Native American to elaborate his own culture at his own pace, which he had been doing quite successfully since the last great glacier of the Ice Age withdrew from New England 10,000 years ago and left a land where plants, then animals, then people could live. The people in time learned to cultivate domestic plants, but no one to this day has found ways of domesticat-ing most of the animals that were native to the area.

On the other hand was the freedom of newcomers who had inherited metal tools, gunpowder, a written language, and domesticated animals and brought them across the Atlantic, risking much in order to practice their religion and expand their part in a burgeoning capitalist economy—two things they had not been able to do in their homeland.

Seldom have peoples, each seeking to live freely, understood each other so little as did the English colonists and the Algonkian Indians, both uneasily sharing the same terrain. And seldom have the aspirations of one group been more completely frustrated by the coercive techniques at the disposal of the other.

Beginning in 1620, English settlers had been demanding that the thin postglacial soil of New England yield them a livelihood. It did, grudgingly and sometimes indirectly. In addition to raising crops and cattle and hogs, the settlers cut trees from the great forests and shaped them into sailing vessels. Soon they took up ocean trade. In doing so, they often evaded the restrictive laws of their homeland. Just as often they ignored the rights of kidnapped dark-skinned, non-Christian peoples, whom they transported and delivered into slavery at great profit to themselves.

In the course of all this activity the New England English developed a society in which overriding power

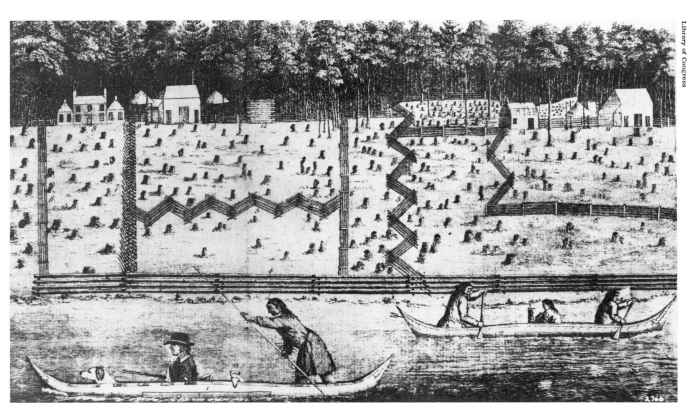

In this early print, Indians witness the destruction of their forest by farmers who have cleared it.

lay in the hands of churches which were Puritan in theology and congregational in form. Each church was controlled by male members, who in turn were greatly influenced by the preachers and teachers they employed. The clergymen, while professing to believe that each congregation should control its own affairs, developed ways of cooperating with each other. And this led to shaping a remarkably unified community. Since only those males who were church members could vote in civil elections, the churches controlled all political life—including, of course, relations with the original population on the Atlantic seaboard. The touchiest of all relations turned out to concern real estate. After an initial period of simply taking what land they wanted, the Puritans began to buy it. They drafted deeds for the nonliterate Indians to sign, and by this method large areas passed steadily from Native American to English control.

At the same time, the Puritans went to school to the very people from whom they were acquiring the land on which both buyer and seller had to depend. The Puritans learned to grow corn and to prepare it as food, to plant beans and squash among the hills of corn in the fields, to build fish traps in the rivers and tidal waters as the Indians had done for centuries. They entered the wilderness on trails that had long been used. Words, too, the white settlers borrowed, and they used and sold skins and furs which the Indians taught them how to take in the woods.

The texture of life all over New England was different from the texture of life in old England, thanks largely to Indians. But even as they taught the foreigners how to manage in the strange environment, Native Americans found that they themselves were being displaced—and changed. Work became easier with the steel knives they got from settlers. (Their own name for Englishmen was "Steel Knives.") English guns made them better hunters and much more deadly warriors than they had been in the days of bow and arrow. To buy foreign artifacts made of metal, the Indians could offer land in exchange. They could also barter land for rum, which prospective English buyers had in great quantities. The rum gave quicker and more sensational visions than any potion or herb the Indians knew. From the settlers they got habit-changing utensils, cloth, gewgaws, drink, and one thing more—sermons. An ardent minister, John Eliot, learned a dialect of the Algonkian language and preached in it tirelessly. After thirty years of labor he managed to produce a Bible translated into Algonkian.

Eliot's missionary efforts brought a profound change in the life of several Algonkian tribes. By 1675, nearly 1,200 Indians had adopted Christianity. These converts, who became known as Praying Indians, were gathered together into fourteen special villages. In their new surroundings, the converts be-

Even as white settlers moved inland, a few voices advocated some equality for nonwhites.

gan the never-easy process of discarding their own culture and adopting the ways and beliefs of strangers who came promising a larger life than they would otherwise have.

Everything the English got from the Indians helped the English to survive in their new surroundings. Many things the Indians got from the English threw them out of balance with the land in which they lived. The guns which made it easier to kill game also made the game more scarce. Strange new diseases to which Indians had not developed immunity swept through the mat- or bark-covered wigwams in Indian villages. Most distressing of all, the Indians discovered that they had less and less land on which to grow food. Often they were surprised to find that Englishmen who gave rum in exchange for land would not let Indians—after they had sobered up—return to the land which had always been theirs.

One especially strange thing accompanied the Englishmen—their laws. For reasons that Indians could not accept, Englishmen felt that English laws should govern Indians. Wampanoag, Narraganset, Nipmuck, Massachusetts Indians—all Algonkian—had their own ways of maintaining order in their villages. They could see no justice, but much insult, in having outsiders dictate how they must behave among themselves. Also it was difficult to see any reason why Indians should go to English courts to

complain about Englishmen whose cattle or pigs destroyed Indian cornfields. Why shouldn't these Steel Knives who did harm to Indians in the Indian homeland be handled by Indians according to Indian customs?

From time to time Indians burst out angrily against indignities. But punishment in English courts was always severe and usually prompt, and it was not always easy for Indians to evade the courts and their verdicts.

In 1637, the English waged a sudden violent war against the Pequot tribe in what is now Connecticut. The Pequot had shown little inclination to submit to Englishmen and much ability to resist them, sometimes with violence. In one action of the war, about 600 Pequot men, women, and children were trapped inside their wigwams and burned to death. This genocidal blow persuaded the few surviving Pequot and some other Indians as well to become entirely subservient to the English.

Certain Indians, unlike the Pequot, had tried to cooperate with their white neighbors. Intergroup cooperation, however, did not form a major part of their tradition. Alliances between bands and tribes were probably not frequent in the millenia before Europeans moved into America in great numbers. Nor was offensive warfare a major part of life. Each Algonkian village had a large stretch of forest in which its men

American Museum of Natural History

(Above) An Indian calumet used in ceremonies. (Right) Seventeenth century trading as seen by a 19th century artist. (Opposite left) A contemporary depiction of an attack on a Pequot fort in the 1600s. (Opposite right) An artist's conception of an Indian chief.

Brown Brothers

34

were free to hunt or to burn off trees in order to create fields for corn. Occasionally young men from one band poached in the hunting territory used by another. Or a group of young men from one village raided another village, much in the spirit of a sporting event. But these raids did not summon into existence any intertribal judicial system.

When Englishmen first began to press against the Algonkian around Massachusetts Bay, cooperation among Indians was not the first thing these Native Americans thought of. Quite the contrary. Indeed some leaders felt that Englishmen might be useful as allies against the Iroquois, who had been expanding into Algonkian territory, or against other Algonkian who were backing away from Iroquois pressure.

One who thought he saw an advantage in alliance with whites was Massasoit, leader of those Algonkian known as Wampanoag, meaning Eastlanders. (It was in his territory that the Pilgrims settled in 1620.) Massasoit was quick to accept a mutual assistance pact and readily put his mark on a treaty drawn up by the English which read:

1. That neyther he nor any of his should iniure or doe hurt to any of our people.
2. And if any of his did hurt to any of ours, he should send the offender, that we might punish him.
3. That if any of our Tooles were taken away

when our people were at worke, he should cause them to be restored, and if ours did any harme to any of his, wee would doe the like to them.
4. If any did vniustly warre against him, we would ayde him; if any did warre against vs, he should ayde vs.
5. He should send to his neighbour Confederates, to certifie them of this, that they might not wrong vs, but might be likewise comprised in the conditions of Peace.
6. That when their men came to vs, they should leaue their Bowes and Arrowes behind them, as wee should doe our Peeces when we came to them.

Forty years later conditions had changed greatly, and some troubled young Wampanoag began to consider alliances against the British, not with them. By the 1670s, several tribes of Algonkian began to talk of pooling their strength. This effort finally culminated in widespread guerrilla activity, which English-oriented historians have called King Philip's War. "King Philip" was a nickname given by Englishmen to an important leader, or sachem, of the Wampanoag tribe, whose own people called him Pometacom, or Metacomet or Metacom. Although this man's position as sachem was hereditary, he lacked the power of a European monarch, and since his name was not Philip except to his enemy, it is more appropriate to call the military action he helped to inspire the Algonkian War of Liberation . . .

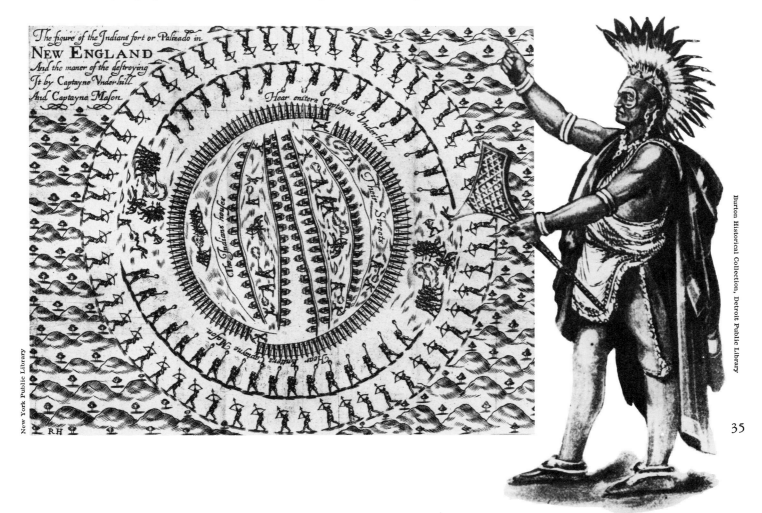

35

8

Indian Wars of Liberation

1675   New England   1680   New Mexico

Thousands of Native Americans rose in defense of their lands and their lifeways against Protestant Englishmen in New England and against Catholic Spaniards in New Mexico. In the Río Grande valley, Pueblo Indians were victorious, and for twelve years they lived in freedom on their own land and worshiped as they wished.

After the old Wampanoag sachem Massasoit died, it was not clear whether his son Wamsutta, the new sachem, would follow the old man's policy of cooperation with the English. Indeed, there were rumors that the Wampanoag intended to forge an alliance with their neighbors, the Narraganset.

The fact was that Wamsutta saw no advantage in his father's conciliatory policy. Encouraged by his wife Weetamoo, who was a hereditary sachem in her own right, he decided to hold his head high and lead his people in a course that would save their self-respect and independence. Accordingly, when the authorities at Plymouth ordered him to come and explain his intentions, he ignored the summons.

Plymouth immediately sent troops out to seize the young sachem. They found him without difficulty. He and some of his tribesmen were resting in a wigwam after a hunt. Their guns stood outside. The Plymouth men seized the guns, then easily took the unarmed Wampanoag prisoner.

While Wamsutta was a captive in the home of one of the Plymouth officers he fell ill and soon afterward died. Many Wampanoag suspected foul play. But if there was any, it did not benefit the English. Wamsutta's younger brother Metacom—age twenty-three—became sachem, and Metacom was far more militant than Wamsutta.

Now the old pattern repeated itself. In the land of his ancestors, Metacom was ordered by foreigners to appear and report on his intentions. Metacom was only too painfully aware that the Englishmen were well armed and his warriors were not. His only course at this time was to obey the summons. At Plymouth, in 1662, he renewed the original treaty of alliance that had been signed by his father, Massasoit, more than forty years before.

Five years passed. The Wampanoag accumulated many more grievances—and many more guns—but still Metacom knew they did not have enough to drive the enemy out of their homeland. So when he was again summoned to Plymouth, he again protested that his aims were peaceful.

As he met the English, Metacom stood facing a society with which he was willing to live but which would tolerate him only on its own terms. And the terms were ever more unacceptable.

Each year there was less land for hunting and farming, and each year more of his people got drunk on English rum. In sober rage more of them took to killing settlers' pigs that destroyed their corn patches. Angry young Wampanoag were even threatening to kill Steel Knives who insulted them. Clearly Metacom had to make a choice. He had to side with the angry young men—he was young, too—or with the all-consuming English monster.

Metacom knew that standing alone, he and his 1,000 people could not win against 40,000 English. There were 40 well-armed Steel Knives for every poorly armed Wampanoag. He needed allies—which meant forgetting the frictions between his own and other Algonkian people. Two groups seemed most likely to respond—the Nipmuck and the Narraganset.

These three tribes together—the Wampanoag, the Nipmuck, and the Narraganset—totaled 8,000 people. They could provide a force large enough to act as a magnet to other Indians.

Least likely to respond were the hundreds of Praying Indians at Niantic and other places. These converts had learned white men's ways and might forget they were Indians in a time of crisis.

Metacom began quietly sending ambassadors to the Nipmuck and the Narraganset to suggest that these proud, independent tribes cooperate instead of quarreling with one another.

Meanwhile the Steel Knives called Metacom to reaffirm for the third time the treaty of alliance that his father had signed. This time he and seventy of his men were forced to give up their weapons. But he steadfastly rejected the religion which they tried to persuade him and his followers to accept. (He once told Roger Williams that he cared no more for Christianity than he did for a button on his coat.)

At home in Montaup—which the English called Mount Hope—Metacom urged his people to store away as much corn and as much dried fish as possible. His ambassadors took the same suggestion to distant villages. If war came they would need emergency supplies.

Men from Montaup and other towns walked along woodland trails to faraway Albany, where they brought more powder and more guns than usual. When French traders slipped down from Canada, Indians got additional guns and ammunition from them. Englishmen, too, sometimes sold guns they brought ashore from pirate vessels.

Metacom soon discovered he was not alone. His uncle offered support. So did Metacom's wife and the sachem Weetamoo, widow of his brother Wamsutta. With these and others Metacom found himself among able leaders. He was by no means commander in chief of the Algonkian. But he was a thoughtful man, and his greatest contribution seems to have been building alliances and planning ahead.

From the beginning, Metacom had a special problem. Many young Wampanoag men wanted to move too fast. They could hardly wait to get rid of the English. Tension began when a certain Wampanoag named Sassamon turned traitor. Sassamon had converted to Christianity, learned to read and write, and even attended Harvard for a while. Then he got into some kind of trouble and returned to his people. Because he spoke and wrote English, he became Metacom's secretary. In this capacity he knew all that Metacom was planning. Sassamon ran to the English with his news, and then one cold winter day he went to fish through a hole in the frozen pond. His body was found under the ice.

Plymouth officials knew that Sassamon had turned informer. Rightly or wrongly they suspected he had been killed by Metacom or by Metacom's agents. The English quickly found three frightened Wampanoag to accuse of the murder. After their trial and execution, Metacom's hotheaded warriors yearned for revenge. And he shared their anger fully.

About this time the governor of Massachusetts sent an ambassador to Metacom asking him to keep the peace. Metacom reflected the mood of his people when he replied: "Your Governor is but a subject of King Charles of England. I shall not treat with a subject. I shall treat peace only with the King, my brother. When he comes, I am ready."

Metacom's pride was great—but so was his sense of the practical. In this he had support from a holy man at Montaup who spoke to the young men in prophetic idiom. They could win a war against the Steel Knives, he said, only if the enemy began the attack and spilled the first blood.

The hotheads, whose pouches were full of bullets, devised a response that was at once an acceptance and an evasion. They did not shoot anyone, but they began to taunt Englishmen they met in the neighboring white village of Swansea and on the trails in the nearby woods. Their taunting was aimed at getting the Steel Knives to fire the first shot. Little by little they pulled ahead in the race they were running with the thoughtful Metacom.

It was hard for many of the young Indians to believe that countless Englishmen would rush to avenge the death of any white settler. Metacom, of course, had been to Plymouth and had observed how strong the English were. Boston was even larger and stronger, and there were scores of other English towns full of Steel Knives. Although he reported this to the

Fifty years after the death of Metacom, who was a Wampanoag, several engravings of Iroquois Indians appeared in London. After another fifty years passed, Paul Revere, borrowing from these engravings, concocted this caricature, which he offered as a likeness of Metacom, whom he called King Philip.

A COLONIAL DEBT TO INDIANS

Colonists owed their survival to the Indians who had learned how to live in the American environment and who passed their knowledge on to the newcomers. The Indians' special food plants, special ways of catching fish and game, special travel routes, all became invaluable to settlers.

At the same time, colonists learned useful new words and adopted them into the American language, which gradually began to evolve in a direction different from that taken by the English spoken in England. Language, along with many other features of life, expanded in a distinctive way in America and became one of the many indications that European colonies in the Western Hemisphere would sooner or later take on an existence separate from the colonizing homelands in the Old World.

Here are words from Indian languages that had entered American English by 1776 and that still remain in use: canoe, catalpa, chipmunk, hickory, hominy, maize, menhaden, moccasin, moose, mugwump, ocelot, opossum, papoose, pecan, pemmican, persimmon, podunk, poke (the plant), pone, powwow, raccoon, sachem, sagamore, samp, skunk, squash, squaw, succotash, tammany, tapioca, tepee, terrapin, tomahawk, totem, wigwam, wampum, woodchuck.

In addition to words that were borrowed in more or less their original forms, Indian words were translated into English and then added to the vocabulary: big chief, bury the hatchet, medicine man, pipe of peace, war club, war dance, war drum, war paint, warpath, war whoop.

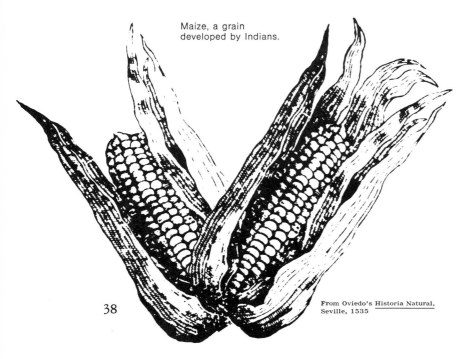

Maize, a grain developed by Indians.

From Oviedo's Historia Natural, Seville, 1535

38

to the young Indian men, they were not willing to listen.

On June 20, some of them entered Swansea and shot cattle, but not people. Three days later an enraged Englishman shot and wounded a Wampanoag. This was the spilling of blood which the young warriors wanted. The next day they killed nine Englishmen in Swansea. They had won the race against Metacom.

Farsighted though he was, Metacom had not yet worked out all his plans for the war that he knew must come. He and his people were in Montaup on a peninsula connected to the mainland by a narrow neck of land—the worst possible place if the Steel Knives decided to attack. The enemy could easily take the narrow neck of land and trap the Indians on the peninsula. Their only escape would be by water.

Metacom quickly assembled as many canoes as he could. In some he sent women and children westward across the bay to the Narraganset. He and his men paddled eastward, heading for shelter in a large swamp, where Steel Knives would not know their way around.

On June 25, following an eclipse of the moon, during which the Englishmen saw all kinds of omens, armed soldiers prepared an attack. Of course they found no one at Montaup. They followed the Wampanoag into the marshes, but the trailless waste—and Indian snipers—frustrated them, just as Metacom knew they would. "It is ill fighting a wild Beast in his own Den," the Reverend William Hubbard wrote. And the Reverend John Eliot, whose lifework was the conversion of Indians, said, "We were too ready to think that we could easily supress that flea"—by which he meant Indians—"but now we find that all the craft is in catching of them, and that in the meanwhile they give us many a soare nip."

By the end of July all the Wampanoag had left the swamp safely and were headed for Nipmuck territory. The English set out in hot pursuit and almost overtook their quarry, but this time, and many more times to follow, the Indians eluded them. Presently the Wampanoag divided their forces, possibly hoping that this would increase their chances of winning allies. Metacom, with one contingent, went on to the Nipmuck, who soon joined in the war. The sachem Weetamoo led another group to a haven with the Narraganset, and before long these people entered the war.

Throughout August, Indian raiding parties struck at English villages along the Connecticut River valley. Apparently the general plan was to drive the Englishmen from their most remote outposts and then herd them toward the sea. The colonies of Connecticut, Plymouth, and Massachusetts Bay now became officially involved in the war. Rhode Island did not. There the government was at the moment under control of Quakers, who wanted no part of violence. But individual Rhode Islanders did join the fighting, and Rhode Island was not spared attacks.

By late fall Canonchet, a powerful and respected leader of the Narraganset, had cast his lot with Metacom. Canonchet's cousin also lent energy to the work, as did a respected sachem, Quaiapen, whom the English called Old Queen. Canonchet's people, who were much more numerous than the Wampanoag, had already begun to aid the refugees. As a defense measure they decided to build a fortified village in the midst of a marshy place called the Great Swamp. Perhaps 3,000 people gathered there inside a protective palisade made of upright logs firmly embedded in the earth. Beyond the palisade a great expanse of tangled roots and swampy water formed a kind of natural moat.

At one place the palisade was still incomplete when the winter cold froze water and mud solid. It was to that place that a Narraganset traitor led 1,000 English soldiers one bitter day in December. The well-armed Englishmen crossed the frozen moat and poured through the one gap in the log wall. The Narraganset fought back as best they could, but soon the whole place was in flames. Canonchet, with some of the leaders, escaped. So did the majority of others in the town. But hundreds of people were burned to death—"barbekewed," one minister put it; "fried," said another.

After the disaster at the Great Swamp, the surviving Narraganset knew that they had to plant gardens if they were to get through another winter. In early April, Canonchet with about thirty men moved through the woods toward a place where a large cache of their seed corn had been hidden. Suddenly a party of Pequot Indians, acting as mercenaries for the English, surprised the Narraganset, and before Canonchet could flee, he was captured. The English offered him his life if he would join their side, but he refused, saying, "I shall

(Above) The English attack and burn a Pequot village. (Below) As warfare in New England increased when Europeans invaded the area, both Algonkian and Iroquois Indians relied increasingly on defensive palisades that resembled the Iroquois structure shown here.

die before my heart is soft, or I have said anything unworthy of myself." The English thereupon ordered three Pequot sachems to execute him. He got shot, and his severed head was taken to the English officials at Hartford, Connecticut.

Metacom and other leaders had continued to inspire or direct military actions against English settlements. Town after town went up in flames until a dozen were utterly destroyed. Fifty-two towns out of the ninety in all of New England were attacked and damaged. Indians had balanced defeat in the Great Swamp fight by many separate victories in small isolated engagements. But victory in an overall sense seemed further than ever from their reach. Soon the tide began to turn against them. In one battle the English killed the leader Quaiapen and 170 of her Narraganset followers. Some Praying Indians who joined the war on the English side killed an important Narraganset sachem late in 1676. A Nipmuck leader was betrayed by another Indian, led to Boston Common, tied to a tree, and shot by his betrayer. (One wonders if he died where Mary Dyer was hanged because she fought for religious freedom.)

About this time a settler named Benjamin Church caught Metacom's wife and his nine-year-old son. Church also found ways of persuading Ashawonka, the leader of the Sacconet, that the Indian cause was hopeless and that her only future lay in siding with the English. She provided Church with many of her best warriors, and now the war became a bitter struggle of Indian against Indian.

Metacom knew that the war was lost. Too great eagerness on the part of his own young men had frustrated the plans for unity that might have saved his people. In the time that was left him, he decided that he wanted one thing more than anything else for himself and his remaining handful of followers. The sachem Weetamoo, in her separate hiding place, had the same wish—to return home to Montaup. Metacom shaved his head, removing the patch of hair on top which was an Algonkian man's challenge to enemies meaning: "Here is my scalp lock. I dare you to come and take my scalp."

When Metacom heard that his wife and son had been captured he said, "My heart breaks, now I am ready to die." And he went back to Montaup to do just that.

(Above) Benjamin Church was the most aggressive military leader among the colonists in the war of 1675. (Right) Warfare between invading whites and defending Indians continued for more than two centuries after 1675. Here, unidentified Indians in uncharacteristic battle formation meet white soldiers of a later period.

At Montaup he had one last outburst of anger. One of his followers proposed that the remaining Wampanoag surrender. Metacom ordered the man shot. The dead man's brother sneaked out of camp, found Benjamin Church, and offered to betray Metacom's whereabouts. Church, well armed and full of aggressive energy, quickly found both Metacom and Weetamoo. Soon both were dead.

Metacom had not known that a special committee of Puritan ministers was assembled to debate whether to execute his son or to send him into slavery. The Reverend Increase Mather favored killing the boy, but liberal ministers won the debate. He and his mother were sold for one pound each and shipped off to spend the rest of their lives in the West Indies. With them, more than 500 other Indian captives were sold into slavery from the port of Plymouth alone. Many more had been sentenced to serve individual Puritans as slaves in New England for periods up to thirty years.

The combined military forces of the Plymouth, Massachusetts Bay, and Connecticut colonies effectively destroyed the national liberation movement of the Wampanoag. The Praying Indians fared little better than their non-Christian brothers. So great was the Englishmen's fear of all Indians that they attacked one village inhabited solely by converts and moved most of the other converts out of their villages and confined them in a concentration camp on Deer Island in Boston Harbor. There, much of the Native Americans' newly acquired English culture dropped away, and their zeal for Christianity never reached very high levels again.

To remind those Indians who survived the war that they had better let white men dictate the terms of their existence, the officials at Plymouth raised the severed head of Metacom high on a pole in town for all to see. It remained on display for twenty-five years.

The valiant effort of the New England Algonkian was over, but they were not the only Indians who reached for freedom from colonial rule. And Englishmen were not the only colonists in what is now the United States. Pueblo Indians in New Mexico suffered under Spanish control, and they, like the Algonkian, rebelled. But they took a longer time to prepare, and their revolution had a different end.

Rachel Folsom

(Left) Colonial Spanish ox goad used in New Mexico. *(Above)* Missions were made of adobe and when abandoned in 1680 soon became ruins. At Taos the mission destroyed in the revolution was rebuilt when the Spaniards returned. Then it was destroyed again in 1847. This is what it looked like after the second destruction, and no doubt also after the first. *(Opposite)* Taos Pueblo as it looks today. Here Popé planned the revolution of 1680.

In 1680, led by Popé, a holy man from the village that Spaniards called San Juan, Pueblo Indians rose up, following a carefully worked-out plan. They utterly defeated the foreigners and drove them out of New Mexico. For twelve years no Spaniard remained in Pueblo country to tell any Indian how he or she must work or worship. When Spaniards did return, they came with great military strength and a greatly modified plan for rule. The Pueblos were not asked to make a complete surrender, and their successful rebellion in 1680 is probably the reason that Pueblo Indians still survive in their homeland today.

In their colonial area the Spaniards had somewhat different objectives from those the English pursued. Both wanted profit, but the English sought it primarily by acquiring land on which they could work. This often meant that the land had to be denuded of people who were already living there. Spaniards, on the other hand, wanted people whom they could force to work the land. Accordingly they did not try to

destroy Indians in New Mexico. Rather they tried to intimidate and subjugate them. One means to that end was the separation of Indians from their religion. For this reason the Catholic missionary effort in New Mexico was intense. Along the Río Grande both ecclesiastical and civil officials worked zealously from 1598 to 1680 toward eliminating Indian religion. They burned all the religious equipment they could get their hands on, and they punished everybody they found holding ceremonies. In 1675 they imprisoned and whipped forty-seven holy men—medicine men. These leaders, from many different villages, were released only after a mass march of Christian Indians from the village of San Juan to the capital at Santa Fé.

One of the holy men, Popé, resolved at that time that the rule of foreigners must end. For five years he worked to unite the many Pueblo villages in one resistance effort. It was not simple. For one thing, the people spoke seven distinct languages. Popé communicated through multilingual traders and medicine men, who traveled from village to village. In each place he had to seek out leaders who could be trusted— who were loyal to their people. Usually this meant men who had not been bribed in some way by the Spaniards.

At last Popé perfected a military plan that only he and a few others knew in detail. On a given day, there was to be a rising throughout the upper Río Grande valley with simultaneous attacks on every outlying Spanish settlement. The idea was to destroy all of the small, isolated places at the same time so that none could get help from another. This done, the rebels would deal in a special way with the two large, well-defended settlements.

In each Pueblo village only the *hour* of the rising was known. Only Popé and a handful of advisers knew the exact *date.* When that day approached, they sent out runners carrying knotted cords. The knots told how many days were to pass before the rising was to begin at dawn.

On August 10, 1680, Pueblo Indians with some Apache

allies attacked the outlying villages exactly as planned and destroyed almost every Spaniard in them. Then the attacking parties joined together in two armies, one moving on the Spanish capital at Santa Fé from the south, the other moving from the north. At Santa Fé and at Sandía, the other colonial stronghold, Spaniards huddled together waiting for news that would give them hope. The biggest news would be the arrival of a supply train from Mexico City. It was already due. And that was exactly why the rising had been scheduled for this date. The Indians knew that the Spaniards were low on supplies. They also knew something the Spaniards did not. The supplies would be held up. Because the Pueblos were great weather-watchers, they had foreseen that unusual high flooding of the Río Grande would keep the wagon train from crossing into New Mexico.

To heighten Spanish anxiety, Indians saw to it that no messengers passed back and forth between Sandía and Santa Fé. False rumors began to circulate among the frightened colonists in each place. Those in Sandía were led to believe that all the Spaniards in Santa Fé had been killed. So they fled southward, away from the capital, which could have used their help. Meanwhile, in Santa Fé, Spaniards believed the false rumor that everyone at Sandía was dead. Surrounded by a very large Indian army that cut off their water supply, they abandoned the city.

The Indians could easily have annihilated the retreating Spaniards. Instead they let their former rulers go in peace. They merely jeered the refugees on their way to what is now Juárez, Mexico, where they remained.

The victory of the Indians was complete and might have been permanent had they realized that it was important to maintain in peace as well as in war the intertribal unity they had developed. But Popé died, petty quarrels developed, and the well-armed Spaniards were able to return. Never, however, did they resume their efforts to destroy Indian culture and Indian religion in that area.

PLACES TO SEE

ARIZONA

Hopi Reservation: Old Oraibi.

MASSACHUSETTS

Boston: Old State House / Boston Common.
Bourne: Aptuxcet Trading Post.
Deerfield: Site of Bloody Brook Massacre.
Mendon: Monument of Battle with the Nipmucks.
Plymouth: Town House Site / Massasoit Statue, Cole's Hill.
Rochester/Middleborough: Assawompsett Pond.
Springfield: King Philip's Stockade, Forest Park.
Swansea: Miles Garrison House.
Wayland: Wadsworth Monument.

NEW MEXICO

Santa Fe: Palace of the Governors Museum.
San Juan Pueblo.
Taos Pueblo.
Tesuque Pueblo.
Pecos National Monument.
Other Pueblos: Acoma / Cochiti / Isleta / Jemez / Picuris / Sandía / San Felipe / San Ildefonso / Santa Ana / Santo Domingo / Zia / Zuñi.

RHODE ISLAND

Wakefield: Great Swamp Fight Monument.
Wickford: The Updike House.

For more information, see Gazetteer, page 212.

9

Bacon's Rebellion

1675   Virginia

Nathaniel Bacon, though an aristocrat himself, was a leader in helping the poor whites of Virginia to rise against their wealthy oppressors—but at the same time they were themselves oppressing the Native Americans.

When in 1649 Puritans in England beheaded King Charles I and established a republican regime, the colonial governor of Virginia, Sir William Berkeley, went into a rage. Berkeley had been one of the king's closest advisers and had once lived in the royal palace. Since he believed that monarchs ruled by divine right, it followed that he, as the king's representative, should have absolute power in Virginia. Now, fearful of the common people around him, he denounced any semblance of republicanism. To show where his heart lay, he refused to recognize the Commonwealth government in London, and in the tiny capital of Jamestown he proclaimed the dead king's son, Charles II, king of England.

When officials of the Commonwealth got around to it, they sent a fleet to Jamestown and removed the governor from office—but not from Virginia. Berkeley retired to his estate at Green Spring, only a few miles from Jamestown, where he occupied himself with increasing his already considerable wealth. And he bided his time. It came soon enough. The Commonwealth was overthrown; Charles II did in fact become king of England; and Berkeley resumed his post as governor of Virginia, more hostile than ever to notions of representative government.

Berkeley had always run the colony's affairs to suit himself. He appointed all members of the Virginia Council of

State. Soon after his arrival, when a new House of Burgesses was elected, he made sure by devious means that all members of that body were subservient to him. Then he refused to call a new election. Year after year his obedient henchmen went through a kind of dumb show, pretending to represent the people. But there was small chance they would do anything to antagonize the governor. He had seen to it that they drew high salaries, plus additional allowances as officers in the colonial militia or as justices of the peace or as county officials of one kind or another. Through them Berkeley not only controlled the government; he and his followers also owned the best land. Newcomers, who had been arriving from England by the thousands, had to become tenants of the big landowners or move out into the wilderness onto land that was usually poor and often menaced by Indians whom they were displacing. But move they did, and they insisted on planting tobacco, the crop that had very obviously brought wealth to the first Virginia settlers who lived along the coast.

For some time there had been a good market for tobacco in Holland. But after Charles II came to power in 1660 that market disappeared. Very soon Parliament, with the king's approval, passed the Navigation Acts, which made it illegal for Virginians to sell tobacco to Holland or to buy goods in that country. All tobacco had to go to England. All goods purchased by Virginians had to come from England. These simple-minded regulations were supposed to divert to English merchants the huge profits the Dutch traders had been making. But things did not work out that way. English warehouses began to overflow with tobacco because the markets that had been buying tobacco in Holland would not buy from England.

Soon Virginians were getting only about one-sixth of the former price for their crop. This was a blow to rich planters as well as to poor, but the rich could stand the loss. They grew food as well as tobacco on their large estates. Some raised other crops for which a market remained open. But the small farmer suffered intensely. He had no such resources. At the same time he was still expected to pay exceedingly high taxes imposed by the government in Jamestown. And his betters had only begun to devise schemes for squeezing him. First the king decided to grant two of his special friends ownership of the whole colony of Virginia. Now tobacco farmers had to bear the expense of sending representatives to London to plead with the king. He did relent and withdraw the grant—but at a price: Landowners in Virginia, in order to keep their land, were required to pay the king's two friends an annual fee, called quitrent. The initial payment was supposed to cover accumulated quitrents for eleven years. In many cases this sum was more than the market value of the land.

People on the frontier could not endure such financial burdens. Nor could they elect useful representatives to the House of Burgesses in Jamestown. Governor Berkeley still refused to allow an election. General dissatisfaction was also widespread in and around Jamestown itself. Indentured servants, who never liked their lot, were angry because Berkeley refused to allow them to serve in the militia, there to draw wages and attain some status in the world.

Against the day when he might be forced to hold an election, Berkeley had wangled a law providing that none of the men could vote unless they owned property. This meant that all the men who were former indentured servants were disfranchised if they had not yet obtained land. And, of course, no indentured servant, slave, or female could vote.

The slaves had their own grievances in this troubled period. There was an epidemic of rebellion among them in 1672. Berkeley managed to stop it—then predictably turned its aftereffects against the poorer taxpayers. He allowed the execution of any slaves who resisted authority, and he provided for large payments to compensate the owners. These payments, of course, came out of the general treasury, to which small landowners already made disproportionate contributions. Nor did grievances end there. Taxation was not based on land ownership or on income. It was a poll tax— one imposed on each person. This meant a poor man paid exactly the same amount as the wealthiest planter.

Behind all of Berkeley's actions was a philosophy which he expressed in part in 1671: "I thank God, *there are no free schools,* nor *printing* . . . for learning has brought disobedience, and heresy, and sects into the world, and *printing* has divulged them, and libels against the best government. God keep us from both." This attitude, added to economic and political grievances, did not increase Berkeley's popularity.

By 1675, Virginia was a bomb ready to explode. And a young aristocrat named Nathaniel Bacon had shown in various ways that he was capable of setting it off.

Bacon already had a history of bursting any restrictions placed around him. At Cambridge University he had been in some kind of scrape which led his father to put him under the care of a private tutor, who happened to be a talented man. He gave Bacon a good education, traveling with him all the while on the Continent. But this expensive training, which included a return to Cambridge, did not make young Bacon tame and docile. He decided to marry a wealthy young woman whose father forbade the match. Nathaniel and the lady married nonetheless, and she was promptly disinherited. About this same time Bacon got into some kind of business tangle, not at all to his own father's liking, and he was sent off to Virginia. There the young man had a cousin who was already well established and another influential relative, the wife of Governor Berkeley.

Berkeley greeted Bacon as a welcome addition to Virginia aristocracy and promptly appointed the slender, dark-haired twenty-seven-year-old to the prestigious Council of State. He also helped Bacon to buy two tracts of land, one about thirty miles up the James River at a place called Curles Neck, the other on the present site of Richmond, which at that time was on the very frontier.

Bacon plunged into life as a tobacco planter. Immediately he began observing at first hand the desperate needs of his farmer neighbors, and they soon came to value him. He had an obvious talent for leadership, was a member of the governor's council, and understood the small planters' problems because he shared them. Before Nathaniel Bacon had been two years in the colony, he became a fuse attached to the bomb that was Virginia.

In no time there appeared a match to light that fuse. Native Americans on the frontier had been promised

This likeness of the elegant and autocratic Sir William Berkeley, 17th century governor of Virginia hangs in the Capitol at Richmond and is a copy by Mrs. Jeffrey Montague of a portrait done by Sir Peter Lely.

reservation lands by Governor Berkeley. He wanted them at peace so that he could buy furs from them. There was more to be earned in the fur trade—and from selling licenses to other traders—than from selling land to tobacco growers, who would only further depress the price of tobacco.

If the fur trade was to prosper, Berkeley had to do his best to avoid war with the Native Americans. But the new settlers had other ideas. They wanted land of their own, and they moved into areas that Berkeley had promised to reserve for the Indians. The Indians naturally objected and offered resistance. Englishmen killed Indians and Indians retaliated.

To complicate matters still further, Virginia began to feel the effects of hostilities between Indians and whites in distant New England, where in 1675 Indians had launched a war of national liberation, perhaps the bloodiest in Ameri-

can history. Indians who survived that conflict recoiled westward, and tribes as far away as the Great Lakes felt the pressure coming from the east. The Seneca, wanting territory in which they could live freely, responded to the pressure on their eastern flank by moving against the Susquehanna Indians on their southern flank. The Susquehanna had to move farther southward to the very border of Virginia. There all the land was taken up by other Indians or by the newly arrived white settlers. So the Susquehanna were desperate. They took food wherever they could find it. Often they raided white farmers on the frontier who had a few pigs and cows and small corn patches.

These raids were the match that lit the fuse which Bacon had become.

On one foray Indians killed the man in charge of one of

In this 19th century engraving Virginia's Governor Berkeley defies 17th century rebels.

46

Nathaniel Bacon's plantations. Neighboring farmers also suffered from attacks. At a meeting in Merchant's Hope, frontiersmen armed with rifles asked Bacon, the council member, to get the support of Governor Berkeley for a war against the Indians. Bacon sent to Jamestown a request for permission to lead militia against the marauders. Then, without waiting for authorization, he started out in pursuit of those who were presumed to be troublemakers.

Berkeley was in no hurry to upset the arrangements on which fur trading was based. He ordered Bacon to disband the little army he was leading. Bacon ignored the order and moved out beyond the frontier toward an island in the Roanoke River, where he expected to get help from the Occaneechi Indians. They agreed to join in fighting the Susquehanna. But they refused Bacon something else he wanted —food for his troops. It was early spring and the Occaneechi had nearly exhausted their winter stores. Since it would be months before the next harvest was ripe, they needed every kernel of corn they had left.

Bacon was furious at being denied. He launched an attack on the friendly Occaneechi and virtually annihilated the community. Immediately he became a hero to frontiersmen, all of whom hated Indians.

As word of Bacon's action spread, so did his popularity throughout Virginia. His defiance of Berkeley and his sympathy with the settlers' basic economic grievances appealed to both the tobacco farmers and the servant class. Volunteers flocked to his army, among them a number of slaves who had no quarrel with Indians but who did want to be free. Backed up by his troops, Bacon demanded that the old Assembly be disbanded and that an election be held to choose new burgesses.

Berkeley was loath to agree. But he could see that Bacon was gathering support from farmers close to Jamestown as well as from those near the frontier. It seemed obvious that Bacon's friends would win the votes. And so Berkeley decided he had no choice. He called an election, and Bacon promptly won a seat in the House of Burgesses. (The governor had, of course, dismissed him as a member of his own council.) More than two-thirds of the other new burgesses were followers of Bacon, who was now only twenty-nine years old.

Bacon set out for Jamestown, traveling by boat and taking with him some of his armed supporters. When Berkeley's men saw him coming they fired on him, and for the moment kept him away from the capital. Bacon managed to enter the town secretly by land at night. But while he conferred with friends, his presence became known, and before he could escape he was captured. To Berkeley he insisted that all he really wanted was a commission to lead forces against the Indians. The governor, uncomfortably aware of the size of Bacon's forces, promised to grant the commission. He let Bacon go free, but he delayed in sending the necessary document.

Impatient with the governor, Bacon returned to Jamestown at the head of an armed body of men. His troops lined up two deep and waited in front of the brick building in which the governor, his council, and the House of Burgesses were sitting. Where, Bacon demanded, was the commission he had been promised? After a good deal of nervous negotiation Berkeley produced the document.

More important, the burgesses soon enacted a series of laws severely limiting the governor's power, giving protection to the rights of common citizens, and easing the economic plight of the small farmers. One law extended the franchise to free men who had no property.

As this overturn of authority was going on in Jamestown, a report reached the capital that Indians had once again attacked the frontier. Bacon, with his troops, dashed off, leaving Jamestown undefended. Berkeley, with armed supporters of his own, now resumed control. But the governor could not muster nearly as many men as Bacon could.

This drawing, based on research, shows Jamestown building which included statehouse in 1675.

When Bacon returned, Berkeley fled across Chesapeake Bay to the Eastern Shore of Virginia. This region had long been settled, had no population of newly arrived farmers, and was far from the frontier. There Berkeley had friends on whom he could rely.

Bacon now held the capital, but he found this achievement more a liability than an asset. A pro-Berkeley army was approaching Jamestown by land, and a number of vessels, commanded by Berkeley's supporters, controlled the James River. Bacon quickly saw that he was bottled up and probably doomed if he chose to stay and defend the capital. Since mere possession of the small cluster of buildings would not weaken Berkeley, who was safe among friends, Bacon decided to abandon the town. But first he made sure it would not be a valuable trophy for Berkeley to recover. Bacon himself set

On September 19, 1676, while Governor Berkeley was taking refuge on the Eastern Shore, Nathaniel Bacon and his men burned much of Jamestown. More than two centuries later, Howard Pyle, a famous illustrator, visualized the event this way.

fire to the church. At least twenty-five houses, several of which belonged to Berkeley, went up in flames.

Next Bacon sent a commando expedition to the Eastern Shore with orders to capture Berkeley. But the governor turned the tables on the ill-equipped band. Its leader was captured and hanged. At the same time the people on the Eastern Shore resisted Bacon's call to rebellion and supported Berkeley instead.

Finally Bacon recalled troops from the west and began pursuit of some Berkeley supporters. The end came quickly. Bacon contracted dysentery. He was exhausted from his campaigns, infested with lice, and in his weakened condition fell prey to a fever and died.

Berkeley had promised himself he would hang Bacon's body in an iron cage as a warning to all who beheld it. Once again he was frustrated. With foresight Bacon's men dug a grave in the yard of the Poplar Spring Church and buried a coffin there. But when Berkeley ordered the coffin dug up, he discovered it contained only rocks. Bacon's body was never found.

Resistance to Berkeley continued, but no one among Bacon's followers had his obvious magnetism. The army he had built up fell apart. Many of its officers were captured. In a jail only a few yards from Berkeley's palatial residence at Green Spring, his prisoners awaited terrible vengeance. In England King Charles II, himself no democrat, was astounded at Berkeley's ferocity. He said, "That old fool has hanged more men in that naked country than I did for the murder of my father."

The king sent a new governor to manage the colony while Berkeley returned to England to explain, if he could, what had been going on in Virginia. Berkeley delayed his departure as long as possible, all the while doing everything in his power to punish his enemies. Soon after he arrived in England he sickened and died, a man of seventy-one years, before he had to face justice.

The success of Bacon's rebellion was short-lived, but it did win some increase in the legal rights of citizens. At the same time Americans had begun to use increased force to replace Indian society with a society of their own. This rising against tyranny by an oppressed group of poor whites was also a tyrannous action against another oppressed group—the Native Americans. In its ambivalence Bacon's Rebellion had much in common with other persistent trends in American history up to and beyond the events of 1776.

PLACES TO SEE

VIRGINIA

Glenns: Poplar Spring Church Site
Green Spring.
Jamestown: Site of Third State House
Occoneechee State Park.

For more information, see Gazetteer, page 212.

10

The Holy Experiment

1681 Pennsylvania

In Pennsylvania William Penn and his Quaker followers began to put into practice many of the freedoms that were established as national policy when the new nation was formed, a century later, in Philadelphia.

Dreams of exciting futures in America were the daily stuff of life for boys in the London of the 1650s. Vessels riding low in the water crowded the Thames, disgorging bales of furs or barrels of tobacco or sugar and occasionally even puzzled groups of American Indians—some chiefs, some slaves—all dark and muscular and outlandishly dressed. And then after a time of bustle and tugging at new sails and new ropes, these same ships moved majestically down the Thames, laden with tools and textiles and gunpowder and emigrants, who were weeping and praying or staring bold and bleak out toward the ocean and seeing who knows what beyond the horizon.

Among the London boys, none felt more drawn toward far corners of the British Empire than did William Penn, who had been born close to the great river in 1644. Penn's father, an admiral in the British navy, fought in the wars for possession of colonies and control of colonial trade. In one engagement he defeated the Dutch. In another, forces under his command won the Spanish island of Jamaica, giving England her first colony in the Caribbean. Although he had not been a leader in the struggle that made Ireland a colony, the admiral owned valuable estates there.

Young Penn received a little military training, learned a bit of law, and studied some classics and theology at Oxford.

Before he was twenty-three he had also gained practical experience administering his father's colonial estates in Ireland, and he had used his military knowledge to help put down a mutiny among troops stationed nearby. Here was a young man apparently headed for a conventional career among the rulers of England's empire. His dream of a colonial career did materialize, but its contours were far from conventional.

What gave the special quality to Penn's life and to the colonial role he played was his religion. As a student he had been attracted to a group who called themselves the Religious Society of Friends, more generally known as Quakers. (The name "Quaker" was supposedly first used in derision by a judge when a leader of the Friends admonished him in court to tremble at the word of the Lord.) Young William Penn espoused the heretical views of that despised pacifist sect, and Oxford soon expelled him. Admiral Penn could do no less. He whipped his son and drove him from home.

After a reconciliation William Penn went to look after his father's colonial interests in Ireland, where for a time he seemed a proper establishment figure. Then one day he attended a Quaker meeting in Cork. Arrest and jail followed. If there had been doubt about where William Penn stood, the matter was settled now. He stood with the Quakers, who were mostly poor and almost always persecuted. From then on he was in and out of one jail after another. All the violent efforts to kill his pacifist views had failed.

On one occasion Penn tried to answer an Anglican priest's verbal attacks on Quakers. The priest refused to let him talk. Penn then wrote out his reply and published it in a pamphlet. Because he had not obtained an official license to publish, he was locked up in the Tower of London. There he wrote another pamphlet, one that became a famous statement of Quaker doctrine: *No Cross, No Crown.* Between prison terms Penn was constantly busy advocating freedom of religion and freedom of speech. In one trial he eloquently defended the proposition that a judge could not dictate the verdict that a jury must bring in.

What was the special nature of Quaker beliefs that so moved William Penn as they had also moved Mary Dyer? Quakerism began, as did much that was important in colonial life, with the Protestant-capitalist revolution. On the religious level that revolution sought at first to replace the church with the Bible. But the upheaval did not end there. Some of those who became Bible readers went on to argue— as Anne Hutchinson did—that neither the church nor the Bible could be the ultimate authority on matters of conscience or theology. Individuals, without the guidance of clergymen or the sacred book, could receive direct religious insight— could commune directly with God. Everyone in the world was part of divine creation and could have direct access to divine guidance.

From this theory sprang various democratic concepts. One was that priests and ministers were unnecessary. Another, the belief that all people were equal in a religious sense, had its effect in daily life. If all people—and this Quaker innovation meant women as well as men—had direct access to God, then priests and bishops and lords and kings were no better than the lowliest laborer. Hence there was no reason to use especially respectful forms of address in speaking to the rich and

William Penn as a young military officer in Ireland.

49

powerful. No one need say "your honor" or the shorter "you" instead of "thee" or "thou." In those days everyone used "thee" or "thou" in addressing children or servants or others lower in caste. To Quakers the informal pronouns were good enough for any man or woman, and they invariably used them. Important people did not like this lack of humility on the part of Friends.

These utterly consistent users of egalitarian language carried their stubborn democratic theories into all departments of life. At that time men wore hats indoors as well as out and were expected to remove them only in the presence of someone of higher social rank. But hats stayed on the heads of Quaker men, except at their religious meetings, when they considered themselves in the presence of God. They refused to bare their heads in court when they stood before judges, and many a Quaker went to jail for this defiance of authority.

By and large, the Quakers were more Puritan than the Puritans. They opposed all outward show of piety. Indeed, they objected to ostentation of any kind. They refused to take oaths because they believed that people should tell the truth at all times, not simply when they had sworn not to lie. If anyone wanted biblical authority for their objection to oaths, they quoted Matthew 5:34, in which Jesus said in the Sermon on the Mount, "but I say unto you, swear not at all. . . ." Since officeholders had to swear to carry out their duties, Quakers were barred from public service. In many ways English life excluded them, and at times there were hundreds —even thousands—of them in jail.

It is perhaps surprising that William Penn spent no more time in jail than he did. Probably the reason lay in his aristocratic origins, signs of which always clung to him. He never dressed quite as plainly as most other Quakers. He wore a very un-Quakerish wig to cover his bald head. But he stuck to other attitudes of his sect. In the presence of his good friend King Charles II, he stiffly refused to remove his hat. Charles was merely amused. On one occasion, so the story goes, Charles said it was customary for only one man to keep his head covered when the king was in the room. Thereupon he removed his own hat, leaving William Penn the only man with unbared head.

QUAKERS AND PRICE TAGS

Quakers believed in sincerity and honesty, and this doctrine led them to question the universal practice of haggling over prices in the marketplace. Was a merchant being honest when he asked more for a commodity than it was worth? Were customers being sincere when they offered less for an article than it was worth? To the Quakers it seemed that the whole customary bargaining process was immoral. They insisted on selling goods at fixed prices— apparently the first merchants to do so. This ended bargaining, but it did not end profits. Many Quaker merchants from the earliest days to the present have been very successful participants in capitalist economy.

The Quakers' disdain of outward show led them to reject music as part of their religious meetings and art in their buildings, public or private. Visual art was somehow too closely akin to the sensuous appeal of pagan idols or popish images. Avoidance of decoration went right through life. Most Quakers dressed very plainly, and they lived simply. Many of them, in the early days of Quakerism, could not have lived otherwise if they had wanted to. They were poor. Members of the lower classes—the first recruits to the Society of Friends—seemed to find their new religion a way to protest the attitudes of those of higher social rank. But it was not part of Quaker theory that people should be content to remain poor. Like all who were influenced by Calvinism, the Friends believed that it was virtuous to work hard. They advocated honesty in all their dealings—and deal they did. They engaged in trade, in spite of persecution that was often obviously designed to eliminate them as competitors of businessmen who held more orthodox religious views.

As honest, hard-working people, Quakers were just the sort who could develop the economy of undeveloped America. In England they were misfits. Therefore England would gain doubly if they could be shifted to America. So reasoned King Charles II when in 1681 William Penn suggested the establishment of a new colony in a vast stretch of land north of Maryland. Penn's proposal had another advantage from the king's point of view. It would enable him to pay off 16,000 pounds he had borrowed from the Penn family. So Charles II made William Penn proprietor of a huge area in America. Merely by having the royal seal affixed to the Charter for the Province of Pennsylvania, the king did at least three things that he thought advantageous to himself: He exchanged tens of thousands of acres of Indian land that he really did not own for an acknowledgment that he was free of a 16,000-pound debt. He put people of a type admirably suited to pioneering and building up business into a vacuum that, if left empty, might soon be attractive to imperial rivals. And he got rid of a domestic headache—the Quakers themselves. Later he could even dump dissidents of other kinds into the new colony.

Because the king and William Penn happened to be personal friends, they found it relatively easy to work out this deal. Their unlikely friendship was only one of several oddities about the founding of Pennsylvania. Charles II was antidemocratic and pro-Catholic. The Quaker Penn, though of aristocratic origin, was a very vocal democrat. Nevertheless, he planned to collect quitrents as any feudal lord would do. It was clearly his purpose to make money from the land where he was to be proprietor. He intended to sell acreage, not give it away.

Penn left no illusion about another of his plans. Pennsylvania was going to be a true haven for people in trouble with laws governing religion. He had already had experience setting up such a refuge. For several years before he asked for the Pennsylvania grant, he had been one of twelve Quaker proprietors of West New Jersey. There he and his colleagues had worked diligently to provide a place of safety for their coreligionists. It was during this time that Penn became convinced that a larger Quaker enterprise across the Delaware could be both a practical and spiritual success.

This modern map (1933) shows the Philadelphia area before settlement began there.

Nearly a hundred years after William Penn made a treaty with the Leni-Lenape, Benjamin West commemorated the event with a painting, on which this engraving is based. The original work, *Penn's Treaty with the Indians,* is at the Pennsylvania Academy of the Fine Arts, in Philadelphia.

Because of the spiritual aspects of his project, he sometimes referred to the province of Pennsylvania as a Holy Experiment. The practical business of his experiment involved first transporting thousands of persecuted Quakers, then settling them efficiently into the vast domain over which he had been appointed ruler.

One novel thing he insisted on from the start. He would grant the settlers certain democratic rights—many more rights than they were enjoying in England and more than they could enjoy in any other colony except Rhode Island. Remembering the horrors of English penal laws, he provided that in his colony only two crimes would be punishable by death: murder and high treason. In Massachusetts there were fifteen capital crimes. These included witchcraft, lying, blasphemy, cursing, and even the striking of parents by their children. In England the number was much greater—200 according to one tally.

In a constitution that Penn called a Frame of Government, he provided for universal manhood suffrage. He guaranteed the right of all to worship God as they saw fit. He guaranteed an annual election by ballot to the Assembly, and of course there was no oath required of those chosen to serve.

Quakers could be officials in Pennsylvania.

In every possible way Penn made ready for a mass migration into his province. He traveled to Germany and recruited many Quakers and other nonconformists for his venture. In England he encouraged all kinds of dissidents to become settlers. The first of these were mostly English and Welsh Quakers, but other people soon followed. And when they arrived the immigrants found that commissioners, who had been sent in advance, had prepared well for them. A city was completely planned out. With streets in a regular gridiron pattern, Philadelphia was to be, according to one commentator, "the squarest and levelest city that our planet had ever seen." Its site, between two rivers, the Schuylkill and the Delaware, made it accessible to commerce, and the hinterland was good for farming. Philadelphia offered excellent prospects for all kinds of enterprise—and all kinds developed, as William Penn had hoped.

Penn arrived in his domain late in October 1682, and the scene at his landing dramatized the startling contradictions in his life. He, a Quaker who eschewed ceremony, was made the center of an almost medieval pageant in the little town of New Castle where he came ashore. The Dutch, the Swedes, and the Finns in the village greeted him, their new ruler, by offering him, as symbols of submission, water and soil and turf and a twig. Penn, a theoretical democrat, was faced with the reality that some at least in his realm regarded him as a feudal lord—which he was.

The non-English people of New Castle, members of the Lutheran and Dutch Reformed churches, may have wondered what this man of another nationality and another faith had in store for them. It is not likely that they suspected how liberal he would be toward them and their ways. Nor is there any evidence that they had yet reached out for some of the civil rights they were about to receive.

Consistent with his belief that all people were equal, William Penn soon began to treat the Indians he met with the same respect he showed to members of his own race. He even practiced speaking to the Leni-Lenape chiefs in their own language—a kind of ultimate courtesy. Before a month had passed he and they had worked out a treaty of peace. The Leni-Lenape, hard pressed by the Iroquois, were badly in need of friends, and the Friends certainly did not want enemies. The agreement between Native Americans and new Americans was well conceived and was sealed not with oaths but with a dance. And, though dancing was not encouraged by Quakers, Penn had the grace to join in. Because of his courtesy and evident good faith, the Indians trusted him and gave him an Indian name. Sometimes he was Miquon. At other times he was Onas. Both words meant "quill," which, of course, was what Penn used as a pen.

The treaty, agreed to under an elm tree in Shackamaxon —now a part of Philadelphia called Kensington—was durable, so durable that Voltaire said it was "the only treaty between savages and Christians that was never sworn to and never broken." The exact terms of the agreement have been lost. No copy of it has survived, but whatever its terms, they seem to have satisfied both the Leni-Lenape and the Quakers for a period of seventy years. During that time Quakers ruled Pennsylvania, and people of various nationalities and various faiths poured into Philadelphia, making it the largest city in the colonies. Before long, non-Quakers outnumbered the Friends by six or seven to one. Still the original settlers held all the most important elective as well as appointive offices.

But Pennsylvania did not exist unaffected by imperial rivalries in the larger world. England began to insist that the colony take active military part in a war that was building up with the French, who controlled Canada. This war, a part of a general conflict between France and England, ran counter to the pacifist Friends' beliefs. In 1756 the Quaker members of the Assembly refused to stand for reelection. Power passed to non-Quakers, and they immediately declared war.

One provision of their declaration suggests the vastly changed relations between Indians and whites in the decades that had passed since the signing of the treaty of peace in 1682. The governor and the appointed Council of Pennsylvania now offered bounties for the scalps of Indians who were allied with the French. The rate of pay, figured in 1973 dollars, was more than $200 for the scalp of any male over twelve years old and nearly $100 for the scalp of any female.

How this brutal policy of genocide came into being is not a part of this story. It is enough to say that the Leni-

LOG CABINS AND APPLE PIE

Peter Stuyvesant in 1654 resisted the entry of Jews into New Amsterdam because they might become commercial competitors of Dutch burghers. A year later he ended another kind of rivalry in the New World. He took over, by force, the Swedish settlements, which included many Finns, along the Delaware River.

Among the European powers, the scramble for colonies was intense. England, France, Portugal, Spain, Holland all wanted a piece of America and so did Sweden for a while. Ten years after he had crushed the Swedes' colonial outpost, Stuyvesant and the Dutch were themselves crushed by the English.

In 1664 a British ship sailed up the Delaware and took the Dutch town of New Amstel. Renamed New Castle, it later became part of the holdings of the duke of York. The duke, in turn, made the land along the western shore of Delaware Bay part of the colony which Quaker William Penn founded. On Penn's visit to the colony in 1682 he landed first at New Castle and took formal possession of the area which became known as the Three Lower Counties of Pennsylvania. Differences soon made trouble between Penn's Quaker-dominated English settlers and the older mixed population along the shore. In 1704 the Penn family gave the Three Lower Counties their own separate legislature, and when the Declaration of Independence was signed in 1776 they became the state of Delaware.

The Swedes and Finns, whose settlements began early and ended early, left little mark on America. But they did contribute one important architectural feature to the New World—the log cabin. This type of structure from heavily forested Scandinavia could flourish in the deep woods along the Eastern Seaboard. Very soon the frontier practice of building houses from whole logs became as American as apple pie. And how American is that? Apple pies were popular in Elizabethan England long before the first one was baked in the New World.

A 1650 Swedish cabin on Tinicum Island.

Lenape found rulers of Pennsylvania who followed William Penn—including his sons—more and more greedy. In one instance they redefined the outlines of a parcel of land in a way that infuriated the Indians. The Leni-Lenape had granted white men an area within a line that could be walked in a day and a half. The Pennsylvanians had swift runners to do the "walking," and to make it easy for them to travel a great distance in a day and a half, they sent men with axes out ahead of the runners to clear away all underbrush.

Trickery and subsidies for the slaughter of Indians were not among the creative trends that pointed toward the great political achievement of 1776. However, creativity—a great deal of it—did exist within the Pennsylvania community, both while it was under the control of Quakers and later. In the early years, Quaker pressed against Quaker, insisting on even more democracy than William Penn had initially granted. Poor Quakers, who were mostly farmers, made radical demands of the wealthy Quaker proprietor Penn. Their spokesman, David Lloyd, a Welshman and a lawyer, insisted that the county courts should have increased power. These courts were more responsive to the wishes of the poor than the Supreme Court, which sat in Philadelphia and was influenced by well-to-do merchants. The merchants, for their part, liked the Supreme Court and wanted more power centered in its hands.

This insurgency—all nonviolent—began early during the proprietorship of William Penn. It went on during the stormy years after Charles II died and James II came to the throne in 1685. After William and Mary replaced James, the pressure of David Lloyd and the poor and the farmers still continued. When Penn made his second visit to Pennsylvania in 1699, he was perplexed and hurt by what seemed to him ungrateful demands. But before he left in 1701 he granted the colonists more rights than he had provided for in his original Frame of Government. He called the new constitution a Charter of Privileges, saying, "Ye shall be governed by laws of your own making, and live a free and if you will a sober people." The charter served as the basis for the government of Pennsylvania as long as it continued to be a colony.

The year 1701—a time of democratic advance—was interesting in another respect. At that time Penn drafted a will in which he set his slaves free. The fact that he ever had slaves indicated clear limits to his doctrine that all men were equal, and in this he was not alone. Other Quakers in the colony had slaves. But many opposed the practice. Already in 1688 German Friends, who lived just outside Philadelphia in Germantown, passed a resolution "against the buying and keeping of Negroes." Their statement marked the beginning of the campaign against slavery in America.

Only a few years before Penn granted the Charter of Privileges, he had made another governmental proposal that showed the kind of long-range vision of which he was capable. To the Board of Trade and Plantations, which supervised England's empire, he suggested a plan for the union of the American colonies. He argued for what amounted to a United States of North America. But he reckoned without the fears of board members. They shrewdly saw that if the colonies were united they might be hard to rule. It suited the board better to keep them apart and even suspicious of one another. Penn's plan for union had to wait nearly eighty years to come into effect.

Such large schemes for the general welfare were a characteristic product of Quaker thinking. So, too, was a liberal attitude toward people of different views. As a result, Philadelphia became a city of great variety, full of many contrasting ideas and customs. It was a place of stir and excitement, ahead of all other American cities. Nonconformity flourished, but so did conventional business. The union of intellectual dissidence and economic diligence ultimately led restless, ambitious Philadelphians to look for ways out of restraints imposed by England. Many such Philadelphians, along with others in the colonies, came to believe that the only practical way to be free of forcible restraints was to resist them by force. And although the Quakers were ultimately responsible for much of the ferment that led to the Revolution, most of them would not take up arms when the outbreak came in 1776. They were pacifists and did not believe in the use of force. When violence did begin, the great majority stood aside and took no part in the military actions or even in the coercive actions that preceded actual armed combat. Only a minority, who were excluded from the Society of Friends and who called themselves Free Quakers, supported the Revolution. By and large, pursuit of many of the democratic goals of the Quakers of 1682 was carried on in 1776 by non-Quakers and by non-Quaker means.

The pathway to independence was not simple and direct.

PLACES TO SEE

DELAWARE

New Castle: Immanuel Church / Old Dutch House Museum / Old Presbyterian Church / Amstel House Museum.

NEW JERSEY

Burlington: Site of First Quaker Meetings, 1677.

PENNSYLVANIA

Merion: Merion Meeting House.
Morrisville: Pennsbury Manor Reconstruction.
Philadelphia: Arch Street Meeting House Museum / Christ Church / City Hall; William Penn Statue / Dock where Penn landed / Old Swedes Church (Gloria Dei National Historic Site) / Historical Society of Pennsylvania / Kensington (Shackamaxon), Monument / Penn's Cottage / Philosophical Hall, Independence National Historical Park / St. George's Methodist Church / St. Joseph's Roman Catholic Church / St. Peter's Church / Slate Roof House Site / Stenton Mansion.

For more information, see Gazetteer, page 212.

THEY CAME AS COLONISTS

The land of America was inviting, and New Englanders flattered themselves by adopting a seal *(Right)* that showed an Indian inviting settlers to come and help. *Left:* The silver cup used for Communion at Boston Church, was donated by John Winthrop.

Silver Collection
of the First Church in Boston,
on loan to the
Museum of Fine Arts, Boston
(Photo by David F. Lawlor)

Massachusetts Art Commission
(Photo by George M. Cushing, Jr.)

Earliest Settlers
—East

British Museum

John White, an early settler on Roanoke Island, did this watercolor of an Algonkian village. This painting is one of a series done from life, and it gives as accurate a picture of Native Americans as exists.

Doris DeWitt/Van Cleve

In Plymouth, Massachusetts, many of the 17th century occupations are reenacted.

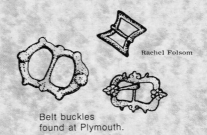

Rachel Folsom

Belt buckles found at Plymouth.

Robert Lightfoot III/Van Cleve

The Castillo de San Marcos, originally built to protect St. Augustine, is now a national historical monument.

56

In the reconstruction of Jamestown, Virginia, houses are still built as they were in 1607.

Above: The seal of Plymouth Colony. *Below:* Pilgrims at the first Thanksgiving, as seen by a 20th century artist. According to accounts of the time these lively colors are more accurate than the subdued tones often used by earlier artists.

The Holy Experiment

The Peaceable Kingdom, by Edward Hicks, whimsically shows the underlying goodwill of Penn's Holy Experiment, where babes are safe even with leopards. The painting is in the Worcester (Massachusetts) Art Museum.

This painting of the port of Philadelphia in 1754 is in the collection at Independence National Historical Park.

The German settlers of Pennsylvania, now known as Pennsylvania Dutch, were skilled craftsmen. This intricately designed plate was made in 1780.

Colonial Life and Death

Despite the arduous life of Puritan women, some managed to create delicate needlework, as demonstrated in this 17th century tapestry.

Puritan children, David, Joanna, and Abigail Mason, as painted in Boston in 1670.

These tombstones in Hingham, Massachusetts, date from the 1700s. Note the death's heads, a popular tombstone decoration of the times.

The candles in this 17th century standing rush light are made of mutton tallow. Colonists used many devices, such as reflectors on candle-holders, to offset the gloom in their often windowless houses.

59

A Diversity of Cultures

Touro Synagogue, in Newport, the oldest Jewish temple in North America, is a symbol of the religious freedom established by Roger Williams and an exquisite example of 18th century architecture.

Dutchmen like these painted by Frans Hals in 1641 were managers of the Dutch West India Company, which operated New Netherlands at the time the first Jews arrived there.

In 1734, James Oglethorpe returned from Georgia to England, accompanied by the Native Americans who had sold him land. In this painting, the English backers of the colony meet formally with Tomochichi and other representatives of the dissident Creek.

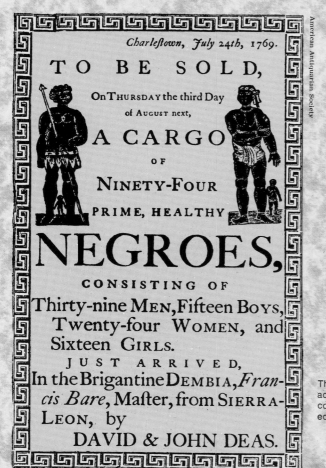

Charlestown, July 24th, 1769.

TO BE SOLD,

On THURSDAY the third Day of AUGUST next,

A CARGO

OF

NINETY-FOUR

PRIME, HEALTHY

NEGROES,

CONSISTING OF

Thirty-nine MEN, Fifteen BOYS, Twenty-four WOMEN, and Sixteen GIRLS.

JUST ARRIVED,

In the Brigantine DEMBIA, *Francis Bare*, Master, from SIERRA-LEON, by

DAVID & JOHN DEAS.

This broadside, published in 1769, advertises an increasingly important commodity in the colonial economy—slaves.

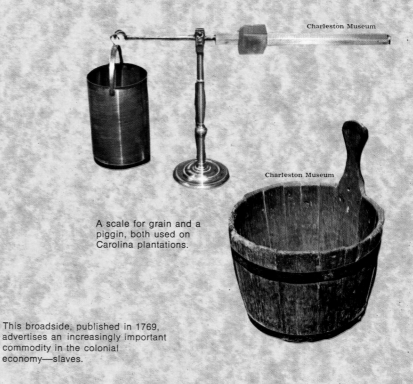

A scale for grain and a piggin, both used on Carolina plantations.

Earliest Settlers —Southwest

Mrs. Mary Garriott

The petroglyph recreated above is in the Indian Petroglyph State Park, New Mexico. The original drawing dates from before Popé's Rebellion, or the Pueblo Revolt, of 1680.

Right: Junípero Serra founded the Carmel Mission in Carmel, California, in 1770, and attempted to convert the Native Americans of the area to Catholicism. *Below:* A painting shows Serra with other Spaniards and Native Americans.

PART TWO

Toward Self-Expression & Self-Government

The high things that are said in favor of rulers and of their dignitaries, and upon the side of power, will not be able to stop people's mouths when they feel themselves oppressed.

—ANDREW HAMILTON

It is the duty of every good citizen to point out what he thinks erroneous in the commonwealth. —JAMES OTIS

The Glorious Revolution in America

1689   Boston and New York

When pro-Catholic King James II was forced by Parliament to abdicate and the Protestant William and Mary became monarchs of Britain, this peaceful transition was called by Protestants "The Glorious Revolution." In America the transition was not so peaceful, and popular actions in Boston and New York drove from office colonial officials who favored King James II. In New York Jacob Leisler led the actions.

Events in England often had profound effect on the distant American colonies. This was certainly true in 1688–89. In these years radical Whigs and conservative Tories in Parliament jointly found a unique formula for guaranteeing that the English monarchy would be Protestant and not Catholic. Their unlikely coalition forced the abdication of James II, who was pro-Catholic and whose Catholic wife had just borne a son destined no doubt to be raised in her faith. Fortunately for Parliament, James had a daughter, Mary, by his first wife, who was a Protestant, and Mary's Protestant husband was Prince William of Orange of the Netherlands. These two, Parliament decided, should be brought to the English throne.

This change of monarchs was accomplished without bloodshed, and jubilant Protestants called it the "Glorious Revolution." When the news reached America, popular resentment against James and his colonial policies exploded in

a variety of ways. New Englanders had particularly disliked the king's revocation of their colonial charters, which gave them some control over their own affairs through town meetings and locally elected officials. At the same time James had fused several colonies together in what was called the Dominion of New England, and to administer this new agency he had appointed Sir Edmund Andros, who very quickly made himself disliked. Andros tried to collect unpopular taxes and customs duties; his tastes were those of a feudal lord, differing greatly from those of the Puritans he had been sent to rule; and he was a professional military officer.

News of the king's abdication delighted Bostonians. Now perhaps they could get rid of Andros. The Reverend Cotton Mather took a lead in urging people to restore their old form of government. There was no need, he said, to wait for emissaries and instructions from the new monarchs. The time to act was now.

Early on the morning of April 18, 1689, messengers hurried between the North End and the South End of Boston. By nine o'clock drums beat throughout the town and the cry went up, "All are in arms!"

Organized groups of armed Bostonians seized officials who were serving under Andros. Shouting threats, the citizens chased Andros to the fort, where he took refuge with some of his followers.

Meanwhile military groups from all over Massachusetts were also gathering. Fifteen hundred militiamen waited at Charlestown across the river, ready to invade Boston, if necessary, to get rid of Andros. Their help was not needed. Andros could not muster support. An armed frigate in the harbor did try to send him some weapons. It dispatched a rowboat full of small arms and "hand-grenadoes" to the fort, but these never reached their destination. Rebels seized the rowboat, thus increasing their own armaments.

Andros quickly saw that his position was hopeless. He surrendered to the militiamen clamoring outside the fort and as their prisoner returned to the Town House, the government building where only the day before he had been an autocratic ruler. There, spokesmen for the citizenry told Andros in no uncertain terms that he himself was to blame for his plight. After explaining what their goals were, the rebels put Andros back in the fort and held him there under guard.

There was much coming and going to and from the fort under the new regime. Women as well as men entered the place—to prepare meals, to do laundry and other chores—and their presence gave Andros an idea. With the aid of his handful of supporters he managed to have a woman's clothes smuggled in. Disguised in skirts and shawl, he walked past the first guard. But he wore men's shoes, and they gave him away. He was led back to his cell.

Although Bostonians were rebelling in support of King William and Queen Mary, it turned out that the new monarchs felt a good deal less than enthusiastic about the uprising. They wanted some form of government in Massachusetts that would be more tractable than the old town-meeting form of organization to which the Puritans had become attached. William and Mary were anti-Catholic, no

Nineteenth century depiction of the removal of Governor Andros in Boston.

Governor Andros is led to prison after being deposed (19th century illustration).

doubt about that, but anyone who thought they loved representative government was mistaken.

Very soon the citizens of Plymouth, Rhode Island, and Connecticut followed the example set by Boston. They threw out officials of the Dominion of New England who had served under Governor Andros and returned to the governments they had had before their charters were revoked. No

matter what objection anyone had to some features of these charters, they gave better protection to the rights of Englishmen in New England than had the Dominion regime.

In New York the situation was different. England had seized this area from Holland in 1664, and the population was overwhelmingly Dutch. Among the 850 or more families on Manhattan Island, exclusive of Blacks, whom no one bothered to enumerate, 500 or more were Dutch. Some 200 were French Huguenot, all refugees from Catholic France. There were also 20 Jewish families, refugees from Catholic Portugal. Only 130 families were English. In 1687 the governor of New York described the religious mix of the seaport this way: "New York has first a Chaplain belonging to the Fort of the Church of England; Secondly, a Dutch Calvinist; Thirdly, a French Calvinist; Fourthly a Dutch Lutheran—Here bee not many of the Church of England; few Roman Catholics; abundance of Quakers preachers men & Women especially; Singing Quakers, Ranting Quakers; Sabbatarians; Antisabbatarians; Some Anabaptists; some Independents; some Jews; in short of all sorts of opinions there are some, and the most part of none at all. . . ."

The governor had tried to impose uniformity by insisting that the Dutch, the French, and the Jews all conduct their official business in English. Merchants had to use English weights and measures instead of the ones they had long been accustomed to. More irksome, they could buy and sell only within those parts of the world controlled by England, a restriction which greatly limited their economic freedom. In addition they had to pay exorbitant taxes and customs duties.

After the British takeover in 1664 King Charles' brother, the duke of York, ran this conquered area like a feudal domain, and he gave it his name. It became New York. The duke made huge grants of land along the Hudson River to his aristocratic English friends, but refused to give even small tracts to common people, thus forcing ordinary citizens to become tenants on the large estates. On any Dutchman who already owned land he imposed a new tax—a feudal quitrent payable to him each year. Wealthy Dutch landowners and merchants, as well as poor artisans and tenants, all had to face assaults on the Dutch Reformed church to which they belonged. English officials forbade the old practice of paying the expenses of the church out of public funds. At the same time the English began to appoint Anglican priests to serve in Dutch Reformed churches.

Added to all these indignities was a widespread belief, not without foundation, that English officials in New York were busy draining off public funds for their own private enrichment. The governor, for example, suspended the right to trial by jury, then pocketed the fines he assessed against persons he found guilty of infractions of the laws. These laws were often arbitrary in the extreme. Graft was common.

Life became even more difficult for colonial businessmen when the authorities in London limited the number of coins that could be legally circulated in the colonies. England did not want local commerce or manufacturing to develop in America, because the colony was to be held primarily as a source of raw materials for English businessmen, not as a location for potential competitors. The milling of grain, for example, was forbidden except in Manhattan, where it could

be carefully overseen and taxed. People far out on Long Island could not trade directly with Boston. They had to transship all goods through New York—another device to aid tax collectors. In countless ways most New Yorkers found economic opportunities severely restricted.

Understandably, then, the duke of York was held responsible for these abuses and was not beloved in the province that bore his name. But mere dislike turned to alarm when in 1685 King Charles II died and the duke of York became King James II. Now Protestants and Jews in New York had new reasons for uneasiness. The man in charge of collecting customs in New York was a Catholic. So, too, was the head of the militia. Many people believed that Lieutenant Governor Francis Nicholson leaned toward Catholicism, as did the new king.

Anti-Catholic attitudes among New Yorkers were more than an evidence of prejudice. People in Manhattan knew very well that France and England were engaged in a struggle for control over colonies and trade. Nearby Canada was French and therefore Catholic, and New York might expect military trouble from that direction. Moreover, the Catholics of Canada might find allies among whatever Catholics there were in New York. These coreligionists, so the theory went, might be a fifth column ready to turn New York over to new masters. For most New Yorkers the prospect of falling under French control was frightening. France offered them no especially rosy economic future, and their religious liberties would certainly be drastically curtailed under French rule. The Huguenot refugees among them were testimony to that.

New Yorkers responded to all these fears and grievances by engaging in acts of civil disobedience. Many merchants refused to pay the exorbitant duties required of them. One such tax resister was Jacob Leisler, a German who had arrived in New Amsterdam in 1660 at the age of twenty—a penniless soldier in the employ of the Dutch West India Company. In his new home Leisler married a rich widow,

GERMAN AND DUTCH WORDS IN ENGLISH

More Germans entered North America before 1776 than did people from any other country except England, and many of their words— especially those referring to foods—entered the language of the transplanted Englishmen around them: dumpling, kaffeeklatsch, noodle, pretzel, sauerkraut, schnapps, schnauzer, schnitzel, smearcase, spiegeleisen (a metal composition), spiel, struedel, wiener schnitzel.

The Dutch colonists contributed these words to American English before 1776: boodle (meaning loot*), boss, bush* (backcountry)*, cookey (or cookie, cooky), coleslaw, cruller, dominie, dope, dumb* (stupid)*, patroon, Santa Claus, pit (as in peach* pit)*, sleigh, span (of horses), spook, stoop* (small porch)*, waffle, and —possibly—Yankee.*

and by using her capital well he became one of the half-dozen wealthiest merchants in the city. He also became a vestryman in one of the parishes of the Dutch Reformed church. In this position he gained some prominence by putting up strenuous objections when Lieutenant Governor Nicholson tried to appoint an Anglican priest to run the parish. Finally Leisler was active in the militia, a fact which commended him to his neighbors as their anger increased against the policies and appointees of James II.

Merchant, vestryman, militiaman, Jacob Leisler came to be regarded as a person who could help New Yorkers to liberate themselves. Hope for relief rose with the news that James II had departed. But then nothing happened. Nicholson and his henchmen remained in office. Finally, on the evening of May 30, 1689, a militiaman, perhaps under Jacob Leisler's command, appeared at the fort on the lower end of Manhattan Island. There, oddly, he announced that he was taking over sentry duty from the regular British soldier.

When Lieutenant Governor Nicholson heard of this impertinence he promptly lost his temper and shouted that he would burn the whole city before he would tolerate such insubordination. Whether he would have carried out his threat no one knows, but New Yorkers believed him quite capable of doing so. And in response to his anger they themselves set a fire of quite another kind. Revolution swept the city.

Word had arrived that Governor Andros was in jail in Boston, and there was also the exhilarating news that all over New England people had thrown the supporters of James II out of office. Most New Yorkers felt that their lot would certainly improve under William and Mary. They even supposed that the new monarchs would feel well disposed toward them if they took over the city from the former king's men, who were most reluctant to give up power.

One who rejoiced when William and Mary came to the throne was Jacob Milborne, son-in-law of Jacob Leisler. Milborne was in Holland at the time of the Glorious Revolution, and he started back to New York as fast as he could travel, which wasn't very fast in the seventeenth century.

Meantime militiamen took over not just sentry duty but the whole fort. Rebels then invited Mayor van Cortlandt to proclaim William and Mary king and queen of England. On June 22, the mayor, pleading that he had no official word from the new regime, declined to read the proclamation that had been prepared for him. The militia thereupon made their control of the fort exceedingly secure and on June 28 chose Jacob Leisler to be their captain.

Lieutenant Governor Nicholson fled.

At the same time the rebels set up what they called a Committee of Public Safety—an organization completely new in the colonies. The committee, a kind of defense apparatus, was made up of two elected delegates from each county, who were to direct the affairs of New York pending the arrival of word from William and Mary. This the committee proceeded to do. It chose Leisler to be lieutenant governor, and on August 16 he was also given the title of commander in chief of the province. To show it meant business, the Committee of Public Safety jailed all those who resisted its authority, but no one was executed.

After the pro-Catholic James II abdicated, his daughter Mary and her husband William, both Protestants, became the monarchs of England in the Glorious Revolution of 1689.

It was in the midst of these events that Jacob Milborne returned from Holland. On September 29, soon after his arrival, an election of local officers took place. The franchise was extended to all Protestant property owners—an advance in the direction of democracy greater than any that New Yorkers had enjoyed before.

In February, although no official word had yet come from William and Mary, Leisler called for the election of an assembly to handle affairs for the colony as a whole. Never before had such a representative body been elected in New York.

Once the assemblymen were in office they set about remedying abuses. They levied taxes to support the government, revoked excessive taxes that had been imposed by the previous regime, and dissolved certain monopolies. Significantly they resolved that all towns and settlements should have equal freedom to mill flour and bake bread.

Leisler knew that if the colonies were to solve their problems they all had to cooperate with one another. Early in 1690 he tried to establish an intercolonial congress, the first in America. Its purpose was to plan joint action against the French in Canada, who seemed to be a constant threat on the northern borders of New York. The congress launched a military campaign against the French, but it proved ineffectual.

The course of the New York government was not easy. Although it supported William and Mary, the king and queen did not reciprocate by supporting the Leisler regime. Months and months passed with no word about the inten-

JOHN LOCKE, PHILOSOPHER OF REVOLUTION

In 1690, an English physician and philosopher published two treatises on government that were destined to link the Glorious Revolution of 1689 to the American Revolution of 1776.

The author, John Locke, had been living as an exile in Holland. In politics he was a Whig. This meant, in a broad sense, that he advocated increasing the control that people could exercise over their own lives. He favored a more republican, even a more democratic, form of government than had hitherto existed. Such ideas were very radical in the 1680s. They led to the even more radical theory that Locke developed in his treatises. Men, he said, had certain natural rights. Among these was the right of revolution.

From his exile in Holland, Locke actively supported the Glorious Revolution, which brought to power the Protestant William and Mary—who were less steeped in authoritarian ideas than their predecessor, James II. The downfall of James, doubtless to Locke's delight, then led to dramatic overturns in the colonial governments in New England, New York, and Maryland.

Locke's theories about natural rights greatly influenced the men who became leaders of the American Revolution of 1776. The Declaration of Independence eloquently and simply summed up their beliefs: "We hold these truths to be self-evident, that all men are created equal." Other phrases from the Declaration reflected Lockean ideas—for example: "Life, Liberty and the pursuit of Happiness." He would probably have used a different word for the last of these three rights. Instead of "happiness" he would have said "property." But he would have no quarrel with the document's humane direction.

tions of the new monarchs. Meantime the men who had been ousted from office and influence were not idle. They mobilized what support they could against Leisler. They stimulated protests and disorders.

One opponent even made an attempt on Leisler's life. On June 6, 1690, John Crooke, a cooper by trade, who for unknown reasons had a strong aversion to Leisler, attacked him on the street, using a cooper's adz as his weapon. The attack failed, and Crooke lived on to be active against a very different set of rebels in 1712. If he was punished at all under Leisler's regime, no record of the sentence has survived. In general, penalties handed out to Leisler's political opponents were very gentle compared to those imposed before—and after—he held power. Even under duress, Leisler was a mild and generous man.

He and his supporters governed the colony for a year and a half before William and Mary took any step to assert authority. Then what the monarchs did created great confusion. A British officer, Colonel Henry Sloughter, was made governor of New York, and Major Richard Ingoldesby was ordered to give him military support. But Ingoldesby sailed from England with his troops before Sloughter did and arrived with no clear authority to do anything but obey Sloughter's orders. Leisler received Ingoldesby courteously and gave him and his men shelter in City Hall.

Of course City Hall was not the fort, where Ingoldesby, a military man, thought he should be. Soon he made clear that he did not consider it proper for him and his men to remain as guests in New York. He began to give orders—orders which Leisler was slow to obey. Leisler was not sure that Ingoldesby came with the authority necessary to govern New York. Nor did Leisler have reason to feel that Ingoldesby was friendly to the reforms that had been made during New York's own Glorious Revolution. So Leisler stalled.

By March 16, although Colonel Sloughter had still not arrived, Ingoldesby had obviously begun preparing to seize control of New York by force. It was Leisler's turn to give orders. He told Ingoldesby to stop preparations.

Three days after Leisler's ultimatum Colonel Sloughter reached New York. The city he entered appeared to be involved in civil war. Those who opposed Leisler, mainly landowners, rich merchants, and former officials, were quick to tell Sloughter their version of events. They had long looked with dismay on their own loss of influence, and they shrewdly saw that Sloughter would join them in resenting the rise to power of men from the lower class.

The Dutch had surrendered New Amsterdam to the English only a few years before Leisler's rebellion.

68

On March 30, Sloughter ignored a cooperative letter from Leisler and sent Ingoldesby with troops to the fort. There Ingoldesby offered all of Leisler's militiamen full guarantees against prosecution if they would lay down their arms and march out. The militiamen knew that they had merely been waiting for duly appointed representatives to come from William and Mary. Ingoldesby and Sloughter seemed to be these representatives. So they laid down their arms.

Now Leisler and his closest advisers had no protection. Sloughter immediately had them arrested. Leisler was put in chains.

Next day the captives were brought into a court presided over by one of the most active enemies of the Leisler regime. After a week-long trial Leisler, his son-in-law Milborne, and six others were sentenced to death. All of Leisler's property was confiscated and his family left without resources.

Outcry against the sentence was fierce and widespread. Leisler's supporters began to circulate a petition asking for reprieve. Sloughter responded by pardoning six of the eight, but the sentences against Leisler and Milborne remained. Throughout the colony sheriffs had orders to arrest anyone found circulating petitions that asked for clemency.

Leisler and Milborne appealed to the crown, hoping for a reversal of the verdict against them. But before the result of their appeal could reach New York, Sloughter gave in to pressure. Leisler's friends believed that his enemies got Sloughter drunk and then persuaded him to sign the execution order. Or possibly he was bribed to do so.

It was said at the time that no carpenter could be found who would build a ladder up to the scaffold which stood in what is now Park Row, close to present City Hall Park in New York. But by the rainy morning of May 16, a ladder had been made—or borrowed—and a large crowd gathered around it. Presently they heard an extraordinary sound. From the scaffold Leisler and Milborne joined in singing the Seventy-ninth Psalm:

> O God, the heathen are come into thine inheritance; thy holy temple have they defiled; they have laid Jerusalem on heaps. The dead bodies of thy servants have they given to be meat unto the fowls of the heaven, the flesh of thy saints unto the beasts of the earth. Their blood have they shed like water round about Jerusalem. . . . Let the sighing of the prisoner come before thee; according to the greatness of thy power preserve thou those that are appointed to die; and render unto our neighbours sevenfold into their bosom their reproach. . . .

The song ended and each of the condemned spoke. Milborne, a young man, was bitter and angry. He would meet his persecutors, he said, "before God's tribunal."

Leisler, modest and earnest at the end, as he had been all the time he was in office, spoke in a different vein. He had been chosen by a majority of the people, he said, to undertake the "great & weighty matters of State affairs"—a task that required men who were more "Cunning powerful Pilotts" than he and Milborne. Nevertheless he and his son-in-law had done their best to strengthen "this confused City & Province [and] thought it a very serviceable Act that our poore endeavours should not be wanting in any thing that

BLACK HERO OF 1689

While the revolutionary Leisler regime controlled New York, a black man saved the city from destruction by one of Jacob Leisler's enemies. His name is not known. We do not even know whether he was a slave or free, but there were not many free Blacks in New York in 1689, so the likelihood is great that the city's savior was a slave.

At any rate, a man, whom Leisler called a Papist, managed to set three fires in the turret of the church inside the fort where an office building now stands at number one Broadway. Just below the turret 6,000 pounds of powder were stored. If the fires had reached this powder a tremendous explosion would have destroyed much, perhaps all, of New York. However, the black man discovered the blaze and it was extinguished—the record does not say by whom, but it is not likely that he merely stood by and watched while others doused the flames with leather buckets full of water or sand.

was needful for the Support of ourselves & posterity." He ended with a prayer for "peace & unity" and preservation of the colony "from greedy outragious Enemies abroad & Spiteful inveterate wretches at home."

Neither the psalm nor Leisler's kindly sentiments nor Milborne's angry ones prevailed. The sentence was carried out. And in Boston the Reverend Increase Mather said, "These men were not only murdered, they were barbarously murdered."

Powerful people in London also showed displeasure with the executions. In 1695 Parliament ordered Leisler's property returned to his heirs, and in New York the Assembly voted a very sizable sum of money—2,700 pounds—to the heirs of the man who had tried to put New York government on a course in line with the desires of the people.

Leisler's supporters kept in touch with one another. For many years they were the source of continuing agitation against arbitrary government. The end to the Glorious Revolution in New York was not altogether inglorious.

PLACES TO SEE

MASSACHUSETTS

Boston: King's Chapel / Old State House (Town House Site) / Copp's Hill Burying Ground.

NEW YORK

New York (Manhattan): The Battery (Fort Site) / Park Row (Site of Leisler's Hanging).

For more information, see Gazetteer, page 212.

Intolerance in Maryland

A great fumbling toward freedom made 1689 a memorable year in Maryland as in other colonies. However, the origins of Maryland were unique, and they dictated a unique course for the Glorious Revolution in that province.

When Charles I created the colony in 1632, he had special objectives. For one thing, he wanted to establish a barrier that would limit the northward expansion of Virginians, who had a troublesome fondness for their legislative Assembly. Maryland was to be such a barrier, explicitly designed as a feudal domain and granted to George Calvert, the first Lord Baltimore, who as sole proprietor would wield almost absolute power. At the same time Charles saw an advantage to setting up a buffer against any southward spread of New England's troublesome Puritanism. An antidemocratic Maryland under Lord Baltimore, who was a Catholic and would presumably fill it with Catholics, who were not wanted in England anyway, seemed to solve several problems at once. But there were frustrations from the outset.

To begin with, Lord Baltimore died before the first ship sailed for Maryland. Then when colonization did start under his son, the second Lord Baltimore, too few of his coreligionists crossed the Atlantic. The majority of settlers were Protestant. To counteract this imbalance, the second Lord Baltimore granted the choicest pieces of land to Catholics and gave them positions of power in the government of the colony.

Neither the king nor Baltimore had devised a formula that would work. The colonists did not forget the House of Commons they had known in England. Soon they found out about the Commons-like Assembly which existed across the Potomac in Virginia. Before many years had passed, the idea of a legislative body of their own took irresistible hold on the minds of men in Maryland. They insisted on, and they got, the right to elect delegates to an assembly.

By 1649, when the Protestant Commonwealth in England executed King Charles, both the Catholics and the Protestants in the Maryland Assembly found themselves in a novel posture. Neither branch of Christianity had hitherto seen much use for the idea of religious liberty, but now both branches had reason to espouse freedom of conscience. As a measure of self-protection from the Protestant majority that surrounded them, as well as from the militant Protestant government that controlled England, the Catholics in the Assembly supported a religious Toleration Act. The Protestants in the Assembly, who sat there only because the Catholic Lord Baltimore allowed them to do so, went along with this act, and in so doing were as out of character as the Catholics. They resolved:

> Nowe person or persons whatever within this province shall henceforth bee anywaies troubled for or in respect to his, or her religion . . . professing to believe in Jesus Christ.

For a while all Christian sects in Maryland enjoyed equality, and there is no record that Jews at this time suffered real discrimination. But before long the Toleration Act was revoked. By the time of the American Revolution it had become an antique curiosity.

Meantime migration to Maryland continued, and the religious imbalance increased. Fifty years after the first shipload of settlers arrived, Protestants outnumbered Catholics about twenty to one. Nevertheless, power remained disproportionately in Catholic hands.

Charles Calvert, the third Lord Baltimore.

Long after stormy events took place in Maryland in 1676 colonial tax collectors aften met vigorous resistance, as this 19th century illustration suggests. *(Opposite)* Although it was white men who stole the Indians' land, 19th century white artists liked to portray Indians as thieves.

One-third of the military officers and half of the government officials were Catholic, and only those Protestants who supported Lord Baltimore and were approved by him were appointed to office. The richest plantations remained in the hands of Catholics or of Protestants loyal to the Catholic proprietor.

When Charles Calvert became the third Lord Baltimore in 1675, he went to live in Maryland, the first proprietor to do so. Immediately he found himself in the midst of perfervid politics. Tensions grew with the ever-increasing religious and economic imbalance. Small farmers, almost all Protestant, had many grievances. For one thing, the land they held was largely on the frontier, close to the very real danger of attack by Indians, who resented their intrusion and their total insensitivity to the rights of Native Americans. Maryland farmers knew that in 1675 the Indians in New England had mounted a massive attack on settlers. The same might happen at any time to them. If such an assault did come, the poor farmers were geographically in the position of having to protect the rich farmers in order to protect themselves, and they felt they got too little military and financial support for the risks they took in the common defense.

Taxes and levies were another sore point. Sometimes officials demanded tax payments in cash, and in Maryland as in other colonies small farmers had very little hard money. What wealth they did have was in the form of tobacco, and if they had to pay taxes, they wanted to pay in tobacco.

To these grievances the proprietor had added another. At the very moment when he seemed to be acquiescing to a demand for a legislative Assembly, he tried an irritating political maneuver. First he allowed the election of four delegates from each county. Then he decided which two of these four could go to the capital at St. Mary's and take part in the Assembly.

The proprietor hoped, of course, to create an Assembly of pliable delegates subservient to him. His plan couldn't possibly work. Many who were allowed to take seats in the Assembly remained loyal to those who elected them. All of the rejects were furious— and so, too, were the voters.

Other sources of irritation were the local sheriffs and tax collectors, all appointed and prone to behave, said complaining farmers, "proudly and maliciously," with "huff and hector."

All in all the small farmers in Maryland felt much put upon. They had fewer political rights than had Englishmen in England. Moreover they felt constantly threatened, not only by Indians who wanted to keep their land for themselves but also by the French in Canada who wanted all of America under the control of Catholic France. It seemed logical to the Protestants that Catholic Marylanders and Catholic Canadians would indeed conspire together against them.

Frustrations, limitations, hardships, and dangers —both real and imagined—had begun early and continued with only one brief interruption. During the Commonwealth period, when militant Puritans ruled England, Maryland had a Protestant governor for about a year. Apparently he was intended to act as a kind of brake on the power of the Catholic proprietor, who remained in office. But when the Commonwealth ended, in 1660, so did the new governor's tenure.

Maryland was back to normal—that is to say, in a chronic state of crisis. By 1676 the situation had become acute . . .

12

"Mariland's Grevances Why The Have Taken Op Arms"

1689   Maryland

Popular actions in Maryland during the Glorious Revolution brought the salty, irreverent former priest John Coode to the fore as a Protestant leader who helped to curtail Catholic landlords' autocratic power in the colony.

One day early in September 1676, several dozen angry Maryland farmers came together at a plantation on the Patuxent River. They argued; they discussed and finally agreed on the text of a petition. What they asked was really very simple. They wanted some way to appeal to a higher authority when the proprietor made decisions that they believed unjust.

Somehow the proprietor got wind of the meeting and sent troops to disperse it. This they did. They also captured and executed two of the farmers' leaders, William Davyes and John Pate.

At this point Josias Fendall, the man who had served briefly as Protestant governor in 1656, reappeared on the public scene. In 1678 his neighbors elected him to the Assembly—this in spite of the fact that Fendall had been specifically barred by the proprietor from holding any government position in Maryland. To no one's surprise Fendall was not allowed to take his seat in the Assembly.

Fendall had survived earlier rebuffs, and he was not silenced by this one. Several times in the following years he organized protests in Charles County. Then in 1681 the proprietor had him arrested and tried for subversive activities. Fendall was found guilty, fined 40,000 pounds of tobacco, and sentenced to banishment.

Before he was released from jail, some of Fendall's supporters tried to rescue him. Led by George Godfrey, a rebellious militia officer, they made their attempt, but they failed. Godfrey was captured, tried, and sentenced to death. Later the court seems to have had second thoughts about what effect the execution might have on the excited populace, and the sentence was reduced to life imprisonment.

Davyes, Pate, Fendall, Godfrey—a continuum of leaders—were all disposed of in one way or another. But there was no dearth of men to take their places. Three who appeared were all married to daughters of a farmer who had been an active supporter of Josias Fendall during Commonwealth times. One of these three brothers-in-law was colorful John Coode, who was not only a farmer but also an Anglican clergyman and a perennial agitator.

Coode's abilities had already attracted the attention of the proprietor, who appointed him justice of the peace in his own county and then made him master of a sailing vessel sent out to look for pirates. Official favors did not determine Coode's loyalties. His neighbors obviously trusted him, and in 1676 they sent him as a representative to the Assembly. There, miraculously, he managed to pass the proprietor's scrutiny. He became one of the two out of four delegates from St. Mary's City who were allowed to take seats. In the heat of controversy it appeared soon enough that Coode's language leaned more heavily on the forecastle and the barnyard than it did on the Book of Common Prayer. The delegate from St. Mary's City was a very fountain of salty and earthy profanity.

The year of Coode's election to the Assembly was also the year of Bacon's Rebellion, and it was rumored, though not proved, that Coode crossed the river and took part in some of the actions in Virginia. If he did—and it would certainly have been in character—he was not out of Maryland for long. He had his own affairs to attend to at his plantation on the Wicomico River and at his second home in St. Mary's. Whether before or after Bacon's uprising (the date is not known), Protestant farmers began to gather at Coode's plantation to work out plans for cooperation against the proprietor.

By 1681 Coode was deeply involved in the Protestant movement. At that time he was both a justice of the peace appointed by the proprietor and an assemblyman approved by the proprietor after election by his neighbors. But in spite of his official positions Coode took part in actions with the former governor Josias Fendall, and he along with Fendall was arrested. Coode stood trial for mutiny and sedition, but possibly because of his great popularity he was found not guilty. However, the court rebuked him for his "love to amaze the ignorant and make sport with his wit." Using his arrest as an excuse, the proprietor's officials now sent Coode an order suspending him from his seat in the Assembly. Coode dramatically tore up the order.

To this act of defiance the proprietor replied first by removing Coode from his post as justice of the peace. Then the proprietor and his bureaucracy made a shrewd move. Invoking a principle that Englishmen had struggled for—the principle that the church should not meddle in the affairs of the elected representatives of the people—Coode's enemies got him permanently excluded from the Maryland Assembly because he had at one time taken holy orders in the Anglican church. The Protestant members of the Assembly uncomfortably agreed that church and state should be kept separate in their body. By emphasizing the doctrine dear to Protestants that priests should not be elected to the lower house, the Catholic proprietor paralyzed Coode's friends. Coode's active life as an Anglican priest was apparently long in the past, and he provided evidence that his views were no longer orthodox. They were, in fact, blasphemous by the standards of his age, and some called him an atheist. But in spite of the maverick behavior of his mature years, he paid dearly for his youthful discretion. A rueful Assembly felt it had to deny him his seat.

Although out of office, Coode managed to be a political force. At the same time the proprietor's authority began to dwindle. In 1684 Baltimore left Maryland for England, hoping to resolve a quarrel he was having with William Penn about the border between Maryland and Pennsylvania. While Baltimore was away, hostilities and rivalries in his colony came to the surface, sometimes in surprising ways. It appeared, for example, that the royal tax collector was unpopular not only with poor farmers and artisans but also with members of the ruling clique. One day in 1684 he was murdered by the proprietor's nephew, who was also acting governor of Maryland.

Word of the murder reached England at a time when Baltimore already had enough troubles. He didn't dare return to Maryland for fear that while he was out of England the aggressive King James II would assume royal control of the colony.

Later, while he was still in England, Baltimore sent to Maryland a dogmatic Irishman named William Joseph to act as president of the council. This appointive body of advisers met jointly on occasion with the elected members of the Assembly. In his first address to the joint Assembly on November 14, 1688, Joseph read the members a lecture on the divine right of kings. "There is no power but of God," he said, "and the power by which we are assembled here is undoubtedly derived from God, to the King, and from the King to his Excellency the Lord Proprietary, and his said lordship to us."

Joseph also demanded that the members of the Assembly take an oath of fidelity to the proprietor. These elected representatives had already been forced to take the oath once, and they refused to be further humiliated by having to take it again.

At this juncture Protestant William and Mary became monarchs of Britain. Joseph took no notice. But the advent of the new rulers, together with Joseph's past record of dictatorial behavior, triggered massive defiance. An organization designed to coordinate the activities of artisans and small farmers—and of some large Protestant farmers, too—brought together men from most of the colony. This new political entity called itself "An Association in Arms for the Defense of the Protestant Religion, and for Asserting the Right of King William and Queen Mary to the Province of Maryland and all English Dominions." That was too much of a name for anyone to handle even in the seventeenth century, and the organization soon became known simply as the Protestant Association. John Coode was its central leader.

By July 1689 Coode was gathering militant recruits at his farm in Charles County, and he was joined there by his widely known and well-respected brothers-in-law. One of

In Maryland, the Assembly adopted a Religious Toleration Act after King Charles I was executed in England.

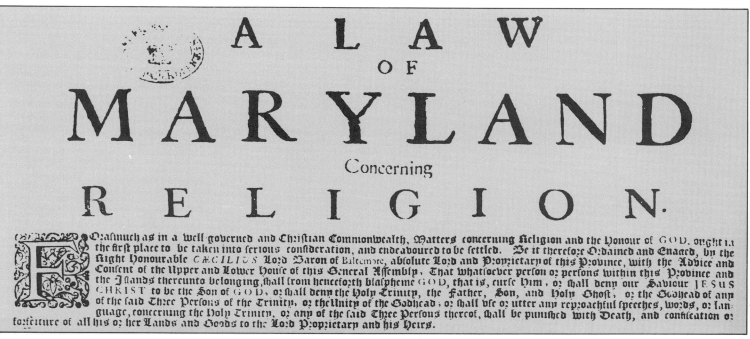

The reconstructed Old State House stands in St. Mary's City.

them, Kenelm Cheseldyne, had been speaker of the Assembly. The other had been a royal official, collector of customs directly responsible to the king, not to the proprietor.

Somebody noticed the unusual doings at Coode's farm and ran to St. Mary's to report. William Joseph called the council into emergency session. Alarmed, the council, on July 16, decided to send an investigator to find out what was going on in Charles County. Coode discovered the spy and held him prisoner. Meanwhile the Protestant Association sped up its preparations. A full company of militia, officers and all, arrived to join Coode's forces.

When it became clear that the men gathering at Coode's plantation were armed and meant business, most of the councillors and many other leading Catholic officials fled from St. Mary's, leaving a man named William Digges in charge. Digges, although a Protestant, had been made one of several deputy governors by Lord Baltimore, who was his father-in-law. As Digges considered what to do, he must have had before him a copy of the Protestant Association's manifesto, one of the first documents of any importance to be printed in Maryland. Its title was: "The Declaration of the Reason and Motive for the Present Appearing in Arms of His Majesty's Protestant Subjects in the Province of Maryland." (The manifesto refers to a single ruler although William and Mary had been in power for several months.)

Now Digges had to weigh his beliefs as a Protestant against the powerful position he held under the Catholic proprietor. But if he was seriously torn between two sets of loyalties, he quickly resolved the conflict and sided with the proprietor. He summoned men to the State House to defend it. With eighty or a hundred armed soldiers, Digges entered the government building and waited.

On July 27, Coode at the head of an armed body which he said consisted of 250 men—his enemies said there were 750—soon reached St. Mary's. Digges' soldiers looked out of the State House, saw Coode's forces, which must have seemed formidable, and decided not to fight. Whether the men in the State House sympathized with the Protestant Association or whether they merely knew that they were outnumbered is not known. At any rate, Digges had to surrender.

Now Coode was in possession of the State House and all the government records. The councillors and others who had fled from St. Mary's began fortifying Mattaponi, the proprietor's residence. Two days after capturing St. Mary's, Coode marched the eight miles to Mattaponi with his army, which seems to have grown. On August 1, he arrived accompanied by two cannon, which had been taken from a merchant ship. These weapons might be useful against the log stockade which had been erected around Mattaponi.

When the rebel army approached the barrier, Coode sent forward a trumpeter, who carried a demand for surrender "In the name of William and Mary." (The supporters of Lord Baltimore still had not acknowledged the Protestant monarchs as their rulers.)

For two hours the council members and others at Mattaponi negotiated with Coode. Then it was all over. The Protestant Association without firing a shot took control of Mattaponi, and with it they gained control of most of Maryland.

Immediately—as they had announced in their manifesto they would do—Coode and his followers called for the election of a new Assembly. When this body met, Coode surrendered all his power to it. But his services were not over. The Assembly sent him and Kenelm Cheseldyne on a special mission to England. There they explained to William and Mary the course that events had taken and appealed for an end to the proprietary rule of Lord Baltimore. This plea was granted. Lord Baltimore lost his proprietorship, although his lands in Maryland were not stripped from him.

The Maryland revolution of 1689 had achieved its major goal. It ended the feudal form of government under which Marylanders had suffered. Now Protestant men in the colony expected to be on equal footing in most respects with their counterparts in England. More they had not sought. They believed, not without reason, that most Protestant men in England in 1689 had more freedom than most other men in the world. Certainly Protestant male landowners in England had more freedom than English Catholics of any category. And before many years that would be the case in Maryland, too. In 1712 Maryland, which had been established for Catholics, denied suffrage to any members of the Catholic faith, barred them from holding office, and forced them to pay taxes twice as heavy as those of non-Catholics.

It now became the problem of members of the Catholic minority in Maryland to fight for their rights, and fight they did—the story will be told in a later chapter—as one of the forces that created the American Revolution.

PLACES TO SEE ✤

MARYLAND

St. Mary's: Maryland's First State House Reconstruction.

For more information, see Gazetteer, page 212.

13

"The Seditious Ffactious and Rebelious Rable of Albemarle"

1670s and 1680s   Albemarle, North Carolina

For more than three decades a group of poor tobacco farmers in an isolated area of North Carolina were able to run their own affairs without any authoritarian interference from England.

The gap between freedoms sought and freedoms gained was probably smaller in the Albemarle district of North Carolina in the seventeenth century than any place else in the western world. There, for more than a generation, a thousand men of English origin, together with their wives and children, lived beyond the control of any outside agency. Their homeland was a virtually independent republic, though they never bothered with the technicality of announcing it as a separate nation. Why should they bother? Such a boast to the world could not increase their liberties. It would quite likely provoke attacks.

So, quietly, the men of Albemarle governed themselves in a kind of Utopia which for them lacked little that tobacco planters could achieve in the seventeenth century—except wealth. They were probably among the poorest of farmers in America, but the fault was not lack of spirit on their part. Their soil was not the best for tobacco growing. Also the price at which tobacco could be sold was often very low.

So the men of Albemarle were poor, but free. And we may surmise that the women also breathed a little more freely because officials from outside were neither adding their increment of restriction to life nor increasing poverty by drawing off wealth from the farm-owning menfolk. Nothing is known about the lot of the indentured servants nor of slaves, if any. Since poverty never became more than the farmers could endure, Albemarle was generally a place of quiet delight in living.

The first settler to establish any kind of title to the wilderness land on the north shore of Albemarle Sound did so in 1659. He was George Durant, about twenty-five years old at the time, the son of a prominent Puritan of Virginia. By arrangement with the local Indians, Durant planted tobacco on land he obtained from them. Other former Virginians soon moved southward into the area. At peace with the original inhabitants and with each other, Durant and his neighbors began a unique experience, which they thoroughly relished. No government and no church supervised their lives. They paid no quitrents to feudal-minded officials. They paid no fees to support ministers. Indeed, no ministers and no missionaries except Quakers conducted services in the Albemarle district. Since the Quakers did not require church buildings for their services, no churches were built. By default, there was achieved a kind of separation of church and state. No strict laws governed behavior on the Sabbath as in other colonies. All marriages were civil and civil only. People were buried without religious ceremony, wherever their families chose to dig graves. There were no formal cemeteries.

Technically the Albemarle settlers lived within the Indian-owned territory of Carolina, which England claimed without consulting the Native American inhabitants, and which Charles II had granted as a feudal domain to a group of men known as the lords proprietors. Like all colonists who grew tobacco and other products for export, the Albemarle men were expected to pay duties to the king and to provide some way in which the aristocratic investors—that is, the lords proprietors—could derive income from labor the settlers performed. But the settlers had not gone into the wilderness to make somebody else rich, and they found a convenient way of avoiding taxes. They managed to get one of their own number, Valentine Byrd, appointed collector of customs. Obligingly Byrd never found any customs to collect.

If any royal revenue officer had been inclined to take his job seriously, he would have found the task impossible without the aid of military force. But where was such force to come from? How could it get to Albemarle? Any expedition sent overland from Virginia would have to make its way through the almost impenetrable Dismal Swamp. From Carolina's capital at Charles Town (now Charleston), an overland force would have to make a long and arduous journey. Much of the country was heavily wooded. Rivers were many and large. Finally, Albemarle Sound itself, reaching far inland, blocked the way. The men who were evading customs lived on the far side of that wide body of water.

There were obstacles, too, for any law enforcer who might try to enter Albemarle Sound from the ocean. Most oceangoing vessels could not pass into the sound through the shallow opening known as Roanoke Inlet. But if naval vessels

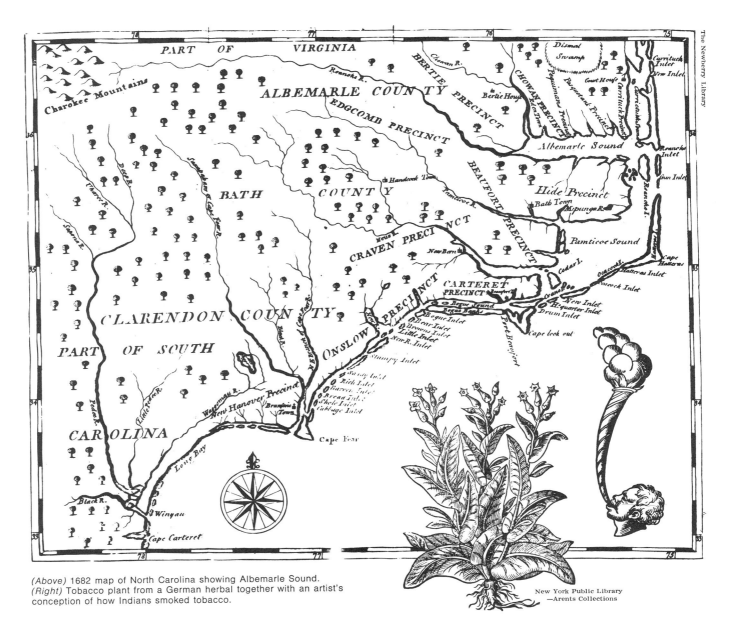

(Above) 1682 map of North Carolina showing Albemarle Sound.
(Right) Tobacco plant from a German herbal together with an artist's
conception of how Indians smoked tobacco.

of any size could not get into the sound, neither could ocean-going cargo ships leave it. This geographic fact provided still another support for Albemarle's unique course of independence. The ships that were best fitted for sailing Albemarle waters were shallow-draft vessels built for the coastal trade. Most of these came from Boston, Salem, and Gloucester. So trade was lively between Albemarle and New England. This went counter to the wishes of the king and British merchants and the lords proprietors. All of them, with the support of Parliament, wanted England to have a monopoly of trade to and from the colonies, which were not supposed to trade with each other or with rival powers.

To further English commercial interests, Parliament enacted a law in 1672 that required tobacco growers to pay a penalty of a penny for each pound of tobacco they shipped to some destination other than England. When the farmers of Albemarle heard of this tax, which became known as plantation duty, they simply declined to pay. Their friend Valentine Byrd, the collector, did not try to collect.

Royal instructions emphasizing the importance of enforc-

ing the act were sent to Carolina, and the lords proprietors urged their agents to follow the instructions. If the plantation duty was not collected, they feared that the king might revoke their charter. These feelings were shared by some of the Carolina landowners who were especially favored by the proprietors. But George Durant and the other small farmers remained adamant. They simply would not pay.

In Albemarle and elsewhere another troublesome idea arose. Farmers insisted on reforming the Carolina Assembly, making it more responsive to their needs. This caused considerable uproar, and out of it came a governor who was friendly to the Albemarle farmers. At the same time a new customs collector, a Quaker, was appointed. George Durant and the other farmers of Albemarle supported his appointment. But the Quaker seems to have been a humorless sort of fellow and a prisoner of legal scruples. As collector he thought he was supposed to collect. Needless to say, he quickly fell from favor among the men of Albemarle. Just as quickly he rose in the estimation of the proprietors' friends. Two of these, who enjoyed their only importance as appointed colonial officials, were Thomas Miller, a onetime apothecary, and Thomas Eastchurch, a young man more than usually eager to get a wife.

Miller and Eastchurch, willing though they were to carry out the proprietors' instructions, found themselves helpless. They needed more power. Besides, Eastchurch wanted to be governor of Carolina; so to obtain the desired power and appointment, the two men sailed for England. The Albemarle farmers were not far behind. To protect their interests George Durant also went to England. There he told the lords proprietors, without mincing words, that if they made Eastchurch governor there would be an insurrection.

The proprietors chose to ignore Durant. They appointed Eastchurch governor and sent Miller back to Carolina as collector.

Eastchurch, still a bachelor, started out for Carolina, then decided to stop off in the West Indies to look for a wife. He appointed Miller to act as governor in his stead, and on July 9, 1677, Miller reached Charles Town.

Durant returned to Albemarle somewhat later, a passenger on a shallow-draft vessel that brought much-needed supplies. The master of the vessel was a Bostonian, Captain Zachariah Gillam, known in Albemarle as Old Zach. Gillam traded anywhere from Hudson's Bay to Albemarle Sound, obeying the laws of king and Parliament only when it was convenient to do so.

Although Miller, the acting governor, was not always sober, he knew two lawbreakers when he saw them. He promptly had Durant and Gillam arrested.

Then the storm broke. Many of the thousand men of Albemarle came to the support of Durant, their leader, and of Gillam, who provided one of their chief ways of getting their tobacco to market. The surviving records do not reveal exactly what happened at this point. Perhaps men armed with brand-new cutlasses milled around outside the private home where the prisoners were held. There was a good supply of these weapons aboard Gillam's vessel, and it is known that they were distributed soon after he arrived. One thing at least is sure. Durant and Gillam were soon free. Almost simultaneously Eastchurch arrived in Virginia after having dallied—successfully—in the West Indies looking for a wife.

In Virginia Eastchurch tried to raise troops, and he sent orders for the insurgents to disperse. Instead of dispersing, they put Miller in jail. Now came the problem of how to confine him. The only instruments for this purpose that had existed in the Albemarle district were stocks and a pillory. These had become symbols of the proprietors' authority, and the rebels had by now thrown them into the river. So they had to improvise chains to restrain their captive until they could ready a jail, for which they had apparently never felt the need before. On the bank of the Pasquotank River they constructed a log building about ten feet square and locked Miller inside. They also arrested the Quaker tax collector and kept him elsewhere. Then, with faces straight, they appointed John Culpeper collector. Culpeper had unique credentials. He came from an aristocratic family, but he had had experience as a rebel in Charles Town and had been banished from that city. Culpeper understood very well that his duty in the Albemarle was to perform no duties.

From what illness we do not know, Eastchurch died in Virginia less than five weeks after he assumed his post as governor of Carolina. The former acting governor, Miller, was in jail. But that did not mean no government existed in Albemarle. At Durant's house farmers met and elected five delegates from each of the four Albemarle precincts. These delegates formed themselves into an Assembly and in turn elected a court of five members. Thus the men of Albemarle established their own government.

For about two years matters went along quietly. Then in 1679 the two prisoners escaped from their separate jails— the Quaker tax collector and Thomas Miller, former apothecary, former acting governor, and perennial nuisance. It has not been recorded how they escaped, but they somehow made their way to England. There Miller lodged serious charges against Culpeper and Gillam as leaders of the "seditious, ffactious and Rebelious Rable of Albemarle."

In 1680 Culpeper, who happened to be in England, was summoned to court to answer Miller's charges. But the lords proprietors now took a hard look at the realities in Albemarle and decided they must find some way to smooth matters over. Surprisingly, they let the court know that they found no fault with Culpeper. Thereafter the case against him faded away. The proprietors also looked at Miller and found that even when he was sober he did not reassure them. They decided not to send him back to Carolina.

A new governor was appointed, then another and another, but for various reasons not one of them assumed his duties. Durant and his followers remained in full control in Albemarle. One governor-select, Seth Sothell, had good reason for not appearing. He was captured en route to Carolina by Algerian pirates and held prisoner for three years until he finally paid the ransom the pirates demanded. When he did appear he brought with him an attitude no different from that of his predecessors. He was determined to collect plantation duty from the poor farmers and even had the bad judgment to put George Durant in jail. Soon after that—the year was the fateful one of the Glorious Revolution, which brought many a reversal of roles—Sothell, not Durant, was held prisoner. Exactly how this came about is not clear. But when Sothell finally left jail it was not to resume his post as governor. George Durant and the men of Albemarle had prevailed.

Until Durant died in 1694 he remained what he had always been, an essentially free man. He did not live to see the drab administrative events that gradually brought the isolated Albemarle district under control within the British colonial empire.

PLACES TO SEE ❧

NORTH CAROLINA

New Hope: Leigh Mansion.
Batts Island.

For more information, see Gazetteer, page 212.

The Witchcraft Hysteria

In Salem Village, Massachusetts Bay Colony, nineteen people were hanged in 1692 after they had been tried and found guilty of witchcraft. The chain of circumstances that led to the executions began when young girls accused their elders of being witches. In this bizarre drama some historians have seen a tragedy that could have been avoided if magistrates had followed proper legal procedures. Some have thought the episode was the outgrowth of personal feuds, while others have interpreted it as the result of mass hysteria. Still others see in it the lamentable result of ancient superstition that lingered on in the midst of a society that had the true—that is to say the Puritan—version of the Christian religion. Puritan leaders had their own theory: According to Cotton Mather, the whole sorry mess was the work of the Devil. Finally there are those who, looking backward from our own recent McCarthy episode, interpret the Salem witch-hunt in the political, as well as literal, sense of the words.

There is something to be said for most of these interpretations, but they do not exhaust the possible ways of looking at the evidence. No matter how it is told, the story of witchcraft in Salem Village largely concerns girls and women, and the reason is not hard to find. Females in seventeenth century New England were lifetime inmates of the maximum security section of the prison which was Puritan society. They could hold none of the positions of power in the community. They could not be ministers or magistrates, nor could they practice any of the other professions. As a rule they could not own property. Married women were virtually owned as slaves by their husbands, and girls were doubly owned—slaves to their slave mothers. Few of the freedoms we romantically associate with childhood existed for boys in colonial New England, and fewer still for girls. Youngsters had to work as soon as their immature muscles could coordinate well enough to do simple household tasks. They worked all the rest of their lives, and their lives were usually very short. Since women died at a much earlier age than men, it was not unusual for a man to outlive three or four wives.

So harsh an existence led girls and women, like all people who seek to relieve their miseries, into special ways of reaching out for more life than the surrounding society allowed them. For some girls in Salem Village, exposure of alleged witchcraft became a route toward freedom. "Crying out"—that is, accusing others of being witches—developed into a curious and dramatic means of breaking through manifold confines. At the same time, ministers and magistrates used witch-hunting to maintain intact the society in which they wielded power.

Witchcraft in the seventeenth century was a many-sided structure, part new and part a relic of

religious beliefs held by ancient European peoples who were conquered and submerged by Christians. Seventeenth century Christians, believing there were supernatural causes for natural phenomena, also believed that witches existed and could produce changes in the natural or human world by using magical techniques or supernatural powers. As a rule, men in authority equated sorcery with evil. But there were professed witches who claimed they could do good, as well as harm, by their practices.

These practicing witches were actually religious leaders who operated in competition with leaders of the various Christian sects. They were also advocates for the lower classes, in one way or another opposed to the governing authority. Many witches were healers who treated the sick. In other words, they practiced medicine in competition with male doctors, who systematically excluded women from medical training. Doctors, like folk healers, made use of herbal medicines, but much of orthodox medicine in the seventeenth century was totally unscientific. It merely sounded more impressive than witchcraft because the dogma on which it was based was contained in books, often in Latin, and available only to the learned. Valueless though a doctor's training was for the most part, no one could practice medicine without it.

A witch's herbal remedies may have been as effective as those used by doctors. If she cured as many patients as a doctor did, perhaps it was because she got her knowledge of herbs through experience rather than texts. She relieved certain symptoms simply because patients had faith in her procedures. On the other hand, because fear of witchcraft was intense, she could also cause pain and perhaps even death.

In the Middle Ages tens of thousands of women were executed in Europe because they practiced witchcraft or because they were accused of doing so. The exact number who perished, usually by burning at the stake, cannot now be determined. However, a few random figures have been salvaged from later records. They tell, all too eloquently, of massive attacks on women who in some way resisted male domination of important social activities and institutions. In 1515 in the city of Geneva, 500 women were executed as witches. In Scotland from the year 1560 to 1600, the number who met death was about 8,000.

In 1597 King James VI of Scotland, soon to become King James I of England, wrote a tract in which he urged that the courts accept testimony of even very young children in the trials of witches. The England to which James moved and in which Puritanism developed was preoccupied with witchcraft, and Puritans shared with other Christians the obsessive notions that led to witch-hunts.

European immigrants in the New World soon found that Native Americans had their own traditions

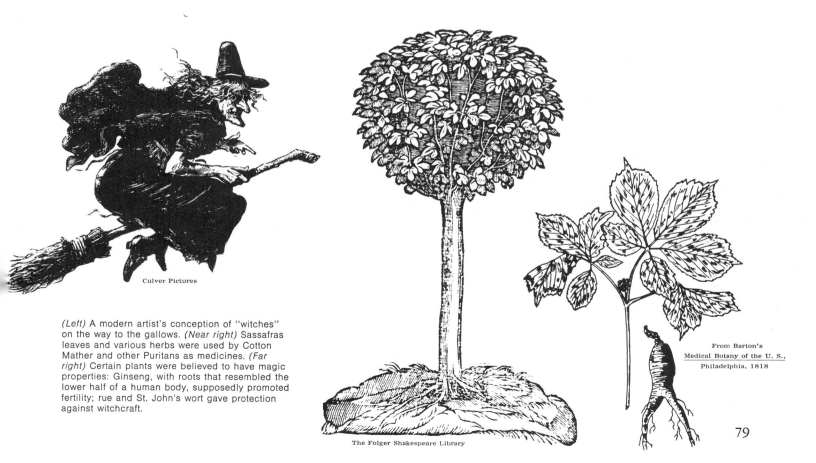

Culver Pictures

The Folger Shakespeare Library

From Barton's
Medical Botany of the U. S.,
Philadelphia, 1818

(Left) A modern artist's conception of "witches" on the way to the gallows. *(Near right)* Sassafras leaves and various herbs were used by Cotton Mather and other Puritans as medicines. *(Far right)* Certain plants were believed to have magic properties: Ginseng, with roots that resembled the lower half of a human body, supposedly promoted fertility; rue and St. John's wort gave protection against witchcraft.

79

of healing and their own religious practices. So did the Africans brought to America as slaves. Both the African and the American Indian beliefs and rituals were condemned by Christians as witchcraft and as works of the Devil. This was true of Spanish and French Catholics and of English Protestants alike.

The Puritan Englishmen in Massachusetts knew their Bible well, and the directive in Exodus 22:18 was clear: "Thou shalt not suffer a witch to live." Until the year 1692 this injunction had not seemed urgent in Salem Village. However, by that time, New Englanders had for a variety of reasons come to feel very insecure. Indians in Massachusetts had risen up in 1675 and tried to drive the white invaders out. More recently a smallpox epidemic had wrought havoc. Two great fires had devastated Boston. Besides fire, pestilence, and rebellion, problems of state had plagued the authorities. In 1684 King James II had revoked the Massachusetts Bay Colony's charter, an act which pulled the foundation out from under the colony's theocratic rulers. Not until 1691 did a new charter arrive, and it removed much power from the Puritan ministers. Even worse, a great many New Englanders believed the new charter called into question their titles to the lands they occupied.

Foreign affairs also caused general fear and apprehension. England was chronically at war with France, and English forces skirmished with French soldiers from time to time on American soil. Invariably the English were defeated. The danger seemed real that French Catholic Canada might overwhelm English Protestant Massachusetts.

To these manifold uncertainties the clergy made a series of responses. The Reverend Increase Mather, later president of Harvard College, proposed as early as 1679 a general meeting of the clergy to see if they could determine what evils had "provoked the Lord to bring His Judgment on New England." Two years later he called for another gathering to record "illustrious providences," meaning remarkable supernatural events, including witchcraft.

In 1684 he published his findings in a document called Illustrious Providences. Five years later his son, the Reverend Cotton Mather, published a lurid report that passed for information about witchcraft. At this time scarcely a minister in all New England had failed to warn people against spirits, sorcerers, demons, and witches and to excite their imaginations on the subject.

For all their religious and psychological aspects, witch-hunts in the seventeenth century had social and political motivations as strong as our twentieth century attacks on those whose offense had been that "they didn't play the game," "rocked the boat," or were "out of line." Then, as now, the heretics represented a threat to established authority . . .

LATE

Memorable Providences

Relating to

Witchcrafts and Poſſeſſions,

Clearly Manifeſting,

Not only that there are Witches, but that Good Men (as well as others) may poſſibly have their Lives ſhortned by ſuch evil Inſtruments of Satan.

Written by *Cotton Mather* Miniſter of the Goſpel at *Boſton* in *New-England.*

The Second Impreſſion.

Recommended by the Reverend Mr. *Richard Baxter* in *London,* and by the Miniſters of *Boſton* and *Charleſtown* in *New-England.*

LONDON,

Printed for *Tho. Parkhurſt* at the *Bible* and *Three Crowns* in *Cheapſide* near *Mercers-Chapel.* 1691.

(Above right) The Reverend Increase Mather and *(above left)* his son the Reverend Cotton Mather were dominant figures in Puritan New England. Both father and son believed that witches, doing the work of the Devil, appeared among people. *(Left)* Late Memorable Providences by Cotton Mather was published before the Salem witchcraft hysteria.

14

From Salem to Sanity

1692 Salem, Massachusetts

Witchcraft had a long history by the time young girls began to accuse persons in Salem of acting as instruments of the Devil. The monstrous trials and tragic executions of so-called witches were finally ended by popular pressure and by insistence on a rational approach to evidence.

Salem Village (now called Danvers) and Salem Town (now called Salem) both took their names from the Hebrew word *shalom,* meaning "peace." But in Salem Village at least, peace was very little known in the seventeenth century. The community had long argued about boundaries with the nearby village of Topsfield, and within the community many neighbors were pitted against each other in controversies about ownership of land. The contentious congregation in Salem Village had already driven two ministers out of its church, and in 1691 a new minister, Samuel Parris, was locked deep in dispute with his parishioners. Only a few years before, the Reverend Parris had left the unsuccessful pursuit of business on Barbados in favor of a more secure position in the ministry. Now he wanted, but could not get, his parishioners to give him title to the parsonage. He also insisted that part of his salary should be paid in firewood— as much as he needed. This demand, too, did not bring the response he stubbornly sought.

While Samuel Parris wrangled about a house and an adequate woodpile, his wife seems to have been ailing. The work of caring for her, the cooking, the laundry, the cleaning, the carrying out of slop jars, the spinning and weaving and bringing in of water from the well—all was done by Tituba, a slave. Tituba also had full charge of the Parris' nine-year-old daughter, Elizabeth, and her eleven-year-old cousin, Abigail Williams, who lived as a member of the household.

Samuel Parris had bought Tituba in Barbados. Her previous owner may have been an Englishwoman who was forced to sell her to pay a gambling debt. It is not clear whether Tituba was descended from Africans or from American Indians or whether she was part African and part Indian. About her husband, also owned by Parris, there was no doubt: he was always called John Indian.

Tituba had grown up on a tropical island where she could absorb large elements of three cultures: native Indian, African (brought by slaves), and English. In all three there were folk beliefs about the curative value of certain herbs, about rituals that brought good luck, charms that warded off evil, and ways of reading the future.

As Tituba went about her enforced labors in the home of the Reverend Parris, whom no one ever found it possible to love, she felt a great need for support from whatever beliefs she had brought with her from Barbados. Certainly they offered her much more than did the grim teachings of her master. Besides, he worked her very hard, paid her nothing, and on occasion beat her.

Tituba's exotic knowledge also gave her practical help in supervising Elizabeth and Abigail. The girls, she discovered, could be kept on a psychological leash if she told them fascinating things she had heard in her own childhood. She recalled tales of red cats, red rats, pigs that did strange tricks, and a mysterious tall man who said he was God. She revealed that she had been a healer in Barbados, where she knew the herbs that were good for certain ailments. Now, when she could steal time, she was exploring the woods near Salem Village looking for roots or stalks or flowers that might be the equivalent of plants she had used at home. These woodland gleanings she made into potions and poultices, much as Anne Hutchinson had done in England and later in Boston.

Often in the winter of 1691–92 Tituba shared her nourishing notions with Elizabeth and Abigail, both of whom had reasons for needing hope and strength in the oppressive Parris household. Palmistry, an art that supposedly told of things to come, gave both Tituba and the girls a way to leave the cramped world of the present and to enter a larger world that just might lie ahead.

Tituba had still another way of looking into the future. (This, too, she had learned in Barbados, possibly from the Englishwoman who owned her.) She broke an egg, discarded the yolk, and put the white into a transparent glass container. There it glistened like a fortune-teller's crystal ball. Peering through this window to the future, Tituba foretold what occupations the girls' husbands would have.

Elizabeth and Abigail found all this very exciting. Similar lore came from their girl friends and from their adult neighbors, all of whom knew something about spells and magic formulas. Witches, they said, rode sticks through the air and held gatherings that were the exact opposite of Christian days of worship—witches' Sabbaths. Common gossip, as well as books by Increase and Cotton Mather,

No portrait of Tituba exists. An artist made this caricature about three centuries after young girls accused her of being a witch.

described how people behaved when they were bewitched.

The sessions in which Tituba entertained and instructed Elizabeth and Abigail added spice to the last bleak months of 1691. Until now the Reverend Parris had paid little attention to the girls. He had sermons to write, parishioners to visit, quarrels to pursue. But in January 1692 he noticed that his never very bright daughter Elizabeth was more than usually inattentive to what went on around her. She often seemed to daydream. When an adult interrupted her reveries, she sometimes looked startled, then screamed and made unintelligible sounds. That was bad enough, but what Parris found really unendurable was her conduct during prayers. At times she stared vacantly, and often she interrupted the most solemn prayers by making little barking noises.

This procedure appealed to Abigail, who was older and brighter than Elizabeth. Soon she joined in the staring and the barking, but she went on with flourishes of her own. She began to crawl around the Parris house on all fours like a dog. On occasion she created quite a sensation by jerking and twisting and seeming to have uncontrollable convulsions.

This strange behavior demanded attention and got it. The two girls, who had learned only a few of their tricks from Tituba the healer, were taken to Dr. William Griggs, the local professional doctor. His diagnosis: Elizabeth and Abigail were bewitched.

Meanwhile the girls had not kept secret their exciting knowledge about red cats and red rats and the antics that

brought very gratifying notice from adults. They talked to older girls who lived nearby—girls sixteen and even eighteen years old. They in turn talked to other young women. Several of these were indentured servants—the next thing to slaves—who had ample reason to welcome any diversion that would brighten their lives. Presently they took to visiting Tituba and listening to her as she went about her chores.

A growing circle of friends began to imitate Elizabeth and Abigail. In houses farther and farther from the parsonage, girls suddenly twitched and writhed and talked gibberish—and became important. Nor did they limit their performances to home. Girls began to appear at the main tavern—called the ordinary—which stood across the road from the parsonage. There they put on really astonishing performances for the customers, who were mostly men. Deacon Nathaniel Ingersoll and his wife, who ran the ordinary, never for a moment believed the girls were bewitched, but the Reverend Parris thought differently. He had read Cotton Mather's tract and kept a copy of that valuable book in his library.

Something obviously had to be done, for the girls were disrupting not only prayers but also more and more other aspects of life in Salem Village. Parris called in half a dozen ministers from nearby communities. Together they fasted and prayed, and together the girls put on more and more elaborate performances.

Who, Samuel Parris asked, had bewitched the girls? Who had afflicted them?

At first the girls denied that anyone had afflicted them. But the ministers and other onlookers persisted. Clearly the girls were bewitched. Therefore a witch or witches had to be causing their trouble. The questioners began to be helpful: They threw out names. Was so-and-so bewitching anyone? Samuel Parris pointedly asked if his slave, Tituba, was the tormentor. At first none of the girls would accuse Tituba. Then the aunt of one of them thought of using a little trick from the repertoire of witchcraft itself in order to trap the sorcerer. Just exactly how her trick was supposed to work is not clear, but she did persuade Tituba and John Indian to bake, in the ashes of the fireplace, a witch cake made of rye mixed with urine from the afflicted girls.

Supposedly the magic cake was to be fed to a dog. But the Reverend Parris discovered Tituba baking it. Enraged that anyone should use the instruments of the Devil to trap the Devil, he berated Tituba, and in the excitement Elizabeth began to talk incoherently, repeating Tituba's name time and again.

That did it. Elizabeth's babblings were taken as accusation that Tituba had afflicted her. The other girls suddenly joined in. Since Tituba was as low as it was possible to get on the social scale, nothing could happen to the girls if they accused her. Besides, everyone knew she collected herbs and used palmistry.

Now the girls quickly achieved new importance in the community. If identifying one witch could bring them attention, identifying another could bring still more. Somehow they sensed—an adult, perhaps Samuel Parris, may well have made the suggestion—that it would be acceptable to accuse Sarah Good. She was a dirty, pipe-smoking woman who lived by begging, although there was plenty of work to be done for pay. She looked ancient, but she had a five-year-old daughter and a new baby was on the way. Goodwife Good—Goody Good she was usually called—was an outcast. All the town disapproved of her deviant behavior and was ready to believe that she did such things as send her Shape (a kind of invisible other self that could travel about independent of the witch's bodily self) to pinch young girls and make them scream.

Goody Good was not the only outcast in Salem Village. Sarah Osbourne did not conform to current standards of society, although she was neither poor nor dirty. She owned a good house—one so good that it is still standing today. But after her first husband died, she had taken another man into her house—William Osbourne—and she had not bothered to marry him until very recently. Moreover, she had not attended church for fourteen months. Right now she was ill and could not go to the meetinghouse for services, but earlier when she could have gone she stayed away. Perhaps she did not like the open hostility shown by members of the congregation, who suspected that William Osbourne was more to Sarah than just a man who did chores around her place.

So the girls added Sarah Osbourne to the list of women they cried out on as witches.

In February 1692, Tituba, Sarah Good, and Sarah Osbourne were arrested and taken to the jail in the nearby town of Ipswich. Sarah Good protested vehemently. Although she looked like a decrepit old woman, she proved to be almost more than the sheriff could handle. She kept jumping down off the horse that was to carry her to Ipswich, and when the sheriff finally brought her into court she continued to be obstreperous. Both she and Sarah Osbourne, who had been taken to jail from her sickbed, denied any guilt. They insisted they had not sent their Shapes to pinch the girls and otherwise torment them.

With the aid of a whip the Reverend Parris got Tituba to confess that she was the source of the trouble—that she was practicing witchcraft. With amazing suddenness all the beliefs and practices that seemed private and good to Tituba became open to view in Salem Village and were rejected as evil by those who had power and authority—and by many others, too. Tituba was defenseless. She lived under a four-fold handicap. First and most important she was a slave. Next she was a member of an alien race. In addition she was a woman. Finally she engaged in practices that competed with both doctors and ministers.

Whether Tituba would have called herself a witch if the Reverend Parris had not whipped her cannot be known, but she owed no debt to any white person and felt no obligation to accept the code of values professed by those who regarded her only as property, and now, dangerous property. She would do anything that seemed likely to give her even a little protection from the attacks of her oppressors. She would, of course, say she was a witch and agree to repeat words that her master put in her mouth, if that would stop the blows. She might even agree to say that certain white women were also witches, if saying so pointed the way to survival.

To examine the three women and decide if they should be held for trial, two magistrates came out from Salem Town.

The Folger Shakespeare Library

Frontispiece of *The Discovery of Witches* by Matthew Hopkins which appeared in 1647.

They took their duties seriously, and Salem Village officials saw to it that they approached the meetinghouse in some style. Guards and drummers and men carrying pennants accompanied them announcing their arrival. The magistrates conducted their examination, listened to protestations of innocence from two of the three women, decided there was ample reason for holding all of them, and set a date for a trial.

Meanwhile the ministers were unwilling to leave the solution of the witchcraft problem entirely in the hands of civil authorities. After all, witches were instruments of the Devil, and ministers were pledged to fight the Devil with all their strength. For the second time a group of clergymen assembled in Salem Village and fasted and prayed. Their arrival heightened the already great community interest in witchcraft, and the afflicted girls, instead of being cured by the fasting and prayers, were inspired to a new outburst of outlandish behavior. One of them, Ann Putnam, whose mother was emotionally unstable and full of animosities, cried out on a woman her mother disliked. This time the accused was no outcast. She was a pillar of the community and generally respected by the adults around her. What the

83

girls thought of her is not known, but she was clearly the kind of orthodox force against which some young people, and some older ones like Mrs. Putnam, could have had resentment. At any rate, a new witch had been added.

From now on the field of the girls' activities widened. The Reverend Deodat Lawson, who had once been a minister in the strife-ridden community, came back to see what was going on in Salem Village and to check on a rumor that his wife, who had died there years ago, had actually been murdered by witches. Abigail Williams put on a great show for the visiting clergyman the day he arrived. She claimed that the Shape of a well-known farm woman, Martha Cory, was there in the room at the moment, trying to make her sign something called the *Devil's Book*, which would show that Abigail agreed to serve the Devil. No one could see the Shape except Abigail, but she wrestled mightily and courageously with it and managed to avoid signing the book.

This all happened on a Saturday in March. The following day the Reverend Lawson conducted services at the meetinghouse, and the girls were there in force. They took over the services, interrupting the minister's prayer with loud, blasphemous remarks. To add to the drama Martha Cory appeared too, proud in her innocence and full of dignity. She knew she had been cried out on and that a warrant was out for her arrest. But in Puritan society warrants could not be served on the Sabbath, so Martha Cory came to church just as she always did.

William Stoughton, lieutenant governor of Massachusetts Bay Colony, acted as chief judge at the Salem witchcraft trials. He apparently never regretted the part he had played in the proceedings.

84

Why had this respectable, middle-aged, pious woman been added to the list of witches? Probably because she thought the whole uproar was nonsense and did not hesitate to say so. When the hearings began, her husband, Giles Cory, had been curious about them. He wanted to ride into the village to see what was going on. But Martha thought it was absurd for the old man to traipse off and waste good time watching silly girls perform antics. She could not persuade Giles to stay at home and tend to his work, so she took the saddle off his horse and hid it. This might have discouraged a lesser man, but Giles was not deterred. He went to the witch hearing anyway, and no doubt let it be known that he was there in spite of his disbelieving wife.

When Martha Cory was brought to the courthouse for her hearing, the girls were all on hand, ready to expand their performances. One of them claimed to see Martha Cory sitting on a beam high above the crowded benches in the meetinghouse, holding a yellow bird in her hand. The public could see very well that Martha Cory had her feet firmly on the floor beside the minister's chair. But the girls insisted that her Shape was overhead with a yellow bird, which they said was her "familiar."

More and more of the traditional trappings of witchcraft—such as familiars, which were assistants in deviltry—appeared as the girls gained experience. And the list of people cried out on continued to grow. There is no need to detail each addition to the list of those who were afflicted or were alleged to do the afflicting. By May 14 all the jails in the area around Salem Village were full. That was the day on which Sir William Phips, the new governor of Massachusetts Bay Colony, arrived in Boston to assume his duties. Phips, a native New Englander and a good Puritan but no scholar—he had not learned to read or write until he was twenty-one—took one look at the witchcraft crisis, appointed a special court of three magistrates to try the cases, and went off to fight Indians.

The newly appointed chief judge was William Stoughton, lieutenant governor of the colony. He and the other magistrates prepared earnestly for their duties, reading everything they could about witchcraft and how to detect witches. One method that attracted them was called spectral evidence—that is, testimony about a Shape, invisible to others, which could be seen by the bewitched. Some ministers warned against too great reliance on spectral evidence, and one of the three judges apparently had misgivings. He resigned after the first trial during which spectral evidence was used to convict a woman.

But the use of such evidence continued. All a girl had to do was claim that she was being pinched or choked or attacked in some way by the Shape of someone who might be miles away. Automatically that person was found guilty of being a witch. Another test involved touch. A girl who claimed to be suffering at the hands of a Shape could be instantly released from pain if the witch whose Shape was causing distress was made to touch her victim. If an accused person touched an agitated girl and the girl calmed down, the accused was obviously a witch.

Recruits continued to join the circle of assertive girls and young women. One was a boy who seems to have languished

A 19th century artist's conception of 'bewitched'' girls performing at a witchcraft trial.

in unhappy obscurity until he burst into prominence by claiming he was bewitched. John Indian also took this route. Of all the afflicted he had the best audience, day in and day out. The Reverend Parris had sent him to Ingersoll's ordinary where he worked for wages—wages that were, of course, paid to Parris and not to John Indian. In the tavern the slave cried out on several witches and had fits that greatly titillated the customers. The fits protected him because they put him among the victims, not the practitioners, of witchcraft, and his accusations led to the arrest of local whites, whom a slave apparently had no reason to love and cherish.

Accusations by the girls continued, and among those arrested was Martha Cory's husband, Giles, who at first had not been so skeptical as she. Giles was about eighty years old and would not live long anyway, so he decided on a unique course of action. He knew that if he was tried he would probably be found guilty although he was completely innocent.

If he was found guilty, all his property would be taken from him, and his heirs would get nothing. However, he could not be found guilty unless he was tried, and he could not be tried unless he pleaded either guilty or not guilty. So he refused to plead either way, knowing full well that English law provided a brutally persuasive method for use in cases like his. The measure was called pressing—that is, piling more and more heavy stones on the accused person until he either entered a plea or entered a grave. On September 19 Giles Cory did the latter. He died under hundreds of pounds of rocks. Three days later his wife Martha was hanged, still professing her innocence.

By October 14 the witch-hunt had spread far beyond Salem Village. About 300 people were in Massachusetts jails waiting to be tried. Nineteen persons, most of whom were women, and two dogs had been hanged as witches, and there was also Giles Cory dead from pressing.

85

Governor Phips, now back from the Indian wars, was aghast. Petitions lay on his desk asking him to let people out of jail while they awaited trial. There was much work to be done in the colony and those 300 pairs of hands were needed. A committee of ministers, including John Wise of Ipswich, had expressed grave doubts about the trials and the kind of evidence the judges relied on. People of higher and higher rank were being denounced. The girls who had begun by accusing a slave and two outcasts now cried out on prominent women in Boston and on an influential minister there. Already one minister who had had the misfortune to serve in Salem Village had been hanged as a witch. There were even rumors that the girls had cried out on no less a person than the governor's own wife. Obviously the whole fabric of Puritan society would collapse if this kind of thing continued.

Some people objected to the trials, not so much because they wanted to save the government as because they denied the reality of witchcraft. The girls, they believed, were merely putting on an act. Skeptics in Boston studied the trials and began to publish critical pamphlets. One, consisting of verbatim trial records and letters, was produced by Robert Calef, a merchant. This document greatly angered Cotton Mather, because it directly questioned Mather's judgment and motives. Calef also pointed out that there was no basis in the Bible for the theory—generally accepted as fact—that witches entered into a covenant with the Devil. In addition, Calef attacked the type of evidence that was being accepted.

"THE BIRTHPLACE OF AMERICAN INDEPENDENCE—1687"

The Reverend John Wise, son of an indentured servant, was a giant of a man, famous for his skill as a wrestler. The people of Ipswich, in Massachusetts Bay Colony, knew him well and loved him. In 1687 he led his parishioners in a general refusal to pay a tax arbitrarily imposed by the governor of the colony. At his trial the jury found him guilty of contempt and high misdemeanor. He was fined fifty pounds and sent to jail.

But Wise was not easily quieted. He suspected with good reason that the jury was packed—that it would bring in any verdict the government wanted—and he did not hesitate to say so. Also with reason, Wise believed that as an Englishman he was entitled to a writ of habeas corpus. His appeal for the writ did not succeed. That injustice rankled. So, too, did a judge's remark: "You must not think that the laws of England follow us to the ends of the earth."

As soon as Wise was out of jail he brought suit for a thousand pounds against the judge who had refused him the writ. Now still another judge imposed a fine on Wise, deprived him of the right to hold public office, and suspended him from the ministry. This went too far for the people of Ipswich. They paid the court costs for Wise and for others who collaborated with him in resisting the tax. At the same time they made vigorous protest against the order removing him from the ministry. As a result Wise resumed preaching only a month later.

After the Salem witchcraft trials began, the case of a man named John Proctor troubled Wise greatly. Proctor had let it be known that he thought all the witchcraft uproar was humbug. When a servant girl in his house joined the circle of the bewitched, Proctor had a cure for her fits. He gave her plenty of work to do and promised her a whipping if she got it into her head to act as if she were possessed. The fits stopped. So long as she stayed in his house she was quite normal. But when the court summoned her as a witness the fits began again, just as Proctor predicted they would.

Not unexpectedly, Proctor's wife was cried out on. Proctor protested. He protested again when he himself was accused. At this point the Reverend John Wise and Proctor's many friends signed a petition in his behalf. In spite of their efforts, Proctor was hanged. But eventually John Wise's efforts to promote sanity and democracy were to have a profound effect on the direction that history took in New England.

Wise had a strong affinity for the common people from whom he came. He was also a well-read intellectual, and the two traits led him into espousing a theory that played a great part in preparing for the American Revolution. From a German writer, Baron von Pufendorf, Wise got the disruptive idea that governments should be set up by men to serve their own interests, not by rulers to control men. This notion directly contradicted the belief, widely held in high places, that an aristocratic few should assume responsibility for ruling over the many and that the authority of government derived ultimately from God. John Wise believed that people had natural rights simply because they were people. This idea grew and won adherents—and became a basic part of the Declaration of Independence.

Wise published some of his ideas on democratic government in two small books which advocated natural rights and democracy. Both were reprinted in 1772, long after his death, on the eve of the Revolution.

The town of Ipswich did not forget that John Wise opposed illusion at the Salem trials, advocated popular control over church and state, opposed tyranny, and led a tax revolt. The official Ipswich seal bears this legend: "The birthplace of American Independence—1687."

Another businessman, Thomas Brattle, whose hobby was science, wrote even more scornfully than Calef about the kind of evidence used to convict witches. Brattle cast doubt on the validity of the confessions of witchcraft, and went on to attack the judges because they endangered the liberty which "was evermore accounted the great privilege of an Englishman." In this novel plea was a theme that would be heard time and again in other context as the revolutionary forces matured in the colonies. Both Calef and Brattle, as men of practical affairs, were accustomed to dealing in realities. In order to survive they had to know the difference between fantasy and objective fact. The witchcraft trials, they found, were based on fantasy—on illusion—for which they had no stomach.

One bit of reality went unnoticed for a long while: Time and again victims refused to confess, even though they knew that not one of the fifty persons who did confess was ever hanged. Some of the fifty apparently pleaded guilty to save their lives or because they were tortured. Some may have chosen this pitiful road to prominence as the only way open to them.

Finally, at one of the hangings outside Salem Village, onlookers protested loudly and openly. The rumbling against trials and sentences had become so great that Governor Phips lost no time in dissolving the court he himself had appointed to conduct the trials. In its place he established another court, which from the beginning refused to accept spectral evidence. The trials continued, but now there were almost no convictions. The governor stayed the sentences of the few persons this court did find guilty, and very soon he pardoned all the condemned who were still alive. He then released from jail all the others who had been accused and were awaiting trial.

The demands of common people, the rational protests of businessmen-intellectuals and of some courageous clergymen, and the governor's desire to have a colony left to govern, all contributed to bringing the episode to an end—or almost to an end.

The Reverend Parris, who had been a zealous seeker for witches and who had used witch-hunting as a way of intimidating his parishioners, failed completely to make his followers shape up as he wanted them to. Instead, the congregation fired him. In time one of the trial judges, Samuel Sewall, rose up in his church in Boston and confessed that in the Salem trials he had been guilty of wrongdoing. Several jurors made similar statements. People who had confessed to being witches recanted, and at least one of the girls who had done the awful accusing finally admitted that her denunciations were false. Some of the other accusers—we do not have the names—went on to lead what records written in 1711 called "profligate and vicious lives." All the accusing girls returned to anonymous obscurity, whether "profligate and vicious" or not, having failed at their grotesque try for freedom and importance. No oppressed individual advanced toward freedom in the sorry Salem affair—neither the girls nor any of the women they accused, nor Samuel Parris nor any of the presiding magistrates. However, people did stop the trials. That was a gain for freedom. So, too, was the sanity that replaced the witchcraft hysteria.

And what of Tituba, who in her own quiet way had started all the uproar in front of a big fireplace in the parsonage? She was kept in jail during the trials and the executions that followed them, safe from hanging because she had confessed. But when Governor Phips ordered the jails emptied, she could not leave. Nor could any other prisoners until their bills for board and room were paid. It was mandatory at that time for all prisoners to pay for their keep while in jail, even if they were subsequently found not guilty of the crime with which they had been charged. Tituba's owner, the Reverend Parris, ever mindful of money, refused to pay Tituba's bill. She was sold to another owner, so that money for her keep could be forthcoming. Her buyer, a weaver, was not at all afraid of having a witch in his establishment. He put Tituba to work at a loom.

The two outcasts, Sarah Good and Sarah Osbourne, who had been accused along with Tituba, were gone by now. Goody Good had been hanged, but not until she had given birth to a baby who soon died, and not until her five-year-old daughter, Dorcas, had joined her in jail, also accused of being a witch. Sarah Osbourne, ill when she was arrested and tried, died before the hangman could get to her.

The trials were over, the jails were empty, and never again would New England see a massive witch-hunt. Rationality grew as a result of the trials and finally became one of the elements that helped to shape the American Revolution.

PLACES TO SEE

MASSACHUSETTS

Danvers (Salem Village): First Church / Rebecca Nurse Home / Holton House / Sarah Osbourne House / Parsonage Site.

Salem (Salem Town): Court House / Charter Street Burying Grounds / Essex Institute Museum and Library / Gedney House / House of Seven Gables / Site of the Pressing of Giles Cory / Ward House / Witch House.

For more information, see Gazetteer, page 212.

A SURGE TOWARD FREEDOM

In Dutch New Netherlands, slaves fared a little better than they did in other places. A bondman, like an indentured servant in New England, had to work for only a specified period and then was released. The prospect of freedom made existence somewhat less burdensome. When the British took over in 1664 they changed not only the name of the colony but also the nature of slavery there. Servitude in New York was for life.

By 1712, in the total New York City population of 6,000, about 5,000 were described in the local records as "Christians," whether they were Christians or Jews. About 1,000 were listed as slaves. Most of them were Blacks, and many had been imported directly from Africa. A few were American Indians. All wanted more out of life than they were getting, and what they wanted most of all was freedom. Knowledge of this plagued their owners with fear. It was worrisome when slaves met to draw water at the several wells in the city. Talk at the wells often went on in African languages that the owners could not understand. And beginning in 1708, the talk was more and more about freedom and how to get it.

In July of that year two slaves came to white neighbors with a gruesome story. One slave was an Indian called Sam, the other a black woman whose name was not recorded. They reported that their owner and all the members of his family had been murdered. Immediately the two were accused of the crime, along with two other slaves with whom they were known to associate. The four were tried very promptly and found guilty. Each of them, according to a contemporary news story, was "put to all the torment possible for a terror to others." The woman was burned at the stake. Sam was placed astride a sharp spike and hanged, still alive, in chains.

The Provincial Assembly of New York then passed laws making the death sentence mandatory for rebellious slaves and providing reimbursement to the owners of any who were executed. The slaves themselves were deeply stirred by the brutal executions and, in the next four years, by other outrages as well. (The records, all kept by whites, do not tell what these outrages were.) At any rate, in April of 1712 a number of the slaves in New York decided that they would endure servitude no longer.

The leaders among the rebels were of three kinds: members of the Cormantine (or Coromantee) tribe from the part of Africa now called Ghana, members of the Paw Paw, or Whidaw, tribe from what is now Nigeria, and two American Indians, whose tribal affiliations are unknown. At least two of the Africans were women. Cormantines in the New World had already established a reputation for fearlessness. Some of them had revolted a few years before in Antigua, where they were described in one official report as "all born heroes." The same report said, "there never was a rascal or coward of that nation . . . not a man of them but will stand to be cut to pieces without a sigh or a groan."

Now in New York the Cormantine and other rebels decided their only hope for freedom lay in killing all the whites who dictated the conditions of slaves' lives and labors. After they had sworn themselves to secrecy, an African holy man performed ceremonies aimed at helping their cause. They needed whatever help they could get. Outnumbered five to one, they had a formidable problem. The whites were well armed and the Blacks were supposed to be weaponless. Such desperate odds required a desperate plan.

The slaves knew that everyone feared fire. Almost all the buildings in New York were made of wood, and a fire anywhere endangered the whole town. Invariably an alarm would bring men running with leather buckets to throw water onto the flames or onto nearby buildings that were threatened. Knowing how property owners responded when fire broke out, the slaves decided to set one and then ambush the fire fighters.

After the moon went down the night of April 6, 1712, twenty-four slaves gathered in an orchard on Maiden Lane that belonged to John Crooke, a barrel manufacturer who had been a well-known opponent of an earlier rebellion among the whites in New York. (He had fought against Jacob Leisler—in fact had tried to murder him.) The slaves, armed with a variety of weapons they had stolen, set fire to an outbuilding near the orchard, then waited in the dark. As the white men rushed toward the blaze, Blacks and Indians leaped out from behind trees, killed nine men and wounded several others.

This first blow for freedom went as planned. The rebels then fled unharmed to hiding places in the heavily wooded northern part of Manhattan Island. But the greater power of the armed whites soon became evident. The governor ordered a cannon fired at the fort on the lower end of the island—a signal for all white citizens to take up arms. The militia formed and began a search, while a messenger rode to Westchester with news of the uprising. Militia from that area soon joined the others, who were already beating the woods. This forestland was an obvious hiding place for the runaways, and unless they managed to get boats they would not be able to escape to the mainland.

It took almost two weeks for the militia to close the trap on all who had participated in the ambush in Crooke's orchard. Eighteen were captured. Six cut their own throats rather than surrender.

In their search for the original twenty-four, militiamen took other prisoners as well— apparently runaways. All together, seventy men and women were jailed and accused of insurrection. Fear among white New Yorkers disposed the magistrates to arrange trials as soon as they could. By promising immunity to two slaves, one of whom was a boy, they got evidence they used to put up a show of due process. Twenty-seven persons were tried, and twenty-one of them were executed immediately.

At this point the governor called a halt. The dubious evidence alarmed him. But more than that, the trials had opened an appalling can of worms in the white community. In an outburst of vindictiveness, slave owners were manipulating judge and jury to carry on personal feuds. One slave named Mars had been placed in triple jeopardy. In two successive trials he was found innocent. But this did not deter the prosecuting attorney, who had a special dislike for Mars' owner, a rival lawyer. The prosecutor managed to impanel a tractable jury, brought Mars to trial a third time, and at last obtained a guilty verdict.

Slaves who belonged to certain popular men were regularly found innocent. Those who had less influential owners were all found guilty. Finally, the governor noticed a discrepancy in the court's figures. By no count did the number of slaves who ambushed the fire fighters exceed twenty-four—and six of those had committed suicide. Yet twenty-seven were found guilty. Under cover of hysteria more than one spiteful man was goring his neighbors by having their slaves accused and found guilty.

The governor could do nothing for those who had been hastily executed. In the beginning he had even spoken with approval of some of the barbarous sentences, which he had thought would intimidate slaves who heard about them. One woman was burned at the stake. A man was roasted over a slow fire designed to let him stay alive for eight hours or more. Another was broken on the rack.

When the governor decided that the whole affair had gone too far, he granted reprieves to prisoners convicted but not yet executed. After a time, pardons for them were forthcoming from London.

The desperate surge of slaves toward freedom was halted, and the uprising had the immediate result of provoking New York officials to adopt especially restrictive laws. But during the next year, 1713, Massachusetts, with an eye on what had happened in New York, abolished slavery. And in 1714 the Quakers of Pennsylvania imposed such a high tax on the importation of slaves as to make the expansion of slavery too expensive in that colony. The courageous Cormantines and Paw Paws and Native Americans had done more than they ever knew to expand freedom in two of the American colonies.

Rachel Folsom

New York Public Library

89

Truth and Libel

Spoken words can frighten, but once uttered they are gone—blown away on the wind. Written words are different. They last, and when their effect is to produce fear, they can frighten over and over again. Knowing this, and being afraid, great tyrants and petty bureaucrats alike have shown special fear of a free press.

Freedom of the press was unknown when European countries began to establish colonies. In England each successive monarch and each successive Parliament in the seventeenth and eighteenth centuries forbade the dissemination of information unless it was to the liking of those in power. Rulers found it easier to keep power if printing presses were not busy turning out material that in any way challenged authority. Printers, therefore, were usually required to obtain licenses in advance, before they could legally set anything in type.

This licensing law was a compelling form of control. But if a printer ignored it and refused to submit material for prior censorship, there were other nets to catch him. The law provided penalties for the publication of anything seditious, and what constituted sedition was very vague. The law also forbade libel. This, too, was vague. A libel could be anything that put an individual in a bad light—anything that might make him subject to criticism or ridicule. And then there was seditious libel, a fuzzy combination of the two. Although a printer might be neither the author nor the distributor of material that displeased the authorities, he could be arrested for seditious libel merely because he set a document in type and ran off copies of it.

If a libelous statement was true, so much the worse. The reasoning went this way: The more a statement weakened authority by discrediting it, the more libelous the statement was. Strange as it may seem, the greater the truth, the greater the libel. There was no basis in law for the notion that truth and power ought to coincide. And if truth and power contradicted each other, it was power that prevailed.

By such means rulers intended to frighten printers and, through intimidation, control what information could reach their subjects. To make enforcement of the regulations easy, court procedure was arranged in a special way. It was the prosecutor's job to convince the jury only that the printer had indeed printed the material in question. Usually that was no problem. Appointed judges then determined whether or not the printer was guilty of sedition or libel. In other words, juries, representing the common people, could have no part in deciding what information people should get.

Printers wanted access to information just as much as any other citizen. But often they also had to fight against control if they were to practice their trade. Since any move for a free press was a move

(Left) Printed sheets, which came slowly from hand-powered machines like this, provoked dramatic trials that advanced the cause of a free press. (Above) In Philadelphia, printer William Bradford espoused press freedom, later in New York he opposed it. (Right) Making paper by hand was part of the whole communications process, and printer Benjamin Franklin was in the papermaking business.

against entrenched power, the struggle for the right to print had revolutionary implications. The search for freedom of the printed word and the effort of people to control their own lives were, and still are, inseparable.

In colonial times it made no real difference whether the rulers were Puritans in New England, Catholics in Maryland, or Quakers in Pennsylvania. None of those who administered the colonies wanted to allow a free press. In Pennsylvania, William Penn, aristocrat that he was, objected to the printing of the liberal laws he himself had drafted. Officials in his province, like those elsewhere, required William Bradford, the first printer in Pennsylvania, to submit for prior censorship anything he wanted to publish. Bradford was actually forbidden to bring out an almanac which referred to William Penn as "Lord Penn."

In 1689 at the time of the general restlessness that marked the Glorious Revolution, Bradford defiantly published Penn's Frame of Government, together with comments on it by a prominent council member. When he was accused of printing the document without having a license for that purpose, Bradford refused to admit responsibility. Instead, he relied on a doctrine of English common law, later included in the United States Constitution as the Fifth Amendment, that a man may not be forced to testify against himself. In the course of interrogating Bradford, a representative of William Penn said frankly, "I had particular order from Governor Penn for the suppression of printing here."

Nevertheless Bradford continued in business and again published something that the officials considered objectionable. When Bradford came to trial, he insisted on a new legal principle. He demanded that the jury, not the judges, decide whether the material he had printed was seditious. According to one story, a curious episode followed. The prosecutor had introduced a chase of type as evidence to prove that Bradford was in fact printer of the pamphlet. Thereupon, it is said, a sympathetic juror poked his cane at the type, pushed it off onto the floor, and reduced it to chaos—or to pi, in printers' language. And so the case against Bradford was never decided.

If the pied type did indeed stop the trial, it failed to bring freedom to Bradford. He spent the next year in jail before he was released by the governor of New York, who for a brief period succeeded William Penn as governor of Pennsylvania. The New Yorker needed a printer. William Bradford needed a job. So he left Philadelphia and set up shop in New York. His contribution toward winning freedom of the press had been made. Now it fell to others to carry on. The next engagement in the long war for the very human and very disruptive right to communicate was fought out in Boston . . .

15

"Freeness of Speech: A Thing Terrible to Public Traitors"

1722 Boston

Freedom of the press was only freedom to print what authorities approved of, until printers began to make strenuous objection. In Pennsylvania William Bradford resisted intimidation, and in Boston James Franklin and his brother Benjamin, both printers, used their newspaper as a weapon against entrenched authority.

Doomsday, the day of terrible reckoning, was fast approaching in the early 1700s—so preached New England's theocrats. And it was a fact that the power of Puritan ministers had been growing weaker for some time as a result of a series of blows.

For one thing the franchise had been extended to males who were not Puritans—that is, not members of the Congregational church. This meant that the church's members had lost their automatic monopoly over political life. In addition, there was a steady increase in non-Puritan immigrants, diluting the original population. Commerce had increased steadily, and Bostonians now found themselves confronted with customs and ideas that fitted ill in the world of Cotton Mather. He and his colleagues also had problems because their image had not been enhanced by their role in the Salem witchcraft trials.

All in all the Puritan leaders had reason to worry, and as happens when rulers feel insecure, they clung apprehensively to control of the press. Just as inevitably the desire for a free press grew as more and more people chafed under restrictions that were not to their liking. But it was no simple matter to establish liberty for the written word, and the effort to do so came to absorb much of the energy of a young printer who would rather have spent his time in other pursuits.

In order to make a living at his trade, twenty-year-old James Franklin set himself up in the printing business in Boston in 1717. He began, modestly enough, to bring out a weekly newspaper, the dull, conventional *Boston Gazette,* which was edited by others. However, before a year had passed he lost the contract to print this paper, which always stuffily supported the Puritan bureaucracy. At that point a few of the livelier non-Puritans in town gave up arguing with each other about the relative merits of radical deism versus conservative Episcopalian doctrine long enough to agree on one thing. They all wanted a newspaper that would be interesting and critical of the Puritan establishment. Now that James Franklin's press was available, it could help them turn out such a periodical. Would Franklin print what they proposed to call the *New England Courant,* a paper that would be rough on Cotton Mather and his followers? Franklin agreed, against the advice of some of his friends who could not see how such a publication could possibly survive.

The *Courant* not only survived, it prospered, and for good reason. It leaped into the center of a controversy that was of great concern to everyone. An epidemic of smallpox was taking a terrible toll in the community, and not a soul in Boston but was interested in reading arguments about how people could or could not avoid the too often fatal effects of the disease. On this subject the *Courant* spoke out vehemently. And Cotton Mather, whom the *Courant* wanted to whittle down, conveniently thrust himself forward to be carved upon. He offered a startling proposal on how to handle the smallpox epidemic. It could be halted, he said, by a new medical procedure known as inoculation. The *Courant* scoffed at the notion.

Predictably, Mather resented the *Courant's* attitude toward his proposal and toward other ideas coming from him and others like him who monopolized New England's pulpits. Of his detractors he said, "The practice of supporting and publishing every week a libel on purpose to lessen and blacken and burlesque the virtuous and principal ministers of religion in a country, and render the services of their ministry despicable, even detestable, to the people, is a wickedness that was never known before in any country, Christian, Turkish, or Pagan, on the face of the earth."

Mather had sensed the real import of the *Courant's* attacks. They were aimed at the power structure in which ministers were the central element. This opposition voice had its value in promoting dialogue, and it marked an important step along the road to a free press. But there was an element of irony in its choice of issues about which to raise a furor. Haughty Cotton Mather had proposed to serve God by inoculating people against smallpox. The upstart *Courant* stoutly insisted that smallpox was God's doing and mere men should not interfere with divine Providence.

THE New-England Courant.

[N° 17

From **MONDAY** November 20. to **MONDAY** November 27. 1 7 2 1.

To the Author of the New-England Courant.

Mr. Matthew Adams

SIR, *Boston, Nov. 4. 1721.*

THO' the Small Pox has made more than half its Progress thro' the Town, yet I presume it may not be altogether unseasonable to insert in your next the following Lines, which were occasioned by the melancholly Prospect which the Author had some time since of the present doleful Circumstances of the Place.

NOW on the Town an Angel flaming stands,
Grasping tremendous Woes in his right Hand,
And in his left, a black and awful List
Of all our Crimes. And shall we dare persist
In hostile Deeds, t'incense an angry God,
And stand the Blows of his revenging Rod?
Stand clear ye fearless Sons of Vice, whose Breasts
With more than bruitish Folly are possest,
T'engage Omnipotence! —— His kindled Darts
Will chase, and reach, and pierce your flinty Hearts.
See! Now th' infectious Clouds begin to rise
With sickly Gloom, to vail the healthful Skies:
The Thunder roars, the Lightning flashes in our Eyes.
Then let him fight that will, my Soul shall fly
For speedy Shelter from the Storm so nigh:
I'll hide me in Love's Chamber, till his Rage
Is overblown, and Mercy mount the Stage.
Then of his sparing Grace I'll gladly sing;
My rescu'd Life to him a thankful Tribute bring.

Besides, who could be sure that inoculation would not spread the disease instead of stopping it?

While the epidemic raged in Boston, killing sometimes hundreds a month, the *Courant* and the only doctor in town who had real medical training opposed the new measure in every way they could.

But Mather, of course, was right about inoculation and his opponents were wrong.

He had learned about this procedure from two different sources. One was his own black slave Onesimus who said that Africans protected themselves against smallpox by giving themselves mild cases of the disease. Mather had also

Front page of newspaper printed by James and Benjamin Franklin.

found two reports in the *Philosophical Transactions of the Royal Society* in London, of which he had been elected a fellow, on successful use of inoculation in Turkey. Armed with this information Mather began to campaign for immunizing everyone in Boston, and he won over to his side Zabdiel Boylston, who practiced medicine and did not lack for patients even though he did lack a medical degree. Boylston began by inoculating his own son and two slaves he owned. From there he went on to immunize others in spite of orders from worried Boston officials not to do so.

Mather's enemies jeered in the coffeehouses. They ridiculed him in print in the *Courant*. Their articles brought readers to the paper, but certainly no advantage to science or to the sick. It would not have been like Cotton Mather and his father, Increase Mather, who was still alive, to forgive and forget the insults. But at first there seemed to be no easy way to silence James Franklin or the paper. Then on June 11, 1722, the *Courant* printed a letter on a different subject, which the Massachusetts authorities thought they could use as an excuse to move against the paper. The letter hinted unmistakably that officials were doing less than they could to protect ships from pirates. Here was impermissible contempt for civil authority, and the council of the colony clapped James Franklin into jail.

While he was locked up, his apprentice, who happened to be his sixteen-year-old brother Benjamin, continued to publish the *Courant*. He also continued to contribute articles as he had been doing for some time under the name of Mrs. Silence Dogood. In one issue Mrs. Dogood wrote the following: "Without freedom of thought there can be no such thing as wisdom; and no such thing as public liberty without freedom of speech; which is the right of every man as far as by it he does not hurt or control the right of another; and this is the only check it ought to suffer and the only bounds it ought to know. . . . Whoever would overthrow the liberty of a nation must begin by subduing the freeness of speech: a thing terrible to public traitors."

After a month in jail, during which time he steadfastly refused to reveal the identity of the author of the offensive letter about pirates, James Franklin was released, and he promptly resumed his irritating attacks on community leaders. On January 14 he criticized religious hypocrites and went so far as to say that they were worse than "those who pretend to no religion at all."

The council had had enough. It ordered James Franklin not to publish anything in the future unless it was approved in advance by the secretary of the province. This imposition of censorship certainly did not end the desire of the backers of the *Courant* to have a paper through which they could express opposition. More than ever they wanted to keep on publishing, but the name of James Franklin could not appear on the masthead. However they used a technicality in order to outwit the council. The *Courant* continued to appear with the teenage apprentice fronting for his employer-brother. Benjamin Franklin was listed as editor.

The new editor made a lively start. He poked fun at the many honorary terms of address that establishment types liked to use: "In old time it was no disrespect for men and women to be called by their own names. Adam was never called Master Adam; we never read of Noah Esquire, Lot Knight and Baronet, nor the Right Honourable Abraham, Viscount Mesopotamia, Baron of Canaan. No, no, they were plain men, honest country graziers, that took care of their families and their flocks. Moses was a great prophet and Aaron a priest of the Lord; but we never read of the Reverend Moses nor the Right Reverend Father in God, Aaron, by Divine Providence Lord Archbishop of Israel. Thou never sawest Madam Rebecca in the Bible, my Lady Rachel; nor Mary, though a princess of the blood, after the death of Joseph called the Princess Dowager of Nazareth. No, plain Rebecca, Rachel, Mary or the Widow Mary, or the like. It was no incivility then to mention their naked names as they were expressed."

Benjamin Franklin, shown here as a young man, began his lifelong career in communications as a printer's apprentice at the age of 12.

94

THE FIRST NEWSPAPER

Benjamin Harris was one of the early fighters for freedom of the press. In England, when he spoke critically of the king, he was sentenced to be pilloried, fined, and imprisoned. He then emigrated to Boston where, in 1690, he started the first newspaper ever published in the colonies. Obviously Harris had not lost his spirit of defiance. He reported news the authorities in Boston did not like, and his paper, Public Occurrences both Foreign and Domestic, *was suppressed after its first issue appeared.*

This satire attacked no specific individual Bostonian. It assaulted the establishment as a whole only by indirection, elusively, and the council could find no sufficient pretext for suppressing the paper. The little journal—a single sheet printed on both sides—continued to make its appearance every Monday, and it continued to make improper Bostonians snicker at those whom they were supposed to regard as their betters.

The circulation of the *Courant* grew, but its prosperity did not last. James Franklin could not endure having his sibling, nine years his junior and also his apprentice, receive all the credit for the stir the *Courant* was creating. As a result the brothers quarreled. The younger ignored the legal requirements of his apprenticeship and left Boston in favor of Philadelphia, which enjoyed a much stronger tradition of liberty. "I took upon me to assert my freedom," Benjamin Franklin said.

James Franklin also left Boston. Before long he was publishing a paper in Newport, Rhode Island, another place where the libertarian tradition was more vigorous than in Boston. This paper did not survive long, and James Franklin himself soon died. His services to a free press were over, but the story of his young brother-apprentice was only beginning. The outpouring of words that Benjamin Franklin had begun while working on the *Courant* was not to stop for the rest of a long life. For nearly seventy years he would continue as a printer and writer and publisher. He was always involved in communication in some way—he even developed a postal system. Tirelessly he built and used freedom of the press, and his doing so was an exercise in delight, an operation in the realm of free enterprise, and the schooling of a whole people who wanted to find some road out of the confinements of life.

PLACES TO SEE

MASSACHUSETTS

Boston: Granary Burying Ground / Site of Benjamin Franklin's Birthplace.

For more information, see Gazetteer, page 212.

16

A Free Press:
"A Curb, a Bridle,
a Terror,
a Shame and Restraint"

1743   New York

*Peter Zenger was arrested for printing material
to which the colonial government objected.
Zenger's defense, unprecedented in English law,
was that a man could not be punished for
publishing something that was true. His victory
in court greatly advanced the cause of
a free press.*

A dozen years after oppositionists persuaded James
Franklin to print the *New England Courant* in Boston, New
Yorkers made the same kind of effort to establish a free
press. In their town the enemy was not a Puritan oligarchy
but a corrupt and dictatorial governor, William Cosby. The
printer, one of many recent immigrants, was a German, John
Peter Zenger, who had served his apprenticeship at the same
time Benjamin Franklin was serving his. As matters turned
out, Zenger's efforts on behalf of a free press went further
than those of either Benjamin or James Franklin or of anyone else in the colonies up to 1735. Moreover, Peter Zenger
(his first name is often omitted) was the central figure in a
historic trial that expanded the boundaries of liberty and

correspondingly limited the powers of a tyrannical administrator.

Gathering around Zenger, supporting him and giving
him legal defense, were some of the most interesting char-
acters in America. One was Zenger's second wife, a Dutch
woman. For nine months Anna Catherina Maulin Zenger
defied authority and continued to publish the very paper
which had so enraged Governor Cosby that he sent her
husband to jail. Another figure in the drama was Scottish
James Alexander, heir to the title of the earl of Stirling, a
former attorney general of New Jersey and a former member
of the councils of both New York and New Jersey. Alexander organized much of the opposition to Governor Cosby.
Andrew Hamilton, also a Scottish lawyer, a man of no
known religion, former attorney general of Pennsylvania
and speaker of the Assembly in that colony, acted as Zenger's
attorney. Others who supported Zenger were Lewis Morris,
who had been chief justice in the province of New York,
William Smith, an attorney, and twelve jurors—average
citizens all—who risked much to make a brave decision.

In the 1730s the time was ripe for the appearance in New
York of a crusading newspaper. That colony had less self-
rule than Massachusetts, Rhode Island, or Connecticut. Its
governor was appointed by the king, and the governor in
turn appointed a council to advise him. He also appointed
judges to sit in the courts. When in 1731 the incumbent
governor died, New Yorkers waited more than twelve
months for the new one, William Cosby, to appear. Almost
immediately one faction of the community saw that they
and Cosby could not get along. The new governor, they said
with reason, was singularly greedy and most unresponsive
to the wishes of the people over whom he had been sent to
preside. Cosby's past was not reassuring, either. He had
already been removed from one post as governor because
his behavior in England's colony of Minorca had been too
outrageous. However, he had important connections and so
managed to get the New York appointment. His wife was
the sister of an influential earl; his family owned large
estates in Ireland; and he was a close personal friend of the
most important member of the board of trade.

Sure of his post, Cosby was in no hurry to take up his
new duties. He remained in England for a year while a New
York resident, Rip van Dam, performed his duties for him.
Then when he did arrive, he tried to get Van Dam to kick
back half the salary Van Dam had drawn during the year he
was acting as governor. Apparently there was some basis in
custom for Cosby's request. But that bit of graft did not
satisfy him. While still in England he had been collecting
certain monies payable to the governor of New York. Van
Dam discovered this and suggested that each of them should
split the sums he had received during the year. Since Cosby
had collected more than Van Dam, Cosby was not interested
in this proposal. He sued Van Dam for the half of the
gubernatorial income that he claimed. During the course of
his case he encountered two very able attorneys who acted
for Van Dam—James Alexander and William Smith.

This first clash was only the beginning. Cosby soon
found he could not get the Supreme Court to make the
rulings that he wanted. So he removed the chief justice,

Lewis Morris, and put in his place James De Lancey who, Cosby believed with good reason, would be more pliable. But Morris had not risen to his high post by accident. He was an active politician, and he immediately began a campaign to regain power.

When an election was called in Westchester County, Morris ran as a candidate for representative to the Assembly. Cosby put up one of his own supporters against Morris. Clearly two political parties were now forming in New York. The one that backed Morris became known as the Popular party. The supporters of Cosby made up the Court party.

In 1733 an election in Westchester County was no simple matter of stepping into a polling booth on the way to work. Voters were farmers for the most part, and they lived scattered over a wide area that included much of what is now the Bronx. There was only one polling place in the whole county—outdoors on the green in front of St. Paul's Church in the village of Eastchester. The day for voting was announced in notices posted on the church door and elsewhere. But the hour was not mentioned. Fearing that this omission was some kind of trick, the Popular party stationed fifty guards around the village green, beginning at midnight before election day. These watchmen would see to it that the votes were not tallied at some moment when Court party members temporarily outnumbered members of the Popular party.

Many farmers had to start riding toward Eastchester the day before election. On Sunday afternoon, October 28, supporters of Lewis Morris found the way to the polls well prepared for them. Feasts were spread out on tables at farmhouses along their routes. By midnight a considerable number had reached New Rochelle. There they built a big bonfire in the street and spent a merry night around it. Then at daybreak, with two trumpeters and three violinists leading the way, they rode boldly forward toward Eastchester. Above them waved a banner. On one side of it big, gold capital letters spelled out KING GEORGE; on the other, LIBERTY AND LAW. Behind the banner rode Lewis Morris, the Popular party candidate, and behind him came two riders carrying flags. By the time this column reached the polling place, 300 horsemen were in the line of march.

Members of the Court party apparently slept a little later than riders in the Popular party cavalcade, but about eleven o'clock in the morning they, too, arrived at the green in a body, led by their candidate, who also had flags and a banner with a slogan: NO LAND TAX. It would be easy to assume from this slogan that the Court party consisted primarily of large landowners. But the economic division between the rival parties was not at all clear-cut. There were landed proprietors in both groups. Lewis Morris came from a family that had very large holdings. On the other hand the man who had replaced him as chief justice came from a family with large commercial interests. Some merchants supported the Court party and the Cosby government. Others favored the Popular party. However, three well-defined groups that supported the Popular party were much less visible in Court party ranks: Quakers, artisans, and the Dutch.

As the Court party riders entered Eastchester, someone counted the horses and got the figure of 170. At the head of their column was James De Lancey, the new chief justice. Beside him rode Frederick Philipse, an associate justice. The two files of horsemen began to circle the green in opposite directions, with what thoughts no one knows about the stocks, pillory, and flogging posts that were in plain sight there. When the columns met, the leaders of the rival parties sedately tipped their hats, and the parade continued. After this decorous demonstration ended, the sheriff arrived, "finely mounted, the housings and holster caps being scarlet richly laced with silver." He read the official announcement of the election. Then drums beat, and the two candidates went to stand at opposite sides of the green, while their supporters gathered around them to be counted. Much the larger crowd assembled at Morris' side.

The Court party did not intend to lose this election. Friends of Governor Cosby demanded a more careful tabulation. It took two hours to assemble tables and chairs to accommodate all the voters and inspectors, but finally the balloting began. Now the sheriff, recently appointed to his post by the governor, began to play with technicalities. Knowing very well the Quakers' religious scruples against taking oaths, he insisted that each pro-Morris Quaker swear on the Bible that he in fact owned real estate and accordingly was qualified to vote. Of course, the Friends refused. By this maneuver the sheriff disqualified thirty-eight Morris voters. Two Quakers who supported the Court party were not asked to take the oath. But when the polls closed at eleven o'clock that night, Morris led—231 to 151, even without the votes of his Quaker friends. Now the trumpets blared again, the violins squeaked, and the weary but jubilant supporters of the Popular party escorted their victorious leader to his lodging.

On November 5, Morris went by sailboat to New York City, and when he arrived at the ferry steps he was greeted by a general firing of cannons on merchant ships in the harbor. A multitude of merchants and artisans met him and paraded with him, shouting and rejoicing, to a banquet at the Black Horse Tavern—a place frequented by adherents of the Popular party.

A few days later Peter Zenger got the *New York Weekly Journal* off to a rousing start, announcing that it stood for a free press as "A Curb, a Bridle, a Terror, a Shame and Restraint to evil ministers [meaning government officials]." In line with this policy the paper carried a detailed account of the Westchester election. Although Peter Zenger was listed as editor, the material in this and later issues of the *Weekly Journal* was no doubt written mainly by the well-known lawyers James Alexander and William Smith, both of whom had urged Zenger to start the paper. To protect them from harassment, Zenger printed their contributions either anonymously or under pseudonyms.

Governor Cosby, already dismayed by the defeat of his candidate in the Westchester election, was now enraged by the *Weekly Journal*'s audacious statement: "The liberty of the press is a subject of the greatest importance, and in which every individual is as much concerned as he is in any other part of liberty." And soon afterward: "[The people] think, as matters now stand, that their liberties and properties are precarious, and that slavery is like to be entailed on them and their posterity if some past things be not amended."

In another issue the *Weekly Journal* ran a piece that no reader could fail to recognize as a description of Francis Harison, editor of a paper called the *Gazette*. (The man who printed the *Gazette* was none other than William Bradford, once in trouble because he defied authority in Philadelphia, but now content to bring out a paper that always reflected Governor Cosby's point of view.) The *Journal*'s lampoon of Harison said: "A large spaniel of about five foot five inches high has lately strayed from his kennel with his mouth full of fulsome panegyrics, and in his ramble dropped them in the *New York Gazette*. When a puppy he was marked thus (FH), and a cross in the middle of his forehead; but the mark being worn out, he has taken upon him in a heathenish manner to abuse mankind by imposing a great many gross falsehoods on them. Whoever will strip the said panegyrics of their fulsomeness, and send the beast back to his kennel, shall have the thanks of all honest men. . . ."

The piece clearly ridiculed a public figure, and many a printer had been taken to court for publishing such a thing. So in January and again in October 1734, Cosby tried to persuade a grand jury to indict Zenger for seditious libel. Both times the jurors refused. Cosby then got the appointive council to order the sheriff to burn four issues of the *Weekly Journal* in the presence of the mayor and the city magistrates.

The sheriff obeyed, but the only person he could get to burn the papers was a man who could not refuse—a slave. The mayor and the magistrates ostentatiously did not appear, and the only witness to the event whose name has survived was Francis Harison, editor of the rival *Gazette*.

Again Cosby had failed. Finally he put pressure once more on the council, all members of which held office only so long as he was pleased with their behavior. The council ordered the attorney general to arrest Zenger and charge him with "false, scandalous, malicious and seditious libels."

On Sunday, November 17, 1734, John Peter Zenger, age thirty-six, was locked up in a cell on the top floor of the City Hall, at Wall and Nassau streets. After trying unsuccessfully for release on a writ of habeas corpus, he asked to be freed on bail. Bail was finally set at 400 pounds—exactly ten times what Zenger estimated his total assets to be, exclusive of his clothes and the tools of his trade. The large sum demanded, plus technicalities in the bail law, made it impossible for Zenger to raise the required amount. So for more than nine months he remained in the city jail behind a locked door. However, there was a slot in the door and through it his wife, Anna, talked to him daily. And weekly the *Journal* continued to appear. No one knows exactly what the brave Dutch woman did to get out the paper. She had her husband's assistant to help her, and two of her five sons were also printers. Even so, she must have

So great was interest in the trial of Peter Zenger that numerous editions of accounts of the trial appeared, including the one in 1756.

Today at Colonial Williamsburg in Virginia a printshop operates much as did the one in which Peter and Anna Zenger put out the *New York Weekly Journal*.

A BRIEF

NARRATIVE

OF THE

CASE AND TRIAL

OF

JOHN PETER ZENGER, Printer of the
NEW-YORK WEEKLY-JOURNAL.

NEW-YORK Printed:
LANCASTER Re-printed, and Sold by W. DUNLAP,
at the New-Printing-Office, in Queen-Street, 1756.

had a difficult time. She risked arrest at any moment, and it could not have been a simple operation for a woman to engage in activities which men always reserved for themselves, not only running a business and editing a newspaper, but also taking part in an important political struggle.

James Alexander and William Smith appeared at the preliminary court hearing as Zenger's attorneys. They seized the occasion, no doubt with Zenger's approval, to challenge the right of the judges who were present to sit in the case. Since the judges held office only at the governor's "pleasure," instead of "during good behavior," they could scarcely be expected to decide anything contrary to his wishes. They replied to the challenge by disbarring the two attorneys. Now Zenger had to be represented by a court-appointed lawyer. This man must have been something of a surprise to Cosby. He objected, in a ritualistic way, to the very unusual list of prospective jurors. The sheriff, instead of bringing in a panel of forty-eight freeholders chosen at random, had produced forty-eight who could all be relied on to support the governor.

After this matter was straightened out, a jury of ordinary citizens was impaneled to sit at Zenger's trial. Meantime James Alexander and William Smith had made some secret arrangements. When Zenger's case was called on August 4, 1735, an elderly figure rose in the courtroom, approached the judges, and announced that he was there to represent Zenger. There was no need to ask his name; he was Andrew Hamilton, the greatest lawyer in the colonies.

Andrew Hamilton, Peter Zenger's attorney, most often remembered as defender of a free press, also helped design Independence Hall.

Hamilton was a Scot of independent spirit. He had been admitted to the bar in London, could practice in any English court, and had risen to great prominence first in Maryland and then in Pennsylvania. Both law and politics had rewarded him. For a while he served as attorney general of Pennsylvania and later as speaker of the Pennsylvania Assembly. Now he was well on in years. No one knows his age exactly because the facts of his birth and youth were hidden in obscurity, but he had certainly passed sixty and some believe he was eighty years old when he appeared at Zenger's trial.

Whatever his age, Hamilton had not lost his vigor or his eloquence. With strong logic and deep emotion he used one of the arguments that had been introduced in 1692 in Philadelphia when the printer William Bradford was tried for sedition. Perhaps Andrew Hamilton had heard of Bradford's case. Perhaps he even wished to embarrass the printer and publisher of the pro-Cosby *Gazette*. At any rate, Hamilton upset the Cosby-appointed judges by insisting that the jurors, not the judges, should decide on the substantive matter of libel. On behalf of Zenger he readily admitted to the jury that Zenger was responsible for the printing, and he went on to plead: "It is not the cause of a poor printer, nor of New York alone, which you are trying. . . . It is the best cause. It is the cause of liberty . . . the liberty both of exposing and opposing arbitrary power (in these parts of the world, at least) by speaking and writing truth. . . . The practice of informations for libels is a sword in the hands of a wicked king . . . to cut down and destroy the innocent."

This was the meat of Hamilton's appeal to the jurors. As intelligent citizens they had a right to know the truth about what was going on in the world. The law did not forbid them to *hear* the facts. It merely provided penalties for those who were tempted to *reveal* facts. The illogic of the law, Hamilton argued, affected ordinary citizens as well as newspaper men. "Our Constitution," he said, "gives us an opportunity to prevent wrong by appealing to the people. . . . But of what use is this mighty privilege if every man that suffers must be silent; and if a man must be taken up as a libeller for telling his sufferings to his neighbour?"

If it was indeed a libel for a newspaperman to tell the truth—or even to poke fun at officialdom—Hamilton said, ". . . there is scarce a writing I know that may not be called a libel, or scarcely any person safe from being called to account as a libeller. Moses, meek as he was, libelled Cain; and who has not libelled the Devil? . . . How must a man speak or write, or what must he hear, read, or sing, or when must he laugh, so as to be secure from being taken up as a libeller? I sincerely believe that if some persons were to go through the streets of New York nowadays, and read a part of the Bible, if it were not known to be such, Mr. Attorney [the attorney general] . . . would easily turn it to be a libel; as, for instance, the sixteenth verse of the ninth chapter of Isaiah: 'For the leaders of this people cause them to err; and they that are led of them are destroyed.'"

The jury of average freeholders obviously agreed with Hamilton. After deliberating only a few minutes they defiantly brought in a verdict of not guilty—meaning that Zenger had told the truth and should not be imprisoned for

A 19th century engraving shows Andrew Hamilton saying, "It is not the bare printing and publishing of a paper that will make it a libel: The words themselves must be libelous, that is, false. . . ."

doing so. As James Alexander later reported, "the numerous audience expressed their joy in three loud Huzzas and scarcely one person except the officers of the court were observed not to join in this noisy exclamation."

Zenger had to spend one more night in jail, but the crowd did not wait for his release to celebrate. They carried Hamilton to a great feast at the Black Horse Tavern, and there some admirers presented him with a box made of gold on which appeared the seal of New York, where he had won his victory over tyranny. The next day when he set sail in a sloop on his homeward journey, the guns of merchant ships in the harbor fired a salvo in his honor just as they had done for Lewis Morris when he came down from Westchester after his victorious election.

Along with all this exuberance went the sober fact that Hamilton had introduced a new principle of English law. He had contended successfully that it was no crime to print the truth about an autocratic government official. The jurors had done their share by heeding Hamilton, who told them, "Every man who prefers freedom to a life of slavery will bless and honor you as men who baffled the attempt of tyranny, and, by an impartial and uncorrupt verdict, have laid a noble foundation for security to ourselves, our posterity, and our neighbors."

A foundation it was, but Hamilton's new principle did not at once become a generally effective part of the law. Officials went on trying to intimidate and silence their critics. The struggle for a free press continued up until 1776. And it was not even guaranteed by the Constitution adopted in 1787 after the Revolution. In that year, Thomas Jefferson felt called on to say that newspapers without government would be preferable to government without newspapers. Freedom of the press finally became a legally assured right only after the adoption of the First Amendment in 1791.

PLACES TO SEE

NEW YORK

Mount Vernon: St. Paul's Church, Headquarters of the Society of the National Shrine of the Bill of Rights.

New York (Manhattan): Federal Hall National Memorial.

For more information, see Gazetteer, page 212.

Utopia in the Wilderness

1733–43   Georgia

James Oglethorpe, a man of vision, established a colony in Georgia that was at once idealistic and practical, attracting a rich diversity of colonists from many different backgrounds and possessing many different skills.

In the early 1730s several astonishingly diverse streams of people flowed toward what they hoped would be a kind of paradise in a part of North America that Spain claimed and England wanted.

Half a hundred of these were refugees who left Salzburg, in what is now Austria, and crossed part of Germany on foot accompanied by two wagons full of baggage and children. These Salzburgers—all Lutherans—had been forced into exile by the Catholic archbishop of their homeland, who was also its temporal ruler. Walking by twos along roads they hoped would lead to freedom, they sang hymns, one of which became famous throughout Europe:

> O Lord, let our flight not occur in winter;
>   this used to be my plea and the aim of my wishes,
> but now I am content to go even in wintertime,
>   because God's warm love will cover us.

While Lutherans were making their way across Europe, forty Sephardic Jews were raising money in London to pay *their* passage across the Atlantic. They had been expelled from Catholic Portugal and now sought a place where they could live in peace and worship as they thought right.

Also in London at this time thousands of unemployed Englishmen begged and starved in the streets. New agri-

cultural methods had thrown many of them off the land, and new industrial methods had not yet provided them with work. For these jobless, almost any change would be for the better.

Another kind of social victim occupied London jails in the 1730s. Their only crime was failure to pay their debts. They had to stay in prison until they satisfied their creditors, but as long as they remained there they could not earn money to do so. Very few could find a way out of this vicious circle. Jails were full and conditions in them appalling.

Prisoners also crowded the jails in Ireland, one of the countries England had conquered in her march toward imperial power. Some of these Irishmen were criminals by any standard in any society. Others had run afoul of the law only because they thought Catholic Irishmen should be free to run a Catholic Ireland.

At this same time, in the university town of Oxford, several young Anglicans were drawn together by a common dissatisfaction with the lack of dynamism in their church. These young men made up what was known as the Holy Club and would eventually create an immense stir among the common people of America.

Also in the early 1730s many Presbyterian Scots in the far northern Highlands of the British Isles were rattling around for lack of any farms to cultivate or enemies to fight. They were traditionally warriors, but in 1715 they had failed in an effort, made jointly with Catholic Highlanders, to replace King George I with a descendant of James II, some of whose ancestors had been Scots. These Highlanders had grown up on small farms that were now being taken over for use as sheep pastures. They saw no future for themselves or their families in Scotland and were ready to go wherever their farming and fighting skills would pay off.

Northern Italy, too, had its share of discontented men and women in the 1730s, some of them employed in an industry that had not yet developed in English lands. These Italians understood how to raise silkworms, how to unwind delicate thread from the cocoons, and then to weave it into lovely cloth. But silk workers were not entirely happy. If they could find some place in the world where they could make a better living, they would like to give it a try.

In America, south of South Carolina, several bands of Creek Indians had just angered other, more powerful, Creek bands and had been sent into exile. The offenders had destroyed a Catholic mission established by Frenchmen who had moved eastward from the Mississippi Valley. This raid seemed like bad tactics to the dominant Creek bands who looked to the French as a possible source of protection against Englishmen from South Carolina. The exiled Creeks, weak and isolated, were now faced with an unhappy prospect: They had either to fight against or to seek support from the Spaniards in nearby St. Augustine, who also had missions and forts in southern Creek territory.

All these people—Salzburgers, Jews, the London jobless, the Irish prisoners, Scottish Highlanders, members of the Holy Club, Italian silk workers, dissident Creeks—were misfits in some way, according to the norms approved by the rulers under whom they lived. And because they all wanted to do something about expanding their lives, they erupted onto the American scene in the 1730s and joined in an enterprise in an area where England had not yet attempted to establish a colony. Here, these social deviants were told, they could live in a model society. Most of them, however, were not acutely aware that their model society would be encouraged because it might enlarge England's empire at the expense of Spain's.

Who could bring such a varied assortment of people together to cooperate with one another toward a common goal? Who could raise money to transport them all to America and get them land to live on? For this task it took a person with a rare combination of skills—a man of sweeping vision, driven by intense motivations. Such was tall, gray-eyed James Edward Oglethorpe, born in 1696 into a wealthy, offbeat family that sided with King James II after that monarch was deposed in the Glorious Revolution.

Oglethorpe, when still very young, became an army officer and remained one all his life. He also persisted in a lifelong devotion to reading inspirational romances. As one of the most influential members of Parliament, he advocated prison reform laws, and no one in that body or out knew more about the utter degradation of life in prison. He had been in jail himself, in 1722, just after he was elected to Parliament for the first time.

The young man had gone up to London from his estate in Surrey, and one night he got drunk. By six o'clock in the morning of April 25, much in his cups, he stumbled into a rough tavern. A brawl started and he ran his sword through a man of the servant class. The man died, and Oglethorpe found himself behind bars. But he was an aristocrat with connections. Sometime before October 8, he was freed. On that day Parliament opened, and he took his seat. No record has been found of any trial or sentence.

Oglethorpe's memories of prison life were soon reinforced. His closest friend, an architect, was arrested because he could not pay his debts. In jail, where Oglethorpe visited him, he could not pay bribes demanded by the jailer. This official, out of malice, put the architect in a cell with men who had smallpox. He contracted the disease and died.

These two experiences produced in Oglethorpe a sense of mission. He began to work in Parliament for prison reform and became chairman of an investigating committee. His reports on the terrible conditions he found were detailed and thorough, and he made sure that members of Parliament saw them. Speaking in his high, shrill voice, he pleaded for reform. In 1730 Parliament passed the law he proposed.

In this same period Oglethorpe wrote *The Sailor's Advocate*, a widely read pamphlet which opposed impressment —another limitation on human freedom of which he had become aware. It was the custom of the English navy to kidnap—to impress—men into service at sea. Oglethorpe was second to none in his enthusiasm for a strong navy, but

Disease was rampant in the English debtors prisons, and often migration to the colonies was the only alternative to death for convicts who could not pay their bills.

Culver Pictures

he wanted it manned by sailors who went to sea by choice, not because they had been snatched off the streets and forced on shipboard.

In the course of his visits to jails, Oglethorpe had found many men who, he was sure, would do well for themselves and for England if they were able to reach the colonies. There they could grow crops and practice trades and start new industries. He was an early believer in the value of the industrial revolution. Unlike most Englishmen, he opposed as outmoded and restrictive the mercantile policies of the government, which held that colonies should trade only with England, producing raw materials and not competing with the homeland in the manufacture of goods.

Oglethorpe also believed that Englishmen in the colonies should be regarded as the equals of Englishmen in England. To Parliament he said in 1732: ". . . our colonies are all a part of our own dominions: the people in every one of them are our own people, and we ought to show an equal respect to all."

As a military officer Oglethorpe thought often about the problem of expanding and defending the American colonies, and he saw in the slums and prisons of London a way to do so. Gradually a grand plan took shape in his mind. He would transform people who were a liability in England into an asset in America. There they could hold territory for England against Spain to the south and against France to the west. He would ask King George II for land between South Carolina and Florida, and he would flatter the king by calling this land Georgia.

The idea had been proposed some years before. At that time the colony was to be a feudal enterprise called the Margravate of Azilia. Nothing came of the scheme, but not because of its exotic name. It failed because its promoter was more given to words than to action. Oglethorpe, on the other hand, was a man who liked to get results. The plan he drew up appealed to the king. Soon a committee of men called "trustees" was named to begin colonizing Georgia—an area defined as stretching from the Atlantic coast all the way to the Pacific Ocean, right through territories claimed by both Spain and France. Oglethorpe was a member of this board of trustees, as were many of the members of the prison reform committee he had headed in Parliament. When it came time to select an administrator for Georgia, the trustees chose Oglethorpe, who was then thirty-six years old. (He was never named governor. For lack of a formal title, many colonists called him "father.")

Now came the problem of recruits for the new colony. Many hundreds applied. The trustees screened these would-be Georgians with care, for they could send only a few more than a hundred on the first ship, and they wanted steady men who seemed likely to be good workers—men with families and sound reputations. Finally the approved party of men, women, and children boarded a frigate bound for America.

The first shipload of settlers consisted partly of men who were unemployed, partly of debtors, partly of Salzburgers, most with families—plus Oglethorpe, one of the most important members of Parliament. On January 13, 1733, the pioneers reached Charleston (called Charles Town at that time), in South Carolina. Oglethorpe wasted little time before going ahead of the settlers into Georgia, where he had something to do that could not be planned out in advance. He had to make friends with the Indians. Unlike most other English colonists, he did not feel that a grant from the king was all he needed. As a matter of decency, and as a practical measure, he sought a grant from the Indians whose land he hoped to use.

After Oglethorpe made arrangements with a Creek chief, the first Georgians founded Savannah.

From the first, Oglethorpe treated the Indians he met with respect. This was not the standard approach. It happened by chance that the Creeks who lived on the land he wanted were at odds with almost everybody, both Indian and white, and were badly in need of allies. In addition, there was among them a woman, part Creek and part English, who spoke English and could act as interpreter while Oglethorpe learned the Creek language, which he proceeded to do.

The leader of the Creeks seems to have developed a genuine affection and admiration for Oglethorpe. He and the Englishman became lifelong friends. All of the Creeks saw in Oglethorpe a welcome contrast to other Englishmen they had known. Willingly they ceded him a large area that included a place called Yamacraw Bluff. This, Oglethorpe thought, would be a good place for a town.

With military efficiency he drew up plans for the settlement, which he called Savannah. It was to be all straight lines and right angles and regularity, and this suited him as a military man. Attractive open parks inside the town suited him as a utopian dreamer. Apparently the idea for the layout of Savannah came from the design of the Chinese city of Peking, which Oglethorpe had seen in a book by a Jesuit priest. He liked what he saw and followed it.

Georgia settlers had lived in the New World only a few months when a ship arrived bearing colonists who had not been sent out by the trustees. These were Sephardic Jews from Portugal who had bypassed the trustees for fear their application might be vetoed. Indeed it would have been. Oglethorpe, the trustee who might have befriended them, was already in Georgia, and the Jews decided to go directly there, without any formal permission. When Oglethorpe, faced with their *fait accompli,* saw that they had talented men among them, including a much-needed doctor, he let

Tomochichi, the Creek who sold land to Oglethorpe, was painted with his nephew while visiting London in 1734. Tomochichi and Oglethorpe became lifelong friends, an unusual alliance for the times.

This map shows Savannah in 1735, two years after the first European immigrants arrived in the colony.

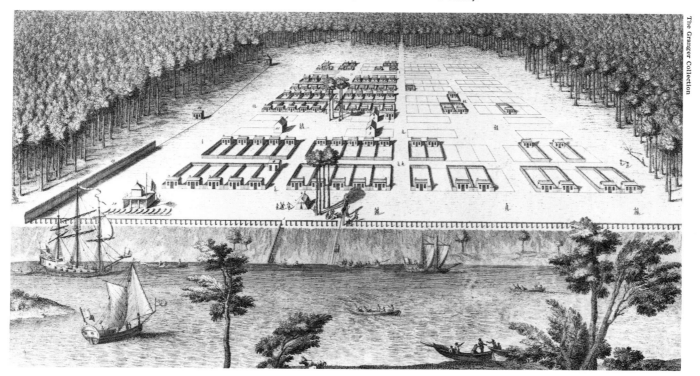

103

Many hymn-singing Lutheran exiles who left Salzburg, Austria, on foot, later became settlers in Georgia. There they found a haven, as did other dissident groups.

had been released from jail into the care of a sea captain who had undertaken to transport them overseas where he could sell them as indentured servants. The captain, unable to dispose of his transports, as they were called, in Jamaica, had sailed up the Atlantic coast hoping to find buyers there. In Savannah he offered the whole lot to Oglethorpe for 200 pounds. Oglethorpe paid the sum, partly because he saw a chance to improve the lives of these onetime prison inmates and partly because he needed a greater labor force in Georgia. Some of the original settlers had died. Now he assigned one Irish man to each widow in the colony to do the work her late husband had been doing. One servant went to each magistrate to do the manual labor he could not perform when he was engaged in official duties.

In a very short time the Irish ex-prisoners, who had become indentured servants, showed resentment of the virtual slavery in which they found themselves. They began planning together to rise and claim liberty. If necessary they would do so at the expense of the lives of those who held them in servitude. At least one of the insurrectionists was a woman. All who agreed to take part in the uprising decided to wear identifying red strings around their wrists. But the whole rebellion had been clumsily planned and came to naught. Possibly it failed in part because of the red string the rebels wore. Its meaning became known and its wearers were betrayed. Ringleaders were arrested and whipped.

The experiment with indentured servants had not been a success. Settlers soon began to clamor for African slaves.

Oglethorpe would not authorize slavery. He had come to be a strong opponent of this institution before he left England, although as recently as 1730 he had had no objection to the kidnapping and sale of Africans. In that year he became a heavy investor in the Royal African Company, which was chiefly engaged in the slave trade. While he was on the finance committee of this company a curious incident happened. One day a man from America brought to the company offices a letter written in a kind of script that no one could read. It came, he said, from a black man who seemed to be an escaped slave lodged in a Maryland jail. Intrigued, Oglethorpe sent the letter to Oxford, hoping that some scholar there would be able to decipher it. A professor who knew Arabic solved the mystery.

The writer of the letter, who became known as Job Jolla, was a well educated Moslem, a Foulah from Gambia, a religious leader in his homeland. He had been forced into slavery, sold in Annapolis to the owner of a tobacco plantation, and sent to work in the fields. From there he ran away and reached the western shore of Delaware Bay, only to be picked up because he had no pass of the kind slaves were required to carry when they traveled. Shortly afterward he wrote the letter in Arabic which, through coincidence, reached Oglethorpe although it was addressed to Job Jolla's father, an exceedingly important religious leader in Africa.

Oglethorpe responded to this prisoner as he had to many others. He wanted him to be free. So he bought Job Jolla from the tobacco planter and then released him. Job Jolla sailed from Maryland to England at the same time Oglethorpe sailed from England to Georgia with the first shipload of settlers. They passed on the high seas, but Oglethorpe

them stay. Later he brought in more Lutheran refugees from Salzburg, and he added to the intercultural mix by sending to Inverness in Scotland a recruiter who found 130 Highlander men and 50 Highlander women and children ready to go to Georgia. Many of them settled in a place they called New Inverness. (Today it is called Darien.)

Gradually Oglethorpe helped to establish small villages on the coast and along the Savannah River, and he designed the town of Frederica on St. Simons Island, which by anybody's definition was inside territory claimed by Spain. At Frederica neat houses lined wide, straight streets under the protection of a fort. Nine miles down the island Oglethorpe built still another outpost called Fort St. Simons, the most southerly military establishment in the English colonies. These preparations were to be of decisive importance a few years later.

While he made sure that his settlers had houses in Savannah, Oglethorpe himself lived in a tent. At Frederica, with its fort to protect the settlers, he put up a home for himself outside the fortifications. This, he thought, would improve morale at Frederica by showing there was nothing to fear from the Spaniards or the Indians.

One day a ship reached Georgia with forty Irish prisoners aboard. They were survivors of a larger number who

University of Georgia Press

learned later that Job Jolla became a valued translator of Arabic documents at Oxford, then returned to his African homeland.

At about the time Oglethorpe learned of Job Jolla, he withdrew from the Royal African Company, and before he left for America he had resolved that there would be no Job Jollas in Georgia. He insisted that slavery must be prohibited there, and so did the trustees. For one thing the trustees feared that slaves, being resentful of their lot, might defect to the Spaniards at St. Augustine and so prove to be a source of military weakness. They said, too, that they could not afford to buy slaves for the settlers. Besides, it would make the colonists lazy if someone else did their work for them.

Slavery was forbidden in Georgia, and so was rum. Perhaps Oglethorpe recalled what he had done when he was drunk. At any rate, he outlawed the importation and the use of hard liquor. In many ways life in Georgia was regulated, and Oglethorpe, as representative of the trustees, did the regulating. He and the magistrates, the constables, and other local officials were all appointed. No provision existed for electing anyone in Georgia. The idealistic plans for the colony included no mechanism for adjusting the government to the needs and wishes of the people.

Oglethorpe's own wishes were benevolent, and many people loved him, including Germans of the Moravian faith, who joined the Lutheran Salzburgers after the colony got started. These Moravians were pacifists and would have nothing to do with Oglethorpe the military leader, but they still revered Oglethorpe the generous humanitarian, the benevolent despot. Even his most severe critics seldom accused him of bad motives. Rather, they said, he had bad judgment.

Critics there were. Many settlers grew dissatisfied. Some wanted the right to have full title to land they farmed—a right which the original plans for Georgia did not provide. Some wanted the right to import and drink rum. Others wanted slaves so that they could produce crops that would compete with those produced by the slave economy of South Carolina.

To handle all the tensions and hostilities that were developing, Oglethorpe felt that strong religious leaders might be helpful. The Anglican priests already in Georgia were weak individuals and totally ineffectual. So, while he was in England on colony business, he looked for the kind of zealous men he thought he needed, and for a time he thought he had found them in the persons of two brothers who were moving spirits in the Holy Club at Oxford, which was trying to invigorate the Church of England. These brothers, John and Charles Wesley, placed so much emphasis on their method of regulating life according to teachings in the New Testament that their detractors called them Methodists. Finally the name stuck to the denomination that grew out of the work they started.

Oglethorpe put John Wesley in a church in Savannah, and Charles Wesley went to Frederica on St. Simons Island, very close to the Spanish settlements in Florida. The emphasis these young men placed on pious behavior and on forms and rules was so great that they stirred up very considerable new resistance, instead of solving problems for Oglethorpe.

James Edward Oglethorpe combines the military career suggested by symbolic armor in this portrait with membership in the House of Commons, and with activities as a social reformer, businessman, and colonizer of Georgia. He advanced the freedoms of many diverse peoples.

Charles lasted only five months at Frederica, then returned to England. John stayed less than two years at Savannah with some visits to Frederica. Then he, too, left Georgia.

The only real result of the ministries of the Wesley brothers in America may have been that they turned away from formalism and developed a style much more moving and acceptable to common people. Another member of the Holy Club, George Whitefield, who followed the Wesleys to Georgia, used just such an emotional approach. His was one of the most sensational revivalist careers in American history.

Whitefield, as a central part of his work, established an orphanage called Bethesda, outside Savannah, which still operates today. This institution, with Whitefield behind it, tells a story of tremendous change that went on in Georgia during its first years of existence. Whitefield, sensing the mood of his supporters, joined them in petitioning the trustees to permit slavery in the colony. In spite of Oglethorpe's adamant resistance, the trustees finally approved. After 1750, when permission was granted, the great orphanage for which Whitefield raised funds all over the colonies, became supported in part by produce from his plantation where the work was done by slaves.

The legal introduction of slavery happened only after

Oglethorpe had left Georgia for good. Meantime, in 1739, rivalry between England and Spain broke out into war, and Oglethorpe, in territory claimed by Spain, was soon engaged in military action. One of his military units, made up of Scottish Highlanders, had been trained on the mainland across from St. Simons Island. These Highlanders were enthusiastic supporters of their commander, who endeared himself to them by wearing a kilt when he came to their town. At Frederica Oglethorpe had regular British troops who had been transferred there from Gibraltar. Other fighting men under his command came from South Carolina. With these and still other forces, he tried in 1740 to capture the Spanish fort, Castillo de San Marcos, at St. Augustine. Although he besieged the place for many weeks, he failed to take it.

When the Spaniards counterattacked on St. Simons Island, Oglethorpe and his men intercepted them before they reached Frederica. With luck on their side, they destroyed the Spanish force at a place that came to be called Bloody Marsh because so much Spanish blood was spilled there. Had the battle ended in defeat for Oglethorpe, United States history might well have moved in a different direction.

Oglethorpe had foreseen that England would do well to establish Georgia in order to contain Spain. He had also helped to achieve this goal. His colony, too, survived, although with arrangements about ownership of land, about rum, and about slaves that differed from those he approved. It was not the Utopia that he had dreamed of.

With Spain defeated and Georgia out of military danger, Oglethorpe went home to resume duties in Parliament, to serve as a general of the army in Britain, and to continue his lifelong practice of eating little, drinking less, and engaging in daily calisthenics. He never lost his interest in America, and as one who had been a benevolent dictator there he had no use for colonial dictators of a harsher sort. Such a man, he believed, was Sir Francis Bernard, once governor of Massachusetts. Popular resistance to Bernard had been great, and he finally withdrew to England. There, on June 5, 1770, he met Oglethorpe, still a crusader at the age of seventy-three. The *Boston Gazette* later reported the following: "Bernard was drove out of the Smyrna Coffee-House not many days since, by General Oglethorpe who told him he was a dirty, factious, Scoundrel who smelt cursed strong of the Hangman."

Oglethorpe, who long ago entered Parliament as a Tory, had developed strong sympathy toward the colonies, much to the disgust of later Tories, including Samuel Johnson, whom he often saw. In 1776, even though he was a general in the British army, he sided quietly with the Americans. When the Revolution was over and the United States sent John Adams to England as its first ambassador, Oglethorpe immediately called on him to express his satisfaction at the course events had taken.

At the age of eighty-six Oglethorpe was still doing his daily exercises. At eighty-eight he attended the sale of the library of Samuel Johnson and bought books there with which to enlarge his own library. He was still reaching out. He was still showing the vitality, the urge to grow, that lay behind the development of a new nation that would include his Georgia.

106

Oglethorpe at age 88 sketched at the sale of the library of Dr. Samuel Johnson in 1785.

PLACES TO SEE

FLORIDA

St. Augustine: Castillo de San Marcos National Monument / Fort Matanzas National Monument.

GEORGIA

Darien: Monument to the Scots Highlanders / Oglethorpe's Oak.

New Ebenezer: Jerusalem Church and Museum.

St. Simons Island: Fort Frederica National Monument / Site of the Battle of Bloody Marsh / Site of Fort St. Simons / Site of Oglethorpe's House.

Savannah: Chippewa Square / Cockspur Island / Johnson Square / Madison Square / Oglethorpe's Bench / Trustees Garden / U. S. Customhouse / Wormsloe Plantation Gardens / Wright Square.

SOUTH CAROLINA

Beaufort: St. Helena's Episcopal Church / 1690 House.

Charleston: Old Fort Johnson.

For more information, see Gazetteer, page 212.

Empire-Seeking in the Ohio Valley

France and England were the most muscular European powers in 1754. Each of them had reached out vigorously for wealth-producing territory in India, Africa, and the New World. In North America, France had her base in Canada. England's base lay to the south along the Atlantic seaboard. South of Canada and west of the Appalachians stretched vast Native American lands coveted by both France and England. The latter, playing the game of empire according to imperial rules, claimed all of that area and more because John and Sebastian Cabot had landed on the shore of North America in 1497–98 and had "taken" all of the continent for England. France could play the same kind of game. She maintained that all territory drained by the Ohio and Mississippi rivers was French because a Frenchman, La Salle, had explored for the first time from the Great Lakes to the Gulf of Mexico in 1669–70. Later, in 1749, another Frenchman had implanted leaden plates at several places along the Ohio River. In effect these precocious no-trespassing signs said: KEEP OUT. FRENCH PROPERTY.

The stakes were enormous in the developing struggle between the two European countries which had been thrust forward onto the world scene by the dynamism of their capitalist economies. Much of the world had not yet entered into the capitalist way of producing and distributing goods, and there was immense profit to be gathered in by whoever spread that system into new areas. France had her own way of extracting profit from North America: French traders persuaded Indians to exchange furs for goods shipped out from France. For this operation live Indians were needed. England's major goal was land from which raw materials could be taken to Europe, and the colonists, particularly in Pennsylvania and Virginia, were inclined to follow English strategy. For their operation Indians were only an obstacle.

As rivalry developed between the European groups, some Indians saw advantages in allying themselves with the French. Others obviously had minimal reasons for becoming allies of the English invaders. Still others had no interest in running risks to aid the French. Indeed, one Indian put it this way to an Englishman: "You and the French are like two edges of a pair of shears, and we are the cloth that is cut to pieces between them."

In 1754 the most distant outposts of France and England came into contact with each other in the Ohio Valley. The Englishmen, who happened to be Virginians, were looking for land, and this meant building forts for protection against Indians who wanted to keep the land. The Frenchmen in the Ohio Valley wanted forts which would serve two purposes: to fend off Englishmen and to accommodate traders who were on friendly terms with the Indians. The contrasting goals of the French and English were irreconcilable, the more so because France and England were rivals all over the world—in India and Africa as well as in America. Inevitably trouble came. It was not possible, given the voracious economics of the rival realms, for peaceful cooperation to develop. So it happened that a wide-flung war started in 1754 in the Ohio Valley, where the only permanent residents were Indians. And this conflict at its beginning point had a very special connection with the American Revolution that was to break out a generation later . . .

An artist's conception of how LaSalle took possession of land in the Mississippi Valley.

18

"A Charming Place for an Encounter"

1750s   Virginia and Pennsylvania

Colonial expansion in the 1750s gave George Washington military experience that was later to prove valuable in the American Revolution. At the same time Washington, as a colonial, was snubbed by English officers, an experience that helped to motivate him as 1776 approached.

Twenty-one-year-old George Washington had inherited a few slaves and more than 2,000 acres. Now he was buying more land with the money he earned by his own labor as a surveyor. Land fascinated him as it did his employer and friend, William Fairfax, who managed a vast estate in Virginia and was reaching out westward for more territory on the Ohio River. George's ailing half brother, Lawrence, also had his eyes on Ohio land, as did Robert Dinwiddie, governor of Virginia, and other politicians and planters. A number of them, with Lawrence Washington acting as their president for a time, had formed the Ohio Company, which received a royal grant of 200,000 acres along the Ohio River. After some advance preparation, the company planned to send out settlers to live there.

A colony was launching a colony, and George Washington felt very much a part of the venture. So active was his involvement and so unique were his talents that he was easily chosen, in spite of his youth, to investigate what, if anything, the French were doing along the tributaries of the Ohio River. Besides gathering intelligence, he would try to make friends with Indians. And he would carry a letter to the highest-ranking French officer in the area warning him, and all other Frenchmen, to stay out.

One of young Washington's obvious qualifications for such a journey was his experience as a surveyor in the wilderness. He had ridden and tramped through a great deal of rugged, unexplored forest, establishing the boundaries of the Fairfax estate. He knew how to live outdoors. He was very strong, a superb horseman, and greatly attracted to the ardors and honors of military life. A love of competition shaped his actions, whether at the card table or on fox hunts or in weight-throwing games or gambling. But he bore himself in such a way as to make older men have confidence in his judgment. His family was of middle means, and an inheritance made it possible for him, if he chose, to get by in life without much effort. But he had too much energy to endure a lazy existence. Some demon drove him to excel. He loomed above everybody wherever he went—more than six feet tall in a day when men were smaller than they are now. And if that was not enough to make him noticed, he was redheaded—another rarity in Virginia.

Had there been Olympic teams in the eighteenth century, George Washington would surely have been on the one from Virginia. There was no larger colonial entity to which he, or any other American, could be loyal. Indeed, one colony was often the rival of another. Certainly Virginia and Pennsylvania vied for land on the Ohio River. While Benjamin Franklin was busy working in the interest of Pennsylvania, George Washington meant to beat out Pennsylvania as well as France in the race to gain control of territory west of the Alleghenies.

All bristling with ambition, young Washington set out in October 1753. His destination was Fort Le Boeuf, rumored to be on one of the tributaries of the Allegheny River. Supposedly this fort was one of a string of military posts that the French seemed to be setting up from Presque Isle (where Erie, Pennsylvania, now is) south to the Forks of the Ohio, the meeting place of the Allegheny and Monongahela rivers.

An interpreter who knew some French accompanied Washington, along with a trader named Christopher Gist who knew Indians, their languages and the country, and several men to help with the horses and packs. By mid-November Washington had crossed high ridge after high ridge in the Allegheny Mountains and had descended to the Forks of the Ohio. So far the French had built nothing at this meeting place of two rivers. It was a strategic location, and the young surveyor decided just where a fort should be put. Later the Ohio Company would dispatch construction workers to the site and militiamen to guard them.

Moving on, Washington found on the north bank of the Ohio an Indian village which Englishmen called Logstown. There he met a Seneca who was a kind of governor sent out by the Iroquois tribes to keep an eye on their not always dependable subject peoples—the Mingoes, the Shawnee, and the Delaware, or Leni-Lenape. The Indian governor, called by the Iroquois *Tanacharison,* was known as Half King among the English, who equated important Indian leaders with royalty. Since Tanacharison was only a representative of distant authority, the English did not want to overdo his title.

Washington had been led to expect that Half King was a loyal ally. Soon he began to have doubts. Half King made it clear that Indians would be hospitable to either Frenchmen or Englishmen as long as they did not build houses in the Ohio River basin. Because the French were building forts, Half King was opposed to them. Knowing that the English were planning both forts and extensive settlements, Washington sensed trouble ahead. Even now he did not know quite what to make of this "friendly" Indian's behavior. Half King seemed in no hurry to provide the guides and protectors Washington thought he was entitled to get.

Finally the Virginians were able to move on. At an outpost called Venango (present-day Franklin, Pennsylvania), French officers received Washington politely, let him know that the French were indeed engaged in large-scale activities, and sent him on to headquarters at Fort Le Boeuf. There Washington presented the letter he carried, warning Frenchmen that they were trespassing and must leave English territory. The letter had no effect. The French commander formally answered the order to depart, saying, "I do not think myself obliged to obey. . . ."

This was the bleak reply that Washington had to carry back 500 bleak miles in January 1754 to the capital of Virginia at Williamsburg. His horses were weak from overwork and undernourishment. The weather was a sheer horror. Bitter cold had not yet frozen the Allegheny River hard enough to support men and horses, so Washington decided to cross by raft. In midstream he could not maneuver the clumsy log craft and was thrown off into ten feet of frigid water. A weaker man might have drowned, but Washington survived and continued his journey, protected from the worst of the cold by Indian clothing.

On the way up the western slope of the mountains he encountered proof that the Ohio Company was not losing any time. One day he met a packtrain laden with materials for use in constructing the fort at the Forks. The next day he met a band of settlers bound for the outpost that was to be established there.

When he reached Williamsburg with his report of French activity, he found himself suddenly a celebrity, a kind of hero. Very soon—although still only twenty-one—he was made a lieutenant colonel in the Virginia militia. On March 15, a few weeks after he had completed his astonishing journey, Washington received orders to start out again. For this next trip to the Forks, he himself had to recruit the military force he thought he would need. He gathered what men he could and left for the west.

As Washington moved with his 159 men across the mountains, he built the first road into the Ohio Valley, thus opening that area for the first time to wheeled vehicles. But before he reached the Forks, he encountered workmen who were fleeing eastward. They said great numbers of Frenchmen had come down the Allegheny River in canoes. The handful of Englishmen at the Forks could not resist this armada and were allowed to leave unharmed. The Frenchmen—who pointedly threatened, but did not use, violence—were soon engaged in building their own outpost where the Englishmen had been at work. They called it Fort Duquesne after the governor of Canada.

George Washington shown at age 25 in an engraving by John de Mare, made from a miniature painting by Charles Willson Peale. Washington was four years younger when he led an expedition deep into Indian country.

Washington, although he had only a few dozen men who were fit for action, hated to miss a chance for a fight. He decided to advance toward the Forks, despite warnings that the Frenchmen, with their Indian allies, numbered many hundreds. Meanwhile the French force did not sit passively at the Forks. Soon Washington received word from Half King that they were out looking for him.

On the western side of Laurel Ridge Washington came upon a spot which he described as "a charming place for an encounter." An encounter did come a few miles away on May 27—an ambush arranged by Washington—and he, totally inexperienced in combat but eager for action, felt a thrill of excitement which he recorded thus in a letter to his younger brother: "I heard the bullets whistle and, believe me, there is something charming in the sound." Not many men have thought of war in that way, but as Washington was getting his first taste of it, the same word had come to his mind twice in a very short time.

Washington won this first battle of his career. And what happened on that spring day in 1754 launched a war that lasted seven years and claimed the lives of 350,000 soldiers and hundreds of thousands of civilians on four continents.

One of the casualties during the ambush which Washington had planned was Joseph Coulon de Villiers, sieur de Jumonville, commander of the French party. He, it developed, was carrying a letter designed to show that he came on a peaceful diplomatic mission. French authorities, of course, called Washington an assassin—killer of a peaceful diplomat. In reply Washington and the English authorities pointed to the large armed party that accompanied Jumonville. If his mission was really peaceful, why did he need so many soldiers? Washington, three months earlier, had accomplished his diplomatic mission to the French without any such large armed escort.

But why had Washington opened fire on the Frenchmen without first determining what they were up to? It would be easy to call him overzealous and a too-eager competitor. He was doubtless both. But it will hardly do to say that these traits caused the French and Indian War, which led to the Seven Years' War in Europe, sometimes known as the Great War for Empire.

The realities were that if Washington had not ambushed Jumonville, some other event would have kindled the military phase of rivalry between the English and French empires. Only by chance was it Washington who struck the match that set off the explosion: the powder and fuse were ready for the lighting. Nevertheless, Washington, eager and aggressive, was exactly suited for the role he played. What he did was thoroughly consistent with his ambition and with his determination to see to it that his team won. At the same time his hasty action reflected the whole expansionist mood of Virginia's planters, of whom he was one. To them, aggressive land speculation on the frontier was a way of escaping the heavy indebtedness forced upon them by English economic policies.

UNITED STATES HISTORY IN CANADA

Two battles on what is now Canadian soil had a profound effect on the thirteen colonies that became the United States. In one engagement, a long siege that ended on June 15, 1744, colonials, largely from Massachusetts Bay Colony, captured the French fortress at Louisbourg, Nova Scotia. In the other, on September 15, 1759, English regulars led by General James Wolfe defeated French forces under the marquis de Montcalm at Quebec. These encounters determined in great part that England, not France, would rule in the far distant Ohio Valley.

English land speculators in Virginia hoped that with the defeat of France they would be able to make money from the sale of Ohio Valley land. This they sorely needed to offset the debts that planters owed to English businessmen. But England had other ideas. Entrepreneurs and politicians in London did not want the Ohio area filled with people who might be difficult to control so far from England. They engineered treaty arrangements with the Iroquois Indians that forbade settlement by non-Indians west of the Alleghenies. So the land speculators found that victory over France gave them very little comfort. Freedom from England's restrictions could be achieved only by freedom from England itself.

On September 13, 1759 English forces commanded by General James Wolfe scaled the steep slopes shown in this old engraving and captured the stronghold of Quebec, thus helping to determine that English—not French—imperial claims and culture would prevail in North America.

As for the relative merits of the English and French claims in the Ohio Valley, it is tempting, since the English won and a culture derived from England now prevails in the area, to assume that the English claims were superior. But if a man from Mars had dropped down on Earth in the eighteenth century, he might not have thought merit was on the English side in the sporadic butchery he could observe west of the Allegheny Mountains and along the St. Lawrence River. Why, he might have asked in cosmic innocence, did either the French or the English think they had any right to a land that already belonged to a third people who occupied and used it?

A truthful answer, which either a Frenchman or an Englishman could have given, would boil down to, "I want my side to win because it gives me the feeling that I am a winner." But more than ego satisfactions were involved in the French and Indian War. The real reasons behind the conflict were the desires of rich men for more wealth and of ruling men for more power. Greed was the force that drove both the English and the French. And, as often happens in wars, those who did the daring were not the same as those who did the dying.

However, vast issues of empire were surely not uppermost in Washington's mind after he had surprised and defeated Jumonville's party. One member of that party escaped capture. Somehow he eluded the Virginia militiamen and their handful of Indian allies and made his way to the Forks,

FRENCH WORDS IN ENGLISH

For a long time France and England competed with each other for control over much of America. Only a few years before the American Revolution, England won out. By that time these French words had entered the language of the English colonists: batteau, brave (meaning an Indian warrior), bureau, cache, carry-all (a carriage, from carriole), chowder, levee, prairie, voyageur.

The following words entered French from an Indian language and were borrowed from French by the English settlers before 1776: bayou, caribou, toboggan.

where he reported the disaster. A large French force took to the trail. At its head was Jumonville's brother, eager for revenge.

Washington soon realized the danger and tried to build defensive fortifications at Great Meadows, an open marshy place in the midst of forest. He ordered a circular palisade of poles driven into the ground, surrounding a shed, which was roofed over with sheets of bark and hides. Outside the palisade those men who were not sick with dysentery piled up a low breastwork of earth. This makeshift fort had only two

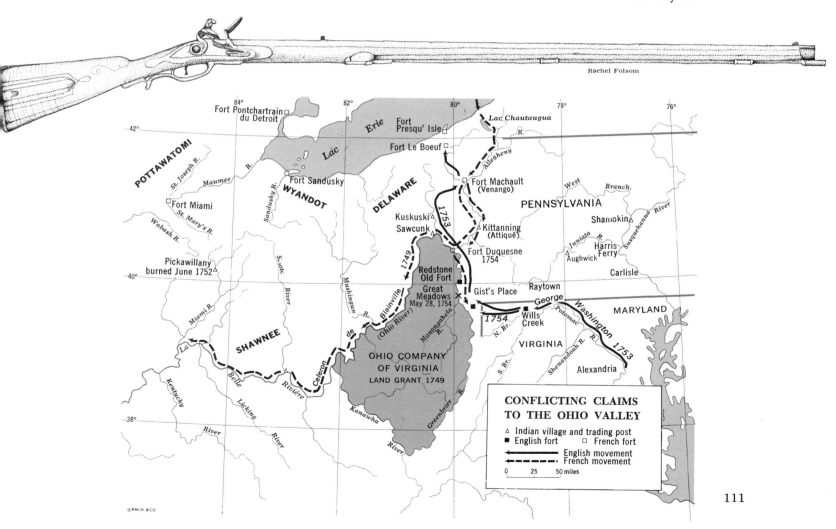

Rachel Folsom

CONFLICTING CLAIMS TO THE OHIO VALLEY

△ Indian village and trading post
■ English fort   □ French fort
▬▬ English movement
▬ ▬ French movement

0   25   50 miles

©RMCN. & CO.

111

George Washington, although thoroughly defeated at Fort Necessity, found the area inviting. He later bought the land on which the fort stood.

military advantages: An enemy approaching it had to cross open ground, and there was water for men and animals within the palisade in case of siege. But there could be too much water in case of rain, as Washington soon found out. And enemies could be sheltered by woods that came uncomfortably close to the palisade.

Enemies did appear—followed by rain. In a driving storm that lasted for hours and drenched the Virginians' powder, the French and their Indian allies surrounded the palisade, which Washington had somewhat grimly called Fort Necessity. Many of the Virginians and some of the regular English army men who had joined them were soon wounded or killed. To save those who were still alive, Washington accepted the offer of his besiegers and surrendered. In a magnanimous gesture, Jumonville's brother allowed his enemies to walk out of the palisade, free men, each with a gun he would need for hunting.

Apparently without knowing it, Washington signed terms of surrender in which he admitted he had assassinated Jumonville. The difficulty lay in his ignorance of the French language and in the failure of his interpreter to give him a correct translation of the rain-soaked surrender document. Even more humiliated than was known at the time, the young officer and his men dragged themselves back across the mountains toward safety.

George Washington had made grievous mistakes in the Jumonville affair and at Fort Necessity, which was a poor excuse for a fort to begin with. He had irritated Indians who were needed as allies. Because of his own great eagerness for

action, he had put his troops in grave jeopardy. He had blundered many times over, but he was not to repeat the same kind of blunder again. His was a mind that could learn from experience.

The report Washington made about his defeat of Jumonville is of special interest. More than half of it was devoted to complaining that Virginia's militia officers received less pay than officers in the regular English army. There had been friction with a British officer who refused to let his men share a camp with the militia or do road building alongside the militia unless they got extra pay. Finally, Washington had been forced to endure an additional indignity when he signed the terms of surrender offered him by the French. Although he was a colonel, he had to place his name below the name of a man who was only a captain but who held a commission in the regular English army.

After so humiliating a defeat as that at Fort Necessity, many a young man might have decided there was really very little charm in military life. Not Washington. He drove on toward a military career with remarkable stubbornness. Knowing the advantages of being in the regular army, he tried in every possible way to get a royal commission—but he never succeeded. The snubs and rebuffs of English officers hurt his pride, and their disdain built up in him a deep resentment that never died. When the war with France quickened, England sent an army and a major general to march on the Forks and secure the Ohio region for King George. The attack on Fort Duquesne was to be handled by professional soldiers, for the English government scorned

Virginia's frontiersmen. Although Washington, the highest-ranking officer in the Virginia militia, knew more about the area of the forthcoming conflict than any redcoat from England, he had no soldiers to command. He could join the expedition only as a volunteer without pay, serving as one of three aides-de-camp to the commanding major general, elderly Edward Braddock.

The veteran general was not interested in advice from a young man who had never been to military school and had no knowledge of the way professionals conducted warfare in Europe. So, following the best European traditions, but ignoring American realities, Braddock brought a great army slowly toward the Forks, where he expected to overwhelm the French. Word spread ahead of him through the forest. At Fort Duquesne the French did not wait for trouble. They hastened to meet it. Though outnumbered, they and a force of Indian allies surprised the English and utterly defeated them. As Washington had expected, Braddock's soldiers were helpless sitting ducks. Drawn up in perfect European formation they were caught in bewildering fire that came from behind trees all around them. The end was quick. And Washington had to read a funeral service for Braddock, who had spurned his advice.

For a second time Washington was obliged to retreat eastward. Still his military dreams had not ended. He desperately wanted a commission in the English regular army, but he had to accept instead a title in the militia and an assignment building up defenses along Virginia's frontier. This experience taught him a great deal about military administration—obtaining, storing, and distributing supplies and arranging transportation. All the while there was no break in the rudeness of Britishers, who looked down on colonials. More than once the proud young Virginian threatened to resign. Finally he did just that. In January 1759 he severed his connection with the Virginia militia. He was already a veteran of more than five years' service, and he carried an abiding grievance against the British military establishment into which he, a colonial, had never been admitted.

Real estate ventures and his own complex plantation now offered direction to his energies and freedom for their release. He continued to expand his landholdings, in one case linking his speculations with his military memories. After the French were finally defeated, he bought more than 200 acres around Fort Necessity—a property that was still part of his million-dollar estate at his death.

When at the age of twenty-seven he took off his colonel's uniform, he stored it carefully away, and he did not forget it. One day nearly two decades later, while he was attending the Continental Congress in Philadelphia, he took it out and wore it.

The young George Washington went west to look after the interests of the Ohio Company. He certainly had no idea that the horizons of his life would shift with an odd kind of logic from real estate to revolution. But out of the tawdry tensions of the French and Indian War came a man with the energy and motivation and talent needed to see through a struggle in which the freedom of millions was at stake. The French and Indian War over real estate in the Ohio Valley trained a natural leader of men who could learn from his mistakes—and could move from bigotry toward an even-handed humanism.

PLACES TO SEE ✿

PENNSYLVANIA

Braddock Park: General Braddock's Grave.
Erie: Presque Isle Fort Site.
Franklin: Fort Venango Site.
Pittsburgh: Point State Park Reconstructed Fort.
Uniontown: Fort Necessity National Battlefield Site / Braddock's Road.
Waterford: Fort Le Boeuf Memorial.

VIRGINIA

Alexandria: Gadsby's Tavern / Mount Vernon.
Fredericksburg: Ferry Farm / George Washington Birthplace National Monument / Mary Washington's House.
White Post: Greenway Court.
Williamsburg: Capitol.

NOVA SCOTIA

Cape Breton Island: Fort Louisbourg National Historic Park.

QUEBEC

Quebec: The Plains of Abraham (Site of the Battle between Wolfe and Montcalm).

For more information, see Gazetteer, page 212.

Gen. Edward Braddock, defeated by Indians in 1755.

Dictionary of American Portraits

19

"A Man's House is His Castle"

1760s   Boston

James Otis, a lawyer, brilliantly articulated the doctrine that a man's house is his castle and that the law must protect his privacy there. Otis stressed the importance of being free from the indignity of unreasonable search, a principle always useful to those who resist tyranny and one which was finally included in the Bill of Rights.

A mountainous man with volcanic energies erupted in Boston in the 1760s. The seethings within him both fascinated and frightened people. He could never seem to sit still. His big body constantly moved and twitched as he talked—and he talked a great deal. His duties as a lawyer were considerable, but he had time left over for other interests. He wrote one book on Latin prosody, which was published in 1760 when he was thirty-five, and another on Greek prosody, which remained in manuscript form. His name, James Otis, appeared on pamphlets of great importance in promoting the self-esteem of colonists. And the newspapers bristled with his letters, usually contentious in tone, always charged with emotion.

Otis' behavior made many men his enemies, and they called him mad—and, after a brilliant but brief career, that word had to be used by friend as well as foe. However, before his mind became a jumble of random, often conflicting impulses, sometimes floating on a sea of alcohol, James Otis acted magnificently on center stage in a major legal con-

frontation with authority. The drama began when he was asked by a group of sixty-three Boston merchants to represent them in a most important law case. Otis took the case and resigned from a good post he held in the colonial government, because he wanted to be free of any conflict of interest.

Otis' sixty-three clients called themselves the Society for Promoting Trade and Commerce within the Province. The name was accurate, but it did not tell the whole story. Much of the trade and commerce they wanted to promote was dependent on the successful smuggling of contraband goods past English customs officials.

Without contraband, New England's biggest industry—the distilling of rum—would have failed. Rum was made from molasses, and molasses was made from sugarcane grown in the West Indies. In 1733 the British Parliament adopted a law known as the Molasses Act, designed to ensure that all profits from the manufacture and shipping of molasses to New England would go only to sugarcane growers and shipowners within the English colonial system. By limiting the freedom of New Englanders to buy where their raw material was cheapest, the act raised the cost of molasses. This, of course, tended to force up the cost of manufacturing rum. But since the colonists could export their rum only to English territories, English merchants were able to keep down the price they would pay. With the cost of molasses up and the price of rum down, New England distillers had to take a low profit or go out of business—or become smugglers. They chose smuggling. Illegally they bought thirty times as much molasses from French and Dutch sources in the West Indies as they bought from English sources there.

Great New England fortunes grew from contraband molasses and from other smuggled goods as well. This was no secret. But British officials found the problem hard to deal with. One device they tried to use was a kind of search warrant called a writ of assistance. An ordinary search warrant permitted a customs collector to look for specific contraband in a specific place. But armed with a writ of assistance he could search anywhere at any time for anything. He did not have to show that there was reason to suspect the existence of what he claimed he was looking for. He did not have to specify what he was seeking or where he expected to find it. Moreover he could compel any passerby to assist in the search—hence the term writ of assistance.

These unlimited search warrants gave great opportunities to informers motivated by spite and to customs men motivated by greed. A collector was entitled to one-third of the value of all contraband goods he seized. But he might easily extract more than a third in the form of a bribe. Bostonians did a great deal of trading in contraband goods, so there was a great deal of bribery.

Almost all merchants—even the most upright Puritans—engaged in smuggling. It became a form of resistance to the hated Navigation Acts which, if enforced, would have choked off much of New England's economic life. Just how much contraband entered the colonies cannot, of course, be known. Neither the smugglers nor those bribed to look the other way kept records of their secret transgressions of the law. One educated guess is that if the laws had been strictly enforced, the crown's annual income from duties in New

England in the 1750s would have been about 25,000 pounds. However, the amount actually collected each year was no more than 2,000 pounds and was sometimes as little as 1,000 pounds. The cost to the government of bringing in this revenue was much greater than the revenue itself.

Clearly the customs officials who had writs of assistance were no blameless crusaders for law and order. A collector could use a writ, once the court had granted it to him, in whatever way he pleased. Against an endless abuse of this instrument, the colonists had only one hope. The writs were good only during the lifetime of the king on whose behalf they were granted. When George II died in October 1760, every customs collector who wanted a writ of assistance had to make a new application. At this point, the sixty-three Boston merchants saw their chance. They decided to resist the applications in court, and they retained James Otis to do the fighting.

Colonial officials were well aware of the importance of the legal struggle over writs. The governor, Francis Bernard, who was new in office, prepared for the event by recovering from storage the portraits of King Charles II and King James II and having them handsomely framed in gold and hung in the Council Chamber of the Town House. He also ordered new scarlet robes for judges to wear as they sat, already impressive in their huge ceremonial wigs.

The merchants, for their part, appeared in a body on the day of the trial—all sixty-three of them—and their considerable presence punctuated every argument put forward on their behalf. Thomas Hutchinson, lieutenant governor of Massachusetts, was chief justice of the court. He was a wealthy man and very conservative—as conservative as his ancestor Anne Hutchinson had been radical. All this made for tension enough. But there was more. Hutchinson's post as chief justice had once been promised—and then denied—to James Otis' father. Hutchinson, certainly aware of the younger man's loyalty to his father and anger at the snub, could be expected to favor writs of assistance as firmly as James Otis opposed them.

To watch the battle between Otis and the authorities, all the lawyers in Boston and the surrounding area assembled at a long table in the Council Chamber. In this dramatic setting, James Otis spoke for more than four hours one cold day in February 1761. There was no court stenographer present, but a young lawyer who sat at the long table took notes, thus saving part, at least, of what Otis said. The note-taker was John Adams, who would soon become a revolutionary and would later serve as president of the republic he had helped to create.

Otis began by making clear that he had taken the case as a matter of principle. "In such a cause as this I despise a fee," he said, adding, "I will to my dying day oppose with all the powers and faculties God has given me, all such instruments of slavery on the one hand, and villainy on the other, as this writ of assistance is. It appears to me the worst instrument of arbitrary power, the most destructive of English liberty and the fundamental principles of law, that ever was found in an English law book."

With this Otis proceeded to his arguments. Such a writ is illegal, he insisted. "It is a power, that places the liberty of every man in the hands of every petty officer. . . . Every one

with this writ may be a tyrant in a legal manner, also may control, imprison, or murder anyone within the realm. . . . A man is accountable to no person for his doings. Every man may reign secure in his petty tyranny, and spread terror and desolation around him, until the trump of the arch-angel shall excite different emotions in his soul. . . . By this writ not only deputies etc., but even their menial servants, are allowed to lord it over us. . . . One of the most essential branches of English liberty is the freedom of one's house. A man's house is his castle; and whilst he is quiet, he is as well guarded as a prince in his castle. This writ . . . would totally annihilate this privilege."

To show how one writ had been abused, Otis followed its remarkable career from the day it was obtained by a collector named Pew. Collector Pew had endorsed the writ over to a Mr. Ware, who, it happened, was accused of breaking the Sabbath laws and was brought to court. In re-

This statue of James Otis by Crawford in the chapel at Mount Auburn, Mass., suggests the great size of the orator who spoke eloquently, arguing that a man's house is his castle.

taliation, Ware then used the writ to search not only the judge's house "from garret to cellar" but also the house of the constable who had arrested him.

In the course of his argument Otis made much use of a doctrine of which much more would be heard in the years to come—the idea that men had natural rights more fundamental than the laws on man-made statute books. A man's right to life, liberty, and property were incontestable. And Otis did not mean that only white men had a right to liberty. He insisted that Blacks should also be free. No man, said John Adams, "ever asserted the rights of Negroes in stronger terms."

Otis argued that the rights of liberty were "wrought into the English constitution, as fundamental laws," and he analyzed those laws from Anglo-Saxon times to the Magna Carta and on down to his day, showing how liberties were insisted on and how tyrants were punished.

The arguments then became more sweeping. Otis attacked the Navigation Acts and the more recent Acts of Trade, under which revenue officers were trying to collect customs. He dwelt on the crippling effect of the Navigation Acts on the economic life of American merchants—and he attacked the Acts of Trade by introducing a concept that was to be of greatest importance. According to Adams he "gave full scope to his talent, for powerful declaration and invective against *the tyranny of taxation without representation.*"

Here was an early form of the slogan that was to be much on the lips of patriots in the years to come: "No taxation without representation!"

"Otis was a flame of fire," Adams said. "With a promptitude of classical allusions, a depth of research, a rapid summary of historical events and dates, a profusion of authorities, a prophetic glance of his eyes into futurity, and a rapid tor-

rent of impetuous eloquence, he hurried away all before him. . . . The seeds of patriots and heroes . . . were then and there sown. Every man of an immense crowded audience appeared to me to go away as I did ready to take arms against Writs of Assistance. Then and there, was the scene of the first act of opposition, to the arbitrary claims of Great Britain. Then and there, the child Independence was born."

Four of the five red-robed judges agreed with Otis. The fifth, Chief Justice Hutchinson saw that some very fast legal footwork was required if he was to stave off defeat for the cause of the crown. Accordingly, Hutchinson agreed that the court had seen insufficient reason to grant the requested writs of assistance. But he got final decision postponed until the judges could be informed about current practices regarding such writs in England.

As Hutchinson hoped, the precedents being followed by the restrictive government of King George III favored unlimited rights of search and seizure. So, ultimately writs of assistance were issued in Massachusetts, but Hutchinson's courtroom victory proved to be very costly for the British Empire.

It was altogether characteristic of James Otis that four years later he was the one who introduced in Massachusetts a resolution calling for a general congress of all the colonies against another form of taxation—the Stamp Act. He made his proposal within a few days of the time Patrick Henry rose in the Virginia Assembly to oppose the same British legislation. The two great orators acted independently of each other, but in accord with intensely felt wishes of large numbers of their fellows.

The work Otis did and the pamphlets he wrote won him an enduring place in the affections of his countrymen. But his emotional instability, which increased in the years before the Revolution, sometimes led to political instability and finally to complete mental illness, broken only occasionally by brief periods of lucidity. However, none of the sickness that marked his middle and later life became epidemic, and Americans' desire for the right of privacy continued. The Fourth Amendment to the Constitution guaranteeing "the right of the people to be secure in their persons, houses, papers, and effects" owed a great deal to James Otis, whose very big body survived his very big mind.

This painting of James Otis hangs in the Old State House, Boston.

Culver Pictures

PLACES TO SEE

MASSACHUSETTS

Barnstable: Crocker Tavern / Great Marshes / West Parish Congregational Meeting House.
Boston: British Coffee House Site / Faneuil Hall / Old South Meeting House / Old State House.
Cambridge: Harvard College.
Milton: Hutchinson House.
Plymouth: Clifford Farms (Warren Estate).

For more information, see Gazetteer, page 212.

20

A Woodland Alliance for Liberty

1765   Detroit

After the French and Indian War, Chief Pontiac led many Indian tribes in a three-year-long attempt to oust the English from Native American lands.

Religion sometimes takes a special form when people are deeply distressed. It becomes an instrument of resistance, even rebellion. Distress there certainly was among Indians along the frontier after the French and Indian War, and people turned eagerly toward a new faith—or rather an old faith newly invigorated.

Until 1760 when the war ended, Indians had been prospering as never before. French traders, who dominated the Great Lakes and the Ohio River valley, had shown a relaxed and even friendly attitude toward them. In general the French acted like guests or tenants on Indian-owned land. Often they took Indian wives. They spoke Indian languages, and they understood the importance to Indians of the giving and receiving of gifts. French traders and officials responded to Indian custom with rum, beads, metal tools and weapons, and most of all, ammunition. In their gift giving and in extending credit, the French had their own objectives. They wanted furs. It was to their advantage to provide Indian hunters with the means of obtaining pelts. When hunters came out of the winter woods, there was usually some lively bargaining. The French got as much and paid as little as they could, but the Indians, from long experience, knew that

powder and lead for the next hunting season would be available, no matter what.

Up until 1760 the Chippewa, Potawatomi, Delaware, Mingoes, Huron, Seneca, and Shawnee had prospered. So had the Ottawa—*Ottawa* means "trader" in Algonkian—along with other tribes farther to the west. The Frenchmen's brass pots, knives, hatchets, rifles, and gunpowder made it easier to hunt and to cook than in the days when Indians had only stone tools and crude pots made of baked clay or of basketry or the bark of trees.

All this changed when the English defeated the French in the Great War for Empire. In the American wilderness a new kind of white men replaced the easygoing Frenchmen to whom Indians had become accustomed, and the newcomers were both scornful and stingy. They seldom took Indian wives. They hurried through bargaining sessions, which under the French had been interesting ways of spending long periods of time. Englishmen never handed out free rum. Most important, they gave little or no gunpowder or lead, either free or on credit.

The many tribes living on the borders of European settlements had become so used to hunting with rifles that they had lost much of their old skill with bow and arrow. Suddenly, with their guns silent because they lacked ammunition, they found themselves facing starvation. Game had already grown scarce during the years when they had all the powder and ball they could use. Now they could not kill enough animals to provide the food they needed.

At this point, when Indians were in real distress, there appeared a religious leader, who urged them to seek salvation by returning to their ancient ways. This meant giving up rum, giving up white man's trinkets, giving up guns. In every way, said the holy man, people must be once more independent and self-sufficient.

The new religious leader was probably what is called a medicine man, and he surely had a name, but the surviving records about him were all written by whites, and these records refer to him only as the Delaware Prophet or the Impostor. As a Delaware or Leni-Lenape, the Prophet had known oppression several times over. First his people had been conquered by the Iroquois and forced to pay tribute. After that the English had driven them from their homeland along the Delaware River. Now in new territory in the Ohio Valley, they faced new difficulties caused by the English restriction on ammunition. To help his people save their self-esteem and keep themselves alive as hunters, the Prophet urged them—and other Indians as well—to return to the old ways. At the same time, he told them, all Indians must unite against the encroaching white men.

As visual aids to his sermons, the Prophet painted symbols on deerskin. One symbol stood for earth, another for heaven, and still another for the English, who barred the Indians' way from earth to heaven. Pointing to these symbols, the Prophet told of visions that had shown him the way to happiness for all Indians. His listeners, who believed in the mystical power of visions, were moved by the holy man's fervor, the more so because he wept as he spoke. Inevitably he won converts.

Among those the Prophet influenced was Pontiac, an

Here Pontiac is rather fancifully depicted in a war council by a 19th century artist. Apparently the tepees, of the type used only by Plains Indians much farther west, were thrown in for good measure.

Ottawa war chief. Pontiac was not the most outstanding member of the Ottawa nation. He had often been passed over when his people chose chiefs to act as ambassadors in dealing with Europeans. As a result his name almost never appears in European records until after he heard the Prophet spell out his vision of unity among all the various tribes of the Great Lakes and the Ohio Valley regions. Suddenly, armed with a religious, revivalistic way of stirring Indians to action, Pontiac began to discuss survival tactics with his fellow tribesmen and with Potawatomi and Chippewa. He repeated the Prophet's message, and added thoughts of his own. One of his talks was remembered afterward by a sympathetic Frenchman. In some such words as these, Pontiac spoke, as an instrument of the Source of Life: ". . . The land on which you live I have made for you, and not for others. Why do you suffer the white men to dwell among you? My children, you have forgotten the customs and traditions of your forefathers. Why do you not clothe yourselves in skins, as they did, and use the bows and arrows, and the stone-pointed lances, which they used? You have bought guns, knives, kettles, and blankets, from the white men, until you can no longer do without them; and, what is worse, you have drunk the poison fire-water, which turns you into fools. Fling all these things away; live as your wise forefathers lived before you. And as for these English— these dogs dressed red, who have come to rob you of your hunting-grounds, and drive away the game—you must lift the hatchet against them."

Pontiac's words gave his people a sense of direction, and gradually his phrases changed. He spoke more and more about lifting the tomahawk and less about giving up guns. In tribe after tribe he stirred a military mood and built up a military organization. He—or an emissary—appeared before one council after another, holding in hand a long belt made up of tubular beads dyed red. This particular kind of wampum belt was an invitation to join as allies in war. Before Pontiac had finished sending out the red belts of war, nearly twenty tribes had received and accepted them. Acceptance meant agreement to take part in a great alliance.

All records of this national liberation movement, inspired by the teachings of the Delaware Prophet, were made by men of European origin, many of them very hostile to Indians. As a result the pictures of Indian resistance that have survived are often unreliable, although Francis Parkman attempted to be fair in his book, *History of the Conspiracy of Pontiac*. The real story of Pontiac's War will have to wait until there is a sophisticated reconstruction of the lives and cultures of the tribes he influenced. We have accurate notes of dates and places of military events in the war, but few observers remembered how the Indians felt or why they did what they did. Certainly the Ottawa, and possibly others, had been very little influenced by French Jesuit missionaries, while at the same time French traders were making their lives easier. In their heads and hearts the Ottawa remained thoroughly Indian, although their hands held European tools.

118

No authentic portrait of Pontiac is known to exist. This engraving has long been used, apparently because no one involved thought it was important to be accurate about Native Americans.

Pontiac, by all available accounts, emerged as the military leader of the Ottawa and of twenty or so other tribes that had varying traditions and languages. Since he could not be everywhere at once on a battlefront that spread over many hundreds of miles, other Indians, a good many of them, served as his active lieutenants, and some were exceedingly successful. The overall strategy, which Pontiac may have proposed and which was obviously agreed upon, called for simultaneous attacks on all English forts and settlements. To implement this plan Pontiac sought allies, and he included as potential friends the French settlers who had been left behind after French military forces withdrew. Indians even hoped that French military units still lingering in the Mississippi Valley would join their effort to expel Englishmen. These units, however, were subject to control from France, and France was in no position to resume the war in which it had just been defeated.

In May 1763, aided only by a handful of individual Frenchmen, the Indians launched attacks on the English, who were well protected in forts that the French had built for use against the redcoats themselves. There were twelve of these strongpoints in all. Two military organizations now faced each other—one native, one foreign—and both depended on armaments from the same source, which the foreigners controlled. To counter this British monopoly of arms, Pontiac proposed the tactics of surprise, ambush, and deceit. It was to be a test of Indian brains against British brawn, and what the brains worked out went this way:

At Fort Sandusky, which was garrisoned by an officer and fourteen men, seven Huron Indians appeared and asked to see the commander. The commander recognized the men, who lived in the neighborhood, and agreed to confer with them. Other Huron lounged around outside the conference room while their leaders sat quietly smoking with the commander. Then at a silent signal, the seven seized and tied the commander, while the loungers silently killed all fourteen of the soldiers. In minutes the fort had changed hands. Not one Indian had perished, and no word of what had happened reached any other fort.

At Fort Miami the plan of attack was different. There, contrary to the usual English pattern of rejecting Indians, the commander had taken a young Indian mistress. However, she was unhappy with the arrangement, and when her tribesmen planned an assault, she willingly joined in the scheme. On the appointed day she went to the commander with a story that an old woman outside the fort was ill and wanted to be treated as Europeans treated their sick. The commander agreed to visit the old woman. Once outside the fort, he was seized, and his garrison, now leaderless, was easily overwhelmed.

Such attacks went on simultaneously or close enough together to prevent the spread of news from one fort to another. At the same time Pontiac sent forces to cut British lines of communication and seize British supplies. When one convoy of ten bateaux, laden with ninety-six soldiers and 139 barrels of supplies, left Fort Niagara bound for Detroit, warriors knew the party would be likely to stop for a night's rest along the northern shore of Lake Erie. Indians lay in wait at Point Pelee. Only two of the bateaux escaped and fewer than half of the soldiers. Most of the supplies vanished into the woods along with the warriors. The loss was a great blow to the English, and the victory, achieved with almost no loss to the Indians, was a great morale builder.

Warriors raided another supply line very close to Fort Niagara at a place called Devil's Hole. Here the Seneca ambushed a wagon train and destroyed it, thereby offending the British, who felt it was a very ungentlemanly trick. The Seneca had chosen a spot along the road where they could hide in underbrush and behind trees. When twenty-five wagons, some drawn by horses, others by oxen, were stretched out single file, the Indians opened fire. In the chaos, drivers could neither go forward nor retreat. On one side of the road rifles fired from Seneca hiding places; on the other a cliff dropped off into the valley. Wagons, animals, and men plunged into the chasm, and only a few survived. The Seneca then ambushed a relief force sent out to rescue the supply train. The Indian victory was complete.

The most spectacular deception unfolded at Fort Michilimackinac. There on June 2, 1763, members of a Chippewa band that lived nearby and a group of visiting Sauk gathered outside the fort and began a casual game of lacrosse. This had often happened before, and no Englishman suspected anything unusual. Indeed many of the thirty-five soldiers in the garrison wandered outside the palisade to watch. At the same time, some Indian women wandered into the fort. Concealed under their robes or their skirts they carried weapons.

At an exciting moment in the game a player made a wild toss of the ball, and it went over the palisade. In a scramble to recover it the players raced through the open gate. Once inside they quickly got weapons from the women; the officers were soon captives and most of the soldiers dead. The Chippewa were in complete control of this important stronghold.

In two crucial places such tactics failed—Fort Pitt and Fort Detroit. Along with Fort Niagara these were the strongest English military posts west of the Alleghenies, and they remained in English hands even after they endured determined sieges.

Pontiac himself led the operation at Fort Detroit. On May 1, he had appeared there with thirty or forty warriors, ostensibly to engage in a calumet dance. The Ottawa knew, although the English did not, that this ritual could be performed for a variety of important purposes. It could be a dance for peace; it could just as well presage war.

Pontiac and his colleagues quietly prepared for war. They brought with them a sacred calumet—a long-stemmed tobacco pipe adorned with significant symbols—and as the Ottawa danced, a few of them quietly dropped out of the exciting ritual and took a good look at the fortifications.

All courtesy, Pontiac asked at the end of the dance if he could return to the fort in a few days for a formal visit. He said he wanted to bring with him a number of men who had not yet returned from their winter hunts. The English commander agreed.

After Pontiac had heard intelligence reports from the men who had dropped out of the dance, he sent messengers to the tribes in the area, asking their leaders to attend a conference. There, according to a Frenchman who was allowed to listen, he spoke in these terms:

> It is important for us, my brothers, that we exterminate from our lands this nation which seeks only to destroy us. You see as well as I that we can no longer supply our needs, as we have done from our brothers, the French. The English sell us goods twice as dear as the French do, and their goods do not last. Scarcely have we bought a blanket or something else to cover our selves with before we must think of getting another; and when we wish to set out for our winter camps they do not want to give us any credit as our brothers the French do.
>
> When I go see the English commander and say to him that some of our comrades are dead, instead of bewailing their death, as our French brothers do, he laughs at me and at you. If I ask anything for our sick, he refuses with the reply that he has no use for us. From all this you can well see that they are seeking our ruin. Therefore, my brothers, we must all swear their destruction and wait no longer. Nothing prevents us; they are few in numbers, and we can accomplish it.

All those who heard agreed to assault Fort Detroit a few days later. A group of innocent-looking Indians was to enter the fort with weapons concealed under their robes. But someone betrayed their plan to the English commander. It may have been a Frenchman; account books show that a French agent rendered some advice at this time for which the English commander paid liberally. Or the informer may have been an Indian man. Apparently Pontiac thought it was an Indian woman. At any rate the scheme failed. Unable to take Fort Detroit by surprise, the Indians had to lay siege.

Meantime at Fort Pitt, other warriors in the great alliance were unable to persuade the commander that he should surrender because his position was hopeless. Here also a siege proved necessary, and the defense was very strong. Neither Fort Pitt nor Fort Detroit fell. Nor did the Indians capture Fort Niagara. With these centers firmly in their control, the English managed to hold out until the winter hunting season began. Then Indian men had to leave in search of meat for their families. Hunting required ammunition. This they could get only from the English, and so they had to make peace—or seem to. The freedom they sought was not the freedom to starve.

On one side, the killing in the summer of 1763 had been done to preserve a way of life; on the other, to get land. And on both sides the slaughter was ferocious. The English, at the suggestion of Britain's supreme commander in America, introduced germ warfare, probably for the first time in history. The officer in charge at Fort Pitt, in the course of a conference with the Delaware who had come to urge him to surrender, gave the Indians presents—two blankets and a handkerchief that had come from the pesthouse, where smallpox patients were kept. Soon afterward a smallpox epidemic broke out among the Delaware and also among the Shawnee, who lived nearby.

British officers conferring with Indian chiefs on the banks of the Muskingum in October 1764. Benjamin West drew the sketch from which this engraving was made. The house in which Benjamin West was born still stands on the campus of Swarthmore College, Swarthmore, Pa.

The Indians, for their part, used any device they could. They scalped victims, following a practice that had been greatly encouraged by the British, who offered bounties to anyone—white men or Indians—for Indian scalps. Some warriors, with the sanction of their religion, sought courage by drinking the blood or eating the hearts of courageous enemies. Also with religious sanction they avenged the deaths of members of their tribes by ritualistic tortures and executions of prisoners. The Indians, fighting with every psychological—and other—means of warfare of which they had knowledge, won some brilliant victories. But all the individual successes of the allied tribes that summer did not add up to winning the war.

From headquarters on Grosse Isle, near Fort Detroit, Pontiac helped guide actions at Fort Niagara, far to the east; at Fort Pitt, far to the south; at Fort St. Joseph, to the west; and at Fort Michilimackinac, far to the north. Before it was over, the war he directed had destroyed about 2,000 English people and in 1763 forced the English government to issue a proclamation that no settlers could move into land west of the highest ridge of the Allegheny Mountains. This gave Indians what they wanted, except that Forts Niagara, Detroit, and Pitt remained British strongholds deep inside Indian territory. However, the words of the proclamation very soon proved to be words only. They changed nothing in reality. Settlers and land speculators from the English colonies disregarded the orders which had been issued by a distant and dictatorial government. Frontiersmen continued to settle on the western lands.

Still Pontiac did not despair. He kept trying to expand the Indian alliance and to increase the pressure the alliance could exert on the British intruders. His red wampum belts went almost as far south as New Orleans, which the Indians called Warm Town. But Fort Niagara, Fort Pitt, and Fort Detroit still remained in British hands.

In the fall of 1764, for the second time during the war, men had to turn from fighting to hunting. To many Indians it seemed that they were no nearer to solving their economic problems than they had been when the war started. Certainly they still lacked the gunpowder and other European supplies to which they had become accustomed. Discouragement spread. It deepened throughout 1765, and at last Pontiac could see no chance of victory in the war he had directed so well. With as much dignity as he could muster, he appeared at Oswego in 1766 before Sir William Johnson, who was empowered to arrange peace. Pontiac agreed to give up fighting.

Some of his followers were outraged. Young men who wanted to continue their war for independence fell upon him and beat him and drove him from his village. Pontiac began to wander aimlessly westward, away from white settlements, and the English did what they could to increase his isolation. They slyly encouraged feelings of jealousy in other Indian leaders. They did not discourage a rumor that Pontiac had withdrawn from the war because he had received a large English pension. No evidence of any such payment has been found, but the rumor helped to isolate the leader who had done more to hold back the English tide of settlement than any other man.

In April 1769 Pontiac was far from his homeland, in Cahokia, a settlement built by the French in what is now Illinois, on the site of the largest prehistoric Indian town north of Mexico. As Pontiac emerged from a store where he had been doing some business, another Indian struck him down with an ax, then killed him with a dagger.

Many Indians felt that Pontiac had failed them. His enemies had increased in proportion to his withdrawal from conflict. As long as he led his people in a violent war for the right to live in peace, he had been safe. When, momentarily at least, he was personally at peace, his life was forfeit to violence. White men buried him in an unmarked grave in nearby St. Louis, across the Mississippi River.

PLACES TO SEE

ILLINOIS
Pontiac: Pontiac Monument.
Starved Rock State Park.

INDIANA
Fort Wayne: Site of Fort Miami.
Lafayette: Fort Ouiatenon Site and Reconstruction.

MICHIGAN
Detroit: Site of Fort Detroit.
Mackinaw City: Michilimackinac State Park; Fort Michilimackinac Reconstruction.
Niles: Site of Fort St. Joseph.

NEW YORK
Niagara Falls: Devils Hole Ambush Site.
Oswego: Fort Ontario Site.

OHIO
Cleveland: Site of the meeting between Major Robert Rogers and Pontiac.
Sandusky: Fort Sandusky Site.

PENNSYLVANIA
Braddock Park: General Braddock's Grave.
Bushy Run Battlefield State Park.
Erie: Fort Presque Isle Site.
Franklin: Fort Venango Site.
Pittsburgh: Point State Park; Fort Pitt Reconstruction.
Waterford: Fort Le Boeuf Site.

WISCONSIN
Green Bay: Fort Site.

For more information, see Gazetteer, page 212.

21

Self-Fulfillment in California

1769–76   Arizona and California

Spanish missionaries and soldiers opened a new world for the poor of Mexico, and Native Americans heroically tried to maintain their freedom and their own way of life.

The race of Europe's empires for control of North America did not end when England defeated France in the French and Indian War. Spain, which had been first to enter the New World, was still in competition, and while thirteen English colonies on the East Coast began moving toward independence, Spain was just starting to crush the independence of Native Americans on the West Coast.

Although for two centuries Spain had claimed what is now California, Spaniards had not moved into the area. No riches were visible there, and formidable difficulties lay in the way. Deserts blocked overland communications, as did Indians who resisted intruders. The sea route was possible but hazardous, and Spain had only a few ships on the west coast of Mexico.

For these reasons Spain did nothing about what she called Alta California (in contrast to Baja, or Lower, California) until after the middle of the eighteenth century. Then the situation changed and very quickly. Word came that Russian fur traders, and behind them the Russian Empire, were looking more and more greedily at the West Coast of North America. Spain, to protect her claims from Russia and also from England, decided to establish military posts, which she called *presidios,* along the California coast. And to protect the presidios, she sent Franciscan missionaries. Their assignment was to transform independent Indians into a subject people who would not contest Spain's occupation of their land and who would also, with their labor, supply the wants of those who had conquered them.

Shortly after the conquest of California started, a Franciscan missionary, Fray Luís Jayme, put the matter in surprisingly modern terms: "Spain's initial purpose in coming into California was not a religious one. The conquest was politically motivated, chiefly for the containment of Russia."

José de Gálvez, the *visitador,* or royal inspector, of all New Spain, was the original organizer of the imperial venture, and he was not above giving instruction for missionary work to Fray Junípero Serra, who was to take charge of establishing the missions. "We must adorn the new missions," Gálvez said, "as if they were cathedrals and the vestments must be of the very finest, that the heathen may see how Our Lord is worshiped, and how the House of God Our Lord is adorned, so that by this means they may be induced to embrace our holy faith."

These orders came from a man who had been exceedingly frustrated by obstacles that the Seri and Pima Indians had placed in the way of his plans for northward expansion. They had so stubbornly insisted on keeping their own way of life and rejecting the practices and even the presence of Spaniards that Gálvez had been pushed beyond the limits of sanity. At one time he proposed to import 600 apes from Guatemala to do his Indian fighting for him. Another day he was the king of Prussia, the king of France. He was God.

Needless to say, Gálvez with his fantasies could not keep an indefinite hold on his post as visitador, but he did plan—presumably in lucid moments—what was called a Sacred Expedition to begin the conquest of Alta California. On January 9, 1769, he was on hand in the southern part of Baja California when the expedition finally assembled. The 300 men who had gathered for the assault on largely unknown territory included soldiers; workmen; sailors, who were to man two vessels laden with supplies and seeds and tools; and four Franciscan missionaries, clad in their coarse robes of unbleached wool.

The *San Carlos* sailed January 11, with some of the men and supplies. The *San Antonio* left a month later. In April the first of two parties that were to travel by land started on its way up the length of Baja California, accompanied by a large herd of cattle. A second land party, commanded by Gaspar de Portolá, who was to be the first governor of California, left in May. With his party was fifty-two-year-old Fray Junípero Serra, in charge of establishing missions.

Serra had distinguished himself as a professor of philosophy at the university near his home on the island of Mallorca, off the coast of Spain. He had also attracted some attention when he moved to Mexico by his highly emotional appeals to Spanish aristocrats to give up their decadent ways. To dramatize the sufferings of hell, he scorched his breast with a burning torch. Now he insisted on walking to Alta California despite an open wound in one foot, which never healed.

The four contingents of the Sacred Expedition all headed

northward along their separate routes toward a spot near the bay of San Diego, which Spaniards had known about since 1542. Although the planning of this venture had been elaborate, its execution was far from perfect. The first ship to leave, the *San Carlos,* was blown off course and took more than 100 days to make the journey. Along the way a good many on board died. When at last the ship did arrive, the crew were so ill from scurvy and lack of water that they could not row themselves ashore. The *San Antonio,* which left Baja California long after the *San Carlos,* had arrived much sooner and with fewer casualties.

The two parties that traveled by land encountered less difficulty. Their main problem was that Indians who had been compelled to accompany them did not relish the journey and kept running away. Understandably weary, the overland contingents finally made the rendezvous by July 1, 1769.

Of the 300 men who had started, 126 survivors assembled on July 16, at a place the Indians called Cosoy, and Serra raised a cross. Sprinkling water, he blessed the cross and the ground around it. Then, under a brushwood shelter, he said high mass and preached a sermon. Soldiers fired guns, and thus San Diego was founded.

Now there began a wait for a relief ship with needed supplies that never arrived because it sank with all hands somewhere at sea. Another kind of wait stretched from days into weeks, then into months—Indians were very slow to appear at the mission and still slower to be converted.

With a whole chain of missions to establish, Fray Junípero Serra did not settle permanently at San Diego. In the

Father Junípero Serra, founder of the California mission system.

Brown Brothers

next seven years he managed to get six of them off to a slow start. The Indians, with good reason, suspected that the Spaniards, no matter whether they wore the leather armor of soldiers or the woolen robes of the missionaries, were after their land. Those Native Americans who did become converts soon had regrets. The women and girls were locked up at night, and they could not leave the mission premises during the day until they had completed all the tasks required of them. Men and boys had to endure the unfamiliar experi-

ence of sleeping, regimented, in barracks. They could not go hunting when they wanted to. In addition, there was the unrelenting humiliation of being treated like children. The Spaniards referred to themselves as *gente de razón,* that is to say, people who had reasoning powers. The clear implication was that Indians lacked intelligence.

Indians outside the missions bitterly resented the practices of Spanish soldiers. Around San Gabriel, mission soldiers amused themselves by racing through Indian villages and shooting at random. Sometimes they lassoed Indian women, then raped them. On one occasion the woman turned out to be the wife of a chief, who then attacked the offending soldier. For this, the chief's head was cut off and put on display for all Indians to see. The incident touched off a local revolt.

Fray Luís Jayme at San Diego wrote in dismay on October 7, 1772, "Very many of [the soldiers] deserve to be hanged on account of the continuous outrages which they are committing in seizing and raping the women. . . . [The Indians in one large village] many times have been on the point of coming here to kill us all, and the reason for this is that some soldiers went there and raped their women, and their soldiers turned their animals into [the Indians'] fields and they ate their crops. Three other Indian villages have reported the same thing to me several times. . . ."

As a result, when Indians saw any Spaniards approaching their villages—it made no difference whether they were soldiers or missionaries—they fled and stayed away, sometimes at the risk of starvation.

Serra reported on April 22, 1773, that Spanish men at San Diego took pottery by force from the Indians and committed sexual assaults every day at all the missions. "It is certain that the poor gentiles [meaning Indians] until now as gentle as sheep, will turn on us like tigers." And this the Yuman-speaking Indians of the San Diego area did. Led by a holy man, whose name the Spaniards did not bother to preserve, they attacked the presidio. The first blow did not succeed, but the will of the Indians to live and be independent had not been broken.

Altogether, the attempt to convert Indians to Christianity and to make them useful supporters of the Spanish imperial venture was not going well. "We cannot make the natives around here work," complained Fray Luís Jayme. "Often we cannot teach them the doctrine because they have to go hunting for food every day."

The problem of getting supplies had not been solved either. Fray Junípero Serra, with a keen awareness of the Indians' determination to remain Indian, opposed the establishment of an overland supply route from Sonora in northern Mexico to northern California. Such a route through Indian land would, he felt, only increase resistance to the Spanish invaders. But Serra's counsel was ignored. Instead, officials in Mexico took advice from an experienced Indian fighter, Captain Juan Bautista de Anza, who had grown up on the frontier.

Anza's father and his grandfather, also Indian fighters, had both spent their lives as members of the officer caste in presidios in the desert wilderness. His father had heard from Indians that there were trails through the deserts that lay

There may be no authentic contemporary picture of the 18th century Diegueño Indians, but this old engraving suggests how some coastal Indians in California appeared to one white artist.

California State Library

between the presidio of Tubac, in the southernmost part of what is now Arizona, and the Pacific coast. Accordingly, Anza felt sure that if he could find and follow the trails, parts of which were already known to earlier Spanish explorers, he could provide Spain what she sorely needed—an inland means of communication between Sonora and Monterey. Such a route would be proof against the hazards of sea travel, which was scanty in any event for lack of ships on the Pacific Ocean. And so, though there is no evidence that Anza savored this irony, he set about using Indian knowledge of the desert in order to conquer Indians. The first step in the conquest was to be a reconnaissance. Anza was not the kind of man who would venture carelessly with a large expedition into a vast, almost waterless area, without knowing exactly what he was doing.

By chance Anza found in Sonora, the day after Christmas 1773, an Indian who had just crossed the arid waste through which Anza wanted to make his way. The Indian—he had been given a Christian name, Sebastian Tarabal—was a native of Baja California, who had been taken to the San Gabriel mission in Alta California. There, forced labor at the mission so embittered him that he, with a wife and friend, ran away. Doubtless Tarabal tried to follow Indian trails of which he had heard, and he did get through the Borrego Desert, but the farther he traveled from San Gabriel the more confused he became. Finally, guided by a Yuma chief named Palma, he reached Sonora instead of Baja California. Somewhere along the way, his wife and friend died of thirst.

The experience that Tarabal had gained was something that Anza thought he could turn to good use on his reconnaissance. No one has recorded what pressures or what incentives persuaded Tarabal to return to San Gabriel after he had made such an enormous and painful effort to break away from that place. At any rate, Anza was able to include him in the exploring party which set out January 9, 1774.

At every stage of this first journey, Anza had the good sense to use information about desert trails—and trials— gathered from Indians, whom he always identified as "the heathens." He had with him not only Tarabal but an interpreter who knew the Pima language. Later, the Yuma helped him to cross the Colorado River and advised him about trails to the West. Two Yuma even accompanied him for some distance. Then Tarabal found he was in country that he recognized, and he was able to lead Anza's party to the Borrego Desert; up into Coyote Canyon, which offered water and grass; and on to a pass through the mountains. From there it was easy to reach San Gabriel, near present-day Pasadena.

Anza could now make serious plans for a large-scale expedition, which would serve two purposes. It would establish the needed inland supply route, and it would make possible a new kind of settlement in California. Anza proposed to take along not just soldiers and missionaries but also a whole colony of hard-working people who had been brought up in the Catholic faith. Back in Mexico City he received virtually unlimited funds from the royal treasury, and in this respect his project differed from the many expeditions and settlements that Europeans had made on the East Coast. Those had all been financed by private initiative of one kind or another and not by the central government of any of the colonizing powers. Anza's venture was entirely government-subsidized.

Anza knew what kind of colonists he wanted. They must be family men so poor that they would feel they were advancing themselves if they merely received food and clothing for the journey. Such people would be drawn to endure hardships by nothing but hope, and no matter how bad life was in California—or on the road there—it would seem better than it had been in Mexico. Prospective colonists of this kind were numerous in the vicinity of the city of Culiacán, in western Mexico. All of them were reported to

124

be descendants of men in Cortez's army, which meant they were part Spanish and part Indian. All were only too glad to travel some 1,700 miles in search of a better existence.

After gathering his recruits and collecting animals, Anza moved northward to headquarters at Tubac, where his winter crossing of the desert would start. In his party were 240 people, 155 of them women and children. He had 340 saddle horses ready for the journey, 165 pack mules, and 302 cattle. Tents had been prepared for the officers, soldiers, and missionaries, and a big round one for Anza. The settlers, for the most part, would have to concoct shelter from blankets and sticks, but they all had new clothes—"from shoes to hair ribbons," Anza said. He had even provided petticoats for the little girls.

On October 27, 1775, everything was in readiness. Five Indians, each of whom could interpret from a different Indian language, were on hand. Father Font, a Franciscan and a member of the expedition, said mass and preached a sermon on a text from Luke: "Fear not, little flock." He likened Anza to Moses, compared the settlers to the children of Israel passing through the Red Sea to the Promised Land, and urged them not to molest the heathen—the Indians whom he hoped to convert.

Then Anza gave the order: "Everybody mount." Font broke into a religious chant, which the settlers joined, and the journey to California began. Four soldiers rode out ahead. Then came Anza. Behind him rode the chanting Franciscan, followed by the settler families and most of the soldiers. After the straggling crowd of men, women, and children, came a group of armed guards, and behind them the pack mules. The inexperienced muleteers had trouble that first day. Packs kept slipping off the animals. Following the mules came the saddle horses that were not being ridden, and last of all the cattle, which three cowboys herded along. Father Font noted in his diary, "Altogether they made a very long procession."

It was a very colorful procession, too. Father Font was, among other things, an astronomer. From time to time he paused and used his quadrant to find the exact location of the expedition. In the evening he unpacked his psaltery, a kind of harp, and played on it. Another Franciscan in the party, Father Garcés, had a flair for the dramatic. When he wanted to impress Indians encountered along the way, he unfurled a large banner he had brought with him. On one side was a representation of the Virgin Mary and the Infant Jesus, on the other side a graphic portrayal of a soul suffering the tortures of the damned in hell.

On the first day out a woman had a baby. She died, but the child survived, and after that not one colonist died on the entire journey. Three more babies were born along the way.

Anza followed a slightly different route from the one he had explored on his reconnaissance trip. Because the silt in the bed of the Colorado River had shifted, he could not ford it where he had made his first crossing. Later, in the Borrego Desert, he encountered different weather too—much colder than in 1774. Rain drenched the travelers in this normally parched area, and as they ascended into the mountains, they had to make their way through snow. The settlers

had never seen snow before, and now they were not only cold but frightened. Some of them almost froze to death, and some animals did freeze. But at last the long procession started down the western side of the mountains and into warmer land. On January 4, 1776, Anza led his expedition into the unprepossessing little village of San Gabriel.

One person who was particularly happy at the outcome of her adventure was the spirited young widow María Felícia Arballo de Gutiérrez who, with two small daughters, had joined the expedition seeking a new life. In San Gabriel she met Juan Francisco Lopez, a soldier, whom she promptly married. It may be significant that Father Garcés—he who was always unfurling his flamboyant banner—not Father Font, performed the marriage ceremony. María and Father Font had had their differences along the way. On one occasion, when Anza issued liquor and allowed a fandango to go on all night, María had danced and sung "naughty" songs, to Father Font's dismay. He could not get her to stop singing, nor could he persuade Anza to order an end to the performance. But when an earthquake shook up the revelers, he did insist dourly that it was a punishment for her gaiety.

While the Anza expedition gathered at Tubac, Indians in the vicinity of San Diego had been growing restless. The soldiers' repeated brutal assaults on Indian women and the looting they did in the Indian villages had driven normally peaceful men to a state of rage. It may also have happened that they had heard of the Spanish plan to send large new forces into California. This news could have come with Indian traders, who often traveled from villages in present-day Arizona and New Mexico to the Gulf of California or the coast. Or Spaniards in San Diego itself may have been talking about the Anza expedition, and the knowledge certainly would have increased the Indians' sense of outrage and alarm.

Other events also prompted some Indians to consider desperate measures in defense of their traditional way of life. The number of little Indian huts beside the mission was increasing. This meant the number of converts was increasing. Moreover on October 3, 1775, there had been a big religious festival at the mission, and sixty new converts had been baptized.

All things considered, the Indian holy man who had led the earlier attack on the San Diego presidio thought the time had come for action. So, too, did two men among the supposed converts. They ran away from the mission, and soldiers conducting a search could not find them. What the soldiers did not know was that these men, and presumably the holy man, too, were going from village to village organizing an attack on the presidio and the mission at San Diego. Almost every village they visited agreed to support the assault, and a good-sized army came into being.

As in the earlier foray, the holy man seems to have been the main leader. He—or somebody—worked out careful plans. The leaders decided to storm the presidio on a day when only a half-dozen soldiers were on duty and at an hour when the soldiers and everybody else were likely to be asleep. A simultaneous strike would be made at the mission.

Two separate Indian armies assembled. Spanish estimates of their combined force varied from 400 to 1,000. Even if Spanish figures were exaggerated, there were several score Indians to each Spaniard capable of bearing arms.

Under cover of night the armies approached their separate objectives which, though six miles apart, were within sight of each other. The leaders lacked precise ways of synchronizing their attacks, and the men assigned to take the mission arrived at their destination before the other group did. Immediately, according to plan, they took up positions at the doors of the huts in which converts lived. Even if a convert was of a mind to, he could not give warning of the attack or join in defense of the mission. Other Indians not assigned to watch the huts went to the sacristy, broke open chests and took what they wanted, then proceeded to the guardhouse. Not a Spaniard had wakened, in spite of the considerable activity.

In the guardhouse was something too tempting to resist —fire. Somebody, apparently running ahead of schedule, seized a brand from the fire and set the guardhouse ablaze. At last the Spaniards were roused. The handful of soldiers tried to get into their leather armor and use their weapons, and they did well enough to make problems for the attackers. The Indians also inflicted casualties. A blacksmith dropped dead. A carpenter was mortally wounded. Minor wounds hampered most of the soldiers.

In the confusion one of the two missionaries escaped harm, but the other, Fray Luís Jayme, was taken outside the village and executed. Fray Luís was the Franciscan who more than once had complained to authorities about the brutal behavior of the soldiers. By morning, survivors at the mission had fled the charred ruins, carrying their dead and wounded toward the presidio.

If the Indians' plans had worked out perfectly there would have been no presidio standing when they arrived. But, for some reason that is not quite clear, the army assigned to take the presidio did not attack it, although they could easily have done so. Possibly the premature burning of the mission sent them racing off to aid their fellows, who needed no help. When the mistake was discovered it was too late. The Spaniards and a frightened handful of converts were all inside the fortress, with weapons and ammunition ready.

A message went immediately to the commander at Monterey. He set out with soldiers and on January 3, 1776, reached San Gabriel on his way to San Diego. The next day Anza arrived from the opposite direction, having crossed the desert with his large expedition. Together Anza and the commander hurried to San Diego with a contingent of picked soldiers. Anza, as an old Indian fighter, wanted to ride through the villages looking for and punishing the men who had taken part in the attack on the mission. Just how he was going to tell who they were is not clear, but there can be little doubt that he would have used the most decisive and brutal forms of punishment. His training on the frontier had led him to have great faith in force.

The commander, however, procrastinated. Twenty days went by and still he did nothing to coerce the Indians into submission. Anza, intolerant of any shilly-shallying, departed to resume his trek northward toward a place on the shore of a bay the Spaniards had named for St. Francis. The rest of his journey over a well-known trail was uneventful. When he had chosen a place for a settlement, he himself returned to Tubac.

On June 29, 1776, Fray Junípero Serra founded the mission now known as Mission Dolores. The building of San Francisco had begun. Some of the original settlers who occupied Indian land around the bay prospered mightily. One of them, Luís María Peralta, eventually claimed the whole area on which the cities of Oakland, Alameda, Berkeley, Albany, Emeryville, and Piedmont now stand.

In his own way Anza did in 1776 the same kind of outgoing thing that George Washington did when he ventured into Indian territory in 1753. These men and many others on the frontier helped to expand a way of life for one group of people at the expense of another group. So the year 1776 in California was a time of breakthrough for men whose ancestors came from Europe and who wanted to make a life for themselves on American soil. It was not a year celebrated by the original owners of the land. At the time when the Continental Congress in Philadelphia was preparing to throw off colonial restraints, soldiers and missionaries were just beginning to impose such restraints in San Francisco. While impoverished men from Mexico sought a way to fulfill themselves in California, Indians were also trying to keep their own freedoms alive—and these unreconciled efforts coincided in time and tendency with other efforts far to the east, where the Declaration of Independence was being dreamed of and drafted. What Spaniards and Indians on the West Coast and Englishmen and Indians on the East Coast did not know—and it still remains to be learned— was how people can achieve reasonable fulfillment of themselves without cruelly limiting others in the process.

PLACES TO SEE

ARIZONA

Coolidge: Casa Grande Ruins National Monument.
Tucson: Mission San Xavier del Bac.
Tumacacori National Monument.

CALIFORNIA

Borrego Springs: Anza-Borrego Desert State Park.
Carmel: Mission San Carlos Borromeo del Rio Carmelo.
King City: Mission San Antonio de Padua.
San Diego: Mission San Diego de Alcalá / The Presidio / Serra Museum Library.
San Francisco: Mission San Francisco de Asís The Presidio.
San Gabriel: Mission San Gabriel Arcangel.
San Juan Capistrano: Mission San Juan Capistrano.

For more information, see Gazetteer, page 212.

A modern painting suggests the arduous creative struggle engaged in by Benjamin Franklin and John Adams as they attempted to improve on Thomas Jefferson's language in the Declaration of Independence. (See the story of Jefferson's reaction to their editing, on page 189.)

127

Courtesy of Longines-Wittnauer, Inc.

Tensions Mount

Above: On March 5, 1770, rioting provoked by the British troops broke out in Boston. The conflict was called the Boston Massacre, and Paul Revere issued this rendition of the action.

Right: In response to the Stamp Act, a Pennsylvania newspaper printed this protest. *Below:* Residents of Providence, Rhode Island, captured and burned the British revenue ship *Gaspée* in Narragansett Bay on June 10, 1772.

The TIMES are
Dreadful,
Dismal
Doleful
Dolorous, and
DOLLAR-LESS.

Patrick Henry, in an address to the House of Burgesses concerning the Stamp Act, phrased his opposition so strongly and so well that he came into sudden prominence. Outside the doors of the chamber stood a young student named Thomas Jefferson, who overheard the "torrents of sublime eloquence." Although Jefferson was conservative in education and temperament, Henry's impassioned speech moved him deeply. The painting is at the Patrick Henry Memorial Foundation in Roanoke, Virginia.

Artists and Craftsmen Carry On

Henry Francis du Pont Winterthur Museum

Michael Bertan/Van Cleve

Newark Museum

Above: A set of colonial pewter ware. *Far left:* The home of Paul Revere in Boston. *Left:* A silver tankard from the late 1700s. *Below left:* The family of Charles Willson Peale, a well-known artist, was painted in 1773. *Below right:* The Old North Church, where the signal was given that the British were moving on the colonials.

New York Historical Society

Michael Bertan/Van Cleve

A General Was Needed

Braddock's Defeat, by Edwin W. Deming, depicts Braddock's forces, still in formation, being decimated by the French and Indians, who are using, to the classical European military tactician, highly unorthodox strategy. Braddock lost his life in this battle in 1755, and the young George Washington, whose advice was not heeded, read the funeral services for the unyielding general.

This painting, showing George Washington with a blue ribbon indicating that he was a commander, can be seen at the Brooklyn Museum.

A reconstruction of a tidewater plantation at Wakefield marks George Washington's birthplace. He lived here on his father's plantation until he was three, then moved to what became known as Mount Vernon.

This engraving of the battle at Lexington is the most accurate of several early representations. It was done in 1775 by Amos Doolittle, a Connecticut militiaman who was an eyewitness. The Doolittle picture shows a massacre without resistance. See also page 156. *Right:* A North Carolina Revolutionary soldier carried this drum.

Plan of the Town of Boston with the
Attack on BUNKERS-HILL in the Peninsula of CHARLESTOWN.
the 17th of June 1775.

This map shows Boston at the time of the Battle of Bunker Hill, when the Revolutionary forces, under Colonel William Prescott, surprised themselves and the British by giving a very good showing against well-trained European troops. Only days after this success, a much-heartened George Washington arrived as commander in chief to bring order to the forces. . . . A careful examination of the map will reveal many significant sites, such as the Liberty Tree, Faneuil Hall, and the Town Hall.

Many public meetings took place in Faneuil Hall, built in 1742 and named for Peter Faneuil. It was here that Bostonians met on December 16, 1773, with Sam Adams as chairman. After this meeting, a select group departed for Boston Harbor to dispose of taxed tea.

131

Innovators and Communicators

Poor Richard, 1733.
AN
Almanack
For the Year of Chrift
1733,
Being the Firft after LEAP YEAR:

By RICHARD SAUNDERS, Philom.

PHILADELPHIA:
Printed and fold by B. FRANKLIN, at the New
Printing-Office near the Market.

Above: One of Benjamin Franklin's highly successful publications was *Poor Richard's Almanack*. *Right:* Franklin was one of the founders of the Philadelphia Fire Company.

Philadelphia Contributionship

This plaque on a house indicated that the home was covered by fire insurance, another of Franklin's enterprises.

Franklin was often a visitor in the gracious Van Cortlandt home in New York. This dining room is at Sleepy Hollow Restoration in Tarrytown, New York.

Thomas Jefferson built Monticello, near Charlottesville, Virginia, and lived there from 1772 until his death in 1826. He is buried on the grounds of the estate. *Below:* Rembrandt Peale painted Jefferson from life in 1800.

Below is a section of the *Presentation of the Declaration of Independence*, by John Trumbull. The picture hangs in the Library of Congress Annex in Washington, D. C.

Independence

In part designed by Andrew Hamilton, who
defended Peter Zenger, the State House was the
meeting place for the Pennsylvania General
Assembly. Although work on the main building
continued until 1748, meetings were held there as
early as 1735. In 1750 work began on the tower
and steeple, and in 1753, the Liberty Bell graced
the belfry. The delegates adopted the Declaration
of Independence in this building, and later, the
Constitution was written here. Independence Hall
has been restored to look as it did in 1776.

The Declaration of Independence was adopted
on July 4, 1776, and after being carefully
engrossed on parchment paper, was signed on
August 2. In 1823, John Quincy Adams had a
facsimile made, which damaged the original.
Thereafter, it was shown only occasionally,
and in 1894, it was finally sealed in a steel case.
The Declaration is on display in the National
Archives Building.

PART THREE

Final Steps Toward Independence

What country can preserve its liberties if their rulers are not warned from time to time that their people preserve the spirit of resistance? . . . The tree of liberty must be refreshed from time to time with the blood of patriots and tyrants. It is its natural manure.

—Thomas Jefferson

The Parson's Cause

Tobacco growers in Virginia, whether they operated small farms near the frontier or large plantations in the older part of the colony, had one problem in common—they were in debt. Year after year their income from tobacco was less than the cost of the goods they had to buy from England. "These debts," said Thomas Jefferson, "had become hereditary from father to son for many generations." And he added, "The planters were a species of property annexed to certain mercantile houses in London."

If the price of tobacco fell, a farmer would have to go deeper into debt in order to import the commodities he needed from London. If the price of tobacco rose, the benefit of the increase would go to the merchants, who could then collect the interest due them on debts.

Government fees and taxes were regularly paid in fixed amounts of tobacco, and one such tax supported the established church. Whether or not a farmer was an Anglican, he had to turn over each year a certain number of pounds of tobacco to the vestry of the parish in which he lived. The vestry in turn paid an annual salary of 16,000 pounds of tobacco to the parson it employed.

In a bad year, when crops were small, this fixed tax could take a very big bite out of a farmer's income. Both 1755 and 1758 were bad. Drought greatly reduced the yields, and so, to give farmers some relief from the church tax, the Virginia legislature voted in those years to allow payment of the parsons' salaries in paper money instead of tobacco. For every pound of tobacco that had formerly been due, the taxpayer now paid two pence. Since the price of tobacco had almost tripled because drought had reduced the crop, this Two Penny Act was to the growers' advantage. A man could now pay the church tax with about one-third the amount of tobacco he would have had to surrender under the old law. Most farmers rejoiced, particularly the increasing number who were dissenters and resented being forced by the state to support a church of which they did not approve.

Clergymen, of course, disliked the new law. They could no longer benefit when the price of tobacco rose. Soon they began to lobby in London where, without much difficulty they got the Two Penny law annulled by the privy council, acting for the king. Then individual clergymen brought suit in courts in Virginia to recover the difference between what they had actually been paid and what the privy council said they were owed.

The most famous of these law cases (called "causes") was heard in Hanover Court House in 1763. During the trial Patrick Henry, an obscure young country lawyer, leaped into sudden, astonishing prominence . . .

Tobacco grown and processed by the unpaid labor of slaves of African origin became a source of great wealth to large landowners in the southern colonies, where the soil and climate particularly suited the tobacco plant. As the number of slaves increased, so did the rebellions of slaves against their owners.

22

"Give Me Liberty or Give Me Death"

1760s and 1770s   Virginia

For a dozen years before the Revolution Patrick Henry roused Englishmen in Virginia to insist that they had the same rights as Englishmen in England. His special contributions were those of an orator skilled at voicing and channeling popular resistance to tyranny.

Patrick Henry had tried—and failed—to make a livelihood growing tobacco. Then he had tried—with no better luck—to be a storekeeper. While he floundered around wondering what to do with his life, he often went hunting with his neighbors. He liked venison; he liked camping out; and he liked people. Many backwoodsmen were his good friends, and as long as he lived he spoke with a backcountry accent. His dress and manners were those of the common people. Few suspected that he could do more than simple reading and writing, for he had a comfortable way of hiding the knowledge of Latin he had got from his father, who had gone to a university in Scotland.

One day when he was twenty-four years old, already married, and the father of three children, Patrick Henry decided to be a lawyer. How long he studied is a matter for debate among scholars—possibly a few months, perhaps only a few weeks. Somehow he squeaked by the bar examination given to him by four prominent lawyers in Williamsburg. Then he began to practice in the little village of Hanover, eighteen miles north of Richmond. There he com-

bined serving drinks in his father-in-law's tavern with pleading cases in the courthouse across the road. Legend has it that Patrick Henry was very lazy and largely unemployed as a lawyer. Actually in his first three and a half years of practice, he handled 1,185 cases.

People around Hanover were poor, and many of them disapproved of the Anglican church. Some were Quakers, others Baptists or New Light Presbyterians. Henry himself belonged to the Anglican church, but his mother, who was a dissenter, often took him to services conducted by Samuel Davies, a New Light Presbyterian minister. Davies was a spellbinder. Apparently young Henry paid close attention to the preacher's technique. But when, if ever, Henry himself practiced public speaking is not clear. Certainly he had no reputation as an orator when some of his neighbors came one day and asked him to defend them in a lawsuit so hopeless that no other lawyer would touch it. They were being sued by the Reverend James Maury, an Anglican minister. Maury sought to recover the difference between what the vestry of his parish had paid him under the Two Penny Act and what he claimed he was owed.

The court, with Patrick Henry's father, John Henry, acting as a judge, ruled that Maury was indeed entitled to back salary, and on December 1, 1763, a jury of common men was assembled to determine how much he should be paid. At this point Patrick Henry rose in Hanover Court House and began an oration that shook Britain's empire.

What Henry said was not taken down in the courtroom. The only contemporary report is in a letter written by the parson James Maury shortly after the trial. But what Maury said about the sallow, unprepossessing lawyer who opposed him and what spectators recalled years later coincided on essential points. Henry spoke with great eloquence. He even moved the judge—his father—to tears.

Before this, Henry had handled only petty cases, and no one recalled anything of note he had ever said in a courtroom. Now, after a stumbling start that embarrassed everybody present, he drew strength from some unsuspected inner source and eloquently voiced the desire of Virginians to direct their own affairs. Until recently, he said, an agreement, a kind of contract, had existed between the people of Virginia and the government in London. But the royal government had broken the contract by nullifying Virginia's Two Penny Act of 1758. Therefore, the agreement was no longer binding on the colonists in Virginia. The Two Penny Act ought to be considered the law of the land; and "A King by annuling or disallowing laws of this salutary nature, from being the father of his people degenerates into a tyrant and forfeits all right to his subjects' obedience."

This was stronger heresy than a few members of the audience could stomach, and they shouted, "Treason! Treason! Treason!"

The jury was not intimidated. After deliberating only five minutes they returned with the verdict: the Reverend Maury should be awarded exactly one penny and not one whit more.

This verdict, in defiance of the powerful privy council, made the lawyer who obtained it a sudden hero. At the next election voters in Louisa County chose him to represent them in the House of Burgesses.

137

In this room in Colonial Williamsburg, Virginia's burgesses heard Patrick Henry's oratory.

Patrick Henry was now a spokesman for backcountry people—poor, unorthodox, and so numerous as to be an important political force. On May 20, 1765, give or take a day or two, he appeared in Williamsburg in ill-fitting country clothes to begin his service in the House of Burgesses. To take office, a new delegate had to swear that he was not a Catholic, not a dissenter, not one who supported the descendants of the Stuart kings who hoped to regain the British throne. With these requirements satisfied Henry began to participate in the routine business of the burgesses. It was ironic that one particular piece of legislation should have seemed routine—a measure aimed at preventing insurrections and conspiracies among slaves. There seems to be no record of any comment that Henry made on this restrictive measure. He certainly did not stir the imagination of witnesses by speaking out against it. Why would he? He himself was a slave owner, albeit on a small scale. The freedom he had defended in the Parson's Cause was freedom for men who were on his social level or higher. Those at the very bottom of society, the slaves, were no poorer for his efforts—nor did they gain by them. But his eloquence helped more men to do more and enjoy more than had been possible before he spoke. His contributions were specific and necessary—but limited, not universal.

For some weeks before Patrick Henry arrived in Williamsburg, Virginia's leaders had been considering what, if anything, they could do about an offensive new tax law known as the Stamp Act, which Parliament had passed in March. So far the colonies had done nothing about it. All were outraged by it. The stated object of the act was to raise funds for maintaining on American soil regular troops from England. It required that all legal documents be written on paper to which a tax stamp had been affixed. Newspapers and pamphlets had to be printed on similar stamped paper. In other words, Americans who wanted to do business or to communicate with one another in public ways had to pay a fee for the right to do so. Then—insult added to injury—these same fees financed soldiers sent to keep an eye on restless colonials.

On May 29, which happened to be his twenty-ninth birthday, Patrick Henry, tall, thin, unimportant looking, rose before the burgesses in Williamsburg. In his hand was a blank page torn from a lawbook on which he had written the wording of several resolutions he wanted to propose for adoption. These resolves, as he called them, emphasized that Virginians were Englishmen entitled to all the rights of Englishmen in England. But since Virginians were not represented in Parliament and had no voice in making tax laws, the Stamp Act was not binding on them.

No man listening to Patrick Henry on this day, his ninth day in the House of Burgesses, doubted that he had heard a masterful oration. Many who were not even inside the capitol heard the speech, for the day was warm and the doors and windows of the building were open. One of those gathered outside the main door was a young law student, Thomas Jefferson, who later recalled the "torrents of sublime eloquence" that came from the youthful backcountry statesman. But once again the words themselves vanished. No one took notes on what Henry said that spring day in Williamsburg.

Bostonian Society

MEDITERRANEAN REBELS IN FLORIDA

The largest single migration of settlers that had yet crossed the Atlantic brought their hope for a better life to Florida in 1768. Spain had given up that area to England five years before, and all Spaniards had left. To attract population, authorities in London bestowed 60,000 acres of land on a company of English investors, for whom the Scottish physician, Dr. Andrew Turnbull, was to act as recruiter and administrator in residence.

The doctor started from a sound premise: The settlement most likely to return a good profit to the investors would be made up of people accustomed to hard farm work and a warm climate. If they had ample reason to want to leave the Old World, so much the better. Turnbull, who had a Greek wife and knew Greece well, immediately thought of the Mediterranean area, particularly the island of Minorca, which England controlled at that time. There a large number of Greeks had settled, refugees several times over, first from Turks who had conquered their homeland, then from Corsica, Gibraltar, and other places. Some Minorcans, as well as Italians and Corsicans, also wanted change. All together many more recruits signed up than Turnbull had provisions for, and before his eight ships sailed 200 stowaways also hid themselves aboard, making a total of about 1,400 passengers.

At this point Turnbull's canny judgment failed. Unmindful of his settlers' temper, he decided to exploit them as sharecroppers on ninety-nine-year leases, and they had to work at least five years to pay for their passage. Another source of labor Turnbull counted on was a shipload of 500 African slaves. But the vessel sank off the Florida coast, and none of the slaves reached shore. The brutal overseers Turnbull had hired to control the slaves and the white immigrants now gave their whole attention to the immigrants. All were over-worked. Many perished of malaria; others soon began to suffer from hunger. It took only four weeks ashore for the farmers to realize that Turnbull's Florida paradise was in fact a hell from which they would be lucky to escape alive.

One morning a ship appeared in the harbor near the place they called New Smyrna, after the town in Greece from which Turnbull's wife came. At sight of it the settlers stopped work. Three hundred of them clambered aboard and were soon prepared to sail for Cuba. But the overloaded vessel rode too low in the water to clear the sandbar at the harbor entrance. To lighten it, the refugees jettisoned precious stores, then found themselves sailing into gun range of a British naval vessel, which had been quickly dispatched from St. Augustine to put down the revolt.

The refugees lacked arms of any kind, and a single cannonball whizzing across the deck showed them that their cause was hopeless. They surrendered and returned to grueling labor. Most of them—in fact most of the original 1,400—were dead before a decade had passed.

New Smyrna failed those who came seeking a free, secure life. Florida as a whole was not freedom-oriented and was not involved in the ferment which culminated in the American Revolution. The new British colony had a sparse population, and British control was very strong. It was to Florida that Tories fled from colonies in the north, and there patriot prisoners were held during the Revolution. The Greeks and other Mediterranean people had made their bid for freedom, and it was their misfortune that the authority they faced had overwhelming power.

The cultivation of indigo, used for dying cloth, was to be the basis of the New Smyrna economy.

139

"KINGS HAVE BEEN BRO'T TO BY MOBS"

Tenant farmers on the eastern side of the Hudson River faced a curious choice in the 1760s. They could pay high rent to white men who claimed ownership of 1,600,000 acres of the land that the farmers worked, or they could pay lower rent to Indians who were reasserting claim to that same land, which they had never ceded to anyone. The white landlords, partly Dutch in origin and partly English but now all English-speaking, belonged to four families— Van Cortlandt, Van Rensselaer, Philipse, and Livingston. In good feudal tradition, these four families refused to sell land to the tenants, who farmed it under leases that usually ran for 999 years. The Indians, on the other hand, offered the tenants short-term leases with opportunity to buy.

The four landed families would not negotiate better terms. The courts, controlled by the landlords, would not confirm the Indians' title to the land. And so an explosion was inevitable. With no hope of peaceful reform, the tenants felt they had no choice but to withhold rent and then to resist the sheriffs who came to evict them for nonpayment. Leaders began to emerge throughout the area that now comprises Columbia, Albany, Dutchess, Putnam, Rensselaer, and Westchester counties in New York State. Among the militants was William Prendergast, a thirty-eight-year-old farmer on the Philipse estate.

Prendergast, already familiar with English colonial practices in his native Ireland, believed that the tenant farmers "could not be defended in a Court of Law because they were poor: therefore they were determined to do themselves justice: poor men were always oppressed by the rich." And, said he, "Kings have been bro't to by mobs before now." (The thought was applicable, although the tenants' immediate enemy was not the royal government.) At times, sixty or eighty armed men would appear at evictions, to intimidate the sheriff's posses. Many tenant farmers were arrested, among them William Prendergast.

Regular troops guarded the court when Prendergast was brought to Poughkeepsie for trial. Because the landlords had retained every lawyer in the area, Prendergast could not find legal counsel and so had to act as his own attorney. During his trial the colonial world witnessed an unprecedented event to which the newspapers paid great attention: Against all the traditions of male-dominated society, his wife, Mehitable Wing Prendergast, rose time and time again in court to help conduct his defense. One paper reported: "She never failed to make every remark that might tend to extenuate the offense . . . not suffering one Circumstance that could be . . . thought of in his Favour to escape the Notice of the Court and Jury."

Nevertheless the court and jury, both dominated by landlords, found Prendergast guilty of treason and sentenced him to be hanged until almost dead; then his bowels were to be cut out, his genitals cut off, and both burned before his eyes while he was still alive.

Mehitable Prendergast did not give up. She leaped on a horse, rode seventy miles to New York City, and pleaded with the governor to grant a reprieve. Her plea was persuasive. The governor ordered the execution stayed until he could learn whether the king would grant the pardon which he recommended. Mrs. Prendergast raced off with the news and reached Poughkeepsie only three days after she had left. Meanwhile the sheriff had advertised for an executioner, promising good pay and a disguise "so as not to be known and secured from Insults." No applicant came forward.

Mindful of the farmers' massive resistance, the king pardoned Prendergast, and the governor's wife paid all the fines that had been imposed on sixty or seventy other farmers found guilty of some crime in connection with the uprising.

This outcome somewhat quieted the tenants, who had been sorely disappointed on another score. They had confidently expected help from the radical Sons of Liberty in New York City. But no help came. The urban dissidents who were resisting the Stamp Act could see no need for coalition with rural rebels who were merely opposing landlords. Indeed a member of the Sons sat as one of the judges in the court that sentenced Prendergast to death for treason.

The farmers failed to get lower rents or the right to buy land, and the Indians' claims were defeated. Many rent strikers were evicted and forced to move away, but somehow Mehitable and William Prendergast managed to stay on in the Hudson River valley until 1805. In the spring of that year the old couple moved to the frontier in western New York, still seeking greater freedom. With twenty-five children and grandchildren, and, ironically, a slave named Tom, they went in a caravan of covered wagons to settle in the place now called Chautauqua. The struggle that Prendergast led never died out completely. It flared up again before the Civil War and influenced Congress to pass the Homestead Act, which enabled farmers to start new lives in the West on land for which they paid no rent.

The day after his triumph Patrick Henry, wearing buckskin breeches, swung up onto his lean horse and rode off toward home. He left to others the tedious business of winding up the affairs of the Assembly. Only the most important of tasks ever held his interest and attention. He would rather go walking in the woods than bother with details.

Important tasks increased in number and in frequency during the years that followed, and Patrick Henry's influence grew. He was the undoubted leader of Virginia's Committee of Correspondence on May 24, 1774, when a message arrived from the Massachusetts Committee of Correspondence: The British had closed the port of Boston as a means of crushing resistance to Britain's oppressive measures. The burgesses promptly decided to set June 1 as a day of fasting and prayer as a way of expressing solidarity with Bostonians. Thinking beyond Virginia, they said this day would "give us one heart and one mind firmly to oppose . . . every injury to American rights."

Lord Dunmore, Virginia's governor, was in no mood to accept this kind of behavior. He dismissed the House of Burgesses, but the members, including George Washington, Thomas Jefferson, and George Mason, simply walked down Duke of Gloucester Street to the Raleigh Tavern, where they reassembled—with Patrick Henry acting as chairman. There on May 27, 1774, they voted to call for a general congress of all the colonies on the continent. To prepare for such a Continental Congress, the Virginians decided to hold a preliminary convention. At the convention, in St. John's Episcopal Church in Richmond, Patrick Henry strongly urged military preparedness. Supporting his position, he made the third great speech of his career, which included the famous words, "Gentlemen may cry peace, peace—but there is no peace. The war is actually begun . . ." and the conclusion, which every American knows, "Give me liberty or give me death!"

How accurate Patrick Henry was in assessing tensions soon became apparent. A few days after his speech in Richmond, fighting broke out in faraway Lexington, Massachusetts. Before news of Lexington reached Virginia, Patrick Henry was chosen to attend the Continental Congress when it met in Philadelphia. There, men from many colonies would learn from each other and discover that they all had common problems for which there must be a common solution. Afterward Patrick Henry would carry back to Virginia a new sense of the way events must go.

His oratory, learned from revivalist preachers, had helped to prepare America for independence. But great orator though he was, he did not limit himself to speeches. He was an officer in the militia and in time went to Williamsburg as governor. There he served for five terms. After the new, independent republic of the United States was established, he insisted on the adoption of the Bill of Rights, giving more power to the common people than was proposed by the framers of the Constitution. Because a great speaker from the backcountry of Virginia was cantankerous and stubborn and victorious, the quality of life in America has been more loose and open—and impertinent—than it might otherwise have been.

Patrick Henry as seen by an artist a hundred years after he pleaded the Parson's Cause.

PLACES TO SEE

PENNSYLVANIA

Philadelphia: Independence National Historical Park (Carpenters' Hall; Independence Hall).

VIRGINIA

Brookneal: Red Hill Shrine (Grave of Patrick Henry).
Charlottesville: Mitchie Tavern.

Hanover County: Hanover Court House / Hanover Tavern / Patrick Henry's Birthplace / Scotchtown.

Louisa: Roundabout Plantation.

Richmond: St. John's Episcopal Church (where Henry said, "Give me liberty or give me death.").

Williamsburg: The Apothecary Shop / The Capitol / The Governor's Palace / Market Square Tavern / Raleigh Tavern.

For more information, see Gazetteer, page 212.

A Voice of Reason

1774–76   Boston

John Adams, a scholarly, rational lawyer, became convinced of the rightness of colonial opposition to British tyranny and contributed his skills in the work of the Continental Congress.

Revolutionary impulses appeared again and again in the colonial centuries, but none of them approached full, successful maturity until the third quarter of the 1700s. Then the ripening process was rapid. Insurgent activities burgeoned and multiplied. Among the outbursts of energy and aspiration that led to independence, there were paradoxical —but significant—efforts toward restraint and orderliness. Realism and rationality appeared as a balance to romanticism and rambunctiousness. No person had more of this urge toward order amid upheaval than John Adams.

Young John Adams had dragged his feet when his father wanted to send him to Harvard. His teacher in the small town of Braintree was lazy and a bore. If what this man offered was a sample of intellectual life, John wanted none of it. He preferred to be a farmer like his father. At least he could enjoy life working outdoors, and he could not enjoy anything in school. But John's father, who was a shoemaker and harness maker as well as a farmer, strongly believed in the value of college training—perhaps because he had had none. He foiled his potential dropout quite simply by finding a different and better teacher, one whose mind and method John could respect. The elder Adams watched with satisfaction as the new tutor prepared his bright son for college. One day, he was sure, John would be a minister.

But as John studied, his tutor encouraged him to question and to think, thereby stimulating his curiosity and creativity, though neither was a prerequisite for entering Harvard. But searching out the truth became a lifelong habit. John Adams liked to be independent in matters of politics and religion. It was in the latter realm that his independence first appeared. While he was a sophomore at Harvard, he made a significant departure from orthodoxy. During a vacation at home in Braintree, he found the church split in a brutal controversy about theological matters. On one side were the older members of the congregation, including John's father; opposing them was a young minister, the Reverend Lemuel Briant, and the other young people in town. The Reverend Briant questioned some of the standard teachings of Calvinism, among them the doctrine of the Trinity. He did not believe that God was three separate persons. To him God was a single entity. The Reverend Briant had become a Unitarian some time before there was a Unitarian church, and John Adams sided with him, to the great distress of his father.

John's religious rebellion was quiet but persistent. Finally he found he could not enter the Congregational ministry. Although he was surrounded for most of his life by men who believed that the Father, the Son, and the Holy Ghost were separate realities, John Adams remained a philosophical Unitarian.

The break with Congregational theology set Adams apart from most of his fellows, but he still attended church. After he decided to take up law, he also stood apart from political activities, while actions and counteractions were escalating in the tussle between England and her colonies. As a very young lawyer he had been impressed when James Otis gave up an important government post in order to plead against the government's use of search warrants that invaded privacy and smacked of tyranny. In 1765 he felt somewhat concerned when Parliament gave its first approval to the Stamp Act. But he was living in Braintree, outside Boston, apart from the mainstream of political life. Moreover, he had to travel a great deal as he went from town to town trying cases. So he was not at the excited center of New England's protests when word came that Parliament had given final approval to the Stamp Act, which was scheduled to go into effect November 1, 1765.

James Otis led the agitation in Boston and wrote two fiery pamphlets in opposition to the act. John Adams admired his cousin Samuel Adams and James Otis for their protests, but John continued to be busy with his legal work. He was in the town of Falmouth (now Portsmouth, Maine) when the *Boston Gazette* arrived with a report of Patrick Henry's anti-Stamp Act resolves. The full force of the resolves struck John Adams, and he responded in his reflective way by sending an unsigned article to the *Gazette*. The colonies, he said, were governed by generally antiquated, unsuitable laws, some of which derived unchanged from feudal times, when state and church were closely enmeshed one with the other. This scholarly piece was so long that it had to be published in four installments, and its closely reasoned thinking seemed hardly likely to stir large numbers of people into action. But act they did.

On August 14 somebody in Boston made an effigy and hung it from the big elm that was known as the Liberty Tree. The effigy represented Andrew Oliver who, as everyone knew, would be the official responsible for selling the hated stamps. Oliver also belonged to a prominent family—part of the clique of aristocrats who ruled Massachusetts for the crown. After all of Boston had seen the effigy—and no one had torn it down—a crowd carried it to—and right through—the Town House where Lieutenant Governor Thomas Hutchinson and Andrew Oliver were sitting, then on to a new frame building where it was rumored Oliver was going to distribute the stamps. In a matter of minutes, axes laid this building flat. Next, Oliver's home was thoroughly ransacked. Finally the angry—and well-organized—crowd burned the effigy. The meaning of their symbolic act was not lost on anyone.

Less than two weeks later Bostonians burst out once more against the Stamp Act. This time they attacked the home of Lieutenant Governor Hutchinson. The beautiful dwelling of this very rich, very conservative man was wrecked. The next day Hutchinson, who was chief justice of the colony as well as lieutenant governor, had to appear in court without his judicial robes, which the wrathful demonstrators had not spared.

(Above) John Adams. (Below) When he was president of the U.S., John Adams added this, the Long Room, to his home in Quincy, Mass.

WHAT WAS THE STAMP ACT?

In 1760 King George II died. Three years later England and France signed the Treaty of Paris, ending a long conflict that in America was known as the French and Indian War. Under this treaty England annexed a great part of North America that had been ruled or claimed by France, and England became center of the largest empire that the world had seen since the great days of Rome.

George Grenville, as Britain's prime minister, sought funds to finance this immense politico-economic organization. At his suggestion, the acts governing colonial trade were made more liberal, but they were also more strictly enforced. Since previous acts had been very little enforced and were very generally evaded, the new reduction in tariffs made little favorable impression on colonial merchants. Enforcement was what they saw and resisted. Strict obedience cut into their profits and aided their competitors in England.

The colonials resented even more a special revenue-raising measure that Grenville proposed —a tax that took the form of a stamp that had to be purchased and affixed to all legal documents, newspapers, and pamphlets. Objections to the tax were manifold. To begin with, the colonists protested that they were being taxed without their consent. They had no representation in Parliament as most other Englishmen had. In addition, the tax was to be used for financing a standing army of Englishmen on American soil. Against what danger was this army to protect Americans? France had been eliminated as a threat; no armies would be marching down from Canada. Indians were no more of a problem than they had been in the preceding century-and-a-half, during which colonists had made their way into the wilderness unaided. The conclusion was inescapable: Redcoats on American soil would be used against Americans.

Objectionable provisions of the Stamp Act did not end here. Colonists accused of breaking the law were to be tried without benefit of juries in vice-admiralty courts, presided over by judges appointed by the crown.

On May 29, 1765, the Virginia legislature, responding to an appeal made by Patrick Henry, voted to oppose the Stamp Act. The Virginia decision was circulated throughout the colonies, and many parallel resolutions were adopted by local communities as well as by colonial legislatures. The resistance which Virginia had set off was so intense and so widespread that less than a year later Parliament repealed the Stamp Act. This effort to make colonies serve the interests of the politicians and businessmen who were centered in London had failed. And exuberant colonists held celebrations such as America had never seen up and down the Atlantic coast.

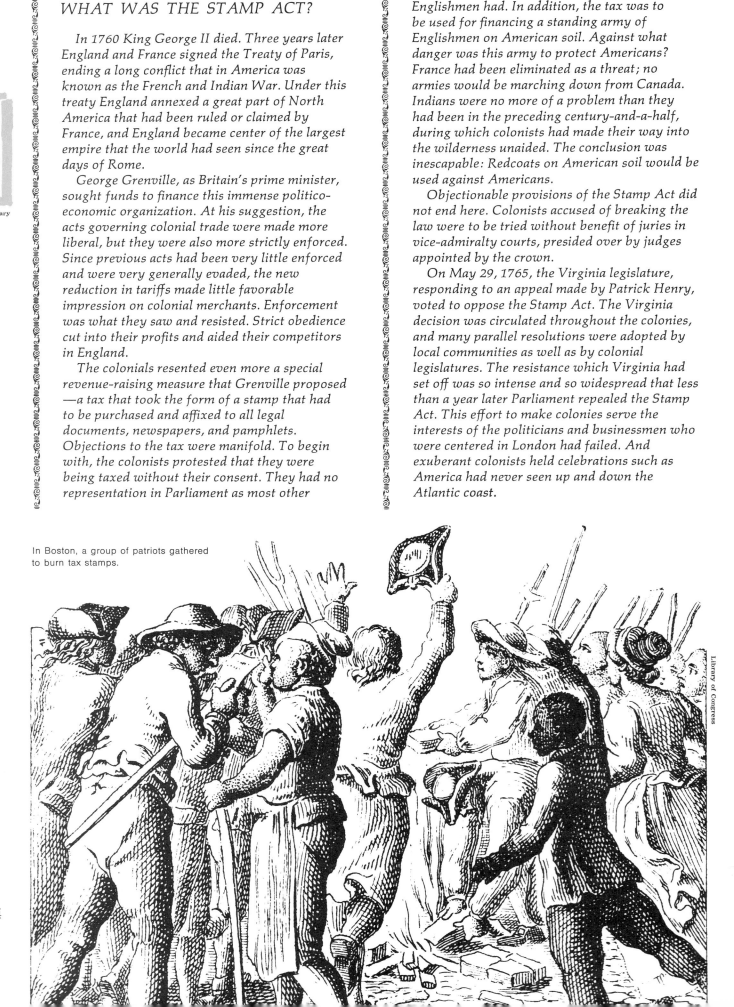

In Boston, a group of patriots gathered to burn tax stamps.

144

John Adams was far from Boston at the time, tending to legal business on the isolated island of Martha's Vineyard. He did not approve of violence, and when he heard what had happened he went to work as a political scientist to draft a document that he hoped would point toward the proper, the orderly governmental way to solve this Stamp Act problem. Knowing that Massachusetts towns customarily handed written instructions to their representatives in the legislature, he wrote out instructions concerning the Stamp Act. These, the Braintree voters adopted as guidelines for their representative. The Stamp Act, they argued, was an illegal law and was null and void.

The Braintree instructions were published in the *Gazette,* and soon dozens of towns had adopted almost identical guidelines.

Articles, pamphlets, and discussions in coffeehouses—as well as instructions—educated New Englanders against the unpopular new taxation, and Massachusetts elected delegates to attend a Stamp Act Congress on October 7, 1765, in New York. One of the delegates was John Adams. At last he was being drawn away from detached theorizing into active participation in a growing movement.

The king and Parliament knew very well how the colonists hated the very idea of the Stamp Act, but plans went ahead to enforce it. On the morning of November 1, when the law was to go into effect, church bells tolled in almost every town up and down the Atlantic coast. At that moment almost all legal business stopped. Lawyers would not buy stamps to make their documents official. Without official documents, courts could not operate. The wheels of justice came to a halt. Many business houses failed to open their doors because their proprietors would not buy stamped paper on which to keep their records. Officials of the crown saw most governmental activity—and a great deal of business life—paralyzed. But how do you force men to buy something they don't want to buy?

By the end of December the citizens of Boston desperately needed courts that functioned so they could settle disputes and conduct other business. Three lawyers were asked to approach the council with a request that the court activities be allowed to proceed without the stamps. One of the lawyers was James Otis, another was thirty-year-old John Adams.

Ever concerned with government procedures, Adams earnestly joined in making the protest, and his words, along with the whole varied and angry resistance movement, had an effect. Parliament revoked the Stamp Act. The opponents of the measure had won. And winning, they had learned the value of cooperation in joint action. Men in Massachusetts, Pennsylvania, and Virginia had also discovered that they were all Americans.

Every city and town celebrated. Crowds held their jubilations on Boston Common in front of the home of the wealthy merchant John Hancock. This elegant gentleman, who had opposed the Stamp Act as ardently as the roughest mechanic, had two great barrels of wine rolled out from his cellar onto the common as a gift to the Bostonians.

King and Parliament responded at once to the colonials' victory. The crown began new efforts to enforce laws affecting navigation and trade, and the chief commissioner of customs in Boston, Charles Paxton, decided on a test case. He would catch an important Boston merchant and punish him for smuggling. The smuggler would be tried in a vice-admiralty court, with no jury and before a judge appointed by the crown.

The prominent man Paxton chose was none other than John Hancock, probably the richest merchant in Boston, whose fortune had come from his uncle, an experienced and skillful smuggler. The contraband Paxton decided to take was aboard Hancock's ship, the *Liberty.* When that episode finally ended with the seizure of the *Liberty,* Paxton still was not through. He had Hancock charged with violation of the Townshend Acts, and Hancock retained John Adams to defend him.

John Hancock, a very wealthy man, sided with the patriots, but John Singleton Copley, who painted this portrait of him, left Boston with the British when they abandoned the city.

SMUGGLING AND JOHN HANCOCK

John Hancock wore the fanciest clothes in Boston, and he had a slave who served as his valet. His was one of the grandest houses in the thriving city. Ships that he owned tied up at his own wharf, the second largest in Boston, discharging or taking on cargo and increasing the very large fortune he had inherited from his uncle Thomas. The uncle, the son of a Congregational minister, had defied Britain's restrictions on colonial trade by becoming an accomplished smuggler. John was not to be outdone by an uncle, nor would he allow interference by officials in his business enterprises.

In 1767 a great deal of new interference began. Britain imposed new duties on many kinds of goods, and Hancock had no intention of paying. Nor would he let customs commissioners or their clerks inspect his ships in search of contraband. He sent out word that not one of these men was to be allowed aboard a single Hancock vessel without his approval. An accident, however, happened on the night of April 8, 1768. His ship Lydia arrived from London, and somehow two customs collectors slipped aboard. When Hancock heard the news, he rushed to his wharf and ordered the ship's captain to keep the tidesmen, as customs collectors were called, from entering the holds where the cargo was stored. The tidesmen left. But one of them returned to the Lydia the next night. Somebody saw him below decks and reported to Hancock. About eleven o'clock Hancock reached the Lydia with eight or ten husky men and a personal servant, who lighted the way with a lantern. Hancock gravely made a careful inspection of the tidesman's credentials, found them faulty on a technical point, and had him removed from the hold. Then with a straight face Hancock graciously offered to let the tidesman inspect anything he wanted to on the deck or above.

The customs official eyed the burly men who accompanied Hancock and decided to leave. By this time a crowd had assembled and now they escorted Hancock up the wharf, "he having the approbation of the spectators," the lieutenant governor ruefully reported to London. On board the Lydia that night in April 1768, British authority encountered forcible resistance which was offered by a leading member of the upper class in America, and America's lower class approved.

In June another ship of Hancock's, significantly named the Liberty, sailed into Boston Harbor with a cargo of Madeira wine. Hancock behaved as he and other merchants always did when their vessels arrived. He sent an agent on board when it tied up at his own pier. According to time-honored ritual, the agent and the captain of the Liberty then invited a customs official into the captain's cabin for a drink and offered him the usual bribe for turning his back while the cargo was unloaded. To their astonishment the official refused the bribe and insisted instead that all the tariff had to be paid on the ship's huge cargo.

This was amazing behavior. Hancock's agent and the captain could think of nothing better to do than tie the collector up and lock him below decks while they and the crew unloaded the contraband as fast as they could—so fast, indeed, that the overwrought and harried captain died, apparently of a heart attack.

Meantime the smuggling operation was completed, and Hancock won that round. Now it was the customs commissioners' turn. They called in sailors from the naval vessel Romney to take possession of the Liberty. Dockside workers, when they saw all this happening, set to work with a will to prevent seizure. They landed a good number of whacks on the sailors, but could not save the Liberty. The Romney towed her out into the harbor, and there the fifty guns of the naval vessel kept effective control over the prize, while an arrowhead sign was painted on her side, signifying that she had been taken by the government.

It was not so easy, though, to keep control over Bostonians who had witnessed this latest affront to American dignity. Protestors followed the customs commissioners, pelting them with stones. Some hotheads broke windows in the commissioners' homes. Others dragged a small sloop that belonged to the commissioners out of the water and burned it on Boston Common. Very soon after this, all of the commissioners in Boston took refuge behind the guns on the Romney.

With John Hancock's defiance and the popular protest that accompanied it, the struggle between Americans on the one hand and the king and Parliament on the other reached a new stage. On April 18, 1769, when the Massachusetts Assembly met, it elected John Hancock speaker. Lieutenant Governor Hutchinson quickly vetoed the election. Next month Bostonians made their reply when they chose new representatives in the senate. Hancock was almost unanimously elected. Only eight Bostonians voted against him. Later Hancock's popularity was such that he served for a while as president of the Continental Congress.

How does one defend a man who has quite obviously defied the law? By challenging the constitutionality of the law that has been defied. This Adams did, and he leaned heavily on the contention that tax laws affecting American colonies were invalid because the colonies had not acquiesced in their passage. Americans, unlike other Englishmen, were being taxed by Parliament, although they had no representatives in that body. Englishmen in England, on the other hand, generally were represented. They could oppose and disapprove of measures that they thought unjust, but Americans were denied this right. Any law that denied Englishmen the right to help decide whether or not they should be taxed was clearly contrary to basic principles of English justice, and hence was unconstitutional.

Appointees of the king, who acted as judges, were not likely to be persuaded by such reasoning. The king, after all,

wanted colonists to obey the laws governing navigation and trade. But fortunately for the colonists, more than fine legal reasoning was operating to further their cause. When the government called witnesses into court to prove that there had indeed been smuggling of Madeira wine on the *Liberty,* not one could be found who had seen any such thing. Every single person called to testify solemnly swore that he had not seen any illegal behavior. Before the trial ended, a large number of God-fearing Bostonians had committed perjury as a way of defying a law they earnestly believed did not belong on the books. And John Adams, who just as earnestly did not believe in perjury, had the odd experience of winning his case because of it. The government finally dropped the smuggling charges against John Hancock.

But Hancock's victory was not complete. The *Liberty* had been seized, and before charges had been dropped, the

Hostile British cartoons were part of the propaganda war that preceded the outbreak of military hostilities. This one, entitled "The Bostonians in Distress," appeared in London in 1774. *(Below)* Men of the sea like this one, probably of a later date, were at the center of much of the friction between England and the colonies. For one thing the British navy kidnapped colonial sailors and forced them to serve on British ships.

ABIGAIL ADAMS

John Adams had a talented and determined partner who urged him forward—indeed sometimes urged him on to more daring ideas than he himself would have thought of. Abigail, his wife, was quite fearless, and in some areas she saw more room for revolutionary development than John did. When he was attending the Continental Congress, after the Revolution had started, she wrote him this: "In the new code of laws which I suppose it will be necessary for you to make, I desire you would remember the ladies and be more generous and favorable to them than your ancestors. Do not put such unlimited power into the hands of the husbands. Remember, all men would be tyrants if they could. If particular care and attention is not paid to the ladies, we are determined to foment a rebellion, and will not hold ourselves bound by any laws in which we have no voice or representation."

Abigail Adams *(above)* said almost two years before Independence, "We have too many high sounding words, and too few actions that correspond with them."

vessel had been sold at auction. Now, still called the *Liberty,* she was being used to pursue other smugglers. This would not be tolerated by some citizens in Newport, Rhode Island, who called themselves Sons of Liberty. In July 1769 they stealthily boarded the *Liberty,* set her afire, and sent her to the bottom.

Day by day the struggle between British authority and colonial freedom grew more intense. The British navy began kidnapping Americans and forcing them to serve as sailors on naval vessels. This practice, known as impressment, made American seamen virtual slaves on the British ships. In April 1769 off the coast of Massachusetts, a naval vessel, the *Rose,* stopped a Massachusetts vessel, and naval officers boarded her. They demanded that four of the American sailors come aboard the *Rose* and serve there. Four were selected but refused to be kidnapped—they swore they would die rather than be impressed. They ran to the forepeak, picking up whatever they could use to defend themselves—including a harpoon. When an incautious British officer ignored their warnings, he died with the harpoon in his guts.

All four sailors were charged with murder. John Adams became their attorney, and as always, he prepared his case carefully. His main argument was to be that the death of the officer was justifiable homicide. Before he began his defense he laid ostentatiously open on a table in the courtroom a volume of the British *Statutes at Large.* As everyone knew, his was the only complete set of British *Statutes* that existed in America, and he had opened this volume to the page on which was printed a law which specifically forbade the impressment of American seamen by the British navy.

It may have been that Adams was the only American who knew about this particular law. But possibly there was one other, Chief Justice Thomas Hutchinson. At any rate Hutchinson looked down on the open lawbook and either knew or suspected the purpose for which it was open. Before Adams could start his argument, which every Bostonian would read in the next issue of the *Gazette,* the chief justice ordered the trial adjourned. Next day, still before Adams had presented his case, and hence before the existence of the statute against impressment could be broadcast, the judges gave their verdict: The killing of the naval officer had been justifiable homicide.

The legal victories that Adams kept winning made him more and more a hero, albeit a reluctant hero, of Bostonians who sought freedom. He even had to endure serenades bawled out at night directly under his window by enthusiastic artisans who were members of the militant Sons of Liberty.

Now a constant tug went on within him. By temperament he wanted order. He wanted a quiet personal life. He enjoyed study. Time and again he wrote in his diary, "At home with my family, thinking." Once, at least, while the revolutionary storm gathered, his love of order and his dislike of violence made him take sides in court with redcoated British soldiers against the angry Boston populace. The British army had occupied Boston on October 12, 1768, because it was a center of resistance to British laws, and Adams hated the occupation as much as anyone. In an attempt to get farther away from the center of redcoat activity, he even moved his home from Brattle Square to Cold Street.

But the move did him very little good in the end. On March 5, 1770, some redcoats confronted a noisy crowd of irritable Bostonians. Among them was a huge man, Crispus Attucks, part African, possibly part Indian, perhaps a runaway slave in search of still greater freedom. With a stick of cordwood in his hand, Attucks faced the soldiers in the street outside the Town House in the evening cold and shouted with hundreds of others. The soldiers, angry and fearful, fired at the dark giant. Attucks fell dead, and so did three others in the crowd. A fifth was mortally wounded. This was the Boston Massacre.

Who gave the order to fire? Witnesses disagreed, but the soldiers and their officer, Captain Thomas Preston, were arrested and accused of murder. John Adams now astonished many people by coming to the defense of the British army men. To his mind the unruly forces of revolt had gone too far. He wanted justice for Americans as much as ever, but then he wanted justice for everyone, including redcoats. In addition, he and some of his patriot friends thought it was unwise to provoke the crown and Parliament into further use of the great military power they possessed. John Adams believed that he was making a contribution to his countrymen by defending those accused of committing the Boston Massacre.

Whether or not Adams served the American cause by this action, he did not lose his influence or his following in Massachusetts. He was chosen as a delegate from the colony to the First Continental Congress in 1774. In this same period he discovered that he was not opposed to certain kinds of forcible action. On December 17, 1773, when a silent, perfectly disciplined group of Bostonians, dressed as Indians, dumped 342 chests of valuable tea into Boston Harbor, John Adams made this entry in his diary: "This is the most magnificent movement of all. There is a dignity, a majesty, a sublimity, in this last effort of the Patriots that I greatly admire."

By mid-June 1775, it finally seemed to John Adams that the military force being used against Americans could be answered only by military force. When he came to this conclusion he took the lead in recommending in the Continental Congress that a Continental army be established to serve all the colonies. Some colonies were ready for military action, but each of them wanted its own militia under its own control. Adams had to win support for a centralized overall army. He not only urged its creation, but he also had strong ideas about who should head it. It seemed obvious that enthusiastic, egotistical John Hancock wanted to be commander of the army. But John Adams opposed his old friend. He looked beyond Massachusetts for a man with real military experience—one who could win support from colonies outside New England. With this in mind, realistic John Adams nominated the American-born leader who had the most military experience, who was wealthy enough to afford full-time generalship, and who could mobilize support from all the southern colonies. Adams proposed the name of George Washington.

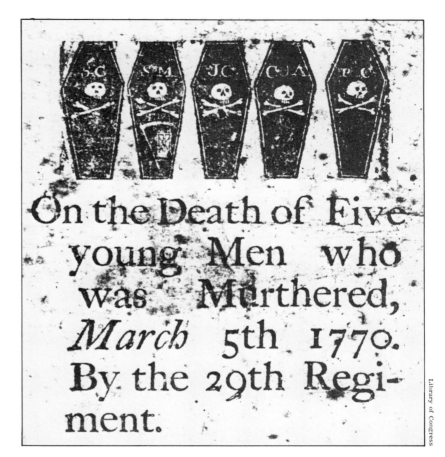

From a handbill on the Boston Massacre.

Library of Congress

PLACES TO SEE ❧

MASSACHUSETTS
Arlington: John Adams' Home Site.
Boston: The Boston Public Library / Hanover Square / Old State House.
Cambridge: Harvard College.
Quincy: Adams National Historic Site / Birthplace of John Adams / Church of the Presidents (Graves of John Adams and John Quincy Adams).
Weymouth: Abigail Adams' Birthplace.
Worcester: The Commons.

PENNSYLVANIA
Philadelphia: Independence National Historical Park (Carpenters' Hall; Independence Hall).

NEW JERSEY
Princeton: The Dean's House.

NEW YORK
Tottenville: Conference House.

For more information, see Gazetteer, page 212.

24

Craftsman and Courier

1775 Boston

*Paul Revere, respected craftsman, joined with
fellow craftsmen as well as with those of the
upper classes in resisting British repression.
Although he is especially remembered for
the warning he carried to Lexington, he was a
tireless courier who made many other important
journeys.*

Boston during the 1760s and early 1770s sheltered a
very mixed crew of agitators. Some of these patriots, as they
liked to call themselves, were wealthy. They regarded themselves as Englishmen overseas and resented the fact that they
could not make the same kind of advantageous business
arrangements that were possible for Englishmen in England.
Others were lawyers who had to live with the fact that
English law gave more privileges and liberties to Englishmen in Britain than to Englishmen in the American colonies.
Farmers near Boston chafed because of taxes imposed on
them by a distant Parliament in which they were not represented. Equally restless under restrictions and constraints
were men called mechanics. These were skilled artisans of
many kinds who saw a limited future ahead as long as they
could not obtain the raw materials they needed except at
monopoly prices from sources within Britain's empire. And
they could sell the products of their labor only to neighbors
and to Englishmen in England. They were forbidden to
trade in the world market. The mechanics were seldom well-
to-do, although they sometimes employed assistants or help-
ers, and they might even have slaves or indentured servants,
who were bound to work for a certain number of years,

then were free to set themselves up in competition with their
former masters.

Ambitious mechanics wanted a larger piece of life than
they were getting, and no one among them was more eager
than a certain ingenious silversmith named Paul Revere, who
practiced other crafts from time to time. He carved false
teeth from hippopotamus tusks and wired them into position
with silver fastenings. He also made engravings on sheets of
copper and at one time printed paper money from such engravings. At another time he made large, sonorous bells. At
still another he manufactured gunpowder. For some of his
skills, particularly his work in silver, Revere is known even
today. But he is more often remembered because he spent as
much energy laboring for revolution as he spent shaping
punch bowls or incising lines on copper. For his revolutionary work he usually got only token pay or no pay at all. His
rewards were of another kind—the love and trust of all the
patriots in the many organizations to which he belonged.

Because he was trusted and was by nature an energetic
man of action, Revere became a courier. From Boston to
Philadelphia and back he rode hundreds of miles delivering
messages, some of them very delicate and confidential, some
so urgent that they had to pass through guard posts the
British established to prevent communication.

This bold and reliable rebel had taken a name that was
easier for the Yankee tongue to manage than Apollos
Rivoire, the name of his French silversmith father, who had
come to New England as a refugee from religious persecution. Paul's Yankee Puritan mother brought him into the
turbulent town of Boston about the beginning of the year
1735. It was not from her but from his father that he got
his coloring. He had dark skin and hair, unlike most of his
neighbors, who were blonde.

By 1760 Paul Revere had begun to join organizations.
Sometimes he was the only mechanic in one or another
group of Harvard graduates engaged in activity regarded
as subversive by the British authorities. Always he was the
member who got things done, so he was welcome. First he
became a Mason, and in that secret order, he met men who
developed into great leaders of the Revolution. Soon afterward he began to take part in annual marches, called Pope's
Days, which often enough wound up in riots between men
who lived in the North End of Boston and those who lived
in the South End. These Pope's Days were, even though
most marchers didn't know it, celebrations of the discovery
of a Catholic plot to overthrow the Protestant government
in London many years before. No matter. In America,
Pope's Days were good training for Bostonians who had
maverick impulses. Anti-British leaders guided the marches
toward expressing political protest.

Paul Revere was active—very active—in support of the
Whig party, a loose organization of restless men. The general direction of Whig momentum was given by small
groups of planners. Three of these were called caucuses, a
word perhaps borrowed from the Algonkian language.
Paul Revere belonged to the North End Caucus, which met
in a tavern usually known as the Two Palaverers. The name
came from the tavern's sign on which was painted two
gentlemen bowing elaborately to each other.

Another group of planners—even more select than the caucuses—met discreetly in a long room above the printshop where the *Boston Gazette* was published. From the Long Room issued a great many petitions, protests, and schemes for counteracting British taxes, British regulations, British authority.

By night Revere went to meetings of either the local Boston organizations or gatherings of the Boston members of the Sons of Liberty, a revolutionary group that was active in most of the colonies. By day he made elegant silver vessels to grace the tables of well-to-do shipowners or merchants or colonial officials. One of his clients was Governor Thomas Hutchinson, a direct descendant of Anne Hutchinson. The governor was as able in his way as Anne Hutchinson had been in hers, and he was as conservative as she had been radical. Paul Revere accepted Hutchinson's money in payment for beautiful mugs or platters or teapots, but he did not accept the governor's ideas.

No one knows exactly where Paul Revere was during the Boston Massacre, but he may have been an eyewitness. Very soon after the event he made a diagram showing the exact location of each of the victims in the street near the old State House. One of his copper engravings also portrayed the scene. In the steady repetition of blow and parry Revere was always involved. When Parliament in 1773 again asserted itself by taxing tea, he and his friends sprang into action as soon as the first ships bearing that commodity arrived in Boston. The identities of those who participated in the famous Boston Tea Party were closely guarded secrets, but from clues picked up in old diaries and letters and other records, some of the names are now known. One person observed lace showing under the disguise of a certain Bostonian dressed as an Indian—lace of the kind that only John Hancock could afford to buy and was known to wear. On the night of the tea party the regular meeting of St. Andrews Masonic Lodge was not held. The minutes noting this fact read: "N.B. Consignees of Tea took up the Bretheren's time." Paul Revere was a member of St. Andrews Masonic Lodge.

News of the Boston Tea Party spread to other ports. Annapolis, then the main port in Maryland, soon had its own tea party. In the North Carolina port of Edenton an amazing thing happened. There, in an age when women were not supposed to take part in politics, fifty of them from many walks of life signed a protest against the tea tax. This protest did not go unnoticed in the place where it would have greatest effect. Its entire text was printed, with all its signers' names, in a London newspaper.

Britain, of course, responded to the "consignees'" action. In May 1774 General Thomas Gage arrived from England with 4,000 soldiers. Gage had orders to stop street demonstrations and to put an end to smuggling—a sideline that was practiced by many of Boston's most respectable businessmen. The Boston populace was required to house Gage's army.

There was instant outcry against this invasion. British authorities retaliated with an order that meant death to the city, if it was effectively carried out. No ship could enter or leave Boston Harbor. This meant that no goods of any kind

Portrait of Paul Revere by John Singleton Copley. When King George III ordered Massachusetts lawmakers to rescind a resolution they had passed condemning the Stamp Act, 92 of them refused to do as ordered.

To honor these nonrescinders, 15 Sons of Liberty commissioned Paul Revere to make a silver bowl that could hold a gallon of punch. On the bowl appear the names of the donors together with a liberty cap and other symbols prescribed by them. Revere's own name also appears on the bowl, which like the portrait above is in the Boston Museum of Fine Arts.

151

could reach Boston merchants and beyond them, the consumers; and nothing that Bostonians made or collected for export could be shipped to market.

Immediately, large numbers of men were out of work. They could earn no money, and without it could buy no food. Even with money it became harder and harder to get anything to eat, and it was not easy to go into the country to look for food. People had to have permission from General Gage before they could leave the city, which was built on a peninsula extending into the harbor. Guards watched over the one road that led to the mainland across the peninsula's narrow neck. Armed vessels kept watch in the harbor for anyone who might try to steal away in a rowboat.

Bostonians felt an ever-growing need to reach out to other colonists who also had troubles with Britain. Each colony had better connections with the governmental center across the Atlantic than with their much nearer neighbors in America. To remedy this lack of communication, revolutionaries began to set up their own way of sending messages to one another. In this critical work Paul Revere played an important part. He was a good rider, tireless in the saddle, and happy to carry messages back and forth between Boston and New York or Philadelphia, making record time.

As Revere traveled with news about the closing of the port of Boston, he passed out handbills aimed at arousing people against the persecution of Massachusetts. Quite prob-

TEA PARTIES

In addition to the famous Boston Tea Party, December 16, 1773, there were "parties" of one sort or another in other places. On Cape Cod, local residents burned tea that had been washed ashore from the wreck of a ship bound for Boston. Boston itself had a second party in March 1774. Again tea was dumped into the harbor. In Greenwich, New Jersey, men dressed as Indians seized tea from the Greyhound, which had been turned away from Philadelphia, and burned it. In Charleston merchants dumped some of their own tea into the Cooper River, and some of it was stored in a dungeon and allowed to rot. In New York the Sons of Liberty turned tea ships back to sea. At Annapolis, in the most violent episode of all, the Sons burned a ship, the Peggy Stewart, laden with tea. And in Edenton, North Carolina, fifty-one women met and signed an anti-tea pledge.

This 19th century engraving offers one interpretation of the efficiently organized dramatization of protest known as the Boston Tea Party.

152

ably Revere himself made the decorations on the handbills —mourning bands, a skull wearing a crown, and a kind of cap which symbolized liberty.

In New York John Lamb, a fellow engraver and one of the chief organizers of the Sons of Liberty, was Revere's host, as he had been on earlier occasions. Revere attended a meeting of the group and found many of the members eager to protest the treatment of Boston. There was excitement at another such meeting in Philadelphia and in every other port up and down the coast.

More and more people began to realize that if Britain could force one city to accept taxation without representation, it could force all the other colonies to submit. In town after town citizens met and passed resolutions which they called resolves, objecting to Britain's tyrannical action.

Britain responded by forbidding town meetings. The answer of shrewd New Englanders to this was to hold county meetings, which colonial officials had neglected to outlaw. At one gathering in Suffolk County, Massachusetts, all the towns in the county were represented and all joined in adopting resolves.

At the same time representatives from the colonies up and down the coast were assembling in Philadelphia for the First Continental Congress. This gathering met in a large, new hall that had been built as a kind of clubhouse for the use of the city's carpenters and builders. There, on September 17, 1774, Paul Revere swung off his horse and delivered the Suffolk Resolves, to be considered with many others that had been rushed to Philadelphia.

It soon became apparent to colonial leaders that if they were to be successful in resisting tyranny they could not allow the British to have a monopoly of the use of force. Patriots began to prepare arms with which to defend themselves, and Paul Revere was asked to learn how to make gunpowder, a chemical compound which colonials might not be able to import. He studied the problem and set to work.

As Revere manufactured powder, other men collected rifles and cannon. Some of this armament was assembled more than twenty miles outside Boston in the little town of Concord. By the spring of 1775 a sizable store of arms was cached there.

On April 18 it happened that two revolutionary assets of even greater value were in the town of Lexington, which lay between Boston and Concord. These assets, irreplaceable really, were the leaders Samuel Adams, a virtual pauper with great talent for organizing and propaganda, and John Hancock, an impressive man who was as rich as Adams was poor. Both men were on their way to represent Massachusetts in the Second Continental Congress which, like the first, would be held in Philadelphia.

At this same time a British spy was being almost as industrious as Revere. He traveled about posing as an American patriot, and while acting as a gunsmith he had learned where the arms were hidden at Concord. He probably knew about the presence of Adams and Hancock at Lexington. At any rate, after hearing the spy's report, General Gage decided to send an expedition from Boston to Lexington and Concord.

Bostonians saw the red-coated soldiers preparing to leave. Although Revere did not know for certain what the British were up to, he felt apprehensive. So he consulted with young Joseph Warren, the most prominent leader left in Boston and a close friend, who happened to be wearing two false teeth Revere had made for him. Together the friends decided that they must warn Adams and Hancock and urge the citizens of Concord to take special care with the stores that had been collected there.

Revere quietly slipped out of Boston in his boat, rowed across the river, then continued on horseback to Lexington to deliver his warning, which was passed on from there to Concord. Immediately afterward he returned to Boston, but on the way paused to confer with leaders of the Sons of Liberty in Charlestown. There he arranged a way of signaling from Boston to Charlestown if and when and how British troops set out from the city. The tall spire of Christ Church—the North Church—could be clearly seen from Charlestown. It was agreed that Revere would have one lantern hung in the steeple if British regulars should leave the city overland by way of the narrow Boston Neck. Two lanterns would mean the regulars were starting across the Charles River in boats.

Back in Boston plans were made to dispatch a young rope maker named William Dawes with messages to the mainland as soon as the British began to move. Dawes was not known as a patriot, and he was a natural-born actor. By pretending to be drunk or half-witted, he might be able to get past the guards on Boston Neck.

By nine o'clock the night of April 18, Joseph Warren knew he should send Dawes to Lexington to warn Samuel Adams and John Hancock that British Light Troops and Grenadiers were crossing the Charles River. Thereafter, it was supposed, the troops would proceed on foot to Lexington to pick up Adams and Hancock and then go on to Concord to destroy the arms assembled by the patriots.

Joseph Warren (above) sent two couriers to Lexington and Concord to warn patriots that British troops were on the way. One courier was Paul Revere, the other William Dawes (right).

No one could be sure that Dawes could get through the regular guards Gage had posted on Boston Neck. And so Warren asked Revere to ride once more to Lexington by way of Charlestown.

Revere immediately went to North Church where, by prearrangement, a friend was ready to hang the lanterns in the steeple. There would be two of them, and they were to shine only briefly—no more than a minute. The longer they shone the greater the danger that the British would see them, suspect a plot, and start a search for the plotters.

From the church Revere hurried home for his riding boots and a warm coat. He picked up two friends to act as oarsmen and turned toward the waterfront where his row-boat was waiting. Now all was in readiness—except one thing. Neither Revere nor his companions had remembered

to bring cloth with which to muffle the rattling that oars made in oarlocks. Quickly, quietly the men moved along the dark street to the door of a house where one of the oarsmen had a girl friend. He gave a whistle signal under the girl's window, then whispered out the need for cloth. In a moment a flannel petticoat floated down, still full of the warmth of the girl who had been wearing it.

Now, if the men rowed well, they could move silently past the guns of the *Somerset,* which was guarding the river. With luck they could get across before the moon rose.

They had the luck they needed, and in Charlestown Revere found that the patriots had seen the lantern signal and were ready to send messengers to Lexington and Concord. But Revere, the famous courier, had arrived, and off he would go instead of local riders. His mount was good,

154

(Opposite page) Paul Revere engraved this view of Boston Harbor after the occasion in 1768, momentous to Bostonians, when British troops landed and occupied the city. The naval vessel *Romney* looms large in the lower right corner and is identified with the number 6. Above that and to the left, labeled B, is Hancock's wharf. On this page is a 19th century interpretation of Paul Revere's ride and a lantern that was hung in the Old North Church on the night of the famous event.

and he left town at eleven o'clock, warned that British patrols were on the road disguised as merrymakers.

At one point along the way Revere could see clearly in the moonlight a grisly iron cage. It had hung there for twenty years and still contained the bones of a slave named Mark who had been executed for leading a rebellion of other slaves. His body had been left permanently on display as a warning that it was hazardous to reach out for freedom.

Soon after this the brilliant moon revealed two British officers immediately ahead. Revere wheeled his horse and, with one of the officers in pursuit, raced away toward a bypass he knew. The officer's heavy horse was no match for Revere's swift mount, and Revere rode on, pausing just long enough at one farm after another to announce that the British regulars were on the march.

Revere covered the twelve miles into Lexington by a little after midnight, well ahead of the British and a half-hour ahead of Dawes. He was in time to warn Adams and Hancock at the home of a minister named Clark, a relative of Hancock's.

Minutemen who had already gathered because they had seen British patrols on the road were warming themselves in Buckman's Tavern. When Dawes appeared, he and Revere had a bite to eat, then they set off for Concord, accompanied by a doctor from Concord who had been in Lexington visiting a young lady. The doctor, a well-known Son of Liberty, was familiar with all the local roads. As it happened he was the only one who got past the British patrols. Revere was taken prisoner. But after holding him for a while, his captors decided to take his horse and set him free on foot.

Fortunately this happened not too far from Lexington, and Revere was able to return there by dawn. To his dismay he found that Adams and Hancock had not yet left. Hancock, who was destined to be president of the First Continental Congress, wanted to shoulder a rifle and join the minutemen on Lexington Green. Sense, however, prevailed, and Revere helped to deliver Hancock and Adams to the home of friends in a village nearby.

Revere then hastened a third time to Lexington, accompanied by Hancock's secretary, John Lowell. Their mission was to get Hancock's trunk from Buckman's Tavern. It had been forgotten in the excitement, and it contained documents that, if they fell into the hands of the British, would incriminate patriots.

Revere and Lowell found the trunk in the upper story of the tavern in a room that overlooked the green where about seventy minutemen were lined up waiting to face a much larger number of British regulars. At that moment the regulars appeared just down the road.

Lugging the big trunk, Revere and Lowell hurried out, across the green and past the minutemen. Then, only moments after they were gone, someone—exactly who has never been discovered—fired a shot: "the shot heard 'round the world."

Adams and Hancock and Hancock's precious papers had been saved. The minutemen lost at Lexington, but later that day they turned the British back at Concord. The war of the Revolution had begun.

PLACES TO SEE

MASSACHUSETTS

Arlington: Jason-Russell House.

Boston: Boston Massacre Site / Boston Museum of Fine Arts / Boston Tea Party Site / Faneuil Hall / Granary Burying Ground / Latin School / Old North Church / Paul Revere's House / Liberty Tree Site / Freedom Trail.

Charlestown: Starting Point of Revere's Ride.

Lexington: Buckman's Tavern/Hancock-Clarke House (Museum).

Milton: Suffolk Resolves House.

Watertown: Abraham Browne House.

Worcester: Worcester Historical Society.

PENNSYLVANIA

Philadelphia: Independence National Historical Park (Carpenters' Hall).

For more information, see Gazetteer, page 212.

This representation of the battle at Lexington is highly imaginative. It was drawn by Hammatt Billings in 1855, and shows heroic resistance by the militiamen. See also page 130.

Library of Congress

25

First Citizen of Maryland

1776   Maryland

Charles Carroll of Carrollton, a very wealthy and aristocratic Catholic, became known as the "First Citizen" of Maryland and was very influential in organizing that colony's support for independence and the Revolution.

From earliest colonial times the English government had considered America a dumping place for dissidents—for people who were out of step with king or Parliament or church. Separatists went to Plymouth and Puritans to Boston. When Lord Baltimore, who had been converted to Catholicism, asked King Charles I for a grant of land in America, he got it. Into his colony, which was established as a feudal domain, could go members of the Catholic minority, thus draining away from England another dissident group and assuring greater unity in the remaining population. Also the Catholic settlers, like their nonconforming predecessors in New England, could be turned to good use. They could do the arduous and dangerous work of opening up new areas, from which the English economy could obtain raw materials and to which it could sell finished goods.

So, in 1632 Catholics were given a place of their own, and their way of thanking King Charles I was to name the new colony Maryland, after his wife. But by 1649 the situation had changed. Charles I had been executed. Puritans had come to power in England. In Catholic Maryland that year members of the Assembly felt they had to take a step in defense of their faith. They adopted a Toleration Act, which granted freedom of conscience to all Christians, including, of course, Catholics. But less than a hundred years later Protestants were in control of Maryland, the Toleration Act was revoked, and the descendants of the original settlers had lost their religious liberty.

Catholics now had to pay twice the taxes that Protestants paid. They were not allowed to hold office or to maintain parochial schools for their children. Many thought of fleeing, perhaps to Louisiana, where the French were in control and where the Catholic Acadian refugees from Nova Scotia had been welcomed. Even Charles Carroll, one of the wealthiest men in Maryland, considered leaving. In spite of his six plantations, the large number of slaves he owned, and other very profitable investments, he was far from free. His wealth, however, did make it possible for him to avoid some of the effects of repressive Protestant control, and he decided to stay. He could pay tuition for his son, also named Charles, at an illegal Jesuit school for Catholic boys in an out-of-the-way place called Bohemia Manor on the Eastern Shore of Maryland.

After two years in this clandestine academy, young Carroll spent sixteen years studying abroad, most of the time in Catholic institutions in France. First he attended St. Omers, near Rheims. Here other Catholic boy refugees from both Maryland and England received thorough training in Latin and Greek. Charles enjoyed these ancient languages and the literatures they opened up for him. He also became proficient in French and well acquainted with French books and theater. From St. Omers he went on to study law in several different parts of France and then in London, where Catholic law students were not exactly welcome and where Catholics could not practice law. Wherever he studied he did something that not all Catholic men were inclined to do: He read the leading non-Catholic thinkers of his age—such men as the rational scientist Sir Isaac Newton and the radical political theorist John Locke.

Finally, in 1764, Charles left Europe and rejoined the large Carroll family in his native Maryland. Soon the small, slender young man began to call himself Charles Carroll of Carrollton to distinguish himself from his father, Charles Carroll of Annapolis; his grandfather, also named Charles; and from other relatives of the same name. By now his father's wealth was much greater than ever, and a few years later a census of his slaves showed that their number had risen to 330.

Charles Carroll of Carrollton now busied himself running a tobacco plantation known as Carrollton Manor, which his father had given him, and helping to administer the rest of his father's many enterprises. He became a good businessman and a good companion, particularly to the more intellectual men in Maryland, regardless of their religion. Gradually, though barred by law from holding public office, he found himself drawn toward politics. For one thing he was angry at being forced to pay a double tax because he was Catholic. He could easily afford the money (according to John Adams he was the richest man in America), but he objected to any tax that was unreasonable and unjust. Any arbitrary official acts offended him, particularly if they were

157

Charles Carroll of Carrollton, a leading Catholic, joined Protestants in supporting the Revolution.

NEW COLONIAL WORDS

English settlers in America created new words for things they found that were new to them or for things they invented. Often they combined existing English words to serve fresh needs. The process of shaping American English had gone far by 1776. In that year the following new combination of English words had already increased the richness of language on the western side of the Atlantic: backcountry, back settlements, ball ground (referring to Indian ball), beef cattle, blue grass, blue jay, bottomland, breechclout, buckshot, buckwheat cake, butternut, catbird, clingstone (peach), double house, fence rails, frame house, ground squirrel, hay scale, hoecake, johnnycake, land office, leaf tobacco, rail fence, salt lick, selectman, shagbark, shingle roof, ship channel, shotgun, sinkhole, slippery elm, smokehouse, snowshoe, spinning bee, springhouse, state house, sugar maple, sweet potato, tarring and feathering, tree toad, worm fence.

raids on the public treasury and would mean increased burdens on taxpayers. In 1770 the governor had engaged in just such an arbitrary act. By proclamation he increased the salaries of colonial officials, and the increase, of course, had to be paid out of funds locally raised. The money did not come from England.

So angry did this decree make Carroll that he finally entered a hot controversy on the subject. To begin with, a supporter of the governor published in the *Maryland Gazette* an article which purported to be a dialogue between two persons identified as First Citizen and Second Citizen. First Citizen gave arguments against the governor's proclamation; Second Citizen answered them.

Carroll wrote a letter of protest saying that First Citizen's arguments had not been well put. He restated them and restated them well. This letter he followed with more, all signed First Citizen. Soon everyone knew that Carroll had written the letters, and people began to call him the First Citizen of Maryland. Which indeed he was.

The letters—written by a man who could not be elected to any office because he was a Catholic—swayed the entire election in Maryland in May 1773. Opponents of the governor won an overwhelming victory. The newly elected representatives to the colonial legislature wrote a letter to the *Gazette* paying tribute to Carroll. When they met in July they declared invalid the governor's proclamation raising salaries, then marched in a body to Carroll's home to thank him again for what he had done.

First Citizen Carroll was no doubt pleased with the gesture, but he deeply resented the status of second-class citizen forced on him because of his religion. Certainly out of self-interest but also as a matter of liberal principle, he became an advocate of religious liberty and cast his lot more and more with those less well-to-do Americans who objected to arbitrary British policies. When General Gage closed the port of Boston, the citizens of Annapolis saw a potential threat to their own port, on which they depended for a livelihood. They selected a Committee of Correspondence to keep in touch with Boston and to plan joint steps for mutual protection. Carroll accepted membership on this committee.

From now on Carroll's involvement in political life steadily increased. By August 1774 he had become a member of the Annapolis Committee of Safety that was planning ways to protect the colonists. When the First Continental Congress met in Philadelphia in September, many of his associates wanted Carroll to be a delegate. But he may have felt that the presence of a Catholic would not help to unify the colonial patriots, almost all of whom were Protestant. Whatever his reasons, he declined to be an official delegate. However, he did attend the Congress as an unofficial adviser.

In October 1774, when the ship *Peggy Stewart* carrying a load of tea arrived in Annapolis, leaders of the community met with Carroll to discuss the problem. No one knows what advice he gave, but those who advocated violence prevailed. Someone set fire to the *Peggy Stewart,* and in this way Annapolis had its own tea party.

At the Second Continental Congress Carroll was again an adviser, and in the spring of 1776 he went as an emissary of the Congress to seek Canadian support for the thirteen

Mount Clare, Baltimore, home of a member of the Carroll family.

colonies to the south. One of his traveling companions was Benjamin Franklin. Neither Carroll, a French-speaking Catholic, nor Franklin, who was always a shrewd diplomat, succeeded in winning over the French Catholic Canadians. But this did not discourage Carroll. When he returned to Philadelphia he found that talk of independence was much in the air, although not enough in the Maryland air to suit him. Maryland's delegates to the Continental Congress had voted against independence. Carroll set about persuading them to reverse themselves. When they did—and when the Congress finally voted for independence—Charles Carroll at last agreed to serve as an official delegate. The day on which he was elected was July 4, 1776—the day independence was proclaimed. For the first time in his life he could be legally voted into office, and he began public service for a government that did not discriminate against people who shared his religious views.

Now, although he had not been a member of Congress when it adopted the Declaration of Independence, Charles Carroll of Carrollton added his name to that document. He wanted to join with the other signers, all of whom knew that they risked their lives by advertising their open refusal to remain under British rule.

Carroll continued in public service. He immediately became a member of the powerful Board of War, and in that post did all he could to give General George Washington support in the war for freedom.

PLACES TO SEE ✦

MARYLAND

Annapolis: Carroll Mansion / Carroll-Davis House / State House / Deshon-Cotton-Carroll House.
Warwick: Bohemia Manor.

PENNSYLVANIA

Philadelphia: Independence National Historical Park (Carpenters' Hall, Independence Hall).

For more information, see Gazetteer, page 212.   159

26

A Professional Revolutionary

1765–76   Boston

*Samuel Adams, one of America's foremost
agitators, although of upper class origin was a
real democrat who worked tirelessly among
both common people and aristocrats to
organize rebellion against British authority.*

A struggle between the haves and the have-nots swirled around the home of Samuel Adams when he was an alert and impassioned eighteen-year-old student at Harvard. Sam Adams' father, also named Samuel but always called Deacon Adams, was at the very center of this controversy. Not surprisingly the haves won, and Deacon Adams lost much of what he owned in this world.

The fight was over money. Farmers had land but no cash. Many townspeople owned houses, but they, too, lacked cash. And they all had debts. It seemed to most country people and also to many townspeople that they would benefit if they could use their property as security and receive for it letters of credit, which they could then use instead of money. The creditors opposed this idea. It seemed to them that letters of credit would be less valuable than metallic coin, and they were probably right. The letter of credit scheme would have helped those who owed debts and hurt those to whom debts were owed. The governor of Massachusetts opposed the scheme, and Parliament passed a law against it. The Land Bank, as the scheme was called, failed.

The controversy about the Land Bank gave Sam Adams

one introduction to politics. There were others. His father, a lifelong holder of small political offices, had created a social mechanism for influencing affairs in Boston. He had founded a club called the Caucus—a small group of men, several of whom were artisans or mechanics. Caucus members met privately, decided what candidates to back in elections, and then campaigned for them. Young Sam observed the workings of the Caucus, and when he was a grown man he kept it alive. But before he made use of it for large social purposes, it may have helped him get a small civil service post.

Working for the town of Boston attracted him more than other occupations. His father had intended him for the ministry. He himself had given some thought to being a lawyer. But neither the church nor the law held his attention for long. Nor did he care for business. He inherited his father's brewery, but he neglected it, and the enterprise failed. Finally he settled on a job as tax collector. Why he chose this usually unpopular line of work is not certain. But how he performed it is well known: He didn't do much tax collecting. Although he held the post for a long time, he managed to be on good terms with a great many reluctant taxpayers. This oddity is worth examining.

It would be wrong to say there was any single reason for his popularity, but one thing was clear. By his negligence he undermined the establishment, and many people liked that. Moreover, depriving the municipality of revenue was only one of his many techniques for overturning society. Sam Adams wanted the common people to replace aristocrats as rulers. He, more than most leaders in America, really wanted democracy, and he made a career of trying to achieve that goal. More than any other man in the colonies—except possibly Tom Paine—Sam Adams was a professional revolutionary. And he helped to finance his activities by using tax money he collected from those who could afford to pay. He was accused of embezzlement, and embezzle he did. But not for his own personal gain. He appropriated funds for a cause. The result was that no jury in Boston ever found him guilty.

Sam Adams was not only an embezzler, he was also an impresario. He took delight in discovering and developing good revolutionary talent. He nurtured committee members, demonstrators, financial contributors. It pleased him to help all kinds of men to see in what direction their greatest fulfillment lay, without making it a habit to step out front himself. Rather he tried to find ways of getting others to be leaders. However, he was always in the wings when actors of his choice were onstage, and he could and did step into the limelight if occasion required. But it was public service not personal publicity that interested him, and he looked anywhere for recruits, not just among his own kind. Although he was a Harvard graduate from a prominent middle-class family, he got along well with common people.

City dwellers today are familiar with street gangs and their rivalries. Their rumbles, their feuds, their petty infringements of the law are part of the texture of urban life. So, too, are their more serious acts of violence. But street gangs did not make their first appearance in the late twentieth century. They existed in many different places in earlier times, certainly in Boston in the 1760s. It was one of the great achievements of Sam Adams that he molded two rival gangs—one from the South End and the other from the North End—into a unified revolutionary force, diverting them from destructive activity into creative political behavior.

It had long been the custom for the South End and North End gangs to meet periodically for physical combat. Each year the big event took place on November 5, which in Boston was Pope's Day (in England and some colonies it was known as Guy Fawkes Day), when the Boston gangs held two separate parades from opposite ends of town. Each group of marchers hauled along a wagon on which there was a large satiric effigy of a pope. Costumed devils paraded in attendance. After a certain amount of marching around and general hullabaloo, the two gangs lit into each other with gusto, and mixed drinking with fighting far into the night.

As the 1760s advanced, Sam Adams saw political usefulness in these street brawlers. It occurred to him that the men and boys who were flailing about, full of dissatisfactions, could be led to deliver their blows against the causes of some of their frustrations. Quietly, gradually, Sam Adams substituted new targets for the gangs to attack. In time he had a force of perhaps 2,000 men who were responsive to his suggestions. What he finally suggested was utter rejection of exploitation by the commercial and political forces that were centered in London. He proposed revolution.

Sam Adams did more than organize. He wrote. Indeed he was a most prolific and effective author of letters to the papers, of pamphlets, of resolutions—all first-rate propaganda, which appeared under more than twenty pen names. What he wrote was usually geared to the needs of a particular moment. Long-range political theories were not his concerns except as he needed certain basic doctrines—for example, the theory of natural rights. Men had rights, he said, before there were any governments. If a government limited those natural rights, the government was wrong and had to be corrected. Another basic point in his philosophy was "no taxation without the consent of those taxed." Such simple propositions appealed to common people, for whom Sam Adams had need as well as respect. He also welcomed Blacks into the activities he stimulated, and he gave freedom to a slave his wife had received as a gift.

Adams was a well-known figure on the streets of Boston, often accompanied by a huge dog he had trained to snap and bark at red-coated soldiers. But he did not have a horse. In this respect he was like any propertyless laborer, except that a workingman was likely to know how to ride. Sam Adams did not learn to ride until he was fifty-three years old and then only because he had to travel on horseback to meetings in Philadelphia.

From small things to large, the list of Sam Adams' activities is a catalogue of answers to political problems. In 1764 he campaigned against one of Britain's perennial tax measures, called the Sugar Act. After the Sugar Act came the Stamp Act. Adams responded by encouraging an organization that came to be called the Sons of Liberty. This group included many artisans and mechanics as well as some pro-

In Boston, and also in Charleston, S.C., men paraded with effigies of the pope and devils on November 5, which was known as Pope's Day.

Samuel Adams, Boston's leading revolutionary, as painted by John Singleton Copley, a Tory. Nahum B. Onthank made a copy of Copley's portrait which is now in Independence National Historic Park, Philadelphia.

161

In the British Empire the parading of effigies as a propaganda technique was well known. This engraving from 1756 shows the practice.

fessional men. A smaller group called the Loyal Nine, under his guidance, was a kind of steering committee for the Sons of Liberty and other activist groups. These, together with a larger, looser group generally called the Whigs, plus the Caucus Club, were all instruments with which Sam Adams stirred resistance. And he was a regular churchgoer. There was only one organization to which patriots belonged and he did not: the Masons. Sam Adams disliked ritual.

It is not actually known that Adams suggested to any group the harassment of the Stamp Act official Andrew Oliver, but he may have done so. It is less likely that he proposed violence against Oliver's house and the Town House of Lieutenant Governor Hutchinson. Aside from finding rowdyism distasteful, Adams feared the severe counterattack that he was sure could come. But if there were going to be riots, he would use them. He would look among the rioters for leaders—leaders who would follow him. Some of those who became his followers were called Mohawks, for what reason no one seems to know. Others were Liberty Boys, for more obvious reasons. Militants all, they prevented the sale of the hated stamps in Boston.

Other cities had their own Sons of Liberty, and Adams, quick to see the need for joint action, urged all such groups to coordinate their activities.

In 1765, the year of the Stamp Act, Adams was elected to the Massachusetts House of Representatives, which was part of the legislative body called the General Court. This body had a certain amount of power, and before another year had passed, Adams had moved into a central position as clerk of the House.

As a result of pressure, some of which he helped to generate, Parliament revoked the Stamp Act. But in 1767 it announced the Townshend Acts, a whole new set of taxes on glass, paint, and tea. A wrathful Adams not only drew up resolutions against the acts, which the General Court adopted, he also encouraged women to brew substitutes for tea. Within a year after the passage of the Townshend Acts, Boston merchants, among others, were so active against the acts that the British government replied with military force.

When in 1768 the naval vessel *Romney* entered Boston

162

Harbor bent on intimidation, Adams mobilized support for John Hancock's resistance. In many other ways, too, Adams cultivated the wealthy Hancock. It was well and good to have mechanics and street gangs on the side of liberty, but the cause could also be served by money, and Hancock had that. He could and did give jobs—a thousand of them all together.

As a way of bringing pressure against the hateful taxes, Adams nurtured a nonimportation movement—a boycott of British goods. At the same time he drafted the Circular Letter, calling for resistance to the Townshend Acts, and this document went out from the General Court to all the other colonial legislatures. When the governor of Massachusetts, objecting to such subversive activities, forbade the General Court to meet, Adams organized an extragovernmental convention of delegates from all over Massachusetts to act as an instrument of the people.

Parliament and the king reacted to these alarming developments by sending troops. In 1768 soldiers entered Boston and took up quarters there. Popular resistance now escalated, and Sam Adams was everywhere, encouraging, agitating, scheming, making use of every complaint the people had. One of their grievances was the impressment of seamen. The effort against this practice ended in a legal victory, and impressment virtually stopped. Hostility did not. Working people continued to detest the sailors from naval vessels and the Lobster Backs, meaning the red-coated soldiers. Street fights kept erupting as Bostonians taunted the soldiers and pelted them with snowballs and mud. The Boston Massacre inevitably erupted from these encounters, and for Sam Adams it meant a new task. He had to convince the more cautious colonies that Boston was not under the control of a lawless mob bent on mindless violence.

As one means of shaping opinion, Sam Adams began in 1770 to develop committees of correspondence. The first of these was established as an official body by the General Court of Massachusetts. Other committees were appointed as part of the democratically controlled governments of towns in New England and elsewhere. Still others were extragovernmental. They all formed an intricate network of communication up and down the Atlantic coast.

Toward the end of 1772, after the Boston town meeting had set up its official Committee of Correspondence, Sam Adams drafted for it a Declaration of Rights. This document went out through the committees' network and soon was adopted in many places throughout the colonies. The Townshend Acts—most of them at any rate—finally had to be rescinded.

Mechanically responding to the growth of organized resistance and intercommunication in the colonies, Parliament in May 1773 took a step that prompted the colonies to renewed assertiveness. Insistent on its right to tax, Parliament symbolically demanded payment of the duty on tea. It might be thought that tea was a trivial matter and that a tax on this luxury could have been accepted in the colonies. But Americans, with few exceptions, believed that they would set a dangerous precedent if they let Parliament collect a duty on anything.

Just possibly the tax on tea might have slipped by without provoking a new wave of resistance but for one event in which Sam Adams was again the prime mover. He, as clerk of the House in Massachusetts, one day received a packet from Benjamin Franklin, who was then in London. The packet contained letters several years old, written by Thomas Hutchinson, the wealthy conservative lieutenant governor of Massachusetts. The letters, addressed to a man in England, expressed contempt for most colonials and for their desire to control their own lives—although Hutchinson was himself an American. To this day no one has discovered how Franklin obtained the letters, and he was careful when he forwarded them to Adams. He gave specific instructions that they should not be published and should be shown to only a few trusted individuals.

Here was a weapon against Hutchinson too good to suppress. Adams, without explaining how he got it, produced an exact copy of the letters, and then had this copy published. Technically he had not published the originals which Franklin had asked him to keep private. It was, perhaps, not a gentlemanly thing to do, but it was certainly practical. The letters greatly strengthened the will of Bostonians to resist Hutchinson and the British authority which he represented.

CLASS AND CLASS AT COLONIAL HARVARD

A student's rank at Harvard in colonial times was determined not by his grades but by the social position of the family from which he came. Take for example, Sam Adams and John Adams. Although they were cousins, Sam ranked fifth in his class, whereas John was only sixteenth. The reason: Sam came from the Boston branch of the Adams family, which was considered socially much more distinguished than the branch which came from the part of Braintree now called Quincy.

John Hancock, never noted as a scholar, was high in his class because his uncle was the richest man in Boston.

From the day of its founding in 1636 up to the Revolution a large number of the leading men of Massachusetts attended Harvard College, shown here as it was in 1725. The three buildings shown still exist.

As tension mounted in Boston
many protest meetings took place in Faneuil Hall.

Some weeks later the committee of correspondence in one of Sam Adams' many organizations, the North End Caucus, voted that tea should not be landed in Boston. This resolution immediately went the rounds of other committees of correspondence. Before the end of November 1773, ships bearing tea arrived in Boston Harbor. Sam Adams, at a huge meeting, offered a resolution that the tea should be returned to England. Now a complex tussle began. The boycott was so effective in Boston that the tea could not be unloaded,

CAUCUS

Caucus is a word of uncertain origin. It may have been derived from caulkers. There were ship caulkers in the group that met in the home of Deacon Adams. Possibly the word comes from Algonkian Indian sources. Many Algonkian words did enter colonial English, and in Algonkian caucauasu meant an elder, counsellor, or adviser.

There is still another possibility. The word may have come from Latin caucus, which came from Greek and meant a drinking vessel. The original Caucus Club in Boston met under the leadership of a brewer, and no doubt many a drinking vessel was drained while the club members made their political decisions.

nor could it be sent back to England without permission from Hutchinson, who was now governor. By December 16, the day before the final day for paying duty on the tea, Boston citizens held a meeting in Faneuil Hall. At least 1,000 people attended, some say 5,000. Even the smaller number is impressive, for there were only about eighteen thousand men, women, and children in Boston at that time. Sam Adams acted as chairman of the meeting which made one last plea to Hutchinson to send the tea back to England. When word arrived that he refused, Sam Adams uttered what was surely a prearranged signal. He said, "This meeting can do no more to save this country."

Immediately a band of his friends and followers, dressed as Indians, went to the ships at dockside, broke open large chests of tea, and spilled the contents into the harbor.

Sam Adams had his hand in the Boston Tea Party and in almost everything else that happened in 1773 and 1774 as tension increased between the colonies and the imperial center of power in London.

Once more Parliament and the king responded automatically and with great harshness. In 1774, what Americans called the "Intolerable Acts" became law. These acts removed from the Massachusetts House of Representatives— an elected body—the right to choose certain officials called councillors. The councillors were now to be appointees "at the pleasure" of the crown. At the same time the governor was given the right to remove and appoint judges. All military and civilian officials responsible for enforcing unpopular laws received special protection, and provision was made for trial in England of those accused of breaking the laws in Massachusetts, where juries were too likely to approve of lawbreaking. Local Boston authorities were obliged to find quarters for unwanted British troops.

Another provision of the new laws, economically brutal, closed the port of Boston. No shipping was to be permitted. This meant death to a thriving community. And to frustrate other colonials outside Boston who had their eyes on real estate west of the Alleghenies, there was the Quebec Act. This took away from speculators in both Virginia and Pennsylvania the prospect of western empires and gave the hope of a bright future to Quebec, where the inhabitants were not even English and Protestant but French and Catholic instead.

Reaction to the Intolerable Acts was immediate. At a town meeting on May 13, with Sam Adams as chairman, Bostonians adopted a resolution asking all colonials to oppose all trade with Britain. This resolution sped out through the network of committees of correspondence.

From now on Bostonians found it increasingly difficult to hold official town meetings or large gatherings of any kind. Meetings were forbidden. People could get together only if they kept the authorities from finding out their plans in advance. Knowing this, and also knowing that he might be seized at any minute and shipped to England to be tried as a traitor, Sam Adams took precautions. On June 17, 1774, the House of Representatives assembled in the Town House and locked the door. Then they proceeded to elect delegates to a congress of representatives from all the colonies—the First Continental Congress. Sam Adams was a delegate.

Tireless agitator that he was, Adams now prepared anti-British resolves that were presented to a local meeting in Suffolk County. Such county meetings had not yet been forbidden. As soon as Suffolk approved of what Sam Adams had written, Paul Revere rode with the document to Philadelphia, where the Continental Congress was already in session. There Adams, quietly keeping in the background, saw his resolves, now called the Suffolk Resolves, influencing the decisions made by representatives of all the colonies.

Even the choice of a meeting place for this First Continental Congress had been mainly Adams' doing. He had insisted on Carpenters' Hall—a building owned by artisans, private citizens. Thus, he reasoned, the workingmen of Philadelphia might be more easily won to support the cause of liberty. There would be time enough later on to meet in the official State House, which today is known as Independence Hall.

That was Sam Adams' way of working, and work he did, though not at earning a living. He was a professional revolutionary. Organizing and propagandizing made up his whole life, and he paid so little attention to himself that friends were embarrassed to send him off in his old clothes to represent Boston at the Continental Congress. They gave him a new outfit, right down to stockings and shoes, and they found tactful ways of filling his pockets with spending money. It would not do to have the intellectuals of Philadelphia or the planters of Virginia think poorly of Boston's leading citizen.

In this colonial cartoon patriots try to quench flames burning America while Britain's Intolerable Acts fan them.

PLACES TO SEE ❦

MASSACHUSETTS

Boston: Dawes House / Faneuil Hall / Latin School Site / Liberty Tree Site / Old State House.
Cambridge: Harvard College.
Lexington: Hancock-Clarke House.

PENNSYLVANIA

Philadelphia: Independence National Historical Park (Carpenters' Hall; Independence Hall).

For more information, see Gazetteer, page 212.   165

27

The Sons of Liberty

1765 New York and Charleston

*Beginning at the time of the Stamp Act,
semisecret, semimilitary Sons of Liberty
organized in urban centers. The Sons included
artisans, merchants, and professional men who
held militant parades, demonstrations, guerrilla
theater actions, and various forms of
sometimes violent resistance. One of their
contributions was the establishment of an
intercolonial communications network.*

Colonel Isaac Barré, an Englishman and a member of
Parliament, had served in America during the French and
Indian War. He knew, better than most men in the British
government, the temper of ordinary people on the western
shore of the Atlantic. Accordingly, when the Stamp Act was
proposed in Parliament, he spoke against it. Americans, he
felt sure, would resent it. In his words the men in England's
American colonies were "sons of liberty."

Reports of Barré's speech went off to the colonies, and
soon after they arrived, men who opposed the Stamp Act
began to call themselves Sons of Liberty. In Boston, inspired
by Sam Adams, they formed a group, also known as Liberty
Boys, and Paul Revere became one of their very active members. But Boston was only one of several seaports where
semisecret, semimilitary Sons of Liberty organizations sprang
up. All along the coast and in the inland port of Albany
and other towns, these organizations maintained contact
with each other. Except in Virginia, they were exclusively
urban. Professional men—particularly lawyers—some merchants, and many artisans belonged. Among them were

wheelwrights, housepainters, joiners, shipwrights, ironwork-
ers, seamen.

In New York three men led the organization—Isaac
Sears, thirty-six; Alexander McDougall, thirty-three, both
daring mariners; and John Lamb, thirty, an instrument
maker and wine merchant. Lamb functioned as an intercolonial secretary, and more than once he was host to Paul
Revere when that energetic Son of Liberty passed through
New York carrying messages between Boston and Philadelphia. Sears may have been the first to propose an intercolonial stamp act congress. And McDougall, the most
publicized leader among the Sons, was central in famous
confrontations with authority. Once when he had been arrested for anti-British activities, his admirers rescued him,
and 2,000 of them paraded him around New York with
uninhibited gusto. Thereafter the authorities handled Mc-
Dougall gingerly, but they did not abandon efforts to
silence him.

A second confrontation with the troublemaker followed
a strong criticism of the New York Assembly, in a broadside
entitled "To the Betrayed Inhabitants," which McDougall
was believed to have written. For what this document said,
he was arrested and charged with libel. He refused to post
bail, and while he was in jail, the political pot boiled. Supporters likened him to the English radical, John Wilkes, who
had been imprisoned for supposedly libelous statements in
the forty-fifth issue of his journal, *The North Briton*. A
great many New Yorkers began to call McDougall the
American Wilkes. Like the English Wilkes when he was in
prison, McDougall found himself besieged with visitors. So
many people wanted to see him and bring him food that he
set visiting hours. In his jail cell he was at home to callers
between three and six o'clock in the afternoon.

One day, with the forty-fifth issue of *The North Briton*
clearly in mind, forty-five men appeared at the jail, bearing
a side of venison on which was blazoned the number 45.
The number was also supposed to represent page forty-five
of the proceedings of the New York Assembly on which,
for some reason, "To the Betrayed Inhabitants" appeared in
full. Then on February 14, the forty-fifth day of the year,
forty-five men came to McDougall's cell, and together they
ate forty-five pounds of steak, which had been cut from a
steer reported to be forty-five months old. Finally, on March
14, came what was surely the most memorable visit of all.
According to the *New York Journal*, "45 virgins marched in
procession to the jail, where McDougall entertained them
with tea, cakes, chocolate, and 'conversation adapted to the
company.' After the repast, was sung the second part of
the 45th Psalm, 'having first undergone some slight altera-
tions.'" Just what changes were thought necessary in this
account of the visit of virgins to an amorous king is not
recorded. Soon after the episode a hostile critic, who said
his research was not even complete, announced that the tally
of virgins was in error. There could not have been more than
twenty-eight.

In spite of all these high jinks, an important question of
freedom of expression was involved. McDougall was accused of criticizing authority, and authority intended to
punish him for it. However, the government had only one

witness who could link McDougall with the offensive publication, "To the Betrayed Inhabitants." This was a printer who agreed to testify that he had seen McDougall reading proof on the document in question. Unfortunately for the government, the printer died before McDougall's case got to court, and he was never brought to trial. After several months in jail, he was released, then summoned before the Assembly and asked if he had written the piece. McDougall, refusing to be made a witness against himself, declined to answer. Thereupon he was jailed for contempt of court. Authority had shown that it had more than one string to its bow.

Other New York Sons erected what they called a Liberty Pole on the publicly owned common. The pole was a rallying point for mass protest meetings, and it also seems to have served as a bulletin board on which anti-British broadsides were posted. From its top, flags often flew—what kind is anybody's guess. One impudent banner may have been the red curtain that the Sons had pilfered from the home of Major Thomas James, commander of the British soldiers in Fort George. At any rate, the Sons did ransack James' home in order to frighten him, and in this they succeeded. They did run off with his red curtain, and they did turn it into a flag.

The Sons had their own flag—of nine horizontal stripes, alternate red and white. There is only speculation about the symbolism of the number nine. Perhaps it represented the Loyal Nine in Boston who directed the activities of the Sons in that city. It could also have stood for the nine colonies that had sent delegates to the Stamp Act Congress. At any rate, a nine-striped flag—flown by patriots—preceded the one with thirteen horizontal red and white stripes which Washington raised over the Continental troops around Boston.

The Liberty Pole had still other uses. Near it the Sons held trials of merchants who were accused of evading a pledge made by colonial groups not to import goods from England. More than one New York merchant thought it prudent to stop selling English imports.

The Liberty Pole, beloved symbol to the Sons, became a target for British soldiers quartered in Fort George. They had had to endure endless insults when they appeared on the streets of New York, and on the night of June 3, 1770, they sought revenge. They tried to bomb the pole. But the bomb did not explode. A few nights later the soldiers returned with axes. Liberty Boys got wind of the attack and quickly assembled. After driving off the redcoats they retired to a nearby tavern to keep watch—and to slake their thirst. By one o'clock in the morning no soldiers had reappeared. The Sons, weary and full of wine, went home.

Immediately, the attackers, who had been lurking somewhere close, resumed their assault on the pole and managed this time to cut it down. To add insult to injury, they chopped it into bits and piled the pieces in the tavern where the Sons had spent the evening.

The hacked-up Liberty Pole now became fuel firing new flames of patriotism among the Liberty Boys. Immediately they applied to the Common Council, the body which had jurisdiction over the commons, for permission to erect another Liberty Pole. The council, wanting to avoid

New York Sons of Liberty defend their Liberty Pole in this 19th century illustration.

167

trouble with the British, denied the request. The Sons, however, were not to be balked. They banded together and bought a lot near the commons. The council could not forbid them to raise a pole on private property, and the Sons set about doing just that. But first they took certain precautions.

They obtained from a shipyard a mast forty-six feet high. Atop this they fastened another, twenty-two feet high, surmounted by a glistening gilt weathervane made of the word LIBERTY. Finally, around the lower section, they placed strong iron bars up more than half its height and held them tight against the pole with numerous hoops of iron half an inch thick. No soldier would be likely to cut this down.

According to the *New York Journal,* the iron-clad Liberty Pole "was drawn through the streets from the ship yards by six horses, decorated with ribbands, 3 flags flying, with the words liberty and property, and attended by several thousands of the inhabitants. It was raised without any accident, while the French horns played God Save the King."

Battles over symbols sometimes gave way to pitched battles between Sons and soldiers. These encounters lacked only firearms to make them bloodier than the Boston Massacre soon to shock the colonies. The most violent of the fights went on at a dump heap, sardonically called Golden Hill. No lives were lost, but many on both sides suffered sword cuts and bruises. The Sons may not have come off with the honors in this brawl which lasted two days. But whether or not they had won the physical combat, they had gained a valuable feeling of unity.

This sense of fellowship extended beyond local organizations. The New York Sons joined similar groups in other cities to resist the tax on tea. In fact, New Yorkers took the lead in proposing to other colonies a general tea boycott. And they had their own tea party, but later than the one in Boston because the ship bearing the first consignment of the objectionable commodity arrived in New York some time

DAUGHTERS OF LIBERTY

In spite of the fact that women were not allowed to take part in political life in the eighteenth century, they found ways of making themselves felt in public affairs. At the time of the Stamp Act crisis some young women who called themselves Daughters of Liberty announced that they would accept the attentions of only those young men who were willing to fight against the act "to the last extremity."

During the nonimportation campaign, women in organized groups worked with great zeal to provide for the colonies cloth and other articles which had formerly come from England. Said one paper of the spinning they did, "That disagreeable noise made by the rattling of the footwheel was counted fine music."

Women also invented all kinds of concoctions made from local plants to take the place of tea. In at least one seaport they had their own tea party. On October 24, 1774, fifty-one women in Edenton, North Carolina, signed a resolution in support of the provincial deputies of North Carolina who had pledged not to drink tea or to wear British cloth. A huge teapot on the Edenton Green and a bronze tablet on the Chowan County Court House commemorate this act.

Women in Newport, Rhode Island, announced their intention to do without luxuries imported from England and asked men to forego "their dearer and more beloved Punch, renounce going so often to Taverns."

In another pursuit normally open only to men —political propaganda—one women, Mercy Warren of Plymouth, performed with vigor. She was the sister of James Otis, and she equaled him in brilliance if not opportunity to exercise her talents. However, she did write many letters, which were published in the Boston newspapers. She also wrote anti-Tory plays at a time when play writing was frowned on even for men in puritanical New England. Later she wrote one of the first histories of the American Revolution.

Mercy Warren's good friend Abigail Adams also spoke her mind on politics in no uncertain terms, but her pronouncements were less public. She directed her comments to her husband, John, and to other men who could influence the course of events. On the question of rights for women and for Blacks she was far ahead of nearly all men. She had this to say to her husband in September 1774, when it was discovered that slaves in Boston were planning to rise and seize their freedom: "It always appeared a most iniquitous scheme to me to fight ourselves for what we are daily robbing and plundering from those who have as good a right to freedom as we have."

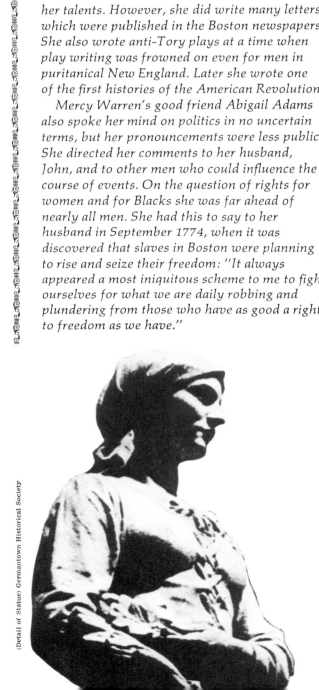

(Detail of Statue) Germantown Historical Society

after Boston had received a shipment. When the vessel did reach New York, the Sons of Liberty told the captain that he would be wise to get what stores he needed and sail back to England with his cargo. A committee appointed by the Sons saw that he did as he was told.

Just at this point another tea ship arrived. Men in New York planned to dress as Indians and dump the chests into the harbor. But their bit of guerrilla theater never came off. Instead a huge crowd gathered spontaneously alongside the ship when it tied up at the wharf. Men clambered aboard without ceremony and threw the chests over the side.

The first tea ship had avoided a similar fate by departing, while a band on shore played "God Save the King." (If the English national anthem had been "God Save the Parliament," the vessel certainly would not have been so honored.) Just to make sure that the captain really did intend to leave, Sons of Liberty, a good complement of seamen among them, commandeered a sloop and escorted the tea ship three leagues out to sea.

A little later the Sons of Liberty again showed their talent for decisive action. As soon as New York got word of the battle at Lexington, Lamb and Sears led the Sons to the Custom House, took possession of it, then seized a quantity of arms at a nearby depository. New Yorkers were going to be ready to fight if redcoats tried to sally out of their fort on Manhattan Island bound for any point on the mainland. The British military forces were prisoners in their own stronghold, and the Sons of Liberty dominated the rest of the city of New York quite as much as the government did.

The situation was slightly different in the busy harbor of Charleston, South Carolina. There the "leather aprons"— the artisans—had even less love of aristocrats than had their counterparts in New York. If anything, the Charlestonians felt more hostile toward men of wealth. Not one artisan sat in South Carolina's Commons House of Assembly. That supposedly representative body was in fact filled entirely with the well-to-do from the countryside or the counting-house.

Artisans felt the need to organize against these two strong groups, and organize they did. And one merchant, Christopher Gadsden, who came from a family of planters, helped them. Gadsden was already well known. In 1760 he had led a company of artisans in a war against the Cherokee Indians—an episode which had a complex history. As far back as the 1750s the Cherokee, under great pressure, had ceded land to white settlers. (One very large tract became ten of South Carolina's present counties.) Not long afterward, soldiers returning from tours of duty in the French and Indian War passed through Cherokee villages and grossly mistreated the inhabitants. The Cherokee in retaliation attacked settlers on the frontier.

The British response was a brutal campaign of extermination. To protect the liberties of his own kind, Gadsden served as an officer in the militia. But he soon grew bitter at the stupidities of the British officers, not so much because he respected the rights of Indians as because he resented the disrespect that the officers showed white colonials. His scorn for the British was no secret. He wrote letters to the South-

Carolina Gazette; he published a pamphlet. From that time on Charleston's artisans admired Gadsden, just as Boston's artisans admired John Hancock. Both these aristocrats were zealous patriots. And both, possibly not by coincidence, owned great wharves and warehouses, which would be more prosperous if England gave up her mercantile policies and permitted the colonies to engage in free trade with all countries. The wharf owners and the artisans had something in common. Both wanted to be free to expand their activities, and the same enemy—Britain—limited both.

Gadsden was well aware that the brightest future for planter, merchant, and artisan alike lay in the direction in which the artisans were pointing when they opposed British restrictions on the colonies. By 1769 he was ready to speak out, albeit not too clearly, in the *South-Carolina Gazette:* ". . . There [is] not . . . the least danger of starving, amongst us. Every man, therefore, who has the *constitutional* command of what is his own, . . . may . . . make himself very easy and contented. . . . But, when oppression stalks abroad, then the case is widely different: For in arbitary governments, tyranny generally decends, as it were, from rank to rank, through the people, til' almost the whole

THE GASPÉE AFFAIR

Most New Englanders took a dim view of the efforts of the British navy to prevent smuggling. Rhode Islanders particularly complained about the activities of the officers and crew of one naval vessel, the Gaspée. Officers of the Gaspée were unduly harsh in their actions when they boarded merchant ships. And Rhode Island farmers complained that men from the Gaspée stole sheep, hogs, and chickens and cut down fruit trees and walnut trees for firewood.

The highest naval officials in America ignored these protests, and Rhode Islanders were too impatient to appeal their case to London. Suddenly, one night in June 1772, the Gaspée ran aground on what is now called Gaspée Point off Warwick, seven miles south of Providence. Word of the accident spread rapidly, and soon John Brown and Samuel Whipple, leading Providence merchants, had got together a number of men at the Sabin Tavern on the northeast corner of South Main and Planet streets. (A tablet placed where the tavern once stood now commemorates this event.) In eight small boats the men rowed out from Providence, surrounded the Gaspée, captured and burned it.

When royal law enforcement agencies began to look for men to be taken to England for trial, they could not find anyone in Providence who could remember anything about the so-called Gaspée affair. The result was that no one was ever sent to England for trial and probable execution.

weight of it, at last, falls upon the honest laborious farmer, mechanic, and day labourer. When this happens, it must make them poor, almost *irremediably* poor indeed! . . . . Which, should it be unhappily the case, they cannot but know, they must then see it out, and feel it out too, be it what may."

The Sons of Liberty in Charleston seemed able to provide content for this last ominous and vague sentence. They did indeed, do a lot of feeling out and they were ahead of the Sons in many other places with proposals for intercolonial policies and activities. But for some reason they never became an actual part of the national organization. This proved to be a mere technicality. The Charleston Sons corresponded with other groups and generally acted in concert with them. And because they included men who were clever carpenters and wood-carvers, they had some distinctive ways of dramatizing their demands. On November 5, 1774, Guy Fawkes Day, when Bostonians paraded in rival gangs hauling effigies of popes through the streets, Charles-

tonians were not to be outdone. They, too, hauled an effigy of a pope along on a specially built movable stage, with a devil beside him—and for good measure, very recognizable likenesses of Lord North, Britain's prime minister, and Thomas Hutchinson, the Tory governor of Massachusetts. Whenever a citizen who opposed the policies of the Sons of Liberty passed this stage—it was parked for a while in front of the State House—the cleverly contrived effigies bowed to the passing Tory as if in gratitude, to the great delight of patriots who were on hand to watch the fun.

The Charleston Sons of Liberty also had their tea party, but there the affair was something of an anticlimax. It was less spectacular than the well-staged Boston party—not because of any predilection of the local artisans for restraint, but because the merchants to whom the tea had been consigned did the Sons' work for them. They boarded the ship that carried it, staved in the chests, and dumped the contents into the Cooper River. A Committee of Observation, apparently sent by the Sons, watched and applauded along with

After Lord North revived the issue of parliamentary taxation on tea in 1773, cartoons like this helped to stir up the political passions of the colonists.

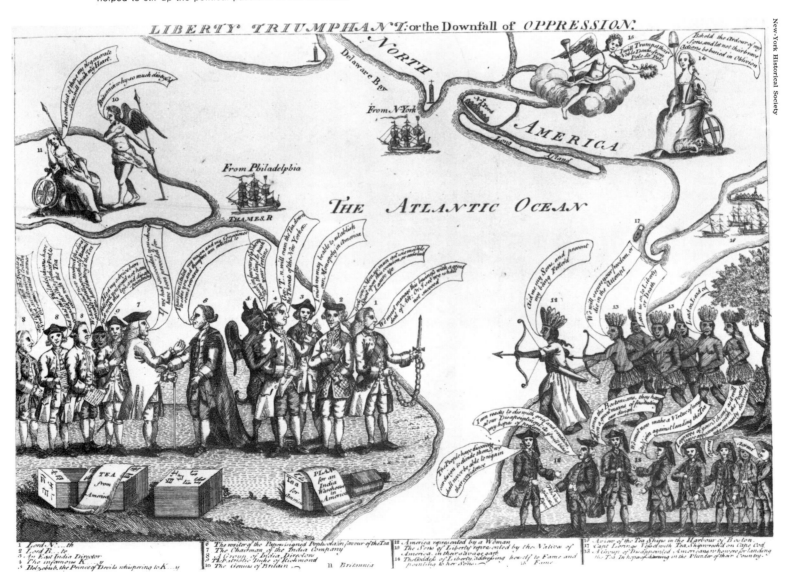

"the whole Concourse of People who gave three heartly Cheers after the emptying of each Chest."

In all their activities the Charleston Sons had the very vocal support of a great many common people—and of Christopher Gadsden. They also had the aid of the *South-Carolina Gazette,* a weekly newspaper which Benjamin Franklin had helped along many years before. An early editor was a French Huguenot refugee who knew not only French but also German and probably Dutch. He had learned printing from Franklin and no doubt a good deal of English as well. In Philadelphia he edited and printed a German language newspaper that Franklin published briefly. Later Franklin found another job for this printer-editor, whose name had changed from Louis Timothée to Lewis Timothy. Franklin sent Timothy to Charleston to revive the *South-Carolina Gazette,* after its first editor died. Soon Timothy himself died, and his Dutch wife, Elizabeth, carried on—the first woman in America to edit a newspaper. In time, their son Peter Timothy took over active control of the paper. (Remembering his father's early years, he named a son Benjamin Franklin Timothy.) Peter Timothy had in full measure the independent spirit of which Franklin approved. He was an ardent Son of Liberty, and he was imprisoned with Christopher Gadsden in Castillo de San Marcos, in St. Augustine, after the British captured Charleston. Except for his imprisonment outside South Carolina, Peter Timothy was mainly concerned with insurgent politics in his own colony.

Long before the Revolution, however, the Charleston Sons had strong links to the whole American scene. With their support, fiery Christopher Gadsden was made a delegate from South Carolina to the Stamp Act Congress in New York in 1765. Later he was one of five South Carolina delegates to the First Contintental Congress in Philadelphia. There he cooperated closely with the radicals from Boston, where the Sons were also strong. When the British closed the port, one commentator remarked: "Mr. Gadsden leaves all New England Sons of Liberty far behind, for he is for taking up his firelock and marching direct to Boston." Although he was not elected to the Second Congress, he was an early advocate of unity among all the colonies and one of the first to speak out for independence from England.

With all their colorful activities, the Sons of Liberty everywhere had opposed—when British actions provoked them—every limitation on American freedom. They were a kind of foundation on which the Stamp Act Congress and the later Continental Congresses were erected. With an intricate network of communications built up, partly with the aid of the postal system and partly with their own couriers, they became an early and very important unifying influence among the colonies. As resistance ripened into revolution, members of the Sons distinguished themselves in three ways. A number of them signed the Declaration of Independence. Many were soldiers and officers in the Continental army. And finally, when the going got rough and Tom Paine said "these are the times that try men's souls," very few Sons of Liberty switched sides in the brutal war. As a group they had a steady record of loyalty to the cause that called them into being.

Christopher Gadsden, Charleston patriot.

PLACES TO SEE

FLORIDA

St. Augustine: Castillo de San Marcos National Monument.

GEORGIA

Savannah: Tondee's Tavern Site.

MASSACHUSETTS

Boston: Liberty Tree Site / Paul Revere Home / Two Palaverers Tavern Site.

NEW YORK

New York City: The Battery / City Hall Park (Liberty Pole Site) / Federal Hall National Memorial / Trinity Church / Wall Street.

SOUTH CAROLINA

Charleston: Broad and Church Streets / Charleston Library Society / Charleston County Court House / College of Charleston / Gadsden's Canal Site / Old Slave Market / Provost Dungeon / Ramage's Tavern Site / St. Michael's Episcopal Church / St. Philip's Episcopal Church / Statue of William Pitt / Thomas Elfe Workshop / South Carolina Historical Society / Tradd Street.

For more information, see Gazetteer, page 212.

28

Conservative Rebel

1770s Virginia

*George Mason, temperamentally a retiring
planter, became an important behind-the-scenes
director of events that led to separation of the
colonies from England. Although ostensibly
a conservative, he articulated liberal doctrines,
some of which took final form in the
Declaration of Independence.*

The American Revolution resulted from astonishingly
varied expressions of the basic human urge to grow—to seek
means of avoiding restraints. Inevitably this expansiveness
led to collisions between colonists—and between colonies—
as well as disagreements between colonies and the English
government. And there were, of course, conflicts and contradictions within individuals. Some of these conflicts, both
broadly political and intimately personal, were manifest in
the life of one important Virginian, George Mason.

In personal matters Mason was conservative and ab-
horred change; yet he drafted some of the most radical
documents of the Revolution. Reluctantly he came to
believe that it was necessary for American colonies to break
away from the colonizing power that had given birth to
them. But paradoxically he was active at the same time in
an effort to establish what was really a colony of Virginia,
west of the Allegheny Mountains. He was a born aristrocrat
but wrote eloquently and sincerely in favor of extending full
rights to all men. He owned a large number of slaves, but he
tried to get others to join him in condemning slavery. He
was a loyal supporter of the Church of England. At the same
time he spoke out strongly for enlarging religious freedom

to protect members of other Christian denominations.

Mason has often been overlooked because he seemed to
be hidden in the shadow of his close neighbor, George
Washington. But Washington did not overlook George
Mason. On many occasions he sought his advice, and often
Washington and other Revolutionary leaders followed his
counsel.

What shaped this man of many contrasts and contradictions who in turn helped shape the Revolution?

George Mason was born and lived out his life on a
large plantation not far from Alexandria, Virginia, which
he inherited from his father, who died when George was
ten years old. George's mother saw to his education with
the aid of a private tutor instead of sending him to the
College of William and Mary, where other wealthy young
men went. An uncle who had a fine library lent him the
books of the great thinkers and guided the boy's reading in
the law. George never became a lawyer; he studied law in
order to be a better businessman and because he enjoyed the
ideas it suggested. He liked clear concepts anywhere he
found them, and he took a kind of fierce pleasure in following thoughts to their sometimes surprising, sometimes
uncomfortable conclusions. For example, theories about
freedom and equality that he found in the writings of John
Locke appealed to him personally but did not square with
his own use of slaves. As time went on he became more and
more uneasy about this institution, from which he and other
plantation owners profited greatly.

When George Mason was twenty-one, he assumed full
responsibility for the land and the ninety slaves he had
inherited. He did his own secretarial work and his own
bookkeeping and took charge of affairs large and small on
his plantation. When he married and decided to build a
home, he himself made the basic design for the house and
checked daily on its construction. To do the carpentry he got
the best craftsman available—a twenty-one-year-old indentured servant named William Buckland. The modest-look-
ing mansion they created—Gunston Hall—still stands as
testimony to George Mason's eye for detail. Although its
designer disdained outward ostentation, on the interior he
sought perfection.

While he was still a young man, Mason began to suffer
from gout. Painful inflammation of the joints often made
him irritable and impatient, and if he had had his way, he
would always have remained at home nursing his ailment,
reading books, watching his tobacco fields, raising fine
horses, and tending to correspondence that related to his
investments in wilderness land far to the west. But Mason
did not have his way. Occasionally it was impossible to
avoid the journey, made agonizing by his gout, to Williamsburg and Richmond. And there—in ways that were equally
painful—he had to deal with men he regarded as fools, who
did an absurd amount of talking and bungling.

Events seemed to conspire against Mason's enjoyment of
peace at Gunston Hall and concentration on private concerns. So, grumbling and protesting, he assumed civic responsibilities. But if he could he avoided tasks that would
take him far from home. More than once he refused to be a
candidate for a seat in the House of Burgesses, which met in

Williamsburg. He did, however, agree to be a justice of the peace in Fairfax County, where he lived. He also became one of the officials who managed affairs for the town of Alexandria, helped to build up the local militia, and served on the vestry of the local parish of the Church of England. In these various posts he got to know his neighbors and most of their problems—all this before he was thirty-four.

In spite of his dislike for travel, the day came when Mason let himself be sent to Williamsburg as a burgess. He served for two years, then swore he would never take on that chore again. He had had all he could stand of tedious meetings. He was tired of hearing windbags make silly speeches. He would waste no more time in politics—except to offer suggestions and submit plans and advice.

So far in his life Mason, like most other men in the colonies, had regarded himself as an Englishman. He was proud of being English, and he revered the achievements on behalf of liberty that Englishmen had made. But in 1765 there came an event that shook his faith in the judgment of those who were running Britain's empire. That was the year in which Parliament imposed the Stamp Act on the colonies. Mason was outraged. The Stamp Act was a departure from the basic principles of English law which he had always respected. As an Englishman who "adores the wisdom and

Culver Pictures

(Above) George Mason, a man of strong intellectual interests and retiring taste, built Gunston Hall (below) which can be seen today with its elegant interior still intact.

Gunston Hall Plantation

Virginia's patriot leaders frequented the Raleigh Tavern in Williamsburg, now reconstructed.

happiness of the British Constitution," Mason felt both obliged and privileged to voice his objections. He wrote an article for an important London newspaper and, one can almost hear him say, his arguments were sound enough to convince even fools.

Perhaps they did have some effect. At any rate they were among many protests of many kinds that came from the colonies, and Parliament did repeal the Stamp Act. But Mason was quick to see that Parliament had really not yielded. It specifically reserved the right to tax the colonies.

With that in mind he returned to his desk. This time he proposed resistance. He urged others to support the actions already being taken by the citizens of Boston, who had stopped importing British goods as a means of forcing Parliament to treat Americans as equals. Virginians, he said, must join with other colonials in the boycott until their rights were recognized. But, beyond that, they should use all manner of public scorn against anyone who continued to trade with Britain.

Mason put his detailed ideas in the form of resolves, hoping they would be adopted by the burgesses in Williamsburg. His neighbor George Washington took the resolves to the capital, where he served in the House of Burgesses. His colleagues adopted them with only minor changes.

The British-appointed governor of Virginia promptly refused to countenance such behavior. He dismissed the burgesses. Forced out of their meeting room at the capitol, they walked down the street to the Raleigh Tavern, where they agreed once more to support Mason's proposals. Henceforth they would boycott British goods and "load with every mark of infamy and reproach" all those who bought from Britain.

Now Mason felt strong pressure to take active part in politics, but he had new and compelling reasons to remain at home. His wife had died and he thought he should be with his children, and of course he wanted to keep an eye on his business interests and his ever-growing plantation. But events soon shook him loose from Gunston Hall. In 1774 British armed forces closed the port of Boston after the Boston Tea Party. Partly in response to this development, and partly because another move by Parliament had affected him personally, he decided to journey once more to Williamsburg.

What distressed Mason—and many others as well—was this: Parliament with the express approval of King George had adopted a measure called the Quebec Act. The colony of Quebec had recently been taken from France. Now by its new act Parliament granted to Quebec a huge tract of land that stretched all the way south to the Ohio River. This grant cancelled earlier ones, which gave parts of the same western land to Massachusetts, Connecticut, and Virginia. Within the new Quebec Colony—on the borders of colonies that were by law Protestant—Roman Catholics were to have freedom for their religion.

The Quebec Act was designed to guarantee that Quebec would side with the king and Parliament and not with the thirteen colonies to the south, which were increasingly rebellious. Moreover, the act directly limited the operations of certain colonists, Mason among them, who had invested a great deal of money in western lands. They had been granted tracts in the Ohio River valley, had built forts, and had begun roads, hoping to sell the land at a profit.

Mason had been one of the prime movers in this speculative real estate operation. The idea seems not to have occurred to him that the land was not for king or Parliament to dispose of. Nor did it belong to speculators or to anybody but the Indians whose home it had always been—and still was. In the 1770s no Americans of European origin were ready to concede that Indians had any right to land which white men wanted.

Mason saw very clearly the meaning of the Quebec Act, both for colonists' personal affairs and for the colonies in general. Here was a situation important enough to merit a trip to Williamsburg. Perhaps he and others could find a way to salvage colonial interests in the western lands.

Mason's search in this direction was fruitless, but something of lasting importance did happen to him in Williamsburg. He met Patrick Henry, whom he had not known before. Henry was ablaze with anger at Britain. His passion and his vision of an independent and self-respecting America stirred Mason deeply.

When he returned to Gunston Hall Mason immediately joined with neighbors in sending food and money to help Bostonians stand firm against British pressure. Then he set about drafting a new series of resolves. These were adopted at a meeting of property owners at Alexandria in Fairfax County on July 18, 1774. Known as the Fairfax Resolves, they were sent all over the colonies and served as models for similar resolutions. Again the most important aim of the resolves was to stop the importation of English goods. This would be a blow to British merchants, and seeking relief, these merchants might persuade Parliament and the king to revoke the measures which the colonies found so offensive.

Mason's logical, consistent mind went on to argue that *all* trade with Britain had to be ended—including the importation of slaves brought to America on British ships. One of his resolves called for an "entire stop" to the slave trade which he called "wicked, cruel, unnatural."

Most slaveholders disagreed with Mason on this ticklish point, but they, together with a great many men who did not own slaves, agreed that Mason had put their beliefs very well in the rest of what he had written. His influence spread, and the campaign against importation of British goods gained support.

To enforce the boycott, there had to be organization. An influential group, called the Committee of Safety, took on the job in Alexandria, and Mason grudgingly agreed to serve on it. As the crisis developed in relations between England and the colonies, a still-reluctant Mason went once more to Williamsburg.

Farther than that Mason would not go. He refused to assume responsibilities beyond Virginia. Specifically, he would not travel to Philadelphia, where delegates from all the colonies were to meet in the First Continental Congress. He did, however, agree to serve on the Committee of Safety for the whole of the colony of Virginia—partly because he wanted to keep bunglers and foolish enthusiasts from moving for independence before they had mobilized the maximum possible support for that step.

When independence came, as Mason was sure it would, new responsibilities would lie ahead. Virginians had to prepare to govern themselves. This meant they had to agree on what kind of government they wanted. To start work on a plan, a committee that included Mason was appointed. Now he had to attend committee meetings, which he hated as cordially as ever. But at night he could work by himself, and he wrote out a series of basic principles for government which were called a Declaration of Rights. What he had to say in this declaration—including his call for freedom of religion—generally met the approval of leading Virginians. It seemed to them a good restatement of the basic English principles of freedom they all had grown up believing in. But there was one exception. Mason's document said: "all men are by nature equally free and independent." He meant that statement to be an attack on slavery, and the other slaveholders knew it. They insisted on a change in the wording to fit their rationalization that slaves were outside society and hence could not be equal to those who were inside. Mason finally gave in on this point in order to get support for the rest of the Declaration of Rights.

On June 12, 1776, in Williamsburg, which the English governor had abandoned, the elected representatives of Virginia property owners approved Mason's declaration and forwarded it to Philadelphia. There it influenced the thinking of many delegates from other colonies and guided Thomas Jefferson as he did the main work of preparing a declaration for all the colonies to approve, announcing their independence.

So it was that George Mason contributed more than anyone except Jefferson to the document that marked the beginning of a great new nation. But Mason was not among the signers of the Declaration of Independence. He was at home in his beloved Gunston Hall with his not so beloved gout.

PLACES TO SEE ❦

VIRGINIA

Alexandria Vicinity: Gunston Hall / Pohick Church / Marlborough.
Williamsburg: Capitol Site / The Apothecary Shop.

For more information, see Gazetteer, page 212.

29

Order out of Anarchy

1775–76   Philadelphia and Boston

Wealthy Virginia planter George Washington shaped chaotic militia groups that had collected around Boston into the disciplined army essential to carrying through the military phase of the Revolution.

From the very day when the American colonies were first established, acts of impertinence, insurgence—even rebellion —showed in dozens of ways that people had the energy and the daring that go into making a revolution. But all was individualism and anarchy. Until about 1760, the drives available to produce basic social change were not directed at a common target—not focused, not organized. Then organizing began. By 1775 protest had taken on military form, and in order to have effective military action, someone had to bring order into the amorphous spontaneity that characterized the colonial militia.

The army that soon came into existence to serve the Revolution reflected the various colonial drives toward self-assertion. The strong egalitarian impulses of many rebels were engines that could produce forward motion, but only if they had tracks to run on. Privates in the militia needed more than anger against injustice or a high sense of patriotism. They needed more than the clumsy muzzle-loading muskets they kept over the fireplaces in their homes. They needed orders and practice at obeying them. They needed officers. Leaders were essential to give effective form to a mass of men who disliked the shape of society as it was and regarded themselves as levelers, meaning that they wanted all citizens to be on one level. They most definitely had not joined the militia in order to reinforce the authority of anyone over them. They had taken up arms precisely because they objected to authority.

In Boston the pervasive antiauthoritarian mood had expressed itself in various ways. After the closing of the port, June 1, 1774, citizens insulted and harassed red-coated British soldiers on the streets. Refugees from the city—and sympathizers—found many ingenious ways of smuggling supplies to the Bostonian patriots who remained in their homes. Meeting outside Boston, the extragovernmental Provincial Congress proceeded to reorganize the Massachusetts militia, in which some high officers were Tories loyal to the king. First the congress obtained the resignations of all officers as a preliminary to adding several new regiments. Then the militia units in each town were instructed to hold elections of new officers. These new ones, of course, did not include Tories, and they in turn chose a general, Artemus Ward, to command the entire Massachusetts militia.

Throughout the province in 1775, volunteer military groups came together for drill, and they collected and stored what powder they could. As the colonial volunteers became increasingly militant, brushes with British regulars were inevitable. A decisive clash came on April 19, 1775, when the British General Thomas Gage in Boston decided to seize the ammunition he was informed had been collected at Concord. After the skirmishes at both Concord and Lexington, the British regulars were forced to retreat without the precious powder, harassed by guerrilla actions all the way. Farmers armed with smoothbore muskets sniped at the redcoats from behind stone walls and trees, but their fire was not very accurate and two-thirds of the regulars managed a safe return to Boston.

Soon after this display of popular courage and defiance in Massachusetts, farmers in what is now Vermont engaged in bold action. Some of them, known as Green Mountain Boys, had been banded together for some time to resist wealthy real estate speculators from New York, who were trying to drive settlers from large sections of Vermont. The New Yorkers' claims to the land were flimsy at best, and men who had been working hard to build up farms were in no mood to turn their property over to absentee land sharks. Accordingly they took up arms and halted many evictions. After news of patriots' activities came from Massachusetts, the rambunctious Green Mountain Boys decided to do a little evicting of their own. On May 10, 1775, they attacked Fort Ticonderoga on Lake Champlain. Leading the Green Mountain Boys was Ethan Allen, a physical giant, a capable propagandist for popular rights and also for radical religious ideas. With eighty-three men, Allen drove out the British and occupied the stronghold, announcing with characteristic color that he did so in the name of "the Great Jehovah and the Continental Congress."

As it happened, Fort Ticonderoga was important to the British because it protected a communication route from Canada to New York. It was equally important to Americans because Allen captured a large number of cannons that were sorely needed by the patriots.

Reports of these encounters reached the Second Continental Congress in Philadelphia along with word that thousands of militiamen had gathered around Boston to confine the British army within that city. All this was good news. However, it seemed obvious to many members of the congress that one important element was lacking. If the colonies were to give effective answer to any large-scale British use of force, they needed an army and a man to command it.

There were very few men in America at that time who had experience at giving orders of a military kind. The officers of the militia were simply leaders in civil matters—in the church, the law, or business—with a sprinkling of artisans and farmers. In other words, the militia formations were commanded by military amateurs. In all the colonies, Charles Lee of Virginia was the only patriot who had had extensive experience as a commissioned officer in the British army. He had served brilliantly, as a matter of fact, but many did not altogether trust him because he was English-born. Moreover, he was an eccentric. In a day when personal cleanliness was less common than it is now, Lee went notoriously unwashed. His slovenliness did not recommend him to aristocratic gentlemen farmers among the rebels in the South, and his habit of enlivening his speech with profanity did not endear him to puritanical Bostonians or genteel Philadelphians. So, as delegates to the Continental Congress began to look for a man who could transform the individualistic colonial militia into a disciplined army, they bypassed Charles Lee.

One choice for commander might have been John Hancock. He was a good executive, and he certainly wanted the job. But the congress looked instead to another delegate from Virginia, George Washington, who had been attending congress meetings daily in a military uniform. Except for Lee, Washington had had as much military experience as any of the American patriots, albeit his martial life had ended years before, during the French and Indian War.

Washington could not have been so naive as to believe that the congress would fail to notice his uniform or to speculate about a military role for him. Still he did not really appear eager to take up army life or to leave the home at Mount Vernon to which he was deeply attached. He seems to have been of two minds. His uniform spoke for one of them. Mount Vernon was the voice of the other, and neither mind made much use of words.

Mount Vernon, seen here in aerial view, was the home of George Washington during much of his life.

It took an outside force to resolve the contrary tugs within Washington, and this force appeared in the short, stoutish form of John Adams of Massachusetts, who was the first to propose formally a continental army and a commander for it. Years later Adams described the brief drama in these words:

> I had no hesitation to declare, that I had but one gentleman in my mind for that important command, and that was a gentleman from Virginia . . . whose skill and experience as an officer, whose independent fortune, great talents, and excellent universal character would command the approbation of all America, and unite the cordial exertion of all the colonies better than any other person in the Union. Mr. Washington, who happened to sit near the door, as soon as he heard me allude to him, from his usual modesty, darted into the library-room. Mr. Hancock, who was our president, which gave me an opportunity to observe his countenance, while I was speaking . . . heard me with visible pleasure; but when I came to describe Washington for the commander, I never remarked a more sudden and striking change of countenance. Mortification and resentment were exprest as forcibly as his face could exhibit them.

Adams' recommendation was more than a polite gesture toward unity among the colonies. At that moment about 20,000 New England militiamen, mostly from Massachusetts and very loosely organized, were camped in a great circle around Boston, immobilizing the British army which occupied the city. The essence of the strategy Adams proposed was this: Individualistic, democratic, radical New England should turn its armed forces over to a moderate aristocrat from faraway Virginia in order to increase the strength of the colonies vis-à-vis England.

Washington hesitated before accepting the command. He doubted that he knew how to handle so many untrained men. He doubted his knowledge of strategy and tactics. He would be facing officers with great experience at organizing campaigns and battles and sieges—men who had learned all there was to know about the grisly art of war. Washington had administered a big farm but not a big army of fighting men. It was obvious to him, however, that little as he knew about running a large war, no one in America, except Charles Lee, knew more. With no sense of elation Washington accepted the generalship, immediately appointed Lee to be a major general, and set out for Cambridge to replace General Artemus Ward, popularly elected commander of the Massachusetts militia. (Of Ward, Lee said the general was a "fat old gentleman who had been a popular church warden.")

Before he had ridden more than twenty miles from Philadelphia, Washington met a courier who was rushing to the Continental Congress with news of the Battle of Bunker Hill. The militia, said the courier, had shown great

John Trumbull, American artist of the Revolutionary period, made this painting of the Battle of Bunker Hill which now hangs at Yale University. Dr. Joseph Warren is shown dying, center foreground.

courage and self-control under attack by professional soldiers. This gave Washington hope that he could create a strong army. Indeed it gave him hope of a larger kind. He was heard to say, "The liberties of the country are safe."

Within days after his appointment Washington reached Boston and began to introduce discipline and a hierarchical chain of command among the militiamen, who were camped in small groups around the city. All officers from corporal up were required to be efficient and honest, and several who lacked one or both of these virtues were quickly demoted.

None of the 20,000 men were in uniform, and none of them wore any symbol of authority. There was no way to tell officers from privates. Uniforms could not be had right away, so Washington designed symbols that were attached to the simple civilian clothes worn by both officers and men. Almost alone he had a uniform, and to it he now added a light blue ribbon that ran over one shoulder and across his breast. For the major generals under him he prescribed a similar but purple ribbon. Ribbons for brigadiers were pink. Aides-de-camp wore green ones. Field officers had emblems of rank in their hats in the form of pink or red cockades. The cockades of captains were yellow or buff. Sergeants wore a red, knotted cloth on the right shoulder. Corporals were distinguished by a knot of green.

Now, in spite of all manner of dress, a man could know who had to be obeyed and by whom. Obedience did begin, awkwardly and uncertainly at times, but the trend toward conformity was there, and military shape started to appear and to resemble in some way the shape of the British army with which it had to cope. The form toward which the Continental army was evolving was not as revolutionary as the objectives of the soldiers themselves. Indeed it was outwardly cast in the image of George Washington, who was among the least revolutionary of revolutionaries. Conservative though he was by temperament and lifestyle. Washington carried through his military assignment with complete devotion and with a certain flair.

Day after day in Cambridge he inspected, instructed, rearranged. He wrote to the congress pressing for a centralized supply agency. He sought canvas for tents. He pleaded continuously for gunpowder, without which he could not attack the British in Boston, and begged earnestly for money, without which he could not feed or clothe the men under his command.

After only a week at his new post he wrote "of the Difficulty of introducing proper Discipline and Subordination into a Army while we have the Enemy in view, and are in daily Expectation of an attack . . . in the mean Time I have a sincere Pleasure in observing that there are Materials for a good Army, a great number of able bodied Men, active zealous in the Cause and of unquestionable courage."

Washington was as zealous and as eager as any soldier in the ranks to end the occupation of Boston by what he called the "ministerial" army. But that curious adjective showed that his break with England was not complete. He preferred not to say that King George was an oppressor and that he was fighting the king's army. Rather he evaded. The king, he implied, was badly advised by his ministers who controlled the army. Perhaps Washington really hoped that if

When the Revolution started, few officers and fewer enlisted men had uniforms. As time passed more uniforms appeared.

In Martin, Horace T. Castorologia or the History and Traditions of the Canadian Beaver. Montreal and London, 1892, p.125.

he could drive the redcoats out of Boston, the ministers would adopt policies with which the colonies could live. Be that as it may, when powder and cannon finally reached him, he was ready—and he moved with quick, firm decision.

Just south of Boston was an eminence called Dorchester Heights, from which artillery pieces could send cannonballs down into the city. After careful secret preparation, which included the building of portable fortifications made of thick bundles of sticks, Washington ordered a group of selected men to move silently onto Dorchester Heights the night of March 4, 1776. Each man in this force carried out a prearranged task quietly in the dark, and when the sun rose the British were astonished to see, looming above them in the distance, an army well able to defend itself and to bombard the city.

This brilliant maneuver was designed to have either one of two results. It could force the British to sail away from Boston, or it could force them to come out of the city and fight against superior numbers in well-fortified positions. The bombardment began, and before long the British chose to leave the city. Jubilantly, Washington wrote to the president of the Continental Congress saying:

> It is with the greatest pleasure I inform you that on Sunday last, the 17th instant, about nine o'clock in the forenoon, the ministerial army evacuated the town of Boston, and that the forces of the United colonies are now in actual possession thereof. I beg leave to congratulate you, Sir, and the honorable Congress, on this happy event, and particularly as it was effected without endangering the lives and property of the remaining unhappy inhabitants.

The first phase of the military struggle for freedom had ended successfully. Washington had given the necessary shape and direction to the energy and courage of the citizen-soldiers. As ships carried the entire British army away from Boston, together with the minority of its population that adhered to the "ministers," patriotic Americans felt more than the thrill of victory. They felt a new comradeship, one with another, and a confidence that would carry them through to the next stage in their effort. They would sorely need the memory of their triumph at Boston. It would be a long time before Washington's soldiers—soon without powder again—would experience another such victory, but at last freedom was on the way.

PLACES TO SEE

MASSACHUSETTS

Cambridge: Christ Church / The Common / Harvard College / Longfellow National Historic Site.
Charlestown: Breed's Hill (Bunker Hill Monument).
Concord: Minute Man National Historical Park.
Marblehead: John Glover Home.
Watertown: Site of the 1775 Provincial Congress.

NEW YORK

Ticonderoga: Fort Ticonderoga.

PENNSYLVANIA

Philadelphia: Christ Church / Independence National Historical Park (Carpenters' Hall; Independence Hall).

VERMONT

Bennington: Site of Colonial Tavern.

VIRGINIA

Alexandria: Christ Church / Friendship Fire Company / Mount Vernon / Pohick Church / Washington's Grist Mill.
Fredericksburg: Hugh Mercer Apothecary Shop / Kenmore / Mary Washington House / Rising Sun Tavern.
Richmond: The Capitol.
Stafford: Peyton's Ordinary.
Williamsburg: The Capitol / The Governor's Palace / Raleigh Tavern / Wythe House.

For more information, see Gazetteer, page 212.

A 19th century artist's view of the evacuation of Boston by General Howe and his troops.

Brown Brothers

180

30

"Where Freedom is Not, There is My Country"

1775–76   Philadelphia

Thomas Paine, a thoroughgoing democrat newly arrived from England, put into memorable words the thoughts and feelings of most Americans and thus at critical moments gave enormous help to their drive toward independence.

"The period of debate is ended," an anonymous writer insisted early in 1776. In other words, more discussions with the English government would not solve the problems of the colonies. The battles of Lexington, Concord, and Bunker Hill—and the continuing occupation of Boston—had demonstrated that peaceful talk was a thing of the past. But "the appeal [to arms] was the choice of the king," the unknown writer went on, firmly adding that the American "continent has accepted the challenge."

Fifty pages of argument accompanied this blunt announcement, and the reasoning, the rhetoric, the imagery, the assembled facts all supported a clear call for a declaration of independence. The pamphlet, *Common Sense,* which put forth these arguments, became an immediate best-seller. Spreading outward from the printshop of Robert Bell in Philadelphia, it sold 120,000 copies in three months. Soon nearly half a million were in circulation—with none of the profits going to the penniless man who wrote it. Scores of thousands of copies reached common people no richer than its author, but the most powerful men in the land read it, too. Three weeks after it came off the press, George Wash-

ington in Cambridge had his copy of *Common Sense,* and its "sound doctrine and unanswerable reasoning," he said in a letter, moved him to give his first nod of approval to what he called "the propriety of separation."

Countless other readers lost their former doubts and hesitations and agreed that it was indeed common sense for the continent America to be independent of the island England. Nothing that had happened before in colonial history had been so convincing.

The man who with this one piece of writing gave sudden clear direction to the lives of three million Americans was Thomas Paine. He was an Englishman, newly arrived in Philadelphia and so little known either in England or in the colonies that the pamphlet would have been just as anonymous had he put his name on it.

When Paine stepped off the ship November 30, 1774, into one of the most literate cities in the British Empire, he had no literary reputation and indeed very little formal education. He had written only one thing—a kind of petition to Parliament. Very few people had ever heard of this appeal and fewer still had read it. There was absolutely no reason to think that Paine might be a successful writer. As a matter of fact, he had no record of success in any field. He had failed as a corset maker, as a tobacconist, as a grocer. Twice he had been discharged from a minor job as an exciseman—a kind of tax collector—the first time because he apparently disliked taking money from poor people. In all Paine's thirty-seven years of life there was only one bit of evidence to suggest that he might be a troublemaker—a fighter for a cause. After he went back to work following his first dismissal he acted as spokesman for his fellow excisemen when they sought better wages. For his efforts as a kind of premature union organizer he got his second and final discharge. Even in marriage, Tom Paine had no success to show. He and his second wife separated after a brief and unhappy time. His first wife had died soon after they were married.

The only thing of value Paine had when he came ashore in America was a letter of recommendation from Benjamin Franklin. The two had met in London while Paine was trying to persuade Parliament to increase the excisemen's pay. Franklin had sensed worth in this intense man, who was so concerned about his fellows. Moreover, Paine, like Franklin, had developed scientific interests in the course of a serious program of self-education and he loved to tinker with inventions. (Later in life he devised a successful iron bridge.) Nevertheless, Franklin's recommendation was cautious. He merely suggested that Paine might do as a "clerk or assistant in a school or an assistant surveyor."

Neither Franklin nor anyone else suspected where Paine's real talents lay. But somehow the owner of a struggling periodical, *The Pennsylvania Magazine,* found out that Paine had a knack with words. He hired the serious Englishman to write for him, and straightaway the circulation of his periodical shot up. Soon Paine was writing almost everything in the magazine. He had an uncanny way of knowing what people were thinking—what they wanted to be told. One thing they liked was political controversy, and Paine had arrived with a headful of political ideas. Some of these he may have got from his Quaker father. Others he certainly got from wide reading in England's most radical books. But none of this political theorizing, which was so attractive to him, could go into the magazine. The owner forbade publication of such material. Paine did manage to slip in one article that opposed slavery. Otherwise he had to keep to himself the thoughts he was having about the future of his adopted homeland.

Paine had been in America almost a year when his political ideas first appeared, on October 18, 1775, in an article for the *Pennsylvania Journal*. Then he set to work expanding his thoughts, and his manuscript soon required a publisher brave enough to bring it out. Such a man was Robert Bell, owner of a bookstore and printshop, who knew very well that he was handling unusually explosive material. It was Paine's friend Dr. Benjamin Rush who persuaded Bell to publish the pamphlet. Rush also suggested the title *Common Sense* for what he considered a very sensible pamphlet, seditious though it might be.

In aphorisms, which eighteenth century readers loved, and with a boldness that must have shocked while it de-lighted, *Common Sense* attacked the idea of monarchy in general. "There is something exceedingly ridiculous in the composition of monarchy," he said. ". . . The state of a king shuts him from the world, yet the business of a king requires him to know it thoroughly. . . ."

"Government by kings was . . . the most prosperous invention the devil ever set on foot for the promotion of idolatry. The heathens paid divine honors to their deceased kings, and the Christian world has improved on the plan by doing the same to their living ones. How impious is the title of sacred majesty applied to a worm, who in the midst of his splendor is crumbling into dust!"

In a simple, earthy way Paine went on to undermine the majesty of British monarchs in particular. Of William the Conqueror, he said, "A French bastard landing with an armed banditti and establishing himself king of England against the consent of the natives is in plain terms a very paltry rascally original." King George III was "the royal brute of Great Britain," and further, "a hardened sullen-tempered Pharaoh."

Tom Paine's words first urged independence, then built morale after war started.

COMMON SENSE;

ADDRESSED TO THE

INHABITANTS

OF

AMERICA,

On the following interesting

SUBJECTS.

I. Of the Origin and Design of Government in general, with concise Remarks on the English Constitution.

II. Of Monarchy and Hereditary Succession.

III. Thoughts on the present State of American Affairs.

IV. Of the present Ability of America, with some miscellaneous Reflections.

Man knows no Master save creating HEAVEN,
Or those whom choice and common good ordain.
THOMSON.

PHILADELPHIA;
Printed, and Sold, by R. BELL, in Third-Street.
MDCCLXXVI.

AMERICAN CRISIS.

No. II.

THESE ARE THE TIMES THAT TRY MEN'S SOULS. The summer soldier and the sun-shine patriot will, in this crisis, shrink from the service of his country: but he that stands it *now*, deserves the thanks of man and woman. Tyranny, like hell, is not easily conquered: yet we have this consolation with us, that the harder the conflict, the more glorious the triumph. What we obtain too cheap, we esteem too lightly: 'tis dearness only that gives every thing its value. Heaven knows how to set a proper price upon its goods; and it would be strange, indeed, if so celestial an article as freedom should not be highly rated. Britain, with an army to enforce her tyranny, has declared that she has a right, not only to tax, but "to bind us in all cases whatsoever:" and if being bound in that manner is not slavery, there is not such a thing as slavery upon earth. Even the expression is impious: for so unlimited a power can belong only to God.

Saying that "virtue is not hereditary," Paine gave readers encouragement to voice their own doubts about the throne. "In England a king hath little more to do than to make war and give away places; which, in plain terms, is to empoverish the nation and set it together by the ears. . . . Of more worth is one honest man to society, and in the sight of God, than all the crowned ruffians that ever lived."

So much for negative arguments. Paine then went on to put forward positive pleas for a republican type of government, responsive to (because responsible to) the people. Only with independence could America avoid involvement in Europe's wars, trade freely with all countries, and prosper by so doing. "But Britain is the parent country, say some. Then the more shame upon her conduct. Even brutes do not devour their young."

Only as an independent country could the united American colonies have diplomatic and peaceful relations with other countries. European nations could intervene to mediate disputes between an independent America and other countries, particularly England, but as long as America was part of the British Empire, such mediation was impossible. It would be meddling in Britain's internal affairs.

To the idealists and humanitarians Paine had a special plea: "Every spot of the old world is overrun with oppression. Freedom hath been hunted round the globe. Asia and Africa have long expelled her. Europe regards her like a stranger, and England hath given her warning to depart. O! receive the fugitive, and prepare in time an asylum for mankind. . . ." And "We have it in our power to begin the world all over again."

Such were some of the arguments in *Common Sense* that molded and gave shape to the hot, fluid anger and frustration of readers and formed emotions into tools and weapons. Now for the second time in his life, Tom Paine had turned into a spokesman for those who had grievances —this time for nearly three million Americans and not merely a handful of excisemen. In *Common Sense* he wrote his heart out—and he wrote so clearly and with such contagious confidence that overnight most Americans discovered he was saying what they felt, and saying it to perfection.

Of course, not everyone agreed with him, but even those who disapproved felt compelled to admit his ability. "A book called *Common Sense*, . . " said a wealthy conservative Philadelphia merchant, "seems to gain ground with the common people: it is wrote artfully."

Six weeks and several editions after its first publication, Paine met crusty General Thomas Lee in New York. "He has genius in his eyes," Lee said. "I hope he will continue cramming down the throats of squeamish mortals his wholesome truths."

Paine did. When Tories attacked him, he answered by writing a series of newspaper articles in the form of letters to the editor, signed "The Forester." These lucid, vehement pieces elaborated his arguments for independence and extended the influence of his ideas still more widely.

Thus, in ways that reenforced each other, Paine's campaign for a "declaration for independence" created a new mood everywhere. By saying the right thing in the right way at the right time he did as much as any other single person

Thomas Paine, propagandist and democrat.

to guarantee that the colonies would slip off the leash on which England had held them. Paine did not write the document which announced this separation to the world. But his work did strengthen Thomas Jefferson's draft of that vivid statement of self-respect, which was to encourage a great many people in a great many parts of the world.

Later Paine himself became important in the world at large. After giving invaluable help to the American Revolution (he continued to be a superb propagandist during the most difficult phases of the war), he went to Europe and became an adviser to Lafayette and other leaders of the French Revolution. Clearly, revolution was his business— the only one in which he was an unqualified success. He spoke truly when he said, "Where freedom is not, there is my country."

PLACES TO SEE

NEW JERSEY

New Brunswick: 60 Livingston Avenue (Paine Residence).

NEW YORK

New Rochelle: Thomas Paine Cottage.

PENNSYLVANIA

Philadelphia: Site of the Aitken Print Shop / Site of Robert Bell's Bookstore.

For more information, see Gazetteer, page 212.

31

"Great Easiness and Command of Writing"

1776 Philadelphia

Among Benjamin Franklin's many talents and interests one was of special importance to the growing movement which sought to solve America's problems by taking the road of independence. Franklin was fascinated by the techniques of communication in every form, and communication was essential to educating and uniting the inhabitants of thirteen separate colonies.

Benjamin Franklin found London an exciting place in the third quarter of the eighteenth century. Here was the very center of the world's largest politico-economic organization. From areas in India, Africa, and America that were dominated by Britain, ships brought raw materials to warehouses along the Thames. Cargoes also came from many countries in Europe. Ivory, tea, lumber, indigo, cotton, rice, spice, tobacco, hemp, wine, and countless other commodities poured into London and along with this palpable merchandise came intangible imports—ideas from all over the world. The mix of exotic goods and foreign notions produced a cosmopolitan atmosphere in a vigorous and growing city. Industrial innovations and scientific advances further enriched London life as English craftsmen transformed raw materials from abroad into products for home consumption or for export.

London's climate of invention and experimentation was pervasive and very congenial to Franklin, who was widely known for his own practical inventions and electrical experiments. He also loved the social life which the city offered in abundance. But none of these pleasures tempted him away from the task that had brought him to England. He had appeared there in 1757 as agent for democratically minded Pennsylvanians, who chafed at the inequalities and inefficiencies of the proprietary government of their colony. What they wanted was greater control over their own lives. Some of them—and for a time Franklin was of their number—believed that if they were governed directly by the king they would have greater freedom than they had under the hereditary control exercised by the Penn family.

At one point in his stay in England Franklin sought to have the king buy the rich province of Pennsylvania from the Penns. He made little headway with this effort. Nevertheless, Pennsylvanians asked him to remain in London to take care of their interests, and in time Bostonians and other Americans also asked his help. He became, in fact, an unofficial ambassador of the colonies to the British government.

As a representative of his fellow Americans, Franklin's real mission was improving communications between the distant provinces and the central power. Indeed communication was an abiding concern of his wherever he found himself. He had begun life as a printer, and printing is nothing if not a means of communication. Very early he had gone beyond composing type to composing thoughts that could be bodied forth in type on paper. He had become a writer, and here was communication in a most fundamental form. To round out the process, he established himself as editor and publisher of what he and others wrote.

In 1729 Franklin launched a newspaper, *The Pennsylvania Gazette,* and he wrote in its first issue that he thought an editor "ought to be qualified with an Acquaintance with Languages, a great Easiness and Command of Writing and Relating Things clearly and intelligibly, and in a few Words: He should be able to speak of . . . the Manners and Customs of all Nations." Franklin did not pretend that he had all these and other requirements for editorship. Rather he was emphasizing the importance he would always give to language as a link between people, and he modestly asked for help in achieving the best possible linkage.

Three years later Franklin brought out *Poor Richard's Almanack.* In this annual he not only offered entertainment and practical information, he also gave immensely influential advice on two problems that he himself often found difficult to keep in harmonious balance. On the one hand, he told ambitious young men how to succeed. On the other, he advised these same young men to be generous, civic-minded members of society. The fact that the two goals were frequently irreconcilable in the laissez-faire world was a problem Franklin never really resolved.

In his own continuing effort to succeed and to render service—more particularly to succeed while rendering the service of communicating—Franklin built up what was virtually a newspaper chain. He sent out to other cities apprentices he had trained in Philadelphia, supplied them

(Left) Among other things, Benjamin Franklin started the first lending library in the New World, in Philadelphia. (Below) A waywiser helped Franklin, as deputy postmaster general of North America, to measure postal routes and determine fair rates for the mail.

Rachel Folsom

with capital, and set them up as printers and editors—his partners in business. Within a few years he was involved in papers in South Carolina, Rhode Island, New York, and New Jersey. In Pennsylvania, he had not only the *Gazette,* but also for a while a German-language newspaper in Philadelphia and another paper in Lancaster. His interest also extended to the British West Indies, where he was a partner in papers in Antigua, Jamaica, and Dominica.

Since paper was essential for the printed word, Franklin interested himself in several paper mills near Philadelphia. He also was in the ink-making business. That was not all. Words, to serve their purpose, had to get from the creating writers to the consuming readers. This required a postal service that would carry not only private letters but also printed newspapers. Franklin became a postmaster, first in Philadelphia in 1737, then in the colonies generally in 1751. In 1753, by royal appointment, he was made a deputy postmaster general, one of two in the American colonies. With great attention to detail he set about making the postal service as efficient as it could be in days when horses provided the fastest means of transportation. He personally

covered most of the mail routes in the New England colonies, where his special responsibilities lay. With an odometer, or waywiser, he measured distances on rough country roads, searching out the shortest routes for riders who carried the mail. Then he ordered milestones set up so that it would be possible to charge postal fees based on mileage.

For some years Franklin ran a bookshop, and because there was a scarcity of good books in America, he thought of a way to get the maximum circulation for each of the precious volumes that did exist. He established the first lending library in the colonies. From Philadelphia, this institution spread to other cities.

Bringing people together by means of the ideas in books, the personal feelings in letters, and the news in gazettes was a matter of direct human concern to Franklin. It was also a matter of business, and business required channels through which people could exchange products and services in peace. Franklin wanted a secure area within which Pennsylvanians —indeed all colonials—could live and conduct their economic affairs. In 1754, at a time when Indians were trying

185

to drive Englishmen away from their lands and when the French were equally interested in preventing English expansion, Franklin was sent to an intercolonial conference on defense. Ever curious, he began to wonder about the secret of governmental strength of some of the Indians. In preparing for the conference, which met in Albany, New York, he looked into the structure of the Iroquois alliance. It was, he found, obviously stable, and there were elements in it that the colonies themselves might well adopt. With this in mind Franklin drafted a proposal for a colonial structure, partly modeled on the Iroquois League. In essence, his plan, which came to be called the Albany Union, provided for closer federation of the colonies for their mutual protection and advantage.

This Albany Union was approved by all the delegates at the conference. But it was not acceptable to any of the colonial governments. Each one felt it would be giving up too much power if it joined with the others. At the same time the English government objected to the plan because it would give too much power to the united colonies. So Franklin's plan came to nothing, but it did show the direction in which his mind was working.

If intercolonial cooperation was not to be the answer to Indian attacks on frontier settlements, what could be done? Words—on which Franklin always placed great reliance—seemed unequal to the task of making an arrangement acceptable both to the Indians who possessed the land and to the Englishmen who wanted it for their expanding way of life. As matters stood in the continuing confrontation between the capitalist economy of the Englishmen and the noncapitalist economy of the Indians, there was no way to satisfy both parties. Franklin now did what lesser men usually do when faced with such a dilemma. He fell back on the use of force. Ironically, he, a believer in the efficiency of reason and good humor, advocated brutality—specifically the use of dogs to track down Indians, and the payment of bounties for the scalps of any Indian men, women, or children who had been exterminated. In this outburst of savagery against people he called savages, Franklin, the compassionate man of reason, poignantly revealed one of the central contradictions of American life. In the good and necessary business of providing freedom for white men, the world of private enterprise offered no alternative to the destruction or subjugation of nonwhite men.

After six years in England, Franklin returned to Philadelphia at the time of Pontiac's War. Almost immediately he found himself again concerned with the unsolved problems of the relationship between whites and Indians. A considerable number of white men, known as the Paxton Boys because some of them were from Paxton, Pennsylvania, had become embittered on two counts. They felt that the well-protected government in Philadelphia was not giving them sufficient protection against the Indians. They also thought, with justice, that they were inadequately represented in the Pennsylvania legislature.

In an act of mindless cruelty, these Paxton Boys at-

This 19th century engraving shows Franklin as agent of the colonies in England's court.

tacked and massacred some Conestoga Indians who had been living in peace as largely acculturated residents of Pennsylvania. The frontiersmen then marched on Philadelphia to force their demands on the legislature and to kill off Indians who had taken refuge in the city. Franklin, newly arrived from England, was sent out to reason with them. He had moved beyond his own proposals for annihilating Indians—made less than ten years before, and was aghast at the slaughter of the Conestoga. But he shared the Paxton Boys' resentment at the undemocratic structure of the Pennsylvania government. And quite probably because of his own anti-proprietary attitudes, he was able to persuade the angry frontiersmen to rely on words rather than guns. They drew up a petition and returned to their homes.

Soon after his diplomacy had saved Philadelphia from what might well have been an armed attack, Franklin was returned to London as agent for the Pennsylvania Assembly. There, once again he patiently dined and wined with men of influence, trying to win friends in high places who would support reforms in the colonial government, trying to provide opportunities for the kind of economy that he believed the rich American continent could support. And over the years he became more and more the representative, not only of Pennsylvania but of American colonies generally.

In 1765 he opposed the passage of the Stamp Act. As a publisher he saw the restrictive effect this tax would have on all forms of printed communication. As a businessman he disapproved of taxes on legal documents. These would slow

the rate of commerce. As a citizen he objected to the tax as an invasion of basic rights. He did what he could to keep the Stamp Act from becoming law, but his lobbying efforts failed.

Franklin now reasoned that it would be better for the empire if Americans, not Englishmen, enforced the act. He nominated a Philadelphian to distribute the tax stamps in his home city, and by so doing, he showed how poor communications were across the Atlantic Ocean. America's resistance to the act was much greater than his information led him to think it would be. But when he found out the facts, he appeared before Parliament—although he disliked public speaking—and urged repeal of the offensive legislation. Parliament listened to the respected American—and to the evidence of great popular resentment—and withdrew the Stamp Act.

Although this particular tax ceased to be a problem, other obstacles to communication and to business remained, and new difficulties appeared. To deal with them, Franklin stayed on in London, using his immense prestige and skill in a variety of efforts, all of which were aimed at reforming the British Empire so that the American colonies could prosper and be comfortable within it. Separation from England was not his goal. Instead he sought improved relations based on increasing participation of the colonies in making decisions on matters that affected them.

Ever respectful of democratic processes and of the importance of facts, Franklin welcomed the efforts of New England town meetings to communicate the feelings of the citizenry to the British government. He was zealous in forwarding petitions to government authorities and tried to solve problems by using good sense and good humor. But as time passed he began to despair and took more and more drastic steps, hoping thus to relieve tensions. One such step had unhappy consequences, although it was intended to convince key political leaders in Boston that the king and Parliament were not solely to blame for all of Boston's problems. The fact was that some of the town's difficulties were caused by important Bostonians who asked the British government to take oppressive measures. As proof of this point Franklin sent, in the winter of 1772–73, to good friends in Boston, a number of letters he had somehow got hold of. Some of the letters were from Governor Hutchinson, others from Andrew Oliver, an important official. Both those Americans had suggested to a prominent Englishman that strong measures be taken in order to bring Bostonians into line with British policy.

The content of the Hutchinson-Oliver letters became public knowledge. But instead of reducing tensions, they increased hostilities both in America and in England. Franklin himself was subjected to extreme abuse from leaders of the British government. In effect, these aristocrats made it very clear that they thought Franklin had not acted like a gentleman when he circulated private correspondence he had come by in some surreptitious way. Franklin, in his own view, had been trying to communicate important information. He always believed that facts should be known and that policies should be based on them. These considerations took precedence over niceties of etiquette, but he had not guessed

187

what uproar his eighteenth century Pentagon Papers escapade would create. And he certainly had not wanted to increase the steadily hardening rigidity of the imperial government.

As a kind of desperate act, Franklin wrote and published two satires that were widely read and warmly approved by friends of America, of whom there were many in England. One of these bitter attacks on governmental policy was called *Rules by which a Great Empire may be reduced to a small one.* In it Franklin said, addressing the king's ministers, "You are to consider that a great empire, like a great cake, is most easily diminished at the edges." The twenty "rules" that he set forth summed up the British stupidities which would indeed break up an empire: greedy governors and judges, harassment by "novel taxes," denial of constitutional rights, haughty rejection of petitions ("though many can forgive injuries," he said, "none ever forgive contempt"), and so on through the grievances of the colonies.

In his other pamphlet, called *An Edict by the King of Prussia,* Franklin lectured King George, satirically propos-

BENJAMIN FRANKLIN —INNOVATOR

No one who helped to shape the American Revolution was more complex—or more creative —than Benjamin Franklin. Here is a partial tally of his initiatives:

He made the first important American contribution to the science of economics, laid the foundations of the State Department, and served as the first United States ambassador to a foreign country.

He founded or helped to found or introduce: the United States postal system; the dead letter office in the postal system; the first American anti-slavery society; the first American debating society; the American Philosophical Society; the University of Pennsylvania; the Philadelphia Fire Company; the first American fire insurance company; the Pennsylvania Hospital; the Philadelphia Society for the Promotion of Agriculture; the Free Library of Philadelphia; subscription libraries in Philadelphia, New York, Newport, Charleston; street paving; street cleaning; street lighting; the rutabaga; and a type of willow tree useful in basket-making.

He discovered that lightning is a form of electricity.

He invented the lightning rod, the Franklin stove, the smokeless chimney, bifocal lenses, a musical instrument called the armonica.

He encouraged the use of mineral fertilizer, the use of plaster in house construction, the construction of ships with watertight compartments, and the culture of silk worms.

ing that the king of Prussia could send orders to England because long ago people from Germany had moved to England and settled there.

After these strong statements appeared, Franklin soon left London. He, a believer in peaceful petition, had reluctantly decided that it would take more than words to achieve the legitimate goals of the colonies. In April 1775 he was on the high seas bound for Philadelphia. At about the time when British troops were marching out of Boston against Lexington and Concord, he was busy dropping a thermometer into the ocean waters to find out what he could about the Gulf Stream, which is warmer than the Atlantic Ocean in which its current flows. He believed that information about the temperature of the Gulf Stream would help him to chart its course. This knowledge might then make it possible for ships to take advantage of the current and thus to speed up communication between America and England.

On May 6, 1775, the day after Franklin landed in Philadelphia, he was made a delegate to the Continental Congress, which was scheduled to open four days later. Events were now tumbling rapidly one over another, announcing, if nothing else did, that a crisis was at hand. In congress, Franklin was the most experienced in diplomacy and the only one with any knowledge of intercolonial administration. Although he had reached an age when most men retire, he was immediately involved in the work of many committees. One of them made him director of the continental network of communication by mail. Other assignments required him to draft petitions on London. On November 29, he was put on a committee, secret in nature, that was instructed to communicate discreetly with the governments of France and Spain, whose support would be essential if American colonies declared their independence from England. This Committee of Secret Correspondence immediately began its delicate work, and out of it in time developed what is known today as the Department of State.

A secret agent from France appeared in Philadelphia in response to the feelers that had been sent out. Franklin, the most prominent man in the city, somehow managed to deal with him privately and to begin the negotiations for arms that would be needed if Americans were to resist successfully the British force that was now being used against them.

The Committee of Secret Correspondence also sent an agent, Silas Deane, to France. Franklin wrote out very detailed instructions. Deane was to pose as a merchant in search of goods for the Indian trade. He was to seek out influential men who were friendly to America, and, if possible, to buy munitions and clothing for a force of 25,000 men. Also he was to find out France's attitude toward American independence and an exchange of ambassadors.

Franklin, who had long hoped that America's future could be assured within the empire, now began with all his energy and talent to provide for America's future outside the empire. Early in the spring of 1776 he set out on a long journey in quest of allies. With him were three other men, all young enough to be his sons. Two were Catholic supporters of independence from Maryland—Charles Carroll of Carrollton and his cousin John Carroll, a Jesuit priest. The third, also from Maryland, was Samuel Chase. Riding part of the way on horseback, traveling part of the way on an open barge, where he had to sleep outdoors on the chilly April nights, Franklin made his way to the Catholic city of Quebec. But even the two Carrolls could not persuade Canadians to support the rebellious colonies. The Canadians remembered too well the long anti-Catholic record of the Protestant Americans to the south.

Franklin had never approved any of the religious persecutions practiced by his countrymen. He hated religious bigotry, but because it existed he returned to Philadelphia empty-handed. The long journey had wearied him. He was seventy years old and ill, but he accepted a position on one more committee. This one was charged with telling the world why Americans felt they had no choice but to declare their independence. At this critical moment, Franklin was concerned as always with communication, but he must have felt relief that Thomas Jefferson was to do the writing he himself did not feel well enough to undertake.

While congress was debating and amending Jefferson's draft of the Declaration of Independence, Franklin saw that the younger man was acutely uncomfortable. Jefferson has preserved the story:

> I was sitting by Dr. Franklin, who perceived that I was not insensible to these mutilations. "I have made it a rule," said he, "whenever in my power, to avoid becoming the draftsman of papers to be reviewed by a public body. I took my lesson from an incident which I will relate to you. When I was a journeyman printer one of my companions, an apprentice hatter, having served out his time was about to open shop for himself. His first concern was to have a handsome signboard with a proper inscription. He composed it in these words: 'John Thompson, hatter, makes and sells hats for ready money,' with a figure of a hat subjoined. But he thought he would submit it to his friends for their amendments. The first he showed it to thought the word 'hatter' tautologous, because followed by the words 'makes hats' which show he was a hatter. It was struck out. The next observed that the word 'makes' might as well be omitted, because the customers would not care who made the hats. If good and to their mind, they would buy, by whomever made. He struck it out. A third said he thought the words 'for ready money' were useless, as it was not the custom of the place to sell on credit. Everyone who purchased expected to pay. They were parted with, and the inscription now stood: 'John Thompson sells hats.' 'Sells hats?' says his next friend. 'Why, nobody will expect you to give them away. What then is the use of that word?' It was stricken out; and 'hats' followed it, the rather as there was one painted on the board. So his inscription was reduced ultimately to 'John Thompson' with the figure of a hat subjoined."

Jefferson may have sensed Franklin's never-ending interest in literary technique. But more than that he was aware of Franklin's sympathetic understanding. There was a strong bond between the aged Philadelphian and the young Virginian. These two profoundly intellectual men, among the greatest in the world at the time, both wanted to advance humankind through intelligence and democracy and capitalist expansion. They were both deists—that is, their religion

rejected, while tolerating, the many forms of more conventional religion. It may have been Franklin who proposed the motto that Jefferson adopted as his own: "Rebellion to tyrants is obedience to God."

"He Snatches the Lightning from the Sky and the Sword from the Tyrant" is the title of this 1780 allegorical engraving by the French artist Jean Honoré Fragonard.

PLACES TO SEE

NEW HAMPSHIRE

Portsmouth: Warner House.

NEW JERSEY

Burlington: Governor Franklin Estate / Site of Samuel Jennings Office / Thomas Revel House.
Perth Amboy: The Westminster (William Franklin House).

NEW YORK

Albany: Schuyler Mansion.
Yonkers: Philipse Manor Hall.

PENNSYLVANIA

Lancaster: Site of the Old Jail / Franklin and Marshall College.
Philadelphia: Site of Franklin's First Printing Office / Sites of Franklin's Houses / Franklin Institute / Keimer's Print Shop / Independence National Historical Park / Christ Church / Christ Church Cemetery / Indian King Tavern Site / Library Company of Philadelphia / Pewter Platter Inn Site / Site of Philadelphia Contributorship

For more information, see Gazetteer, page 212.

32

"All Men are Created Equal"

1776 Philadelphia

In the Declaration of Independence, Thomas Jefferson brought into final and sharp focus many of the widely varied probes toward freedom and growth that had been animating the colonies for more than 200 years.

On a spring afternoon in 1765 tall, young Thomas Jefferson stood listening outside the open door of the Burgess Chamber in the capitol in Williamsburg. Inside, tall, young Patrick Henry was making his momentous denunciation of the Stamp Act. Jefferson was no radical by nature or background. He came from a well-to-do, socially prominent family, and he was studying law under George Wythe, one of the most eminent members of the legal profession in Virginia. But conventional though his rearing had been, Jefferson was stirred by Patrick Henry's emotional backcountry oratory.

Eventually the reticent young aristocrat would step through that same door, into the chamber, and enter on a career of which he now had no slightest dream. Meanwhile the notions that Henry was putting into Jefferson's head stayed there. In time other ideas joined them, forcing him to think in new ways and to test old assumptions. The result was almost literally world-shaking.

There was a sharp irony in the juxtaposition of Thomas Jefferson and Patrick Henry on that memorable day in the capitol. Henry had won a dramatic victory over the Rev-

erend James Maury in the Parson's Cause, and Jefferson knew Maury well. In fact Maury had been his tutor and had done much to give him his love of learning in general and of languages in particular. Now as he listened to Henry, he was torn between two crosscurrents. One flowed from Maury, the other from Maury's greatest enemy.

As matters turned out, Jefferson took the best from both men. In doing so he built for himself a kind of life that was little known in America. Certainly he became a rarity in Virginia—a young man who had little need to work but who was never idle. Even more remarkable, he was a serious scholar, and this in many fields. He used resources he had inherited—several thousand acres and many slaves—to support him as he acquired the best of the culture that his century could offer. And because intellectual curiosity is a strange force that often leads men into uncomfortable dilemmas, he found himself forced to choose between the world view held by men like his establishment-minded tutor, the Reverend Maury, and the insurgent attitudes of the uncouth rebel Patrick Henry. Facts seemed to Jefferson to drive him toward Henry, but he found a way of going in that direction without abandoning any of the intellectual equipment he had received from Maury.

So it was no ordinary occasion for Jefferson when he listened to Henry's speech in the Burgess Chamber. In a few years he would be a burgess himself, a man active in politics, although he really preferred a quiet life of study and research. But Jefferson had the kind of conscience that was more usual in Puritan Boston or Quaker Philadelphia than in pleasure-loving Williamsburg, which he called Devilsburg. And he felt he had an obligation to act as his conscience dictated, even when it was personally inconvenient to do so.

Patrick Henry's oratory did not push Jefferson headlong into radical activity. He returned instead to his lawbooks. And for every month that Henry had spent preparing for the bar, Thomas Jefferson spent a year. Then, although he did not need the money, he worked hard for seven years as an attorney in and out of "Devilsburg."

Most of the time that drowsy village scarcely deserved Jefferson's amused name for it. But in spring and fall, when the court or the House of Burgesses was in session, planters with money to spend came from all over the colony. At these "Publick Times" the dozen inns and taverns filled up, and dice rattled on the gaming tables until the small hours. Women who accompanied their husbands usually stayed in the homes of friends, where entertainment followed, as nearly as possible, the princely style of European cities. Guests sat for hours at table, and the two main courses might offer ten or more different dishes each. Revelers danced at the Raleigh Tavern or in the ballroom of the governor's palace. At the theater they saw Shakespeare or an English company of comedians.

Such busy times brought Jefferson to town, always with his personal servant, the black slave Jupiter, who was exactly his age. Jefferson probably stayed at Charlton's Inn, often dined at the Coffee House or the Raleigh Tavern or Mrs. Vobe's, and took part in much of the capital's gaiety. After 1768, when Governor Francis Fauquier died, Jefferson

Thomas Jefferson often attended social events in the Governor's Palace when he was a young man. The building, reconstructed and elegantly furnished, is open to the public in Colonial Williamsburg.

found Williamsburg much less stimulating than before. In Fauquier's lifetime Jefferson had gone to private dinner parties at the governor's palace whether in the social season or out, and the conversation there had been a source of great delight. Fauquier, unlike many other governors sent to the colonies, was a man of great learning and culture, and he did much to send the young attorney's active mind in pursuit of modern ideas.

Politics was not Jefferson's main concern during this period, but political events helped to terminate his legal career. By late 1774 turmoil in Virginia had almost closed the county courts. Jefferson had little to do, and he decided to retire from practice at the age of thirty-one. Now he hoped to have time free for his beloved studies. He would build Monticello, play his violin, and administer his farm, which had doubled in size with his marriage in 1772. But events in the great world far from the secluded mountain-top he had chosen for a home all kept tugging him away from private concerns. More and more the country gentle-man, to whom personal intellectual growth was a necessity, took part, with his fellow Virginians, in seeking channels for economic and political growth.

A partial summary of Jefferson's activities tells the story: In 1769 he was elected from his county (Goochland, now Albemarle) to serve in the House of Burgesses. There, as a diligent member of committees, he learned much about the

political process. Before long other burgesses became very much aware of his presence. Although he made no spell-binding speeches, he had a feel for the word or act that would stir men's minds. And they needed stirring, he thought, when in 1774 news reached the burgesses that the port of Boston was to be closed. The older burgesses seemed reluctant to protest Britain's action. Whereupon Jefferson proposed—at least he joined others in proposing—a dra-matic plan for nonviolent resistance of the kind that Mahatma Gandhi and the Reverend Martin Luther King, Jr., in later days found effective for moving millions of people. Specifically, the plan called on pleasure-loving Virginians to follow the very New Englandish custom of observing a day of fasting and prayer.

Jefferson, with characteristic modesty, attributed the idea to an informal committee of burgesses who agreed "that we must boldly take an unequivocal stand in the line with Massachusetts." He, along with Patrick Henry, Richard Henry Lee, Francis Lightfoot Lee, and several others, "de-termined to meet and consult on the proper measures in the council chamber, for the benefit of the library in that room. We were under the conviction of the necessity of arousing our people from the lethargy into which they had fallen, as to passing events, and thought that the appointment of a day of general fasting and prayer would be most likely to call up and alarm their attention. . . . We rummaged over

191

[the library] for revolutionary precedents and forms of the Puritans of that day . . . we cooked up a resolution, somewhat modernizing their phrases for appointing the first day of June, on which the Port Bill was to commence, for a day of fasting, humiliation and prayer to implore Heaven to avert from us the evils of civil war, to inspire us with firmness in support of our rights, and to turn the hearts of the King and Parliament to moderation and justice."

The resolution did inspire the burgesses, and they agreed unanimously to the proposal for religious action which had a political objective. Every burgess saw to it that the clergyman in his own parish had a copy of the resolution. On June 1, wrote Jefferson, "The people met generally with

THE NATIONAL MOTTO

After drafting the Declaration of Independence, Thomas Jefferson was appointed, with Benjamin Franklin and John Adams, to recommend to the Continental Congress a suitable national seal. They agreed on a design and then decided that a motto would also be desirable. Jefferson's choice was: "Rebellion to tyrants is obedience to God."

The Continental Congress accepted neither the design nor the motto but did agree that a motto was a good idea. The one that the congress approved was apparently borrowed from The Gentleman's Magazine, *a publication that printed excerpts from many newspapers. It was one thing made from many. This seemed a good description of what the congress hoped for —a unified country made up of many states— "E Pluribus Unum."*

Jefferson did not consider the work of the committee wasted. He adopted as his personal seal the design and motto that the congress had not accepted.

United States Department of State

anxiety & alarm in their countenances, and the effect of the day thro' the whole colony was like a shock of electricity, arousing every man and placing him erect and solidly on his centre."

That Jefferson was alert to political realities and to available political techniques soon became obvious. Other colonies took up the idea of prayer and fasting as a way to rouse people and to put pressure on the British. South Carolina appointed such a day. So, too, did Maryland and Georgia, and in New England the familiar Puritan custom was revived in Massachusetts and Rhode Island. In addition to proposals for prayer and fasting made by official governmental bodies, churches of various denominations in various colonies joined the movement in which Jefferson had played an initiating role.

That same year, 1774, Jefferson planned to attend the Virginia Convention, the unofficial group that had taken over some legislative functions. In advance of the meeting he drafted a document for the convention to consider. Then he fell ill of dysentery but sent his manuscript on ahead to Williamsburg. In his absence and without his knowledge, someone had the document printed under the title *A Summary View of the Rights of British America.* (The person who was willing to run the risk involved in printing this controversial pamphlet was Clementina Rind.) The *Summary View* was based on the doctrine that all men had natural rights—not simply rights granted to them by a king. In other words, rights originated among men, all of whom possessed them equally until they willingly surrendered them. Rights did not originate with a monarch who might let some of them trickle down to other men.

Jefferson did not create this theory. John Locke had done that many years before. Jefferson's function was to use the doctrine at a time when it was widely known and increasingly accepted. He was not, however, advocating the right of the colonies to separate from England. On the contrary, he still held that all British subjects, including those in America, had entered into a contract—a mutually agreed-upon arrangement—with the king. Under this contract the people surrendered some of their rights to the monarch with the understanding that he would render certain services in return. But Jefferson felt differently about Parliament. Colonists, he argued, had never surrendered any of their rights to that body, which they did not help to select, in which they had no voice or vote, and which had not helped them.

Whatever Jefferson thought of Parliament in 1774, neither he nor most other Americans wanted separation from England, and there was no proposal for such a move in the *Summary View.* Although Jefferson's name did not appear on the title page of the document, most people knew that he was the author, and it reached a wide audience. It was even read aloud to a select group in the house of Peyton Randolph in Williamsburg.

Word of Jefferson's skill as a writer of reports and resolutions began to travel beyond Virginia. On June 22, 1775, a Rhode Island delegate to the Continental Congress said in a letter what many others were thinking: "Yesterday the famous Mr. Jefferson, a Delegate from Virginia . . . arrived, I have not been in Company with him yet, he looks like a very sensible, spirited, fine Fellow, and by the Pamphlet which he wrote last summer he certainly is one."

By now it was becoming all too clear that England and the colonies were not equal members of one political entity. England imposed taxes on the colonies and England decided how to spend the money raised by those taxes. England, in one part of the empire, made laws affecting faraway colonies. On the other hand, no person in England was ever taxed without his consent by Virginia or Massachusetts. No Englishman ever had to obey laws imposed by Pennsylvania or New York. English commercial interests could—and did—expand far over the world. American interests were largely confined to the Atlantic seaboard of North America and were limited to serving English interests.

Something had to give.

Early in the spring of 1775, Lord North, the British prime minister, had tried to break the deadlock with a wily proposal. In essence he offered not to enforce the laws that Americans most objected to. This might seem to have been a concession. But at the same time he clearly insisted on the right of Parliament to pass such laws.

Acting for the Virginia Assembly, Jefferson drafted a rejection of the compromise. Then he went on to Philadelphia, where as a Virginia delegate he drafted for the congress another resolution rejecting North's compromise.

Nevertheless certain men in the Continental Congress would not give up hope of reconciliation. At their insistence the congress sent the king what became known as the Olive Branch Petition. In November word came back that the king had refused to receive their appeal. This royal snub increased the feeling of desperation in the congress and in the colonies from which the delegates came. To make things worse, the congress soon learned that the king had declared the colonies in open rebellion.

Clearly the congress had to knuckle under or carry rebellion much further.

The colonies were still not in complete agreement that separation had to come. However, in the winter of 1775–76 feeling moved rapidly in that direction. Tom Paine's *Common Sense* did more than any other one thing to convince people. And even though Jefferson was secluded on his mountaintop at Monticello when the pamphlet appeared, he noted quaintly one day that he had received "two shillings worth of Common Sense."

Paine's arguments and a great deal of direct experience had their effect on Jefferson. He gave up all hope of reconciliation, and he drew up a long list of grievances against the king. (In drafting this list of colonial problems he ignored Parliament, which he consistently maintained had no authority over the colonies.) In June 1776 some items from this list became part of the new constitution that Virginians were drafting. This homework would be put to good use when he returned to Philadelphia.

On June 7, Richard Henry Lee of Virginia rose in the Continental Congress—it was, he said, "the most aweful moment" of his life—and submitted a resolution that "These United Colonies are, and of right ought to be, free and independent States." Everyone knew that this moment had been coming. Still it shocked—and exhilarated.

The Declaration of Independence was read aloud throughout the colonies.

The vote on Lee's fateful resolution was postponed. But four days later the congress did set up a committee of five, including Jefferson, to draft a declaration of independence. Jefferson was asked by the other committee members to assume the task of stating the views that all five men shared.

For seventeen days Jefferson wrote and rewrote in his lodgings in the house of a German bricklayer at Market and Seventh streets. He, who was usually deep in research, did not open a single book in preparation for his task. All that the world could offer of theory about rights and freedom and equality was already in his head. He knew John Locke's

An 1876 representation of the house in which Jefferson wrote the Declaration of Independence.

LIBERTY BELL

In 1701, under Quaker leadership, Pennsylvanians got a new constitution called the Charter of Privileges. The charter guaranteed religious liberty and emphasized separation of church and state. It reaffirmed the voting rights of all males who believed in God, regardless of their denomination. Finally, it increased democracy by permitting the elected Assembly to initiate legislation and to meet when it pleased.

These advances were all treasured in Pennsylvania, and in 1751, exactly fifty years after the Charter of Privileges became law, the superintendents of the State House remembered the tenth verse of the twenty-fifth chapter of Leviticus, which began, "And ye shall hallow the 50th year." The superintendents did just that. They ordered a "bell of about 2,000 pounds weight," which would be used to signal the opening of sessions of court in the State House and to summon legislators to meetings of the Assembly there. Inscribed on the bell were words "well shaped in large letters," also from Leviticus 25:10: "Proclaim liberty throughout all the land, unto all the inhabitants thereof."

For years the bell hung in the State House of Pennsylvania, which is now called Independence Hall. According to tradition it rang out when the colonies announced their independence in 1776. It continued in service for many years after that, and—again according to tradition—it cracked in 1835 while tolling for the funeral of Chief Justice John Marshall.

Now it is displayed on the main floor of Independence Hall, a reminder of democratic attitudes that existed in Philadelphia long before 1776 and that led up to the Declaration of Independence in that year.

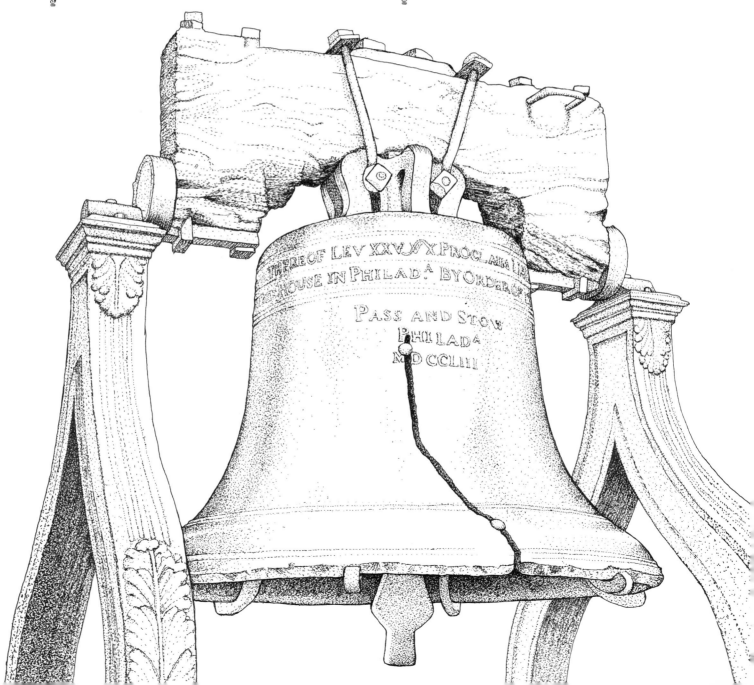

treatises on government and George Mason's *Declaration of Rights*. He knew Tom Paine's *Common Sense*. He needed only to put it all down with simplicity and style. There was no doubt in his mind, either, about specific acts of oppression that the British king had committed. These he catalogued for "a candid world" to see, whether or not it could be demonstrated that the king was wholly responsible.

In his long list of grievances, Jefferson included one outburst against inhumanity that the world does not always recall. He, the uncomfortable owner of 200 slaves, put into his draft of the declaration a denunciation of the slave trade. At one point in this passage Jefferson said, ". . . he [the king] is now inciting . . . [the slaves] to rise in arms among us. . . ." All the delegates, both northern and southern, knew what Jefferson meant. Insurrection had indeed been incited by the royally appointed governor of Virginia, Lord Dunmore. On November 7, 1775, Dunmore had issued a proclamation that sent fear through plantation owners in the South: "I do hereby further declare all indentured servants, Negroes or others (appertaining to Rebels,) free, that are able and willing to bear arms, they joining His Majesties Troops, as soon as may be, for the more speedily reducing the Colony to a proper sense of their duty, to His Majesty's crown and dignity."

Immediately slaves in large numbers had left their masters. Five hundred were soon under arms in what came to be known as "Lord Dunmore's Ethiopian Regiment."

Jefferson preceded his reference to insurrection with a long attack on the slave trade itself. Again he symbolically fastened responsibility on the king, possibly hoping not to alienate certain New England supporters of independence who had profited greatly from that particular trade.

Here are Jefferson's words:

> He has waged cruel war against human nature itself, violating its most sacred rights of life and liberty in the persons of a distant people who never offended him, captivating and carrying them into slavery in another hemisphere, or to incur miserable death in their transportation thither. This piratical warfare, the opprobrium of *infidel* powers, is the warfare of the *Christian* King of Great Britain. Determined to keep open a market where MEN should be bought and sold, he has prostituted his negative [i.e. veto power,—ed.] for suppressing every legislative attempt to prohibit or to restrain this execrable commerce: and that this assemblage of horrors might want no fact of distinguished die, he is now exciting those very people to rise in arms among us, and to purchase that liberty of which *he* has deprived them, by murdering the people on whom he also obtruded them: thus paying off former crimes committed against the *liberties* of one people with crimes which he urges them to commit against the *lives* of another."

John Adams thought this passage was one of the best in the declaration. It was, as he said, a philippic against slavery, but it did not actually call for abolition. Jefferson was no starry-eyed dreamer. In this, as in everything else he wrote, he tried to be practical as well as principled. He believed it was proper and just to end the slave trade. Beyond that he wanted to remove from British hands the weapon of slave revolts that could be used against the

(Above) For a committee, Jefferson wrote the Declaration of Independence, which Congress adopted in the room beyond this doorway *(below)* in what is now called Independence Hall in Philadelphia.

This painting, by the patriot John Trumbull, shows the presentation of the Declaration of Independence.

colonies. If patriots made overtures to the slaves, Jefferson seemed to be thinking, this oppressed fifth of the population could not so easily be stirred up to attack white Americans and thus help the British. Put another way, the desire of slaves for freedom was good reason to admit them to the coalition of merchants, farmers, mechanics, planters, laborers, and lawyers who were taking a course toward freedom.

Jefferson's strategy was exceedingly bold. It meant giving a role to the lowest stratum in Anglican society, a stratum out of which some of the higher strata made a great deal of money. Jefferson seems to have been willing to lose the support of a few thousand planters in exchange for the support of hundreds of thousands of Blacks. But the planters' representatives in congress—where there were no Blacks —were not willing to attack any part of the institution of slavery. They were in the revolutionary movement to better themselves, not to throw away the very thing on which they depended for wealth and power.

Many delegates who owned no slaves hesitated to alienate those who did. And so Jefferson had to listen in acute discomfort as members from all sections of the colonies agreed to remove this section from his draft. He also sat through—and disapproved—lesser changes in what he had written. But he agreed to become a signer of the document,

though he preferred its original, more radical form. In signing, he knew full well that he would be found guilty of treason in an English court if the revolution should fail. And for treason there was a well-known punishment, to which the leader of rent strikers in New York had been sentenced only ten years before. The sentence went this way: "That the Prisoner be led back to the Place whence he came and from thence shall be drawn on a Hurdle [i.e. a sledge— ed.] to the Place for Execution, and then shall be hanged by the Neck and then shall be cut down alive and his Entrals and Privy members shall be cut from his Body, and shall be burned in his Sight. . . ."

Jefferson did not ignore the risk he was taking, but he also knew that the forces of vitality in America could not be confined—could not be stunted—forever. Growth, expansion in every way—that is to say, life, had to prevail.

In his person Jefferson showed, as much as any one man could, the whole expansive, outgoing, probing essence of the revolution for which he had found words in the Declaration of Independence. He was not only involved in the economic and political growth that was being frustrated by British restraints. He favored geographic expansion, with broad democratic rights for settlers in new territories. He wanted growth in every realm of human endeavor. All dur-

ing a life that was to go on for exactly fifty years to the day after July 4, 1776, he pursued learning with intensity and delight. He encouraged education. The study of paleontology and the languages of American Indians fascinated him. He learned French and Italian and constantly read Latin and Greek. Time and again he experimented with new agricultural products and methods. He kept detailed records for his own garden and recorded the dates between which garden products of various kinds were available in the markets. He sought out new inventions and made inventions himself. He was not too busy on the wonderful morning of July 4, 1776, to note that his thermometer read 68° at 6:00 A.M.

"The American Revolution began here."

That statement could have been made, not only of July 4, 1776, but of nearly every episode recorded in this book. The American Revolution began where real revolutions always originate—in the people's effort to live, to reach out beyond, to defy deadly limits. It was only after a great deal of such reaching that climactic military events began. Those marches and sieges and bombardments were really not the Revolution any more than surgery is life. Battles were only a means toward an end—and the end is not yet.

PLACES TO SEE

DISTRICT OF COLUMBIA

Washington: Jefferson Memorial / Library of Congress.

PENNSYLVANIA

Philadelphia: Independence National Historical Park / Christ Church / Site of City Tavern / Graff House Site.

VIRGINIA

Charlottesville: Ash Lawn / Mitchie Tavern / Monticello / University of Virginia.
Richmond: Tuckahoe Plantation / St. John's Episcopal Church / The Capitol.
Williamsburg: Blair House / Bruton Parrish Church / The Capitol / Charlton's / The Governor's Palace / Market Square Tavern / Peyton Randolph House / Raleigh Tavern / William and Mary College / Wythe House.

For more information, see Gazetteer, page 212.

IN CONGRESS, JULY 4, 1776.

The unanimous Declaration of the thirteen united States of America,

When in the Course of human events, it becomes necessary for one people to dissolve the political bands which have connected them with another, and to assume among the powers of the earth, the separate and equal station to which the Laws of Nature and of Nature's God entitle them, a decent respect to the opinions of mankind requires that they should declare the causes which impel them to the separation.

We hold these truths to be self-evident, that all men are created equal, that they are endowed by their Creator with certain unalienable Rights, that among these are Life, Liberty and the pursuit of Happiness.—That to secure these rights, Governments are instituted among Men, deriving their just powers from the consent of the governed,—That whenever any Form of Government becomes destructive of these ends, it is the Right of the People to alter or to abolish it, and to institute new Government, laying its foundation on such principles and organizing its powers in such form, as to them shall seem most likely to effect their Safety and Happiness. Prudence, indeed, will dictate that Governments long established should not be changed for light and transient causes; and accordingly all experience hath shewn, that mankind are more disposed to suffer, while evils are sufferable, than to right themselves by abolishing the forms to which they are accustomed. But when a long train of abuses and usurpations, pursuing invariably the same Object evinces a design to reduce them under absolute Despotism, it is their right, it is their duty, to throw off such Government, and to provide new Guards for their future security.—Such has been the patient sufferance of these Colonies; and such is now the necessity which constrains them to alter their former Systems of Government. The history of the present King of Great Britain is a history of repeated injuries and usurpations, all having in direct object the establishment of an absolute Tyranny over these States. To prove this, let Facts be submitted to a candid world.

He has refused his Assent to Laws, the most wholesome and necessary for the public good.

He has forbidden his Governors to pass Laws of immediate and pressing importance, unless suspended in their operation till his Assent should be obtained; and when so suspended, he has utterly neglected to attend to them.

He has refused to pass other Laws for the accommodation of large districts of people, unless those people would relinquish the right of Representation in the Legislature, a right inestimable to them and formidable to tyrants only.

He has called together legislative bodies at places unusual, uncomfortable, and distant from the depository of their Public Records, for the sole purpose of fatiguing them into compliance with his measures.

He has dissolved Representative Houses repeatedly, for opposing with manly firmness his invasions on the rights of the people.

He has refused for a long time, after such dissolutions, to cause others to be elected; whereby the Legislative powers, incapable of Annihilation, have returned to the People at large for their exercise; the State remaining in the mean time exposed to all the dangers of invasion from without, and convulsions within.

He has endeavoured to prevent the population of these States; for that purpose obstructing the Laws for Naturalization of Foreigners; refusing to pass others to encourage their migrations hither, and raising the conditions of new Appropriations of Lands.

He has obstructed the Administration of Justice, by refusing his Assent to Laws for establishing Judiciary powers.

He has made Judges dependent on his Will alone, for the tenure of their offices, and the amount and payment of their salaries.

He has erected a multitude of New Offices, and sent hither swarms of Officers to harrass our people, and eat out their substance.

He has kept among us, in times of peace, Standing Armies without the Consent of our legislatures.

He has affected to render the Military independent of and superior to the Civil power.

He has combined with others to subject us to a jurisdiction foreign to our constitution, and unacknowledged by our laws; giving his Assent to their Acts of pretended Legislation:

For Quartering large bodies of armed troops among us:

For protecting them, by a mock Trial, from punishment for any Murders which they should commit on the Inhabitants of these States:

For cutting off our Trade with all parts of the world:

For imposing Taxes on us without our Consent:

For depriving us in many cases, of the benefits of Trial by Jury:

For transporting us beyond Seas to be tried for pretended offences:

For abolishing the free System of English Laws in a neighbouring Province, establishing therein an Arbitrary government, and enlarging its Boundaries so as to render it at once an example and fit instrument for introducing the same absolute rule into these Colonies:

For taking away our Charters, abolishing our most valuable Laws, and altering fundamentally the Forms of our Governments:

For suspending our own Legislatures, and declaring themselves invested with power to legislate for us in all cases whatsoever.

He has abdicated Government here, by declaring us out of his Protection and waging War against us.

He has plundered our seas, ravaged our Coasts, burnt our towns, and destroyed the lives of our people.

He is at this time transporting large Armies of foreign Mercenaries to compleat the works of death, desolation and tyranny, already begun with circumstances of Cruelty & perfidy scarcely paralleled in the most barbarous ages, and totally unworthy the Head of a civilized nation.

He has constrained our fellow Citizens taken Captive on the high Seas to bear Arms against their Country, to become the executioners of their friends and Brethren, or to fall themselves by their Hands.

He has excited domestic insurrections amongst us, and has endeavoured to bring on the inhabitants of our frontiers, the merciless Indian Savages, whose known rule of warfare, is an undistinguished destruction of all ages, sexes and conditions.

In every stage of these Oppressions We have Petitioned for Redress in the most humble terms: Our repeated Petitions have been answered only by repeated injury. A Prince, whose character is thus marked by every act which may define a Tyrant, is unfit to be the ruler of a free people.

Nor have We been wanting in attentions to our British brethren. We have warned them from time to time of attempts by their legislature to extend an unwarrantable jurisdiction over us. We have reminded them of the circumstances of our emigration and settlement here. We have appealed to their native justice and magnanimity, and we have conjured them by the ties of our common kindred to disavow these usurpations, which, would inevitably interrupt our connections and correspondence. They too have been deaf to the voice of justice and of consanguinity. We must, therefore, acquiesce in the necessity, which denounces our Separation, and hold them, as we hold the rest of mankind, Enemies in War, in Peace Friends.

We, therefore, the Representatives of the united States of America, in General Congress, Assembled, appealing to the Supreme Judge of the world for the rectitude of our intentions, do, in the Name, and by Authority of the good People of these Colonies, solemnly publish and declare, That these United Colonies are, and of Right ought to be Free and Independent States; that they are Absolved from all Allegiance to the British Crown, and that all political connection between them and the State of Great Britain, is and ought to be totally dissolved; and that as Free and Independent States, they have full Power to levy War, conclude Peace, contract Alliances, establish Commerce, and to do all other Acts and Things which Independent States may of right do.—And for the support of this Declaration, with a firm reliance on the protection of divine Providence, we mutually pledge to each other our Lives, our Fortunes and our sacred Honor.

John Hancock

Button Gwinnett
Lyman Hall
Geo Walton.

Wm Hooper
Joseph Hewes,
John Penn

Edward Rutledge.

Thos Heyward Junr.
Thomas Lynch Junr.
Arthur Middleton

Samuel Chase
Wm Paca
Thos Stone
Charles Carroll of Carrollton

George Wythe
Richard Henry Lee
Th Jefferson
Benj Harrison
Thos Nelson jr.
Francis Lightfoot Lee
Carter Braxton

Robt Morris
Benjamin Rush
Benja Franklin
John Morton
Geo Clymer
Jas Smith
Geo Taylor
James Wilson
Geo. Ross
Caesar Rodney
Geo Read
Tho M:Kean

Wm Floyd
Phil. Livingston
Frans Lewis
Lewis Morris

Richd Stockton
Jno Witherspoon
Fras Hopkinson
John Hart
Abra Clark

Josiah Bartlett
Wm Whipple
Saml Adams
John Adams
Robt Treat Paine
Elbridge Gerry

Step Hopkins
William Ellery

Roger Sherman
Saml Huntington
Wm Williams
Oliver Wolcott

Matthew Thornton

The Text of the Declaration of Independence

WHEN, in the course of human events, it becomes necessary for one people to dissolve the political bands which have connected them with another, and to assume among the powers of the earth the separate and equal station to which the laws of nature and of nature's God entitle them, a decent respect to the opinions of mankind requires that they should declare the causes which impel them to the separation.

We hold these truths to be self-evident: That all men are created equal; that they are endowed by their Creator with certain unalienable rights; that among these are life, liberty, and the pursuit of happiness; that, to secure these rights, governments are instituted among men, deriving their just powers from the consent of the governed; that whenever any form of government becomes destructive of these ends, it is the right of the people to alter or to abolish it and to institute new government, laying its foundation on such principles, and organizing its powers in such form, as to them shall seem most likely to effect their safety and happiness. Prudence, indeed, will dictate that governments long established should not be changed for light and transient causes; and, accordingly, all experience hath shown that mankind are more disposed to suffer while evils are sufferable, than to right themselves by abolishing the forms to which they are accustomed. But when a long train of abuses and usurpations, pursuing invariably the same object, evinces a design to reduce them under absolute despotism, it is their right, it is their duty, to throw off such government and to provide new guards for their future security. Such has been the patient sufferance of these colonies; and such is now the necessity which constrains them to alter their former systems of government.

The history of the present King of Great Britain is a history of repeated injuries and usurpations, all having in direct object the establishment of an absolute tyranny over these States. To prove this, let facts be submitted to a candid world:

He has refused his assent to laws, the most wholesome and necessary for the public good.

He has forbidden his Governors to pass laws of immediate and pressing importance, unless suspended in their operation till his assent should be obtained; and, when so suspended, he has utterly neglected to attend to them.

He has refused to pass other laws for the accommodation of large districts of people, unless those people would relinquish the right of representation in the Legislature, a right inestimable to them and formidable to tyrants only.

He has called together legislative bodies at places unusual, uncomfortable, and distant from the depository of their public records, for the sole purpose of fatiguing them into compliance with his measures.

He has dissolved representative Houses repeatedly for opposing with manly firmness his invasions on the rights of people.

He has refused for a long time after such dissolutions to cause others to be elected; whereby the legislative powers, incapable of annihilation, have returned to the people at large for their exercise; the State remaining, in the meantime, exposed to all the dangers of invasions from without and convulsions within.

He has endeavored to prevent the population of these States; for that purpose obstructing the laws for naturalization of foreigners, refusing to pass others to encourage their migration hither, and raising the conditions of new appropriations of lands.

He has obstructed the administration of justice by refusing his assent to laws for establishing judiciary powers.

He has made judges dependent on his will alone for the tenure of their offices, and the amount and payment of their salaries.

He has erected a multitude of new offices, and sent hither swarms of officers to harass our people and eat out their substance.

He has kept among us, in times of peace, standing armies, without the consent of our Legislatures.

He has affected to render the military independent of, and superior to, the civil power.

He has combined with others to subject us to a jurisdiction foreign to our Constitution and unacknowledged by our laws, giving his assent to their acts of pretended legislation:

For quartering large bodies of armed troops among us;

For protecting them, by a mock trial, from punishment for any murders which they should commit on the inhabitants of these States;

For cutting off our trade with all parts of the world;

For imposing taxes on us without our consent;

For depriving us, in many cases, of the benefits of trial by jury;

For transporting us beyond seas to be tried for pretended offenses;

For abolishing the free system of English laws in a neighboring province, establishing therein an arbitrary government, and enlarging its boundaries so as to render it at once an example and fit instrument for introducing the same absolute rule into these colonies;

For taking away our charters, abolishing our most valuable laws, and altering fundamentally the forms of our governments;

For suspending our own Legislatures, and declaring themselves invested with power to legislate for us in all cases whatsoever.

He has abdicated government here by declaring us out of his protection and waging war against us.

He has plundered our seas, ravaged our coasts, burnt our towns, and destroyed the lives of our people.

He is at this time transporting large armies of foreign mercenaries to complete the works of death, desolation, and tyranny, already begun with circumstances of cruelty and perfidy scarcely paralleled in the most barbarous ages, and totally unworthy the head of a civilized nation.

He has constrained our fellow citizens, taken captive on the high seas, to bear arms against their country, to become the executioners of their friends and brethren, or to fall themselves by their hands.

He has excited domestic insurrections amongst us, and has endeavored to bring on the inhabitants of our frontiers the merciless Indian savages, whose known rule of warfare is an undistinguished destruction of all ages, sexes, and conditions.

In every stage of these oppressions we have petitioned for redress in the most humble terms: our repeated petitions have been answered only by repeated injury. A prince, whose character is thus marked by every act which may define a tyrant, is unfit to be the ruler of a free people.

Nor have we been wanting in attentions to our British brethren. We have warned them from time to time of attempts by their Legislature to extend an unwarrantable jurisdiction over us. We have reminded them of the circumstances of our emigration and settlement here. We have appealed to their native justice and magnanimity, and we have conjured them by the ties of our common kindred to disavow these usurpations which would inevitably interrupt our connections and correspondence. They, too, have been deaf to the voice of justice and of consanguinity. We must, therefore, acquiesce in the necessity which denounces our separation, and hold them, as we hold the rest of mankind, enemies in war; in peace, friends.

WE, THEREFORE, THE REPRESENTATIVES OF THE UNITED STATES OF AMERICA, in General Congress assembled, appealing to the Supreme Judge of the world for the rectitude of our intentions, do, in the name and by the authority of the good people of these colonies, solemnly publish and declare that these United Colonies are, and of right ought to be, FREE AND INDEPENDENT STATES, that they are absolved from all allegiance to the British Crown, and that all political connection between them and the State of Great Britain is, and ought to be, totally dissolved; and that as free and independent states they have full power to levy war, conclude peace, contract alliances, establish commerce, and to do all other acts and things which independent States may of right do. And for the support of this declaration, with a firm reliance on the protection of Divine Providence, we mutually pledge to each other our lives, our fortunes, and our sacred honor.

The Signers

Every patriot who put his name to the Declaration of Independence did so for his own reasons. The signers were a singularly individualistic lot. Some, called "violents" in the Continental Congress, had long believed that the colonies must be entirely free, and the sooner the better. Others, the "moderates," wanted delay and possibly reconciliation. Disagreements, bickering, even conniving, went on among the delegates until July 2, 1776, the day of voting for separation from Britain. Suddenly then the magnet of independence swept them all in and held them together. On that day "the greatest Question was decided, which ever was debated in America," said John Adams, "and a greater perhaps, never was or will be decided among Men."

When debate ended and the colonies resolved on independence, discussion of the Declaration itself still continued. On July 3, and well into July 4, the delegates criticized, amended, and cut the document that Thomas Jefferson and his committee had brought in. Edgy and apprehensive, some delegates continued to voice doubts. It was not so much that they hesitated to support a statement bound to endanger their lives and fortunes, though the peril was real enough. Rather they were men of strong and differing opinions, most of them sharply molded by the groups they represented.

At last, toward evening on July 4, the revised text satisfied almost everyone. (Jefferson whimsically maintained that debate ended only because horseflies from a neighboring livery stable bit and harried the delegates into agreement.) The Declaration was adopted, and by the next morning printed copies were ready to be sent out to all the states—formerly the colonies.

Two weeks later the congress passed a resolution that the Declaration should be copied in a fine hand—"fairly engrossed on parchment"—and signed by all delegates. On August 2, the parchment was ready. John Hancock as president of the congress, set down his big, confident signature first. "There," he is supposed to have said, "George Third can read my name without spectacles and may now double his reward of 500 pounds for my head." All the other members of the congress who were present that day then signed, some in less high spirits than Hancock. To protect the more timid members—and those less notorious than their president—it had been agreed that the printed copies of the Declaration should be circulated throughout the country bearing only the names of Hancock and Charles Thomson, secretary of the congress.

Thomson, called "the Sam Adams of Philadelphia," was not a delegate. He had been a candidate, but his too-radical views on independence cost him the election. Nevertheless, delegates who valued Thomson's abilities managed to have him appointed permanent secretary of the congress. So his name appears in type on the printed copies of the Declaration, but not as a signer of the parchment copy.

One by one during the next months, members who had been absent on August 2 came to Philadelphia and signed. Others who were elected after August 2 also signed. The total list of fifty-six was finally made known in January 1777.

JOHN HANCOCK, for all his long-standing revolutionary convictions, got on well with the moderates in the Continental Congress. He could understand why people on the edge of the wilderness feared to be without British protection. Or why others, proud to be English, dreaded losing the Englishman's privileges that still remained to them. And so, as president of the congress, Hancock resisted the temptation to override the dissenters. Instead, he maneuvered and persuaded and exercised his considerable tact. At times all this diplomacy riled his fellow New Englanders. Still they could hardly doubt his motives. He had so much to lose if the colonies backed away from independence. The British, eager to catch him, would certainly transport him, as the Declaration put it, "Beyond seas to be tried for pretended offenses." With a young wife, and a baby on the way, Hancock had moved to Philadelphia, which was safer at the moment than Boston. But prudence, not cowardice, was his motive, as all the delegates knew. Even wrathy Sam Adams, who would hardly speak to him for a while because he seemed to be siding with their opponents in congress, recognized his generous spirit. So did other delegates who had witnessed his resentment when they did not make him commander of the Continental army. Although his pride was hurt at the time, he later named his son John George Washington Hancock.

NEW HAMPSHIRE

JOSIAH BARTLETT of New Hampshire, it is thought, signed immediately after John Hancock. Since the colonies voted in geographical order from north to south, the delegates from the most northerly province probably headed the list of signers. Bartlett was a physician and a man not to be intimidated in any way by the establishment. When other doctors relied heavily on bleeding their patients, he had his own experimental treatments, including the apparently successful use of quinine for fevers. More than ten years before independence, as a member of the New Hampshire legislature, he had been speaking out against venal British officials. Misappropriation of public lands outraged him, and he refused to be politely bribed into silence. Finally an exasperated royal governor removed the trouble-making doctor from the legislature and from other governmental posts he held. So Bartlett knew at first hand the "invasion of the rights of the people" listed in the Declaration. As soon as Tom Paine's *Common Sense* was published, he used it to help persuade his timid constituents that they would be better off as citizens of a free and independent country. Since Josiah Bartlett was born in Massachusetts, two states can lay claim to him. A statue of him stands in Amesbury, Massachusetts, his birthplace.

WILLIAM WHIPPLE, a practical, quick-witted New Englander, had all the good Yankee merchant's reasons for wanting severance from British control. As a young man he had gone to sea. Many ambitious boys did. They found that a merchant vessel provided a kind of work-study program for future businessmen, combining firsthand experience in trade, including the slave trade, with a chance to make the beginnings of a fortune. Whipple learned and profited from his voyages and then took up life ashore. By 1765, the Stamp Act year, he was a well-established merchant in Portsmouth, firmly on the side of the colonies against Britain. When, in 1776, he was sent to the Continental Congress, he had already begun to devote all his time to public life. Whether or not he was offended by Jefferson's proposed antislavery section of the Declaration, a year later he took along his black slave, Prince, when he was put in command of a New Hampshire brigade at the battle of Saratoga. On the way, General Whipple is said to have remarked that he expected Prince to fight bravely for his country if necessary. "Sir," the slave answered, "I have no inducement to fight; but if I had my liberty, I would endeavour to defend it to the last drop of my blood." Whereupon, according to an account by Whipple's biographer, the general manumitted him on the spot.

MATTHEW THORNTON, born in Ireland, was four years old when his Scottish parents brought him to America. Like Josiah Bartlett, he became a physician and practiced in New Hampshire. According to some who knew him, he was a man "universally loved," a great raconteur of very funny stories but—"invincibly grave"—never laughed at his own quips. Others said he was a sardonic and remorseless collector of the fees his patients owed, yet satirized other doc-

tors who did so. Certainly he relished the impudent humor of the mock funeral procession for the Goddess of Liberty held in Portsmouth on the first day of Stamp Act enforcement. Although he was not appointed to the congress until September 1776, he was allowed to sign the parchment Declaration when he took his seat some weeks later.

MASSACHUSETTS

SAMUEL ADAMS, said one of his biographers, had "all the zeal of a reformer, the confidence of an enthusiast, and the cheerfulness of a voluntary martyr." British authorities in Boston would have agreed, and irritating though they found these qualities, there was another that enraged them even more because they could not understand it. Sam Adams was impervious to their blandishments. Time and again they tried unsuccessfully to woo him with offers of jobs, favors, benefits. Their last effort was made by General Gage, who sent an emissary with what amounted to a bribe if Adams would make his peace with the king. Adams replied: "I trust I have long since made my peace with the King of Kings. . . . It is the advice of Samuel Adams to him [Gage] no longer to insult the feelings of an exasperated people." Later, when Gage offered amnesty to everyone who would give up revolutionary activity, he specifically excepted Adams and John Hancock, whose offenses, Gage said, were "of too flagitious a nature to admit of any other consideration, but that of condign punishment." General Gage's threat had not been lifted at the time that Adams put his signature directly under Whipple's on the Declaration.

JOHN ADAMS traveled by coach, together with three other delegates from Massachusetts, to the First Continental Congress in 1775. They were met a little way outside Philadelphia by several Pennsylvanian Sons of Liberty, who had come to give them a warning: The men from Massachusetts must be very careful what they said in the congress because they were thought to be "desperate adventurers." Any radical thoughts they had about independence must be suppressed, at least until the moderate delegates, who favored conciliation, could be brought around. Adams dutifully heeded the warning. He said little in public. But he grew more and more impatient with John Dickinson, one of the chief Pennsylvania moderates. Finally in a private letter Adams called Dickinson "a certain great Fortune and piddling Genius." The letter was intercepted and published, along with another to his wife, Abigail, spelling out some of his ideas about independence. Naturally Dickinson was furious, and many people in Philadelphia took to avoiding Adams as if he were "infected with the leprosy." Actually the letters did no real harm. Perhaps they even helped to clear the air. But Adams continued for a while to let others in congress do the talking whenever he could. It was not until the spring of 1776 that he began to speak out. Then, according to Thomas Jefferson, he became ". . . our Colossus on the floor; not graceful, not elegant, not always fluent; . . . he yet came out with a power both of thought and expression that moved us from our seats."

ROBERT TREAT PAINE (no relative of Tom Paine), one of the "desperate adventurers" from Massachusetts, did not altogether deserve the title in 1775. He had much less firm convictions about independence than had either of the Adamses. At the same time he was no less a partisan of colonial rights. He had been the patriotic prosecuting attorney at the trial following the Boston Massacre, when John Adams, on moral principle, served as defense attorney for the British soldiers accused of murder. In the congress Paine was known as "The Objection Maker." He was eternally raising questions, not so much from a desire to cause trouble as from the lawyer's habit of analyzing and reasoning. Once convinced that armed conflict was inevitable, he did tireless service on the committee that arranged for muskets, bayonets, and cannons. He also researched the mysterious process of manufacturing saltpeter for gunpowder. Nobody knew why that necessary substance could be leached out of some kinds of soil but not all. Paine encouraged experiments, and the successful ones greatly helped the Continental army.

ELBRIDGE GERRY, like all the other Massachusetts delegates, graduated from Harvard. He was the son of a wealthy merchant of Marblehead, deeply concerned with protecting New Englanders' commercial interests. By the time he was thirty, politics had begun to fascinate him. After election to the Massachusetts legislature he became a member of the Committee of Safety. It happened that the committee met at the time when General Gage made his march on Concord, and Gerry was staying in a house directly in the path of the redcoats. Apparently someone tipped off the British, who approached the house to take the committeemen prisoner. Gerry, with two officers of the colonial militia, fled in their nightshirts, hid in a field, and after the redcoats went on, spread the alarm. Gerry, something of a hero now, carried his enthusiasm for independence to Philadelphia, where his shrewd and tidy business sense was useful in financing the Continental army. A questionable incident later in his political life led opponents to coin the word "gerrymander" when he benefited his party by arbitrarily redrawing election district boundaries in a weird shape resembling a salamander. Although many former associates deserted him, John Adams remained a warm friend.

RHODE ISLAND

STEPHEN HOPKINS, largely self-educated, the son of a Rhode Island farmer, grew up in that colony's tradition of civil and religious liberty. When he was twenty-five years old, he entered town politics and continued to hold office as assemblyman, judge, and governor of the colony for nine terms. In 1756, when many others were only beginning to question British rule, Hopkins argued with much indignation: "What have the King and parliament to do with making a law or laws to govern us any more than the Mohawks have? And if the Mohawks should make a law or laws to govern us we were as much obliged to obey them as any law or laws the King and parliament could make." A few years later he wrote a widely circulated pamphlet on self-government, one of the first to introduce the idea that the colonies might be linked in one country, separate from Britain. In his personal life Hopkins was no less an independent. He belonged to the Quaker Meeting in Providence, and when the Friends decided that he must obey their injunction to set free a black woman he held as a slave, he refused. Whereupon the Meeting "put him from under their care." A year later, however, he himself wrote the act which the Rhode Island legislature passed in 1774, prohibiting the enslavement of Blacks. When he signed the Declaration, Hopkins was still outside the Meeting's care.

WILLIAM ELLERY practiced law quietly and successfully in Newport, built a fine house, had the respect of other liberty-minded Rhode Islanders, and was something of an authority on Greek and Latin grammar. His signature on the Declaration cost him, as it did a number of others, most of his worldly goods. When the British seized Newport, they took pains to burn or destroy much of his property.

CONNECTICUT

ROGER SHERMAN, when he became a delegate to the Continental Congress, had already been a prosperous lawyer, a merchant, a member of the Connecticut legislature, and a superior court judge. At one point Congress put him on a committee to check on an army contract for soldiers' shoes. Sherman, who had once been a cobbler, showed in great detail that the supplier was profiteering. All his immense knowledge of law and government had come from the books he constantly read on his own. Once Patrick Henry asked him why people in Connecticut seemed to be greater patriots than some others. "Because we have more to lose," Sherman answered, ". . . our beloved charter." It was true that Connecticut had been granted, as had Rhode Island, extraordinary freedom from British control. Sherman, no less than others, was a product of that traditional liberty. At a time when even Sam Adams was persuaded to wear a wig and a new red cloak to the congress, Sherman dressed simply, like the strict Puritan he was. Everything about him seemed so measured and uncompromising that one of his friends called him, not unkindly, "a republican machine."

OLIVER WOLCOTT, so unlike Roger Sherman in many ways, was born into a well-established family, went to Yale, started to study medicine but did not stick with it, and finally decided he might like public office. Although he went to church, he was not pious. But in convictions about freedom and self-government, he was just as firm as the other New England delegates. It happened that illness kept him from voting for independence on July 2 or for the Declaration on July 4. But he was on hand later to sign the parchment copy, and no doubt he felt a special amused satisfaction when he put his name to the condemnation of the king. A lead statue of King George, which once stood in New York City, had ended up in Wolcott's garden. It had been pulled down and broken by enthusiastic celebrators of independence; then the pieces were gathered up, loaded in a wagon, and taken to what Wolcott called "a place of safety" behind his house. There the neighbors helped his wife and children melt the lead down and mold it into bullets for the army. His daughter Mary Ann made a total of 10,780 and her young brother Frederick, 936.

WILLIAM WILLIAMS, of Welsh descent, began to question British rule when in his early twenties he fought under English officers in the French and Indian War. Their arrogance and insensitivity to colonial troops irritated him, and his indignation grew when he took up civilian life as a merchant and public servant. Although he apparently did not take a very active part in the congress, he made up for it at home. With his quick, sharp tongue he exhorted patriots, swore at the enemy, and lambasted any neighbors who seemed remiss. At one point he went from house to house wheedling or shaming citizens into giving clothing, lead, or blankets to the army. He himself parted with most of his considerable means to help the Revolution.

SAMUEL HUNTINGTON, the eldest son of a Connecticut farmer, was obliged to stay at home while his two brothers studied at Yale. Apparently without envy, he read and taught himself law, and like many other young men learned to be a patriot in the process. Although he became well-to-do, he lived very simply. All the extravagances of official life in Philadelphia—the entertainment, the wines, and the lavish food—did not change his frugal habits. Some delegates thought him stingy, but none had any doubts about his earnestness or his devotion.

NEW YORK

LEWIS MORRIS had Welsh ancestors who, no doubt, resented English rule. But whatever rebellious spirit the Morris family once had was watered down by the comforts of their life in America. Young Lewis spent a happy childhood on their great estate called Morrisania. He went to Yale, then returned to the peaceful activities of a gentleman farmer. Although Britain's tax measures after 1763 made him uneasy, he did not take part in active resistance. But when New York was told in 1767 to provide extra supplies for the king's troops quartered in the colony, Morris felt completely outraged. Somehow this assault on property rights seemed to him much more tyrannical than any ordinary tax. He spoke out boldly. From then on he became more and more committed to the idea of independence. Although he was a delegate to the Continental Congress, he was absent the day the vote on the Declaration was taken. Later he put his name to it with great satisfaction. Soon afterward British troops vandalized his house, destroyed his large woodland, and confiscated his stock.

FRANCIS LEWIS grew up in Wales. In his early twenties he inherited a good deal of money and used it to finance a trading expedition to America. There the profits from his merchandise encouraged him to settle into an export-import business in New York. Perhaps his Welsh upbringing prejudiced him against the British without making an activist of him. At any rate, when the Stamp Act began to afflict businessmen, he simply retired in disgust to his estate on Long Island. Some years later his son persuaded him to go back into trade, but not for long. By this time he was more anti-British than ever. A very large number of his fellow New Yorkers, however, did not share his opinions. One reason was that Parliament had not come down so hard on New York as on New England. Many ordinary citizens had few complaints, and their relations with British officials remained friendly. It was a relatively small group of wealthy and well-educated New Yorkers who took leadership in the independence movement. Francis Lewis was one of these. When he did begin to have an active interest in politics, he was one of the first to join the Sons of Liberty. And he was one of the first signers to suffer. In the fall of 1776 British troops looted his home and destroyed all his books and papers. His wife was taken prisoner and so cruelly mistreated that she remained a lifelong invalid after Washington managed to have her exchanged for the wives of two Tories. In spite of all this, upright citizen that he was, Lewis used what small resources he had left after the Revolution to pay his debts in Britain.

WILLIAM FLOYD, also of Welsh descent, had a substantial farm on Long Island. He loved to hunt and to give lavish parties and, like his fellow delegates from New York, he had every reason to resent British intrusion into his pleasant way of life. He and Francis Lewis were the only members of their delegation present in the congress on July 4, 1776, and both men were distressed because their delegation was the only one that could not vote for the Declaration. The fact was that their instructions forbade them to vote for any measure until it was approved by the body that had elected them to the congress. Therefore Floyd and Lewis kept silent when the roll was called on July 4, and the vote that day was not unanimous. However, approval did come from New York before the signing on August 2. This explains the difference between the printed version of the Declaration and the parchment version. The former is headed: "A Declaration By the Representatives of the United States of America, In General Congress assembled." The parchment is headed: "The unanimous Declaration of the thirteen united States of America." Like the other New York signers, William Floyd suffered losses. He had to abandon his home—first to occupying troops, then to Tories. Once during the war he did have the satisfaction of outwitting the enemy. What he called "some Carefull persons" managed to smuggle out some of his possessions.

PHILIP LIVINGSTON was a formidable character, more powerful and more conservative than the other New York delegates, but no less devoted to luxury. He disliked British interference with his rights, but he also had contempt for the Sons of Liberty. He was not present when the congress voted on the Declaration. Nevertheless, a thoroughgoing if belated patriot, he signed the document and endured the consequences. He and his family had to flee when the British army took New York. With no great feeling of cheer, but also without grudge, he contributed a great deal of his fortune to keep the new United States going.

203

NEW JERSEY

JOHN HART and the four other delegates from New Jersey made up a special group of signers. Until June 15, 1776, New Jersey had been represented in the Continental Congress by men devoted to restoring harmony with Britain. In this they were supported by the colony's governor, William Franklin, Benjamin Franklin's very conservative son. But after Richard Henry Lee introduced his resolution calling for a break with Britain, patriots in New Jersey decided to take action. William Franklin was ousted and put under arrest. On June 21, new delegates were chosen and sent to Philadelphia instructed to "join with the Delegates of the other Colonies in Continental Congress, in the most vigorous Measures for supporting the just Rights and Liberties of America." John Hart was a good, sound choice as a delegate, and a loyal one. He represented innumerable modest patriots who had not made themselves heard but who now astonished Britain by their dissidence. Living on a farm, scarcely touched by British taxes and trade restraints, Hart and others like him had come to know the taste of liberty. "Independent souls," John Adams called them. Soon after Hart signed the Declaration, Hessian troops devastated his farm and his gristmill near Hopewell. He escaped capture, but from then on the British persistently hunted for him. Sometimes he stayed with friends, never in the same place two nights in a row. He slept in caves and once in a farmer's doghouse. These many months of hardship ruined his health, and he lived only two years after the British retreat from Princeton.

JOHN WITHERSPOON, a Scottish Presbyterian minister, had been in America only about eight years when he became a delegate to the congress. In Scotland he had been known for his scholarship, his wit, and the vigor of his orthodoxy—qualities which led American Presbyterians to make him president of the College of New Jersey, now Princeton. He quickly revised the curriculum, endeared himself to the students, and created a small intellectual revolution in the college. He also raised a good deal of money for it. At the same time his political sympathies moved rapidly toward those of American radicals. This was not entirely surprising. He had sided with the ordinary people in quarrels within the Scottish church. Although they were the conservative, orthodox group, he felt that their rights had to be defended, and he took up their cause and preached it. In America he preached the rights of ordinary people with equal vigor. When a hesitant delegate to the congress said he did not think the colonies were ripe for independence, Witherspoon answered, "In my judgment, sir, we are not only ripe but rotting." He prided himself on the plainness of his sermons. Once when a parishioner remarked that he had a fine garden but no flowers, he said, "No, madam, neither in my garden nor in my discourse." On the signing of the Declaration, however, he allowed himself a slight exception to that rule: "Although these gray hairs must soon descend into the sepulchre," he said, "I would infinitely rather that they should descend thither by the hand of the public executioner than desert at this crisis the sacred cause of my country."

RICHARD STOCKTON was one of two signers who visited John Witherspoon in Scotland and persuaded him to come to Princeton. (The other was Benjamin Rush of Pennsylvania.) Until that trip to Britain Stockton had been only a mild advocate of colonial rights. Although the Stamp Act irritated him, its repeal soothed his feelings, and on a trip to England shortly afterward he delivered to King George in person a copy of a speech by an American praising the king for rescinding the tax. Before he returned home, Stockton stopped in Ireland. There the poverty and suffering he saw appalled and frightened him. Ireland's misery was the direct result of British colonial rule. America, Stockton thought, could be next. From that time on he was attracted more and more to the idea of independence. Not long after he signed the Declaration, British troops occupied and wrecked Morven, his estate near Princeton. A party of Tories then captured him and sent him to a brutal prison in New York. Like John Hart he never recovered from the deprivation, and he died before the Revolution was won.

ABRAHAM CLARK, known as "the poor man's counsellor," grew up on a farm but taught himself a good deal of law, apparently to help his less-educated neighbors in disputes over title to land. At times he annoyed the more urbane patriots—Benjamin Rush called him "cynical"—because he disliked pomposity and any tendency to take advantage of political position. Later in life he angered professional lawyers by sponsoring a law aimed at preventing exorbitant fees. The epitaph on his gravestone called him "Firm and decided as a patriot, zealous . . . as a friend to the public."

FRANCIS HOPKINSON, the fifth "independent soul" from New Jersey, had great wit and charm and was the least solemn of patriots. Few men managed to irritate the British more. He satirized them in very funny articles and essays and won innumerable converts to his opinions on separation. Although he had studied law and worked at it somewhat, his real interests were writing and painting and inquiry into science. He served a brief time as a customs collector, but was ousted because of his anti-British ideas. Like other New Jersey delegates, he lost his books and papers and valuables when the British looted his home.

PENNSYLVANIA

BENJAMIN FRANKLIN, the eldest and most distinguished of nine Pennsylvania signers, was one of only three who actually voted for the Declaration. Two in the delegation voted against independence on July 2, and neither of them signed; two chose to stay away so they would not have to vote. One of these, Robert Morris, did sign later. The other five signers were elected on July 20, when sentiment in Pennsylvania was turning quickly to separation from Britain. On August 2, as the delegates were putting their names on the parchment, John Hancock is supposed to have said: "We must be unanimous; there must be no pulling different ways; we must all hang together." And Franklin answered: 'We must, indeed, all hang together, or most assuredly we shall hang separately."

JOHN MORTON voted with Franklin and James Wilson for independence on July 2. Morton was born on a farm, went to school only about three months, but was well educated at home by his stepfather. Until he was about forty years old he worked both as a farmer and as a surveyor. Then he entered politics as a member of the Pennsylvania legislature and soon afterward was sent to the Stamp Act Congress. There the Massachusetts patriots impressed him with their good sense. From that time on he began to side more with the radicals than with the Pennsylvania moderates. Although for a while he worried about the timing of a break with Britain, Sam Adams' eloquence in the last days of debate in July 1776 finally won him over.

JAMES WILSON, the third Pennsylvanian to vote for independence, had once studied law under John Dickinson, who was foremost among the advocates of reconciliation with Britain. But Wilson entered young manhood influenced strongly by the anticolonialism of his Scottish upbringing. After coming to America in his twenties, he soon began to have an intense interest in land speculation. When his success as a lawyer and businessman increased, his ardor for separation from Britain seems to have diminished somewhat. Still he stood by his vote for independence and later signed the parchment copy. From that time on his sympathies turned more and more toward the wealthy and conservative minority in Pennsylvania, while his own unsuccessful speculating finally bankrupted him. He died penniless in Edenton, North Carolina.

ROBERT MORRIS, from boyhood on, was addicted to trade and finance. As a partner in a vastly profitable Philadelphia mercantile firm, he was one of the first to see that separation from Britain must inevitably come. Although he deliberately stayed away from the congress on the day when three of the other Pennsylvania delegates voted in favor of independence, he was opposed only to the timing of the Declaration, which he considered hasty. Unlike most other signers, Morris had an all-too-realistic idea of what independence would cost. It was a good thing he did. Quite probably no other man could have performed the financial wizardry needed to keep the new United States afloat. He juggled money and credit, first to finance Washington's expensive spies in New Jersey, later to buy munitions and to feed and clothe the Continental forces. In the process, more timid and conventional men accused him of enriching himself at public expense. This was probably not true. But he certainly came through the Revolution with comfortable means. Then all of his wisdom and good judgment succumbed to "western lands" fever. He speculated and lost so much that he was sent to debtor's prison in Philadelphia. There Washington, ever affectionate and tolerant, dined with Morris at his "hotel with the grated doors." Recent archeological excavation has uncovered the foundations of the jail on Walnut Street where Morris spent more than three years before the United States Congress enacted a new bankruptcy law that freed him.

GEORGE TAYLOR, born into a Protestant family in Ireland, left school one day, boarded a sailing vessel, and landed in America without a penny. There was nothing especially strange about this. In the eighteenth century, ships' captains did a good business in such migrants, who were called redemptioners. Taylor, like many other boys and men, agreed that the captain could sell him to an employer in America for a fee equal to his passage money. The man who redeemed young Taylor was a maker of iron. The boy worked off his passage debt, stayed on, and later married his employer's widow. The business prospered. Taylor began to take an interest in local politics and was elected to the Pennsylvania assembly. In 1768 the assembly made him a member of a committee to draw up an outraged protest when Pennsylvania whites who had massacred some Indians were not prosecuted for the crimes. He had equally strong feelings about independence, but was not yet a member of the Continental Congress on July 4, 1776. So many in the Pennsylvania delegation were lukewarm about independence that replacements were chosen on July 20. Taylor, known to his neighbors as "a fine man and a furious Whig," was one of the new delegates who signed the parchment Declaration.

JAMES SMITH, like George Taylor, came from Protestant northern Ireland. He spent his boyhood in Philadelphia, learned some law along with the technique of surveying, and then set out for the frontier in western Pennsylvania. At that time wilderness lands had already attracted speculators. Many an investor bought property only to find that it had questionable boundaries. And so a man who was both a lawyer and a surveyor could be sure of employment. Smith, with his two skills, was busy, and he thoroughly enjoyed the freedom of frontier life, which did not encourage either devotion to the king or admiration for Parliament. Even after he settled down in the town of York he kept his feeling for liberty. That and his dislike of stuffy officialdom made him popular with younger men, who also liked his endless witty stories. Long before he was elected to the Continental Congress he organized meetings and propagandized for independence. Believing in "the logic of the bayonet," he also formed a corps of volunteer soldiers even before the military action at Lexington.

GEORGE CLYMER, left an orphan in childhood, was reared by an uncle who had one of the most successful mercantile houses in Philadelphia. Although he entered his guardian's business, Clymer hated every aspect of commercial affairs. The excitement of a profitable deal, he said, did not last very long, and could never balance the depression caused by a loss. He would certainly have been happier as a writer or scientist or historian, but he had been set on a commercial course, and he had a stern sense of duty which kept him at his work and later made him an active patriot. On principle he opposed the tax on tea and the Intolerable Acts. His republicanism and his pleasure at signing the Declaration grew out of his general philosophy that man had natural rights. Later his humanitarian ideas led him to advocate changes in Pennsylvania's harsh penal code, and he was one of the few men of his time to have any understanding of Indian culture. "The strongest passions of the Indians," he said, "are revenge and benevolence. Revenge in them must be distinguished from the same spirit among the whites: having . . . no public institutions to avenge a wrong, revenge is nearly with them as justice is with us; not so much proceeding from a heart retaining resentment, as from a sense of duty. Their general disposition and habits, are those of kindness." His last official job was negotiating a treaty—with Cherokee and Creek Indians of Georgia—which other white men broke.

GEORGE ROSS, a lawyer, seems to have been until 1775 a rather mild, pleasure-loving, and loyal subject of George III. He had been sent to the First Continental Congress in 1774, believing harmony with Britain could be restored. The next year, although he did not attend the Second Continental Congress, he served on a defense committee of the Pennsylvania legislature. In preparing to meet a possible British armed attack, Ross began to see that conciliation was impossible. On July 20, 1776, he was one of the five new Pennsylvania delegates who replaced the moderates in the congress. In spite of his conversion to the patriot side, Ross was temperate in his judgment of Tories. He thought they were misguided rather than evil and felt obliged to act as defense attorney when some were brought to trial.

BENJAMIN RUSH, a man of boundless energy and innocent goodwill, traveled a straight road to revolution. As a medical student in Scotland, he began to feel that Britain was governed by corrupt men who could only mean harm to the colonies. His zest for living led him to believe in the natural rights of men, including black men. If he had been in the congress when Jefferson's draft of the Declaration was discussed, he would certainly have supported the section against the slave trade. In 1773 he himself had published an antislavery pamphlet that cost him a number of his more conservative patients. (He made up a bit of the loss by charging Patrick Henry a hefty fee of four pounds to inoculate him against smallpox.) In a less controversial pamphlet, published after the Boston Tea Party, Rush advocated a boycott of tea, both on moral grounds (that the tax was oppressive) and for medical reasons (he considered the drink bad for health). Although he shared his colleagues' belief in bleeding his patients, he scandalized many of them by his otherwise independent attitude toward medicine. Recognizing what he called the "imperfections of our science," he thought that doctors would kill fewer patients if they merely prescribed temperance—no drink or tobacco—and plenty of exercise. Most of Rush's patients were plain people, shopkeepers and artisans. His was a large practice, and he used it as a kind of opinion poll when the congress was meeting. Were his patients for or against independence? Their answers were reported to his friends among the radicals in the congress, immediately and at length. Rush was a compulsive and contentious talker. Argument he considered "steel to the flint of genius." But he was much too outspoken to be a good politician. After serving as a delegate in the First Continental Congress, he was not reelected. However, during the first half of 1776, he gave vigorous stirs to the explosive political mix in Pennsylvania, and his efforts helped to bring about, in July, the election of the

five new pro-independence delegates, himself among them. On August 2, he eagerly signed the Declaration in the "pensive and awful silence which pervaded the house."

DELAWARE

CAESAR RODNEY inherited a flourishing plantation, which he managed competently while at the same time he was a busy leader in the Delaware legislature. After the passage of the Stamp Act, he served on a committee that composed a long and flowery remonstrance addressed to the king. When the act was repealed, his committee again addressed the king, assuring him of their gratitude and loyalty. After the passage of the Intolerable Acts, Rodney once more helped to draft an address, "dutifully remonstrating against the proceedings of a British parliament, confessedly the wisest and greatest assembly upon earth." Dutiful though he probably felt toward the monarch, Rodney now began to correspond judiciously with other Americans who were disenchanted with Parliament. Before long he was well on the way to agreement with the radicals in the Continental Congress, where he served from the beginning. Many of his neighbors in Delaware did not share his ideas, and he spent a good deal of time shuttling between Philadelphia and his home territory, trying to convert or at least neutralize Tories. He was on such a mission when, in the evening of July 1, a messenger from a colleague in the congress brought him word that his presence there was urgently needed. At that time the three-man Delaware delegation stood divided: Rodney and Thomas McKean for independence, George Read against an immediate declaration. Therefore, if Delaware's vote was to count, Rodney had to add his *aye* to McKean's. After an all-night dash through a heavy rainstorm, Rodney reached Philadelphia just in time. Still in riding clothes, he cast the decisive vote. News about adoption of the Declaration reached the town of Dover in time to be announced at a turtle feast. Thereupon members of the Committee of Safety sent for a portrait of the king, which was burned after a speech by the committee chairman who said: "Compelled by strong necessity, thus we destroy even the shadow of that king who refused to rule over a free people."

GEORGE READ, lawyer, judge, and public servant, could hardly have avoided ambivalent feelings about independence. He was a close friend of John Dickinson, chief of Pennsylvania's moderates in the congress. Charles Thomson, the radical secretary of the congress, was also a friend and former schoolmate. In 1774 Read helped to collect a fund for the relief of poor Bostonians who had suffered from the closing of the port, sharing in what Sam Adams called their "inextinguishable love of liberty." At the same time he sensed how vehemently many people in Delaware opposed a break with Britain, and since he represented them in the congress he felt obliged to respect their views. So it was that he voted against the resolution for independence in July but supported the new United States once separation was a fact. When the time came to sign the Declaration, he did so with no reservations.

THOMAS MCKEAN, like many other lawyers, entered politics while he was a young man. At that time, in the 1750s, there were two political groups in Delaware. One, headed by the governor, included the judges, magistrates, and various officials, all of whom the governor appointed. The opposition group wanted, among other things, an independent judiciary, which could not be influenced or dismissed at the governor's whim. McKean soon became a leader among the antiestablishment people. In 1765 they sent him to the Stamp Act Congress, where he met James Otis and other outspoken New Englanders. Some of the more timid members of that congress roused McKean's wrath and scorn, and his arguments with them nearly ended in duels. From then on he took part in protests and public meetings. As a delegate to the Continental Congress he voted for the independence resolution and for the Declaration, but for some reason did not sign the parchment copy until 1777. Later that year, he wrote to John Adams that he had had his "full share of the anxieties, cares and troubles of the present war." He was holding official jobs in both Delaware and Pennsylvania and was "hunted like a fox by the enemy. . . . I was compelled to remove my family five times in a few months, and, at last, fixed them in a little log house on the banks of the Susquehannah . . . but safety was not to be found there, for they were soon obliged to remove again, on account of incursions of the Indians." A good many people, even some of his friends, thought McKean high-handed and cold, but most would have agreed with Jefferson that he was also "the soundest, firmest, and most zealous" of republicans.

MARYLAND

CHARLES CARROLL of Carrollton, elegant and graceful aristocrat, was rich enough to spend an idle life in the luxury of his family's several mansions. Instead he put his considerable energy into righting what he considered political wrongs. When he was a child his father sent him to school in France, partly to make sure he had a good education, partly to spare him the misery that Protestants were causing Catholics in Maryland. By the time Carroll returned, the religious persecution had abated, but uproar over the Stamp Act had just begun. Legal training in France and England gave the young man an interest in the relationship of Parliament to the colonies, and he came out firmly on the side of his countrymen. He soon took part in other disputes, went to the First Continental Congress as an adviser, and traveled with Franklin to Canada, seeking French aid in the event of war. In the debate on independence Carroll was all for the break with Britain. However, the Maryland delegates had instructions not to vote for independence without the specific approval of the body that had elected them. This extragovernmental convention, made up of representatives from each Maryland county, had declared itself firmly for reconciliation with Britain. At the end of May 1776, its meetings still opened with prayers for the king and the royal family. Carroll spent a good deal of time discussing and urging new instructions. Finally the prayers, at least, were dispensed with, and before the debate in the

congress ended, the Maryland delegates were freed to vote for independence if they chose. When John Hancock asked Carroll if he wished to sign the Declaration, Carroll took the pen and answered, "Most willingly." Although the Carroll property was indeed vast, neither British troops nor Tories vandalized it.

WILLIAM PACA owned a great estate on Chesapeake Bay and practiced law in Annapolis. As a young man he was elected to the Maryland legislature, where he soon began arguing on the side of the people against royal authority. A proposed measure that would tax citizens, regardless of their religion, to support the Anglican clergy roused his ire, even though he was himself an Episcopalian. Again, when the governor issued a proclamation asserting that he and not the legislature had the right to set certain taxes and fees, Paca joined in the resistance. He and Samuel Chase (also a signer) organized a march that ended at a gallows, where they hanged a copy of the proclamation and then buried it in a little coffin. The impudent ceremony was accompanied by volleys from guns aboard Paca's "elegant armed schooner"—the eighteenth century version of a yacht. (It carried guns only for salutes, not defense.) Paca's high spirits and persuasive tongue helped first to secure him a place in the congress and later to win his constituents over to the side of independence.

SAMUEL CHASE also entered politics by way of the law but, unlike Carroll and Paca, had no great fortune. He made up for it by vigorous activity and "bold, saucy language." In the Maryland legislature he invariably took the side of the people against the royal government. After the passage of the Stamp Act, which he vehemently opposed, the Sons of Liberty in Annapolis burned the stamps and hanged the official distributor in effigy. For his part in the episode, Chase was called by the mayor a "busy, restless incendiary, a ringleader of mobs, a foul mouthed and inflaming son of discord and faction, a common disturber of the public tranquillity, and a promoter of the lawless excesses of the multitude." All of which Chase relished thoroughly. When he was a delegate to the First Continental Congress, the need for conciliatory tactics exasperated him, and no one, except perhaps Sam Adams, rejoiced more when the Second Continental Congress began to swing toward independence. Along with Carroll and Paca, Chase took up lobbying for a change in the Maryland delegates' instructions. As usual, Chase went about it in his own impassioned way. "He hungered and thirsted for independence," says one biographer, "with an eagerness that knew no bounds." He organized petitions and letters against the old instructions, traveled, and spoke at county meetings. Speechmaking came so naturally to him that he often forgot himself and orated at the closed meetings of the congress, when there was no real need for that art. Benjamin Rush, a good friend, remarked that he "rendered great services to his country" but "possessed more learning than knowledge, and more of both than judgment." It happened that Chase could not be present to vote for the Declaration on July 4. The next day he sent an anguished question to John Adams: "How shall

I transmit to posterity that I gave my consent?" Adams replied, reassuring him that when others signed the document he would indeed have "the opportunity . . . of transmitting [his] name among the votaries of independence." In 1796 Washington appointed Chase to the Supreme Court. Some of his colleagues thought his behavior on the bench was "arbitrary, oppressive and unjust," and impeachment proceedings were brought against him. Whatever his faults were, the Senate did not believe him guilty of treason, bribery, or other high crimes, and he was acquitted.

THOMAS STONE, a modest, hardworking patriot and lawyer, was overshadowed in the congress by the three other Maryland delegates. Although his family was very conservative—his grandfather had been a royal governor of the colony—he ultimately sensed that separation from Britain was bound to happen. When the time came, he voted for it resolutely. He served on several committees of the congress, but little else is known about his activities, perhaps because he was ailing, and his wife had been laid low by medical treatment. It was the custom of many doctors at that time to give patients huge doses of mercury before inoculation for smallpox. Benjamin Rush was among the radicals who opposed the practice, and if Mrs. Stone had been his patient she would no doubt have been spared the suffering and early death that the mercury treatment brought about. The quiet, unprepossessing Stone became a great friend of ebullient Samuel Chase. In later life they sometimes worked together on law cases, for which Chase supplied the eloquence and Stone the logical arguments.

VIRGINIA

RICHARD HENRY LEE belonged to an old family of Virginia planters who were well established at the time of Cromwell and the Glorious Revolution. Under the monarchy, aristocratic Virginians had been largely left alone to prosper without interference, and they refused at first to recognize Cromwell's rule. Instead they plotted to bring the exiled Charles, later Charles II, across the Atlantic and make him king of Virginia. One of Richard Henry Lee's ancestors was involved in the scheme, which fizzled when Cromwell died. Still loyal to the crown, young Richard's father sent him to be educated in England. Apparently the usual English classical education had an unusual effect on him. He was fascinated not by imperial Rome but by Greek and Roman republicanism. The theories of Locke about the natural rights of man also impressed him. After he returned home, soon to become a member of the legislature, he entered a controversy about the slave trade. Contending that slavery had been immensely harmful to Greece and Rome, Lee favored a measure that would have imposed such a heavy import duty "as effectually to stop that disgraceful traffic." The only result of his arguments, says a biographer, was "the pleasure of having done his duty." Nevertheless, he went on to the "arduous task . . . of breaking down that wall of proud and perfect separation, which in Virginia had hitherto divided the patricians from the people." Again he was motivated apparently by knowledge of the harmful effect on the Roman republic of segregating the lower classes. Here his ideas had a more practical effect. Under his influence a rather wide group of men got together to oppose the Stamp Act. Although not actually part of the Sons of Liberty, the popular association of rural men he led carried out much the same program of activity in the following years. After the *Gaspée* incident, Lee, together with Jefferson and Patrick Henry, proposed committees of correspondence at about the same time that Sam Adams had the same idea. Lee, who seemed more a New Englander than a Virginia planter, grew more and more outspoken about separation from Britain. "I am afraid," John Adams wrote in May 1776, "they [the Virginians] will get the start of Congress in declarations of Independence. We are certainly ripe for the grand resolution." It was Richard Henry Lee who in June was chosen to present the resolution to the congress: "That these United Colonies are, and of a right ought to be, free and independent States."

THOMAS JEFFERSON symbolizes many freedoms, but most of all political freedom and freedom of mind. That the two were not separate he learned many times over in his long life. After the Revolution, when Virginia's laws were being overhauled, he had particular concern for the problem of religious liberty. It seemed to him that a man was responsible for his own soul, that the state should have nothing to say about what he believed, and that support for churches should come from the individuals who adhered to them and not in any degree from taxes imposed on those of other faiths—or of no faith. Jefferson wrote a bill summing up his ideas, and eventually it became law, substantially as he had drawn it. Later his good friend Benjamin Waterhouse, who was on the medical faculty at Harvard, lost his job because he refused to dissociate himself from Jefferson's social and political opinions. The scientist Joseph Priestley, discoverer of oxygen and a follower of Jefferson, was also persecuted for his ideas and narrowly escaped jail in Massachusetts. Public education, Jefferson thought, could help to free men's minds, not only in Massachusetts but also in Virginia, and there he worked toward establishing a state university. Before he died he left the design of a tombstone for his grave at Monticello. It was to bear a simple inscription, "and not a word more, . . . because by these, as testimonials that I have lived, I wish most to be remembered":

Here was buried / Thomas Jefferson / author of
the / Declaration / of / American Independence /
of the / Statute of Virginia / for / Religious
Freedom / and Father of the / University of Virginia

GEORGE WYTHE, a skillful lawyer, had little formal schooling. His singularly forceful mother, who knew Latin, taught him at home, and together they mastered Greek, too. An uncle taught him law. For some years young Wythe spent most of his time "in the luxuriance of youthful passions [and] the seductions of pleasure." Suddenly, when he was about thirty, he decided to mend his ways. From then on he applied himself to work for his clients and in the Virginia legislature. Greatly influenced by young Thomas Jefferson, who had read law under his guidance, and by Patrick

Henry, Wythe did his share of organizing and politicking for independence. "No man," said Jefferson, "ever left behind him a character more venerated. . . . His virtue was of the purest tint; his integrity inflexible, and his justice exact." During the Revolution, most of his slaves took advantage of Britain's offer of freedom and went over to the British side. Wythe emancipated those who remained, and in his will left a good part of his estate to one of them, a young boy who suddenly and mysteriously died a few days before Wythe's own death. Someone had put arsenic in Wythe's food, and with the black boy out of the way, the whole inheritance stayed in the family. Wythe's great-nephew was tried for the murder but not convicted.

FRANCIS LIGHTFOOT LEE, younger brother of Richard Henry Lee, was a quiet, unobtrusive, but able patriot. Unlike the first three sons in the family, Francis was not sent to school in England. He had a tutor at home where, says a biographer, there were "no strong excitements for the operations of ambition; . . . joy was in every face, and hospitality at every door." On his father's death, the huge Lee fortune provided him with an estate of his own. There he raised tobacco and did experimental farming for pleasure. As a member of the legislature he never tried to match the oratory of his brother Richard Henry, although he helped to write the resolutions and remonstrances that preceded the call for the First Continental Congress. In 1775 Francis Lightfoot Lee replaced an elderly Virginia delegate and served in the congress for four years.

BENJAMIN HARRISON, an immensely wealthy planter, belonged to the rather small group of Virginians who, said Jefferson, had the "forwardness and zeal which the times required." He also possessed an energy and spirit that pleased John Adams when the two met at the First Continental Congress. Before long Harrison had made himself at home in Philadelphia, which meant he entertained with an extravagance normal among planters but rather shocking to New Englanders. Although he proved to be valuable on committees, he and John Adams soon began to rub each other the wrong way. Harrison disliked the northern temperament. Adams wrote, on second thought, that Harrison was "an indolent, luxurious, heavy gentleman, of no use in Congress." Heavy he certainly was, and luxury-loving. But he did his work faithfully, especially on the Committee of Secret Correspondence, which after the Revolution turned into the Department of State. He took the moderate side in some debates, but if the opposition prevailed, he cheerfully carried out whatever the majority decided. His son William Henry Harrison was a president of the United States, and so was his great-grandson Benjamin.

CARTER BRAXTON was the grandson of a famous Virginia planter, nicknamed "King" Carter because of his regal estates. When Braxton was still quite young he inherited several large tobacco and corn plantations. By inclination he would have preserved what a nineteenth century writer called "the peculiar disposition of that country [Virginia] where cupidity and indolence go hand in hand, and serve only as boundaries for each other." But after he had been elected to the legislature, he took part in public affairs and somewhat reluctantly went along with Patrick Henry and the other Virginia patriots. In the spring of 1775, he mediated a curious affair that might have led to the spilling of a good deal of blood. At that time the already edgy Lord Dunmore, governor of Virginia, had the colony's gunpowder secretly removed from the magazine in Williamsburg and put aboard a British warship. News of the seizure brought Patrick Henry, at the head of 150 or so armed men, marching on Williamsburg to demand either the powder or payment for it. Braxton, knowing that Dunmore was prepared to have a company of marines fire on the colonials, persuaded Henry to hold off. Through his father-in-law, Braxton then arranged for the money to be paid to the colony, and fighting in Virginia was avoided at almost the same time it was going on at Lexington. Ever a conciliator, Braxton did not really favor independence, but when the time came he signed the Declaration. During the Revolution he invested heavily in merchant ships, most of which were captured by Britain. He died, said his biographer, greatly impoverished, "a martyr of misfortune."

THOMAS NELSON, JR., belonged to a family of wealthy merchants and planters, most of whom were active patriots. The exception was an uncle of the signer, also named Thomas, who disapproved of the Revolution and retired from public life to the Nelson house at Yorktown. Thomas, Jr., although he had been educated in England, quickly fell in with the radical members of the Virginia legislature. "By heavens," he said, "I am an infidel in politics, for I do not believe [in Britain's honor]." Early in 1775 he advocated the formation of a colonial military force, and during the war he raised a company of Virginia volunteers. He was in command of some troops at the battle of Yorktown. It happened that Cornwallis had taken up headquarters in the Nelson family mansion at Yorktown, which the elder Nelson had not left when the British arrived. Cornwallis allowed the old man to depart under a flag of truce when it appeared that Washington was going to bombard the town. That done, Thomas, Jr., told Washington not to spare his home, which stood on a high spot near the fortifications.

NORTH CAROLINA

JOSEPH HEWES, born in New Jersey of Quaker parents, became a successful merchant, first in Philadelphia, then when he was about thirty years old in the busy little port of Edenton, North Carolina, on Albemarle Sound. For a long time, that part of the colony had been notable for its lack of respect for British authority, and on October 25, 1774, the ladies of the town held their own decorous tea party. Hewes and the other North Carolina delegates were sent to the First Continental Congress with rather bold and liberal instructions. Conciliation was not uppermost in the minds of Hewes' constituents. When, in 1775, the Quakers of New Jersey and Pennsylvania asserted their belief in pacifism and denounced the congress, Hewes broke with the Friends. He now departed enough from Quaker ways to learn how to dance, and even enjoyed it, but he still remained somewhat more sympathetic to the moderates than to the radicals in the congress. Finally, however, when Sam Adams brought out letters proving that majority opinion in North Carolina was for independence, Hewes decided to support the resolution that Richard Henry Lee presented in June. John Adams reported the scene: "Mr. Hewes, . . . lifting both his hands to Heaven . . . cried out, 'It is done! and I will abide by it.'"

JOHN PENN went to a little country school in Virginia for only two or three years before he was eighteen. Then his father died and left him free to do as he pleased with a modest inheritance. At the same time a relative, Edmund Pendleton, offered him the use of his library. Pendleton was a lawyer, and with his encouragement young Penn taught himself enough law to get a license to practice by the time he was twenty-one. Hard work apparently did not make him a bore, and when he moved to North Carolina, he soon had loyal friends who sent him first to the extragovernmental provincial congress and then to the Second Continental Congress. Tom Paine's *Common Sense* seems to have made a thoroughgoing radical of him. Although he never got up in the congress to speak, he was ready to vote for independence long before the other delegates from North Carolina.

WILLIAM HOOPER's birthplace was Boston. He attended Harvard, then began to study law under James Otis at about the time when "the child independence was born" during Otis' battle against the writs of assistance. In those days Boston had all too many young lawyers, so Hooper moved to Wilmington, North Carolina. There he found at first less tension than in New England. But he later became involved in a controversial affair that shocked Bostonians. There had developed in North Carolina a sharp division between people in the affluent coastal settlements and poor farmers scrabbling for a livelihood on the western frontier. Ever since the early 1760s the farmers had been complaining of exorbitant taxes and illegal fees collected by sheriffs, who were said to pocket the money. Their pleas and petitions for relief were ignored, and finally they began to organize into resistance groups. Calling themselves Regulators, they refused to pay taxes, defied law officers, and took some local government into their own hands. This militance soon brought response from the royal governor, William Tryon. In 1771 he sent troops to put down the movement, and among the officers on the expedition was William Hooper. After a brutal battle at Alamance, many Regulators were arrested and seven were hanged. Outraged, the *Boston Gazette* asked how it was possible "for any man, unless he possess the soul of a Cannibal, to wish success to an administration so corrupt, so absolutely void of humanity, and every christian virtue, as that of North-Carolina!!!" Now the eastern merchant-planter groups felt maligned— also fearful that Britain would confuse their sedate remonstrances against the Townshend Acts with the "riotous" actions inland. Hooper certainly supported resistance to the acts, though he failed to understand the plight of the farmers, even as they failed to understand the plight of Indians onto whose lands they had moved. As a delegate to the Continental Congress, Hooper seems to have sided with the New Englanders, but was absent at the time when the vote for independence was taken. His signature on the Declaration did not go unnoticed. The British shelled his house on the Cape Fear River and forced him and his family to flee.

SOUTH CAROLINA

ARTHUR MIDDLETON, handsome, young, somewhat spoiled son of an aristocratic plantation owner, took his father's place in the Continental Congress when the older man resigned because of ill health. Soon he became very friendly with the Pennsylvania moderates and spoke out often. John Adams said of him, "He had little information, and less argument; in rudeness and sarcasm his forte lay, and he played off his artillery without reserve. I made it a rule . . . that he never got, and I never lost, anything from these encounters." And then, surprisingly, Adams goes on to say that they parted "without a spark of malice on either side; for he was an honest and generous fellow, with all his zeal in this cause." Middleton, along with the other great rice and indigo planters, felt a certain ambivalence about separation from Britain: They wanted freedom to run their own affairs, while at the same time they cherished ties with Britain and enjoyed the protection of British arms. Until the actual day of voting, the South Carolina delegates favored postponement of action on the independence resolution. But when the time came, they concurred "for the sake of unanimity." In 1780 when the British took Charleston, they looted Middleton's magnificent house and defaced the paintings in it. He and two other delegates—Rutledge and Heyward—were among those taken captive and confined in the fortress at St. Augustine, Florida. An exchange of prisoners freed them several months later.

THOMAS HEYWARD, JR., studied law at the Middle Temple in London, as did Arthur Middleton, Edward Rutledge, and Thomas Lynch. None of them needed to practice at home. It was simply a custom among many wealthy southern aristocrats to give their sons some English education. Charming and talented though the young men were, Englishmen did not welcome them as equals. The snubs they endured apparently did as much as anything else to turn Heyward into a patriot, and perhaps the others, too. Heyward was sent to the Continental Congress in the spring of 1776 and for the most part followed Middleton's lead. During their imprisonment at St. Augustine, their captors seem not to have shared the disdain for colonials that Englishmen in London had. On the Fourth of July, 1781, they were allowed to have dinner together, and a small American flag appeared on the plum pudding that was served. This in spite of the fact that Heyward had passed the time in the fortress writing a song, "God Save the States," to the tune of "God Save the King." While he was in prison the British raided Heyward's estate. Some of his slaves may have been given hope of freedom if they joined the raiders, or they may simply have been abducted. In any case they seem to have ended, no better off, on sugar plantations in Jamaica.

EDWARD RUTLEDGE, brother-in-law of Arthur Middleton, returned from England and decided to practice law. He turned out to be something of a spellbinder in the courtroom and "never failed to dazzle where he did not convince." He was not yet twenty-seven years old when he went to the Continental Congress. At first John Adams thought well of him, but later described him, perhaps too unkindly, as "a swallow, a sparrow, a peacock . . . jejeune, inane, and puerile." Like the other South Carolina delegates, he held back from independence until the last moment, but it was he who persuaded his colleagues to vote for the resolution.

THOMAS LYNCH, JR., dutifully studied law in England but found he had no taste for it. When he came home he persuaded his father to let him manage one of the family plantations. In 1776 he helped to recruit a company of regular troops in North Carolina, and on the way home fell ill of what was called "a bilious fever." Still ailing, he was sent to congress in 1776. His father had already been elected earlier that year, but a heart attack made it impossible for him to be active. Hoping that Lynch, Sr., could at least sign the parchment copy, Rutledge and Heyward left a space between their signatures. He was unable to fill it. Thomas, Jr., stayed in Philadelphia only briefly after putting his name, not in the empty spot left for his father, but beneath Heyward's. Finally, persuaded that his health might be better in some other climate, he and his wife boarded a ship intending to go to France. The vessel had recently been rebuilt in a way that made it unseaworthy. Apparently it went down in a storm. At any rate the Lynch family was never heard from again.

GEORGIA

LYMAN HALL, born in Connecticut, came to Georgia with about forty New England families and settled at Sunbury in St. John's parish (county) south of Savannah. There he practiced medicine and started a rice plantation. He was not at the First Continental Congress—Georgia alone among the colonies did not send delegates. When word came that the congress had resolved not to import or consume any English goods that could be dispensed with, a great many Georgians opposed the idea, and it was turned down at a general meeting in Savannah. Citizens of St. John's parish, however, still holding to their New England independence of spirit, pledged themselves not to buy in conservative Savannah any English goods except necessities. They also elected Lyman Hall to represent the parish at the next congress. Hall traveled to Philadelphia in May 1775 and was allowed to attend the sessions of the congress. But because St. John's parish did not really represent the whole colony of Georgia, he could not vote. By July, opinion in Georgia had swung around to support of colonial unity. Regular delegates to the congress were elected, among them Hall. True to his nonimportation pledge, he appeared in Philadelphia wearing clothes of homespun cloth made in America. Few other delegates were so dressed. When the British invaded Georgia he and his family moved north, and his home and plantation were destroyed.

BUTTON GWINNETT, born and educated in England, was for a while a merchant in Charleston. Then he bought some slaves and some land on St. Catherine's Island just off the coast to the east of the settlement at Sunbury, where Lyman Hall lived. The two men had similar feelings about separation from Britain and both were delegates to the Continental Congress in 1776. Unlike Hall, Gwinnett was touchy and quick-tempered. In 1777 he quarreled with a man who had called him "a scoundrel and a lying rascal." They fought a duel with pistols at twelve feet, and Gwinnett died of his wound.

GEORGE WALTON as a boy in Virginia was a carpenter's apprentice. Later he learned law on his own and began to practice in Georgia in 1774. That year he cosigned an advertisement of a meeting at "the Liberty Pole at Tondee's Tavern in Savannah," where citizens would consider "their constitutional rights and liberties, as a part of the British empire." The results of this and other meetings did not much please Walton. Evidently Georgians were more interested in petitions and conciliation than in action. However, as opposition to the royal government increased, Walton helped to guide it, although he was not among the first delegates elected to the Continental Congress in 1775. One of them, the Reverend John Joachim Zubly, turned out to be something of an embarrassment. He was so vehemently opposed to independence that he wrote secretly to the governor of Georgia warning of a possible break with Britain. A copy of the letter fell into the hands of Samuel Chase, who accused its author of treason. Zubly thereupon left the political scene. The following year Walton was elected. During the war, he was serving as a colonel in the militia at the time when the British took Savannah. They captured him and, because he was a signer and a member of the congress, they offered to exchange him, but only for a high-ranking imprisoned British officer. While the bargaining went on, his term expired. His captors then agreed to lower the price. They exchanged him for a mere captain in their navy. After his release, Walton continued to serve in the congress and, much later, in the United States Senate.

SUCH WERE THE SIGNERS, brave and fallible, each a patriot in his own fashion. The Tories called them a "pack of Banditti." To John Adams they combined "abilities, learning, eloquence, acuteness, equal to any I ever met with in my life." On the day they declared independence, their country —living, growing, moving outward in every way—had reached a momentous and critical time. The thirteen states united, now formed a separate nation, as free as a nation ever is to elaborate itself unencumbered by a past borrowed from a distant land.

❧ Gazetteer

Both the casual tourist and the serious history scholar find a special value in viewing the scenes of historic events, in visiting the homes of persons who have helped to shape the course of human experience, in stepping in the footprints of those who have blazed new pathways for generations to follow. This gazetteer, while not exhaustive, is presented to help readers do their own exploring of the places associated with the events described in this volume. The numbers given in parentheses refer to the appropriate chapter in the book; the letter "S" signifies a place associated with one or more of the signers of the Declaration of Independence.

Arizona

COOLIDGE. *Casa Grande Ruins National Monument.* One mile north of Coolidge on Arizona 87. Juan Bautista de Anza's expedition paused here for a day of rest October 30, 1775, and some members of the party explored the prehistoric Indian ruin which earlier Spaniards had used as a landmark. (21)

HOPI VILLAGES. *Old Oraibi* was inhabited in 1680. Other villages are near their former sites. Some Hopi ceremonies, open to non-Indians, are essentially the same as those the Spaniards tried to suppress before the war of 1680. (8)

TUBAC. Anza's 1774 journey of reconnaissance and his 1776 expedition both started here. (21)

TUCSON. Anza's expedition camped near here on October 26, 1775. (21)
Mission San Xavier del Bac, 6.7 miles south of Tucson on US 89. Father Francisco Garcés of this mission went with Anza on both his expeditions to California, and Anza passed here. (21)
Tumacacori National Monument, 48 miles south of Tucson on US 89. Anza passed the mission here, which dates from the late seventeenth century. (21)

YUMA. Anza's expedition crossed the Colorado River here, late in 1775. (21)

California

BORREGO SPRINGS. *Anza-Borrego Desert State Park.* The Anza expedition passed through the northern section of what is now a state park, and the map supplied by the California Department of Parks and Recreation shows the

trail he followed in this area. Part of it is closely paralleled by a local road. (21)

CARMEL. *Mission San Carlos Borromeo del Rio Carmelo,* south of Carmel on Lasuen Drive. Father Junípero Serra founded a mission by this name in 1770 at Monterey. In 1771 he moved it to the present site. Serra maintained his residence and headquarters here. His cell can be seen, and the Carmel Mission Library contains books that belonged to Serra. (21)

KING CITY. *Mission San Antonio de Padua,* 20 miles south of King City, near the village of Jolon on the Hunter-Liggett Military Reservation. Serra founded this mission July 14, 1771. The chapel has been restored, the remainder of the mission has been rebuilt. (21)

MONTEREY. *Royal Presidio Chapel,* 550 Church Street. On this site Serra established a mission in 1770. The present building dates from 1789 and is the only remaining presidio chapel in California. (21)

SAN DIEGO. *Mission San Diego de Alcalá,* 10818 San Diego Mission Road, Mission Valley, off Interstate 8. Serra founded this mission July 16, 1768, in Old San Diego, about six miles away. It was moved to the present site in August 1774, and it was here that the Diegueños attacked the Franciscans and others on November 4, 1775. (21)
Presidio, in Presidio Park. The site of this building is close to the Father Junípero Serra Cross. Extensive excavation has been conducted here. (21)
Serra Museum Library, 2727 Presidio Drive. This museum stands close to the site on which Father Junípero Serra founded the first mission in California on July 16, 1769. (21)

SAN FRANCISCO. *Mission San Francisco de Asis,* Dolores Street near 16th Street. This mission, usually called Mission Dolores, was founded June 29, 1776. Construction of the present mission building began in 1782. (21)
Presidio, northern tip of San Francisco Peninsula, on US 101 and Interstate 480. Construction of the Presidio began on July 27, 1776, and it was opened on October 9 by Serra. (21)

SAN GABRIEL. *Mission San Gabriel Arcangel,* Mission Drive and Junípero Serra Drive. This mission was founded September 8, 1771, and in that year it was the scene of an Indian rebellion. Anza stopped here in 1774, in 1776, and when he went with soldiers to San Diego following the revolt of Indians at the mission. Construction of the present building began in 1791. (21)

SAN JUAN CAPISTRANO. *Mission San Juan Capistrano.* The establishment of a mission here was interrupted by the Diegueño Revolt, but it was officially founded on November 1, 1776. (21)

Connecticut

BRANFORD. *The Baldwin House* had been built when John Wise served as a minister in this community before he went to a church near Ipswich, Massachusetts. (14)

FAIRFIELD. John Hancock and Dorothy Quincy were married in this town, August 28, 1775. (S)

LEBANON. *Welles House,* south end of the Common. William Williams was born here. His own home is nearby. Both are privately owned. (S)

LITCHFIELD. *Oliver Wolcott Home,* South Street, opposite the Law School. In the garden behind the house Oliver Wolcott's wife and children helped to make bullets from a leaden statue of George III, which had been demolished in New York City after the Declaration of Independence was read there (private). A walking tour of the Historic District in Litchfield takes the visitor through areas associated with Revolutionary times. (S)
Litchfield Historical Society Museum, south side of the Green, contains memorabilia of Oliver Wolcott. (S)

NEW HAVEN. *Roger Sherman's House* site, 1032 Chapel Street, is marked by a tablet on the existing house wall. (S)
Yale University. Roger Sherman was treasurer of Yale College. Although he was self-educated, the college gave him an honorary M.A. degree. Other signers of the Declaration of Independence who attended Yale were Oliver Wolcott, Philip Livingston, Lewis Morris, and Lyman Hall. (S)

NEW MILFORD. Site of Roger Sherman's cobbler shop is at Main and Church streets. (33)

NORWICH. *Governor Samuel Huntington House,* 34 East Town Street (private). He was buried in the old burial ground at the end of Cemetery Lane. (S)

SCOTLAND. *Samuel Huntington Birthplace* (private). (S)

STONINGTON. Canonchet was executed here. (8)

Delaware

DOVER. *Christ Episcopal Churchyard.* Caesar Rodney's grave. (S)

LEWES. *Caesar Rodney House,* Pilot Road, is privately owned, but may be visited on request. (S)

NEW CASTLE. William Penn landed here in October 1682, to begin his first visit to America. The town, which still has colonial buildings intact, began in 1651 as Fort Casimir, a Dutch settlement. Swedes seized it in 1654. The Dutch reoccupied it in 1655, and Peter Stuyvesant then laid out the *Green*, which remains. It is surrounded by historically important buildings. (10)

Amstel House, built before 1730, was the home of an early governor of Delaware and is now a museum. (10)

Immanuel Church, Episcopalian, built in 1703 by a congregation organized in 1689, suggests the diversity permitted by the Quakers. (10)

Old Dutch House, built before 1704, is now a museum of the Dutch period. (10)

Old State House, Delaware Street, south side of the Green. The east wing had been built at the time William Penn did. (10)

Old Presbyterian Church, Second Street, was built about 1707. (10)

Read House, on the Strand, one block south of Presbyterian Church, was the home of George Read after the Revolution. It is open to the public only on the third Saturday in May. (S)

WILMINGTON. A statue of Caesar Rodney stands in Rodney Square, center of the business district. (S)

Fort Christina site, foot of East Seventh Street. A memorial given to the city in 1938 by Sweden marks the spot where Swedish settlers landed in 1638. A Swedish log house stands in the park nearby. (10)

Old Swedes Church, East Seventh Street. The building, which dates from 1698, was originally a Lutheran church, but is now Episcopal. The adjoining stone farmhouse, built in 1690, is now a museum. (10)

District of Columbia

WASHINGTON. There are numerous memorials to early heroes of this country in the capital city. Among them are statues of Caesar Rodney, Charles Carroll of Carrollton, and Richard Stockton in the Capitol's Statuary Hall; the grave of Elbridge Gerry in the Congressional Cemetery; and the Thomas Jefferson National Memorial, at the south edge of Tidal Basin. The Memorial, built in the style Jefferson used at Monticello, was dedicated on April 13, 1943, two hundred years after his birth. Jefferson's library, which included the library of Peyton Randolph, formed the nucleus of the Library of Congress collection. At the National Archives, between Pennsylvania and Constitution avenues and Seventh and Ninth streets, sealed in a special airtight glass case, the original signed parchment copy of the Declaration of Independence is on display. (32, S)

Florida

JACKSONVILLE. *Fort Caroline National Memorial*, 10 miles from the center of the city, east on US 1A and Florida 10, then left on St. John's Bluff Road and right on Fort Caroline Road. (1)

NEW SMYRNA BEACH. *New Smyrna Historic Memorial*, on US 1 and Florida 90. Ruins still stand here, where 1,400 Greeks, Italians, Corsicans, and Minorcans landed in 1768 to establish a colony in English-controlled Florida. (22)

ST. AUGUSTINE. Full information about the restored part of this, the oldest non-Indian town north of Mexico, can be obtained from the Information Center, 10 Castillo Drive, near the City Gate. (1)

Castillo de San Marcos National Monument, 1 Castillo Drive. Oglethorpe besieged the Castillo unsuccessfully for 39 days in 1740. Three years later he made another attempt, also unsuccessful, and Florida remained in Spanish hands. (17) The Spanish fortress was taken over by England when, in 1763, the Seven Years' War ended with the defeat of France and Spain.

Christopher Gadsden and Peter Timothy, leading members of the Sons of Liberty, were imprisoned here with about 60 other South Carolina patriots after the British captured Charleston in 1780. (27) During the Revolution it served as a prison for captives taken by the British, including Arthur Middleton, Thomas Heyward, and Edward Rutledge, three of South Carolina's Signers. In the Castillo, now administered by the National Park Service, may be seen the cells where the prisoners were probably kept. (S)

Fort Matanzas National Monument, 14 miles south of the city, on Rattlesnake Island. (1) The wooden fortifications were replaced with stronger coquina stone when Oglethorpe threatened this Spanish outpost. (17)

Georgia

AUGUSTA. *George Walton House*, 2216 Wrightsboro Road. This was probably only a summer residence of George Walton. Most of the summer houses of prominent people in this area were built on top of the hill, above the miasmal lowlands, where the main part of the city stood. (S)

Meadow Garden, 1320 Nelson Street, was the home of George Walton after the revolution and is now a DAR museum. (S)

DARIEN. On US 17 stands a monument to the Scots Highlanders who settled here. (17)

Fort King George, one mile east of US 17, was the southernmost English outpost in America in 1721. (17)

Oglethorpe's Oak. Near the courthouse is a stump of a live oak tree once so large that a company of Oglethorpe's men could camp in its shade. (17)

NEW EBENEZER. *Jerusalem Church*, 13 miles north of Rincon, on the Savannah River near Georgia 275, was built in 1769 by the Salzburgers who were among the first settlers of Georgia. There is a small museum in the Parish House. (17)

ST. CATHERINE'S ISLAND. Here are the ruins of a house thought to have been built by Button Gwinnett. His grave may also be here. This island is privately owned. (S)

ST. SIMONS ISLAND. *Fort Frederica National Monument*, 12 miles east of Brunswick, via Torras Causeway and Frederica Road. Here Oglethorpe built a town and a fort to protect English colonists from Spaniards who claimed the territory and who had military forces at nearby St. Augustine, Florida. For several months Charles Wesley, a founder of Methodism, preached here. His brother, John Wesley, also visited and preached here. (17)

Battle of Bloody Marsh site, on Demere Road, is indicated by a marker. (17)

Fort St. Simons site, adjacent to the lighthouse on the south end of the island, is indicated by a marker. (17)

Oglethorpe's House site, on Frederica Road, .3 miles south of Christ Episcopal Church, is indicated by a stone tablet. (17)

SAVANNAH. Chippewa Square, Johnson Square, Madison Square, and Wright Square, are all part of Oglethorpe's original plan for Savannah. The Chamber of Commerce, 100 E. Bay Street, has tape cassettes for rent and folders for self-guided tours through this historic city. A statue of Oglethorpe stands in Chippewa Square. Near the sundial in Johnson Square is a map made of tile which shows Savannah as it was in the 18th century. In the southeast corner of Wright Square is a big boulder placed in honor of the Indian leader Tomochichi, who befriended Oglethorpe. (17)

Bethesda, nine miles from Savannah, an orphanage established by George Whitefield. (7)

Cockspur Island, near Savannah, has a monu-

ment marking the spot where John and Charles Wesley landed, in February, 1736. (17)

Colonial Cemetery, Greene Street, between Fifth and Sixth streets. A monument marks the graves of Lyman Hall and George Walton. (S)

Oglethorpe's Bench, west of City Hall on Yamacraw Hill, commemorates the spot near which Oglethorpe lived in a tent for a year while Savannah was being built. (17)

Temple Mickve Israel, east side of Monterey Square. In this temple is the Sephar Torah brought to Savannah in 1733 by the first Jewish settlers in Georgia. (17)

Tondee's Tavern site, Broughton and Whitaker streets. This tavern served as a gathering place for the Liberty Boys in Savannah. Here the Declaration of Independence was read for the first time in Georgia. (27)

Trustees Garden, East Broad Street, near Savannah River. This garden, part of the original plan for Savannah and now restored, was to furnish vegetables, vines, fruit trees, and mulberry trees—these last to be used in the silk industry Oglethorpe wanted to establish. It has been called the first experimental garden in America. (17)

U.S. Customhouse, Bull and East Bay streets. A tablet on Bull Street marks the spot where John Wesley first preached in Savannah; another on Bay Street marks the site of Oglethorpe's headquarters. (17)

Wormsloe Plantation, southeast of the city on Isle of Hope, off Georgia 204. This plantation was established in Oglethorpe's time. Its gardens may be visited in spring. (17)

SUNBURY. *Midway Church*, on US 17, halfway between Savannah and Brunswick, was attended by both Lyman Hall and Button Gwinnett. Neither home exists today. (S)

Illinois

CAHOKIA. Pontiac was assassinated here, in April 1769. (20)

KASKASKIA. Pontiac spent a good deal of time here when he was trying to organize resistance among the Indians of the Mississippi Valley. (20)

PONTIAC. This town is named after Pontiac, although he is not known to have been associated with it. On the courthouse lawn is a monument to the great leader, in the form of a cairn of boulders with a bronze plaque. (20)

STARVED ROCK STATE PARK. According to a legend of doubtful authenticity, remnants of the Ottawa and Potawatomi tribes pursued portions of the Illinois tribe to this place after the assassination of Pontiac. Those believed to be guilty of the assassination were besieged on top of the cliff and died of hunger—hence the name, Starved Rock. (20)

Indiana

FORT WAYNE. A marker designates the site of Fort Miami at Delaware Avenue and St. Joseph Boulevard, on the east bank of the St. Joseph River. (20)

LAFAYETTE. *Fort Ouiatenon* was located four miles from West Lafayette, on South River Road. Indians captured this fort, June 1, 1763. A part of it was reconstructed in 1936. (20)

Maryland

ANNAPOLIS. Bluffs rising just north of the Patuxent River extend to Herring Creek, south of Annapolis. Here William Davyes and John Pate, leaders of a protest movement, were hanged in 1676. (12) Walking tours of this city are conducted by Historic Annapolis, Inc. Numerous buildings exist as they were at the time of Charles Carroll of Carrollton, and he was associated with many of them. (25, S)

Carroll Mansion, on Duke of Gloucester Street, was the birthplace, in 1737, of Charles Carroll of Carrollton and the home he lived in when he was in Annapolis. (25)

Carroll-Caton House, Lombard and Front streets. Charles Carroll of Carrollton made his home here late in life. (25)

Carroll-Davis House, on the campus of St. John's College. This house, which once stood elsewhere in the city, has been restored. It belonged to a Charles Carroll who was related to Charles Carroll of Carrollton. (25)

William Paca Garden, 1 Martin Street. Recreation of beautifully landscaped gardens of the Maryland signer. (S)

Chase-Lloyd House, 22 Maryland Avenue. This house was begun by Samuel Chase, then sold to Edward Lloyd IV. It is now a home for elderly ladies, and the first floor is open to the public. (S)

Peggy Stewart House, 207 Hanover Street. Thomas Stone lived here for a while. (S)

State House, State Circle. From this building, which still serves as the capitol of Maryland, legislators once walked in a body to the home of Charles Carroll of Carrollton to pay him tribute. William Paca helped to design this building, which is also associated with Carroll, Thomas Stone, and Samuel Chase. (25, S)

BALTIMORE. *Deshon-Caton-Carroll House*, 800 East Lombard Street, was the winter home of Charles Carroll of Carrollton after the Revolution. (S)

CARMICHAEL (near Queenstown). *Wye Plantation*, owned by William Paca, is private, but may be visited with permission of the present owner. Paca is buried on the grounds of the plantation. (S)

CUMBERLAND. Here the Ohio Company established a supply post which was called Wills Creek. George Washington passed through the area several times on trips to and from the western lands. (18)

ELLICOTT CITY. Near here is Doughoregan, a favorite country home of the Carroll family. Charles Carroll of Carrollton was buried in the chapel on the grounds of the estate. (25)

PORT TOBACCO. *Habre-de-Venture* was the home of Thomas Stone, and he is buried on the grounds. It is privately owned, but the garden may be seen on request. The fine paneling of its drawing room is now in the Baltimore Museum of Art. (S)

ST. MARY'S. Reconstruction of Maryland's first State House. (12)

Clocker's Fancy. This dwelling, a few miles from St. Mary's, resembles many buildings that stood in 1689. Privately owned, not open to the public. (12)

Mattaponi, eight miles from town, was the residence of the third Lord Baltimore (private). (12)

WARWICK. *Bohemia Manor*, on local road off County 213 or County 282. Charles Carroll of Carrollton attended the Academy here when he was a small boy. Services are regularly held in the Catholic church attached to the manor. (25)

Massachusetts

AMESBURY. *Josiah Bartlett* statue. He was a New Hampshire delegate to the Continental Congress, but Amesbury was his birthplace. (S)

ARLINGTON. On the Green, near the intersection of Mystic Street and Massachusetts Avenue, is a marker that identifies the site of a house in which John Adams once lived. (23)

Black Horse Tavern site, Massachusetts Avenue near Medford Street. Here, before the Battle of Lexington, Elbridge Gerry and two colonels of the Massachusetts militia were spending the night when British troops arrived. The tavern was surrounded, but Gerry and the others slipped out, hid in a cornfield until the British left, then spread the alarm in the neighborhood. (S)

Jason Russell House, 7 Jason Street. Some of Paul Revere's silver is displayed here. (24)

BARNSTABLE. *Crocker Tavern*, on the south side of Main Street, was built about 1754, when James Otis lived in this town. (19)

West Parish Congregational Meeting House, in West Barnstable just off US 6. Otis may have attended this church, which was built in 1717. (19)

BOSTON. A marked walking tour, called "Freedom Trail," begins on Boston Common. It covers the section of Boston associated with the signers and the pre-Revolutionary period. The walk takes approximately one to two hours and includes many of the places listed below. On Essex Street at Washington Street, under a *Liberty Tree*, 355 Sons of Liberty attended a meeting on August 14, 1769. From there they proceeded to Robinson's Tavern in Dorchester. The names of all those present were recorded, including those of John Adams and Sam Adams. (23, 26, 27) The birthplace of Benjamin Franklin was near 17 Milk Street. (15)

Boston Common. Here, possibly near the present Frog Pond, Mary Dyer was hanged, June 1, 1660. Somewhere on the Common is her unmarked grave. (7) Here a Nipmuck leader of the 1675 war was executed. (8) The mansion of John Hancock faced the Common. (S)

Boston Massacre site, 30 State Street. Paul Revere may have been an eyewitness. He made a detailed diagram and a famous engraving showing the event. (24)

Boston Museum of Fine Arts, 465 Huntington Avenue. Here are portraits of George and Martha Washington by the Boston painter Gilbert Stuart and a Copley painting of Paul Revere as are pieces of Revere's work as a silversmith. (24, 29)

Boston Public Library. Here in John Adams' own hand are the notes he used during the trial of British soldiers accused of murder in the Boston Massacre. (23)

Boston Tea Party site. Near where Milk Street ends at Atlantic Avenue is a bas relief plaque showing where Griffen Wharf once stood and where the Boston Tea Party took place. (24)

British Coffee House site, 60 State Street, where James Otis and officers of the Crown had a violent fight. Otis was struck on the head with a cane and it was said that the blow affected his mind. Actually Otis' mental instability already existed, but it was surely not helped by the beating. (19)

Copp's Hill Burying Ground, Hull Street. Cotton Mather's grave is here. (11)

Dawes House, Purchase Street. The Caucus led by Sam Adams met in the home of Tom Dawes. (26)

Dorchester Heights National Historic Site commemorates the fortification of Dorchester Heights, from which came the cannon fire which drove the British out of Boston. (29)

Ebenezer Hancock House, 10 Marshall Street. John Hancock inherited this house from his uncle Thomas. At one time John's brother Thomas lived here. (Private) (S)

Faneuil Hall. On several occasions Samuel Adams spoke here at town meetings, and here he served as clerk of the Massachusetts Convention. John Hancock attended many political meetings here, and James Otis moderated such a meeting when people assembled to protest the seizure of John Hancock's ship *Liberty* on suspicion of smuggling. A statue of Sam Adams stands in front of the building. (19, 24, 26)

Granary Burying Ground, next to Park Street Church at Park and Tremont streets. When John Hancock was buried here, his funeral procession was so formal and elaborate that leaflets giving the order of march had to be printed up. Paul Revere, Samuel Adams, Robert Treat Paine, and Benjamin Franklin's parents are also buried here, as are Crispus Attucks and other victims of the Boston Massacre. (15, 24, 26, S)

Hanover Square. Here, in the Compting Room of Chase and Speakman's Distillery, John Adams met with the Sons of Liberty. (23)

John Hancock's House site, Beacon Street between State House and Jay Street. (S)

King's Chapel. Tremont and School streets. On this site stood Boston's first Anglican church, which was built in 1686 and was attended by Governor Andros and his supporters. The present building is a Unitarian church. (11)

Latin School site, School Street, indicated by a tablet on the wall of a building. Sam Adams, John Hancock, Benjamin Franklin, and many other famous Americans attended this school. (24, 26)

Liberty Tree site, Washington Street facing Boylston Street. On the wall of a business building is carved a tree in commemoration of the Liberty Tree which once stood here. (27)

Old Corner Bookstore, Washington and School streets, is at the site of Anne Hutchinson's home. (5)

Old North Church. In the tower of this church patriots hung two lanterns when the British forces moved out of the city across the Charles River on the night that Paul Revere rode to Lexington carrying word that the British were coming. (24)

Old South Meeting House. On one occasion a meeting chaired by James Otis moved to this place when Faneuil Hall proved too small to accommodate the crowd. (19)

Old State House. On this site once stood the Town House, the seat of government in 1689, from which Cotton Mather proclaimed the overthrow of the Andros regime. (11) In the Council Chamber here James Otis spoke against the Writs of Assistance in February, 1761. A mural in the building depicts the scene at the time of this speech. (19) John Adams sat at a table in the Council Chamber taking notes when Otis spoke. In 1765 Adams with Otis and another lawyer argued here that the governor should open the law courts and allow legal business to go forward without the use of paper to which stamps had been affixed. (19, 23) John Hancock attended many official meetings here. Also in the Council Chamber Sam Adams presented to Lieutenant Governor Hutchinson a plea for the removal of British troops after the Boston Massacre. (26)

Paul Revere's House, 19 North Square, was probably built about 1680 on the site of the home of the Reverend Increase Mather, which was destroyed by fire in 1676. This is the only 17th century building left in the North End of Boston. (24)

State House. Here are statues erected to the memory of Mary Dyer and Anne Hutchinson. A copy of the Mayflower Compact is on display. (5, 7)

BOURNE. *Aptuxcet Trading Post*, off Shore Road. This reconstructed building is the place where Pilgrims began in 1626 to trade with the Narraganset and Wampanoag. Wamsutta and Weetamoo are specifically mentioned as having lived in the territory served by this post. (8)

CAMBRIDGE. It was on Mount Auburn Avenue that the General Court was held in 1637 which tried Anne Hutchinson and banished her. (5)

Cambridge Common. Here on May 17, 1637, in a fateful election held out of doors, Anne Hutchinson's enemy John Winthrop became governor of Massachusetts Bay Colony and soon afterward helped to suppress freedom of conscience in the colony. (5) On the Common gate is a tablet that has this legend: "Near this spot on July 3, 1775, George Washington took command of the Continental Army." (29)

Christ Church, Garden Street at the Common. George Washington worshiped here during the siege of Boston. (29)

Elmwood, corner of Mount Auburn Street and Elmwood Avenue, was the home of Elbridge Gerry when he was governor of Massachusetts. Later it was the home of James Russell Lowell. (Private) (33)

Harvard College was attended by James Otis when there were only three buildings around the Yard. (19) Eight of the signers attended Harvard: John Adams, John Hancock, Samuel Adams (who received both a Bachelor's and a Master's degree here), Elbridge Gerry, Robert Treat Paine, William Ellery, William Williams, and William Hooper. Adams and Hancock were members of the Massachusetts Assembly when its meetings were held in Harvard Hall. The Continental army used the college buildings as barracks during the siege of Boston. (23, 24, 26, 29, S)

Longfellow National Historic Site, 105 Brattle Street. Here George Washington made his home and headquarters while he conducted the siege of Boston. Later the poet Henry Wadsworth Longfellow lived in this house. (29)

Wadsworth House, at the edge of Harvard Yard. General Artemus Ward lived here during the siege of Boston. (29)

CHARLESTON. Here Paul Revere landed, near the present Army-Navy Yard, borrowed a horse, and started his famous ride to Lexington. (24) *Breed's Hill*. Here what is mistakenly called the Battle of Bunker Hill was fought. It is commemorated by a monument. Two artillery pieces, one called "the Hancock," the other "the Adams," are placed here. Both were turned over to the Committee of Safety in February 1775 as a result of a motion made by John Hancock when he was president of the Second Provincial Congress of Massachusetts. (24, 29)

CONCORD. *Minute Man National Historical Park*. The Visitor Center, on Liberty Street, has an exhibit room and audiovisual programs. (24, 26, 29, S)

Wright's Tavern, in the center of town on Lexington Road. With John Hancock as president, the extragovernmental Provincial Congress of Massachusetts met in Concord to organize resistance to Britain. Committees met in the tavern, and members of the Provincial Congress dined here. (S)

DANVERS. Danvers was called Salem Village in 1692. At 69 Centre Street stood the parsonage where the chain of events connected with witchcraft started. Tituba, Elizabeth Parris, Abigail Williams, and the Reverend Samuel Parris all lived in the parsonage. Archeologists have excavated the site and have found hundreds of artifacts, many of which were no doubt in use in the parsonage in 1692. Some of these artifacts are on display in museums. (14)

First Church. This building is on the site of a meeting house in which the Reverend Samuel Parris was minister and where many episodes of the Salem witchcraft frenzy took place. (14) *Nurse Home*, 149 Pine Street. This building, according to tradition, was built by the husband of Rebecca Nurse, who was hanged as a witch in 1692. The old family burying ground is nearby. (14)

Osbourne House, on Massachusetts 62. In this house lived Sarah Osbourne, who was accused of being a witch and who died in jail. (14)

DEDHAM. *Woodward (Fisher) Tavern* site. On the Norfolk County Registry, across Dedham Square from the courthouse, is a plaque marking the site of the tavern where the Suffolk

County Convention met, inspired by Samuel Adams, to draft the Suffolk Resolves, which were later adopted in Milton. (26, S)

DEERFIELD. The scene of an engagement in 1675 known as the Bloody Brook massacre. After Indians attacked Deerfield, the houses here remained empty for seven years. A mile-long street of colonial houses survives. Some were built soon after 1675. (8)

EAST FREETOWN. In nearby Rocky Woods, Metacom is supposed to have spent the last night of his life. (8)

IPSWICH. A number of colonial houses in the town suggest what life was like when John Wise lived here. One, the *Howard House*, 41 Turkey Shore Road, at the east end of Green Street Bridge, was built about 1680. The *Rebellion Tablet* marks the spot on which citizens of Ipswich met in 1687 under the leadership of John Wise to protest an arbitrary tax. The *John Wise House* was built in 1701. The *Whipple House*, 53 S. Main Street, was built about 1640. (14)

LEXINGTON. *Buckman's Tavern*, Bedford Street. Here Paul Revere recovered John Hancock's trunk, that was filled with papers which, if discovered by the British, would have been very damaging to the patriots' cause. (24) *Hancock-Clarke House*, 35 Hancock Street. This was John Hancock's grandfather's parsonage. Hancock and Sam Adams were staying here on April 18, 1775, the night before the Battle of Lexington, when Paul Revere warned them the British were coming. (24, 26, S)

MARBLEHEAD. *Elbridge Gerry House*, 44 Washington Street. Gerry was born here. (S) *John Glover Home*, 11 Glover Street. Washington appointed the mariner John Glover to command the *Hannah* as a privateer. The *Hannah* was the first ship in what became the U.S. Navy. (29)

MARLBORO. Here in 1676 was a village of Praying Indians who, although supposedly friendly to the English, were attacked by colonial troops on March 6, 1676. (8)

MENDON. A monument here marks the site of the battle in which Nipmuck Indians destroyed the settlement in the Indian war of liberation. (8)

MILTON. Here stood the country house of Lieutenant Governor Thomas Hutchinson, the chief opponent of James Otis. (19) *Suffolk Resolves House* (also called Daniel Vose House), 1350 Canton Avenue. In this house were adopted the Resolves which Sam Adams helped to prepare and Paul Revere as a courier rushed to the Continental Congress in Philadelphia. Privately owned, but will be shown on request. (24, 26, S)

NORTH ANDOVER. *Gov. Simon Bradstreet House*, Osgood Street, was Anne Bradstreet's home. (7)

PLYMOUTH. Massasoit signed a treaty of alliance with the English here in 1620. Later his son Metacom renewed the treaty. After he led a war against the English, officials displayed his head atop a pole, and it remained there for 25 years. About 1700 Cotton Mather personally removed the lower jaw. (8) *Clifford Farms*, the Warren estate on Eel River, was the home of Mercy Otis Warren, sister of James Otis, who helped plan the First Continental Congress at this place. (19) *Cole's Hill*, Carver Street. The first Pilgrim cemetery. (3) A statue of Massasoit stands here. (8) *General Society of Mayflower Descendants* is housed in the Edward Winslow House, North Street, part of which was built in 1754. (3) *Harlow Old Fort House*, 119 Sandwich Street. Displays of Pilgrim life. The house was built in 1677. (3) *Jabez Howland House*, Sandwich Street. Built in 1667. Early furnishings. (3) *Mayflower II*. A full-size replica of the original *Mayflower* is at State Pier. (3)

Pilgrim Museum, Court and Chilton streets. (3) *Plimoth Plantation*, two miles south of Plymouth, off Massachusetts 3A. A reconstruction, as it was in 1627, of part of the village which the Pilgrims built. (3,4) *Plymouth Rock*, in Waterfront State Reservation, is what is left, after countless tourists have chipped off souvenirs, of a boulder on which the Pilgrims may—or may not—have landed. (3) *Sparrow House*, 42 Summer Street. Built in 1640 and restored. (3) *Spooner House*, North Street. Now a museum. Built about 1749. (3) *Town House* site, where the trial of the murderer of Sassamon was held in June 1675, is marked by a tablet on Leyden Street opposite the end of Carver Street. (8)

QUINCY. *Adams National Historic Site*, Adams Avenue near Newport Avenue. The "Old House" here was John Adams' home after the Revolution. A stone building nearby houses the Adams library. (23, S) *Church of the Presidents*, 1266 Hancock Street. In this Unitarian church are buried John Adams and his son John Quincy Adams, both of whom were presidents of the United States. (23, S) *John Adams' Birthplace*, 133 Franklin Street. (23) *Quincy Homestead*, 34 Butler Road, was the home of Dorothy Quincy, who married John Hancock. The coach that Hancock used when he was governor of Massachusetts may be seen in the coach house. The home, open to the public, has a secret room where colonial soldiers were said to have had refuge occasionally when pursued by the British. (S)

ROCHESTER/MIDDLEBOROUGH. *Assawompsett Pond*. Partly in Rochester, partly in Middleborough. Here the body of a Christian Indian, Sassamon, was found under the ice. The execution of three Indians accused of his murder was one of the immediate causes of the war of 1675. (8)

SALEM, called Salem Town in 1692. The site of the pressing of Giles Cory is between the Howard Street burying ground and Brown Street. (14) *Charter Street Burying Ground*. Here are the graves of a number of people who lived at the time of the trials, including judges who sat at the trials. (14) *Court House*, Washington and Federal streets. In this building are documents relating to witchcraft, also an exhibit of pins that were supposedly used by witches in Salem Village to torture their victims. (14) *Essex Institute*, 132 Essex Street, is a large museum with many exhibits illustrating the colonial period and some specifically related to the witchcraft trials. An excellent library has material about the trials. (14) *Gedney House*, 21 High Street. Part of this house existed in 1692. (14) *House of Seven Gables*, 54 Turner Street. Part of this and two other houses on the grounds, the Hathaway House and the Retire Beckett House, existed at the time of the trials. (14) *Pioneer Village* in Forest River Park at the east end of Forest Avenue is a reproduction of Salem as it was in 1630, a year before Roger Williams first stayed there. (4, 14) *Ward House*, behind Essex Institute. This house built in 1684 has period furnishings and exhibits. (14) *Witch House*, 310½ Essex Street, was built in 1642, shortly after Roger Williams was banished. This was the home of Jonathan Corwin, one of the judges of the witchcraft trials. According to tradition some of the preliminary examinations of those accused of witchcraft took place here. (4, 14)

SHREWSBURY. *Artemus Ward House*, Massachusetts 140. Until George Washington took command, Ward was commander of the volunteers who besieged Boston. His home was built before 1775. (29)

SOMERVILLE. A tablet on Prospect Hill Avenue, in what was then part of Charlestown, marks the place where a Liberty Pole stood on January 1, 1776. Until that day a red flag had flown from the pole, but beginning the new year a new flag appeared. It consisted of thirteen red and white horizontal stripes, symbolizing the thirteen colonies that were moving together toward freedom. In the upper corner, next to the staff, was a small version of Britain's flag, symbolizing the still continuing connection of the colonies to England. This flag greatly resembled that of the East India Company, whose tea had been dumped into the nearby harbor at the time of the Boston Tea Party. (29)

SOWAMS. Here on the Warren River was the home of Massasoit. (8)

SPRINGFIELD. *Forest Park.* Here is a site known as King Philip's Stockade. From this point Metacom is supposed to have directed an Indian attack on Springfield. (8)

SWANSEA. The first blood of the war of 1675 was shed in and near this town, and here the home of the Reverend John Miles was turned into a garrison. A building which some historians believe was his house still stands and is known as the Miles Garrison House. (8)

TAUNTON. In the church here Metacom met with commissioners from Massachusetts Bay Colony on April 12, 1671. (8)
Robert Treat Paine statue, Summer Street. (S)

TIVERTON and FALL RIVER. Both these modern cities are within the territory called Pocasset, which belonged to the Wampanoag. Here was the home of Weetamoo (Sweetheart), the sachem who resisted the English in the war of 1675. (8)

WATERTOWN. A stone tablet at Mount Auburn and Marshall streets marks the site where the Provincial Congress met in 1775. George Washington met with them on July first, on his way to Cambridge. (29)
Abraham Browne House, 562 Main Street, existed at the time Paul Revere lived in Watertown, which was the temporary capital of Massachusetts while the British occupied Boston. The Abraham Browne House now contains a museum. Other homes which survive from this period are at 425 Main Street and 136 Main Street. In Watertown Revere printed paper money so that the revolutionaries could have their own currency and not be dependent on British currency. (24)

WAYLAND. *The Wadsworth Monument,* on Concord Road, marks the spot near which Metacom defeated the colonials by starting a forest fire. Twenty-eight Englishmen were killed and are buried under the monument. (8)

WEYMOUTH. At 450 Bridge Street stands a portion of the house in which Abigail Adams, wife of John Adams, was born. (23)

WINTHROP. *John Hancock House,* 40 Siren Street, in the Point Shirley area, was Hancock's summer home. (S)

WORCESTER. *The Commons* existed at the time John Adams taught school here. (23)
Worcester Historical Society, 39 Salisbury Street. Here is John Hancock's trunk, which Revere helped to rescue as the Battle of Lexington was beginning. (24)

Michigan

DETROIT. The site of Fort Detroit is in the downtown area of the modern city. Two miles north of Fort Detroit, Pontiac's forces ambushed an English force and defeated it on July 31, 1763. (20)

GROSSE ISLE. Pontiac used Grosse Isle as a base during the siege of Detroit. (20)

MACKINAW CITY. *Fort Michilimackinac.* The site of this fort, which has been extensively recon-

structed, is at the south end of Mackinac Bridge in Michilimackinac State Park. (20)

NILES. Fort St. Joseph was located here. The Potawatomi captured it May 25, 1763. (20)

Missouri

ST. LOUIS. In a cemetery at 2nd Street between Walnut and Market, next to the old cathedral, Pontiac may have been buried; or he may have been buried 20 feet east of Broadway and 50 feet north of Market; or the site of his grave may be in a space bounded by Broadway, Walnut, and 4th streets. At any rate, all accounts suggest that he was buried within a definite limited area in St. Louis. (20)

New Hampshire

DERRY. *Matthew Thornton House* (private). (S)

KINGSTON. Josiah Bartlett's home and grave are here. (S)

MERRIMACK. *Thornton's Ferry Cemetery.* Matthew Thornton is buried here. The inscription on his gravestone reads, "An Honest Man." (S)

PORTSMOUTH. *Moffatt-Ladd House,* 154 Market Street, was the home of William Whipple. (S)
Warner House, Daniels and Chapel streets. Here in 1762 Benjamin Franklin personally supervised the installation of one of his inventions, a lightning rod. (31)

New Jersey

BORDENTOWN. At two different periods, Tom Paine lived here. (30)
Hopkinson House, 101 Farnsworth Avenue. This was Francis Hopkinson's main home. According to legend, when the house was occupied by the British during the war, an officer decided to burn it down. But then he looked over Hopkinson's library, which was so fine that the officer could not bear to destroy it, and he countermanded his order. He did, however, carry off the signer's telescope and other valuables. (S)

BURLINGTON. Here, under a tent improvised from sailcloth, the earliest Quakers to settle in New Jersey held their first meetings, in 1677. (10)
Governor Franklin Estate, south side of Delaware Street, between Wood and Talbot streets. Here the Grubb House, owned by the Veterans of Foreign Wars, stands on the site of the home of William Franklin, illegitimate son of Benjamin Franklin, the last royal governor of New Jersey and a Tory. Benjamin Franklin visited here. (S)
Samuel Jennings Office site, in a garden between 206 and 212 North High Street. Samuel Jennings, a Quaker, was deputy governor of New Jersey from 1680 to 1684. In the building he had used as an office, Benjamin Franklin set up the first copperplate press in America and helped to print paper money for New Jersey. (31)
Thomas Revel House, 8 East Pearl Street. When Franklin was 17 and had run away from Boston, he missed the boat from Burlington on which he wanted to complete his journey to Philadelphia. A woman in this house took pity on him and gave him some gingerbread. (31)

HOPEWELL. *Old School Baptist Church,* West Broad Street. Near here stands a monument to John Hart, who donated the site for the church. He is buried in the churchyard. (S)

NEW BRUNSWICK. At one period during the Revolution Thomas Paine lived at 60 Livingston

Avenue. The house was built in 1760 by Henry Guest. (30)

PERTH AMBOY. *The Westminster,* 149 Kearny Avenue. Here remain parts of a house in which Governor William Franklin once lived. Benjamin Franklin visited him here in a vain effort to persuade him to support rather than oppose the Revolution. Later, William Franklin was arrested by patriots and imprisoned in Connecticut. (31)

PRINCETON. *Morven,* on the edge of the town, was the estate of Richard Stockton. It is now the official residence of New Jersey's governors. Stockton's daughter Julia was the wife of Benjamin Rush, also a signer, who visited at Morven. British troops occupied the house during the war and managed to dig up two chests of valuables that Stockton had buried on the grounds. They failed to find a third. (S)
Princeton University. Nassau Hall and the Dean's House on campus had both been built before John Witherspoon became president of the institution, which was then called the College of New Jersey. He lived in the Dean's House, then the President's House, and John Adams was among his visitors there. Later Witherspoon moved to his estate, Tusculum, at the edge of Princeton, which is open to the public. Witherspoon is buried in the President's Lot at Princeton Cemetery. (23, S)

RAHWAY. *Presbyterian Church Cemetery,* St. George Avenue near Westfield Avenue. Abraham Clark is buried here. (S)

TRENTON. *Friends Graveyard,* northwest corner of East Hanover and Montgomery streets. George Clymer is buried here. (S)

New Mexico

PECOS NATIONAL MONUMENT. Here a pueblo, now abandoned, housed perhaps 2,000 people in 1680. The community was deeply divided between followers of the native religion and followers of Christianity. Under Spanish direction the latter built the largest church in New Mexico on this spot. It was destroyed in 1680. Archeologists have done a great deal of work in both the Spanish and pre-Spanish parts of the site. (8)

SANTA FE. *Palace of the Governors.* The Spaniards gathered in this building when the rebellion broke out, and the Indian army besieged the place until the Spaniards finally had to leave. It now houses the Museum of New Mexico, where 17th century Indian and Spanish materials may be seen. (8)

SAN JUAN PUEBLO. Popé lived here during most of his life. (8)

TAOS PUEBLO. Popé lived here during the last stages of the preparation of the revolution. (8)

TESUQUE PUEBLO. This village, nine miles from Santa Fe, served as the organizational center when the revolution broke out. (8)
In addition to those listed above, there are these other pueblos, still inhabited and on or near their 1680 locations: Acoma, Cochiti, Isleta, Jemez, Picuris, Sandia, San Felipe, San Ildefonso, Santa Ana, Santo Domingo, Zia, Zuni. People in all these villages want to carry on their lives undisturbed. Visitors should respect this wish and obey local regulations, which vary from one village to another. Most of them have regulations about taking photographs. Guests should find out whether cameras are permitted and what rules there are about their use.

New York

ALBANY. Near here in 1765, 400 Liberty Boys ransacked a house because its owner refused to promise that he would not take a job distributing tax stamps. (27)

Schuyler Mansion, southwest corner of Clinton and Schuyler streets. This elegant Georgian house was built by Philip Schuyler, who was appointed by George Washington to be one of the major generals in the Continental army. Alexander Hamilton was married here. Benjamin Franklin stayed here as a guest of Philip Schuyler while on his trip to Canada in 1776. (29, 31)

CHAUTAUQUA. Here are the graves of William and Mehitable Prendergast, leaders of the tenants' revolt in the Hudson River valley. (22)

CROTON-ON-HUDSON. *Van Cortlandt Manor,* off US 9. In this house lived one of the landlord families against which tenant farmers rebelled in 1766. (22)

IRVINGTON. *Philip Livingston House,* Broadway and Livingston Avenue, was acquired by Philip Livingston after the Revolution (private). His great house on Brooklyn Heights was destroyed by fire. (S)

MASTIC. *William Floyd Home.* (S)

MOUNT VERNON. *St. Paul's Church,* 897 South Columbus Avenue, which in 1733 faced on the Eastchester Green, was the scene of an important election reported in the first issue of Peter Zenger's *Weekly Journal.* The present building, which dates from 1763, has been designated a National Historic Site and is headquarters of the Society of the National Shrine of the Bill of Rights. The historian of the church believes that Anne Hutchinson's Westchester home was on or near the site of the church. (5, 16)

NEW PALTZ. *Huguenot Street.* On this street are fine examples of houses of the kind that many farmers lived in at the time of the 1766 revolt. However, New Paltz was not part of the big manor area and was not involved in the revolt. (22)

Luycas Van Alen House, on New York 9H, south of US 9. This house is typical of many in which farmers lived at the time of the tenant's revolt. (22)

NEW ROCHELLE. *Jacob Leisler Monument,* North and Broadview avenues, was erected in 1913. (11)

Thomas Paine Cottage, North and Paine avenues. Paine lived here after the Revolution, on a farm that was given him for his services. It was confiscated from a Tory. (30)

NEW YORK CITY. Between State and Whitehall streets stands a flagpole that commemorates the arrival of 23 Jewish immigrants in 1654. At the corner of St. James and Oliver streets, near Chatham Square, is part of the cemetery which was established by Sephardic Jews in 1682. There are other early Jewish cemeteries, in Greenwich Village and on 21st Street near Avenue of the Americas. (6) At Vesey Street, in the headquarters of the New York County Lawyers' Association, is a plaque honoring Andrew Hamilton, who defended Peter Zenger. (16)

Battery Park. In this area stood a fort which Jacob Leisler's men took over. (11) Here also a cannon was fired to summon all white citizens to arms to fight against the slave rebellion in 1712. And this was the site of a demonstration against the Stamp Act by the Sons of Liberty. (27)

City Hall Park. Here, when it was called the Common, the Sons of Liberty erected a Liberty Pole. Because the pole was destroyed more than once by soldiers and by others, one of the Sons of Liberty finally bought a piece of property and set up a Liberty Pole on it. Apparently he felt the pole was safer when not under the protection of officials who were responsible to the king. (27) On Park Row, opposite the park, is the site of the hanging of Jacob Leisler and his son-in-law. (11)

Federal Hall National Memorial, Wall and Nassau streets. An entire room here is devoted to the memory of John Peter Zenger. Dioramas illustrate episodes in his struggle for freedom of the press. Zenger spent nine months in the jail on the top floor of the building which stood on this site in 1735. His world-famous trial was held on the second floor. (16) In 1712, the trials of rebellious slaves had been conducted here (see pages 80–81). In 1765, when the City Hall stood on this spot, the Sons of Liberty held a meeting here on November 5, attended by 5,000 people who opposed the Stamp Act. Another large Sons of Liberty meeting held here on July 7, 1770, favored nonimportation of goods from England. (27)

Hutchinson River and Hutchinson River Parkway. Both of these were named for Anne Hutchinson. (5)

Spruce Street, near Park Row or Franklin Street. Jacob Leisler and his son-in-law were buried near here. The exact location of the graves has never been found. (11)

Trinity Church, Wall Street and Broadway. At the instigation of the Sons of Liberty, the rector preached a sermon here on May 21, 1766, in celebration of the repeal of the Stamp Act. Francis Lewis is buried in the churchyard. (27, S)

Wall Street. This street was narrow at one end, and here during the nonimportation campaign merchants who wanted to import British goods attacked Sons of Liberty, who were parading in favor of nonimportation. To everyone's surprise, the merchants defeated the Sons of Liberty, who were mainly husky artisans and sailors. (27)

NIAGARA FALLS. In Devils Hole near Fort Niagara, which still stands, Senecas ambushed an English wagon train in September 1763. (20)

OSWEGO. Here at Fort Ontario, foot of East 7th Street, on July 25, 1766, Pontiac with several other chiefs from western and Iroquois tribes met with Sir William Johnson to sign a peace treaty. (20)

TICONDEROGA. *Fort Ticonderoga* (restored), two miles east of town, was the scene of an early victory of the Revolutionary forces. Ethan Allen and 83 Green Mountain Boys, accompanied by Benedict Arnold (not yet a traitor) captured the British stronghold on May 10, 1775. Cannon from the fort were later used in the siege of Boston. (29)

TOTTENVILLE (STATEN ISLAND). *Conference House,* at the foot of Hylan Boulevard, was built before 1688. Here in September 1776 John Adams, Benjamin Franklin, and Edward Rutledge, acting for the Continental Congress, met with British General Howe in a vain effort to avert war. (23, 31, S)

UPPER MILLS. *Philipsburg Manor,* 381 Bellwood Avenue. This National Historic Landmark was one of the homes of the Philipse family against whom rent strikers rebelled in 1776. A member of this family sat as a judge at the trial of Peter Zenger. (16, 22)

YONKERS. *Philipse Manor Hall,* 29 Warburton Avenue. In this, another home of the Philipse family, there is a portrait of Benjamin Franklin by Tuckerman. (22, 31)

North Carolina

ALBEMARLE SOUND. It remains for future historians to find and preserve sites connected with the most dramatic scenes of the Albemarle contribution toward the tradition of freedom. Until this work is done, visitors can know that almost anywhere along the north shore of Albemarle Sound they are on ground where, in the 17th century, there was almost always peace with the local Indians and almost never submission to outside authority. (13)

BURLINGTON. *Alamance Battleground,* eight miles southwest of Burlington on North Carolina 62. Here militia sent by the royal governor fought a group of frontier farmers known as Regulators, who had been protesting high taxes and ruthless officials. The governor had ignored their petitions for redress, one of which complained that tax collectors had seized horses, cows, household furniture—even their wives' petticoats. The governor's militiamen, some of them commanded by William Hooper, defeated the Regulators and set fire to the woods, where some of the insurgent wounded were burned to death. At this State Historic Site are a Visitor Center and exhibits. (S)

EDENTON. Walking tours of Historic Edenton start at Barker House, at the foot of South Broad Street, where there is a museum that offers a slide program. There are places here associated with signer Joseph Hewes, including a tablet marking the site of his store and a monument to him on the village green. The Joseph Hewes house, not open to the public, actually was the home of his nephew, Nathaniel Allen. (S)

Iredell House, Church Street between South Broad and South Oakum. Judge Iredell was a friend of James Wilson, who died in his home. Wilson was first buried in Edenton, but was later reinterred in Christ Churchyard, Philadelphia. (S)

GREENSBORO. *Guilford Courthouse National Military Park,* six miles northwest of Greensboro on US 220. Monuments here mark the graves of two signers, William Hooper and John Penn. (S)

HILLSBORO. *Nash-Hooper House,* near the Presbyterian Church, was the home of William Hooper. He was first buried in the town cemetery on Churton Street, behind the Presbyterian Church, then reinterred in Guilford National Military Park. The park authorities tried to take his gravestone along with his remains, but indignant citizens of Hillsboro removed the stone from the train and set it up again in their cemetery. A monument in the park honors Hooper. (S)

NEW HOPE, Perquimans County. About six miles from here is Leigh Mansion, which is on the site of the land originally taken up by George Durant. In the yard of the mansion, under an old elm, is a slab that is believed to mark Durant's grave. Also in Perquimans County is an area between the Little and Perquimans rivers, called Durant's Neck. Batts Island, at the mouth of the Yeopim River, once belonged to Durant. (13)

STOVALL. Near the town is the site of the home of John Penn, who was first buried in the family graveyard there. Later his remains were taken to Guilford Courthouse National Military Park, where there is a monument to him. (S)

Ohio

DEFIANCE. Pontiac may have been born here, about 1720. (20)

CLEVELAND. Here at the mouth of Cuyahoga River, Major Robert Rogers met Pontiac in November, 1760. (20)

PROVIDENCE. In the Maumee River, about eight miles below this town, is an island on which Pontiac lived with other Ottawas in 1764 and later. (20)

SANDUSKY. Here at Fort Sandusky, Huron Indians were victorious on May 16, 1763. (20)

Pennsylvania

BRADDOCK PARK. Here on US 40, west of Fort Necessity, a monument marks the grave of General Braddock. He was killed and his large English army was defeated near here by Indians in 1755. It is likely that Pontiac took part in this battle. (18, 20)

BUSHY RUN BATTLEFIELD STATE PARK. Two miles east of Harrison City, 26 miles from Pittsburgh, on Pennsylvania 993. Here in a crucial battle British forces defeated Indians, August 5-6, 1763. (20)

CATASAUQUA. *Taylor House*, Front Street. Restored home of George Taylor. (S)

CHESTER. *Penn Memorial Landing Stone*, Front and Penn streets, marks the spot where Penn stepped ashore in October 1682. (10)
Caleb Pusey House and Landingford Plantation, two miles west in Upland. The main house was built in 1683 for Penn's agent and manager. (10)

EASTON. *George Taylor House*, Ferry and Fourth streets. George Taylor lived here for many years. The house is now managed by the Daughters of the American Revolution. (S)

ERIE. The French fort of Presque Isle, which the Senecas captured on June 19, 1762, was at the foot of Parade Street. (18, 20)

ESSINGTON. *John Morton Homestead*, in Prospect Park. John Morton was born here. The house contains interesting Pennsylvania Dutch furnishings. (S)

FRANKLIN. *Venango*, a French fort, was built at an Indian town here. The Senecas captured it on June 16, 1763. (18, 20)

JUMONVILLE GLEN. Three miles north of US 40 on Chestnut Ridge is this ravine, in which Washington surprised and attacked French forces led by Jumonville. This attack is often called the beginning of the French and Indian War, which was part of the Seven Years' War in Europe. A rock formation, called *Half King's Rocks*, is where George Washington joined forces on May 27, 1754, with the Seneca leader, Half King, before attacking Jumonville two miles farther north. (18)

LANCASTER. *Franklin and Marshall College*, College Avenue between Buchanan Avenue and Harrison Pike. This institution was founded as Franklin College in 1787. Benjamin Franklin gave it the largest initial contribution and was said to have been present when the cornerstone was laid. (31)
Old Jail site, 12 North Prince Street. Here the Paxton Boys massacred peaceful Conestoga Indians who were in jail for their protection. Franklin later was persuaded the Paxton Boys not to attack other Indians being protected in Philadelphia. (31)

MANHEIM. *Baron Stiegel Mansion*, on Town Square. Robert Morris lived here for a while during the Revolution. (S)

MERION. *Merion Meeting House*. Built in 1695, William Penn worshiped here. The building is still in use. (10)

MORRISVILLE. Near here is *Pennsbury Manor*, built in 1683. This mansion was Penn's main residence in America. It was reconstructed in 1938, following extensive archeological investigation. (10)
Summerseat, Clymer Street, was the home of George Clymer. Open by appointment only. (S)

PHILADELPHIA. There are countless marked sites in this city associated with its founder, William Penn, and with various members of the Continental Congress, such as The Dock where Penn supposedly landed in 1692; the site of the Slate Roof House, where he drafted his Charter of Privileges; homesites of signers Benjamin Rush and James Wilson; sites of the printshop where Tom Paine edited the *Pennsylvania Magazine* and of the bookstore owned by the publisher of *Common Sense*; and even the site of Benjamin Franklin's kite-flying experiment which proved that lightning is a form of electricity. Various pre-Revolutionary churches still standing are evidence of the religious tolerance and diversity that are traditional in the City of Brotherly Love: Old Pine Street Presbyterian (1768), St. George's Methodist (1769), St. Joseph's Roman Catholic (founded 1733, first Catholic church in the city), St. Mary's Roman Catholic (1763), St. Peter's Episcopal (1761), and others. (10, 30, 31, S) A good place to start sightseeing in Philadelphia is *Independence National Historic Park*. The First Continental Continental Congress met in Carpenters' Hall, 320 Chestnut Street. Patrick Henry, George Washington, and many of the signers attended. Here Paul Revere delivered the famous Suffolk Resolves to the Congress, on September 17, 1774. At Independence Hall, Washington, Henry, and most of the signers attended the Second Continental Congress, which John Hancock served as president after Peyton Randolph of Virginia relinquished the post, on May 24, 1775. Here delegate Thomas Jefferson submitted the Declaration of Independence. A draft of the Declaration in Jefferson's handwriting, with minor changes written in by Benjamin Franklin and John Adams, is kept at the park, as are two of the broadside, or leaflet, publications of the Declaration and the original of William Penn's Charter of Privileges. A famous portrait of Thomas Jefferson by Thomas Sully hangs in one room of Philosophical Hall, a building which dates from 1789. Benjamin Franklin founded the American Philosophical Society in 1769 and was its first president. (10, 22, 23, 24, 25, 26, 28, 29, 30, 31, 32, S)
American Swedish Historical Museum, 1900 Pattison Avenue. Exhibits about the history of Swedes in America from earliest settlement. (10)
Arch Street Meeting House, Arch Street between Third and Fourth. In this building, constructed in 1804, are housed museum exhibits of early Quaker life in Philadelphia and dioramas showing episodes in the life of William Penn. (10)
Betsy Ross House, 239 Arch Street. John Ross, husband of Betsy, was a nephew of the signer George Ross, who undoubtedly visited this house. (S)
Christ Church, Episcopal, Second Street north of Market. This building suggests the cosmopolitan variety of life in colonial Philadelphia. The congregation was organized in 1695. This building dates from 1754 and looks much as it did in pre-Revolutionary times. Benjamin Franklin, Thomas Jefferson, George Washington, and other members of the Continental Congress attended services here. About two-thirds of the signers were Episcopalians. James Wilson and Robert Morris are buried in the churchyard. Five other signers are buried in the Christ Church Burial Ground at Fifth and Arch streets: Benjamin Franklin, Benjamin Rush, Francis Hopkinson, Joseph Hewes, and George Ross. Andrew Hamilton's grave is also here. (10, 16, 29, 31, 32, S)
City Tavern site, west side of Second Street between Walnut and Chestnut. Benjamin Franklin and Thomas Jefferson often dined here. Probably this tavern was more frequented by American patriots than any other in the colonies. (31, 32, S)
College, Academy and Charity School site, Arch and Fourth streets. Benjamin Rush taught medicine here. Two other signers, William Paca and Francis Hopkinson, attended the school. A bronze table marks the site. (S)
Franklin's Houses (sites of), 139 Market (1728-39); 131 Market (1739-48)—this was Benjamin Franklin's printing office (1739-65) and the Philadelphia post office where Franklin was postmaster (1739-52)—; 325 Market (1751-61); 326 Market (1761-65); south side of Market between Third and Fourth streets (1764-90). National Park Service archeologists have done extensive excavation at this last site. (31, S)
Franklin Institute, 20th Street and Benjamin Franklin Parkway. The Franklin Printing Shop in this building is a reproduction of the kind of shop that existed in Franklin's time and includes presses that Franklin may have used. (31)
Graff House site, Market Street at the southwest corner of Seventh Street. Thomas Jefferson rented a second-story parlor and bedroom in a building that was owned by a German bricklayer. Here Jefferson wrote the Declaration of Independence. (32)
Historical Society of Pennsylvania, 1300 Locust Street. Here is a wampum belt that commemorates Penn's successful and long-lasting peace treaty with the Leni-Lenape Indians, and other Penn memorabilia. (10)
Indian King Tavern site, east side of Fourth Street between Chestnut and Market. Here on March 20, 1776, Franklin chaired a meeting of investors in the Grand Ohio Company who wanted to open up the Ohio Valley for colonization. (31)
Keimer's Print Shop site, Market between Third and Fourth streets. Benjamin Franklin worked here. (15, 31)
Kensington, formerly Shackamaxon. In 1827 the Penn Society placed a monument here at the site of the elm tree under which Penn and the Leni-Lenape chiefs signed a treaty of peace in 1682. (10)
Library Company of Philadelphia, Fifth and Library streets. This library was founded by Franklin in 1731. The present building dates from 1869 and contains books once owned by Benjamin Franklin, William Penn, Thomas Jefferson, and George Washington. In it a piece of Franklin's electrical equipment is exhibited. (31)
Old Swedes Church (Gloria Dei National Historic Site), Christian Street and Delaware Avenue. Originally Church of Sweden (Lutheran), now Episcopalian, it was built in 1698, replacing a log church built in 1677. It is the oldest church in continuous service in the United States. (10)
Penn's Cottage, Fairmont Park. This dwelling, which once stood between Chestnut, Market, Front, and Second streets, is by tradition said to have belonged to Letitia, a daughter of William Penn. Penn may have stayed here. (10)
Pewter Platter Inn site, Front Street and Pewter Platter Alley. Here Franklin met with members of the Junto, precursor of the American Philosophical Society, which still exists. (31)
Philadelphia Contributorship site, Fourth Street south of Walnut. Here Franklin founded the first fire insurance company in America. It was also known as the Hand-in-Hand because its symbol pictured clasped hands. (31)
Robert Morris Home, 225 South Eighth Street. Robert Morris lived here after the Revolution. (S)
Robert Morris House site, 190 High Street. John and Abigail Adams also lived here at one time. (S)
Stenton Mansion, 18th and Courtland streets. This was the home of James Logan, William Penn's secretary, built in 1728. It is an excellent example of Pennsylvania architecture, furnished with 18th century antiques. (10)

PITTSBURGH. *Point State Park*. Here is a reconstruction of Fort Pitt, at the fork of the Monongahela and Allegheny rivers. The site was selected by 21-year-old George Washington. There are exhibits of frontier and Indian life. Here Delaware, Shawnee, and Mingo warriors conducted an unsuccessful siege of the British forces, and here British officers gave Delaware chiefs blankets that had been used by smallpox victims, thus introducing germ warfare to the world. (18, 20)

UNIONTOWN. *Fort Necessity National Battlefield*, on US 40, eleven miles east of Uniontown. Here is an exact reconstruction of a fort built by George Washington, which he was forced to surrender to the French. Traces of Braddock's Road are visible here. Washington helped to build the road and he used it in 1754. In Mount Washington Tavern are relics of the military actions at Fort Necessity. (18)

WATERFORD. Here the Seneca Indians captured Fort LeBoeuf on June 18, 1763. (18, 20)

WEST NEWTON. Here Delaware and Mingo warriors destroyed a small settlement on May 27, 1763. (20)

YORK. Signers James Smith and Philip Livingston are buried here. (S)

Rhode Island

BRISTOL. At Mount Hope, east of Bristol, the Wampanoag had their main village in 1675. Metacom lived here. (8).

EAST PROVIDENCE. On Roger Williams Avenue a plaque marks the site of the house in which Williams lived for a while in 1636. (4)

NEWPORT. *Brick Market*, Thames and Washington streets. William Ellery's merchandise passed through this building, which now houses the offices of the Preservation Society of Newport County. (S)
Old State House, North Main Street. The Rhode Island legislature met here when William Ellery and Stephen Hopkins were members. (S)
Touro Synagogue, 85 Touro Street. Nearby is the old Jewish burying ground. (6)

NORTH KENSINGTON. *Smith's Castle*, a house built in 1678 in which Williams is said to have preached when he was a very old man. (4)

PORTSMOUTH. Anne Hutchinson and her husband, William, were among the founders of this town. (5)

PROVIDENCE. A monument marks the place where Roger Williams first stepped out of a canoe onto land in what is now Rhode Island. This spot was once on the bank of the Seekonk River, but man-made land has changed the river's course.
First Baptist Meeting House, 75 North Main Street. Roger Williams was a Baptist for a while, and in 1638 he helped organize the first Baptist church in New England, which was built on this site. The present church was built in 1775. (4)
Roger Williams National Memorial. North Main at Alamo Lane. The original settlement was beside a spring here. (4)
Stephen Hopkins Home, Benefit and Hopkins streets. (S)

WAKEFIELD. *Great Swamp Fight Monument*. Off Rhode Island 2, one mile southeast of the junction with Rhode Island 138. A great battle in King Philip's War was fought here. Roger Williams, although not present at the battle, was one of the two captains in the Rhode Island militia during the war. (4, 8)

WICKFORD. The Updike House, one mile south of town, stands on the site of and contains timbers from what was called Smiths Landing Trading Post, which was destroyed during the war. Roger Williams stayed here in 1675 while he was trying to keep the Narraganset out of the war. (4, 8)

South Carolina

BEAUFORT. On US 21, on Port Royal Island. The first colonists bound for Georgia put up here in barracks in 1733. An old house, built in 1690 and in use at that time, can be seen at Port Republic and New streets. (17)
St. Helena's Episcopal Church, between King and North streets, was attended by Captain William Bull, who helped Oglethorpe to design Savannah. (17)

CHARLESTON. At Broad and Church streets, on October 19, 1765, members of the Sons of Liberty built a gallows 20 feet high and from it hanged in effigy a man who had been appointed to distribute tax stamps. (27)
Charleston County Court House, Broad and Market streets. On November 5, 1774, the Sons of Liberty displayed effigies of the Pope and the Devil in front of this building, which was then the State House. This display was part of intense agitation against the tea tax. (27)
Charleston Library Society, 164 King Street. This library, which began in 1748, has microfilm copies of the *South Carolina Gazette* edited first by Lewis Timothy, a protegé of Benjamin Franklin, then by Elizabeth Timothy, his widow, and then by Peter Timothy, their son and a Son of Liberty. (27)
College of Charleston, between Glebe, George, St. Philip, and Green streets. In the college library is Christopher Gadsden's copy of Tom Paine's *Common Sense*, with Gadsden's underlining and annotations. (27)
Cooper River. Into this river, in November 1774, merchants to whom seven chests of tea had been shipped, broke open the chests and emptied the tea into the water while a large crowd of spectators looked on and cheered. This was the Charleston Tea Party. (27)
Gadsden's Canal site, Calhoun Street between East Bay and Washington streets. This was the head of a canal that Gadsden had dug to drain a large swampy tract of land that he owned. The streets he laid out on the drained land showed his political interests. They included Wilkes, Pitt, Corsican Walk (after Corsican revolutionaries), and Hand-in-Hand Corner, possibly after Franklin's fire insurance company. (27)
John Rutledge House, 116 Broad Street. This was the home of the brother of Edward Rutledge, who visited there often. It is open to the public during the annual spring Charleston Festival of Houses. (S)
Middleton Place Gardens, 14 miles northwest of Charleston on South Carolina 61. This was the estate of Arthur Middleton, who is buried on the grounds. His son started the gardens, which were greatly expanded by later occupants. Visitors may see not only the house and gardens but also living demonstrations of plantation work. (S)
Old Fort Johnson, on James Island. Troops quartered here were under the command of Oglethorpe during the war with Spain. The site is now used as the Marine Biological Laboratory of the College of Charleston. (Private) (17)
Old Slave Market, 6-8 Chalmers Street. In this building planters, merchants, and artisans who were Sons of Liberty bought slaves. The building today houses a museum which shows the creative skill in various crafts of black slaves. (27)
Provost Dungeon, in the cellar of the Exchange, East Bay and Broad streets. Here tea, on which Charleston citizens refused to pay a tax, was stored and allowed to rot. (27)
Ramage's Tavern site, Broad Street. Here the Sons of Liberty often gathered in 1774. (27)
St. Michael's Episcopal Church, 80 Meeting Street. The bells here tolled during a mock funeral of "American Liberty" in which members of the Sons of Liberty took part. After the Revolution George Washington attended services here. (27)
St. Philip's Episcopal Church, 146 Church Street between Cumberland and Queen streets. Christopher Gadsden was buried in the graveyard of this church. By his own request his grave was unmarked. Edward Rutledge, one of the signers, who was often at odds with Gadsden, is also buried here. (27, S)
South Carolina Historical Society. This society has a cockade pin that was worn by Christopher Gadsden during the Revolution. (27)
State Street. On this street was the printshop where Peter Timothy published the *South Carolina Gazette*, which supported the Sons of Liberty. (27)
Statue of Pitt, behind the Fireproof Building on the southeast corner of Chalmers and Meeting streets. In 1766 the South Carolina Commons House of Assembly voted to have this statue erected to honor William Pitt, who spoke against the Stamp Act in the British Parliament. (27)
Thomas Elfe Workshop, 54 Queen Street. Here is restored the home and workshop of an artisan who may have been a member of the Sons of Liberty. (27)
Thomas Heyward House, 87 Church Street. This was the signer's town house. He also had a large plantation in St. Luke's Parish. (S)
Tradd Street. Several houses on this street are much as they were before the Revolution, and Gadsden, Timothy, and other Sons of Liberty must have visited in some of them. (27)

SANTEE. *Hopsewee Plantation*, 12.5 miles south of Georgetown on US 17, was the birthplace of Thomas Lynch, Jr. Open to the public by appointment. (S)

Vermont

BENNINGTON. *Colonial Tavern* site, Monument Avenue. Here Ethan Allen and the Green Mountain Boys planned their attack against Fort Ticonderoga. (29)

Virginia

ALEXANDRIA. In and around this city are many points of interest associated with George Washington and George Mason. The original survey and plan for Alexandria were made by Washington. (18, 28, 29)
Christ Church, Cameron and Columbus streets. Washington often attended services here. (29)
Friendship Fire Company, 107 South Alfred Street. When Washington went as a delegate to the First Continental Congress in Philadelphia in 1774, he bought a red hand pump for this fire-fighting company. A replica is on display here. (29)
Gadsby's Tavern, 128 North Royal Street. Here, at "The Sign of the Bunch of Grapes," George Washington in 1754 recruited the militiamen who made up his first military command. (18)
Gunston Hall, fifteen miles south of Alexandria on Virginia 342, is a house built by George Mason in 1755-58. It has been restored, together with its gardens. (28)
Marlborough site, near Alexandria, was the home of George Mason's uncle. Here Mason went to study law and to borrow books. (28)
Mount Vernon, seven miles south of Alexandria on the Mount Vernon Memorial Highway. In 1752 George Washington became owner of this estate by inheritance. It remained his home until he died, in 1799. He and his wife, Martha, are buried here. (18, 29)
Pohick Church, 12 miles south on US 1. The parish church of Mount Vernon and of George Mason's Gunston Hall. Mason was a vestryman when the church was built, and Washington served here as a vestryman for 37 years. (28, 29)
Washington's Grist Mill, on Virginia 235, three miles west of Mount Vernon. Here is a restoration of a mill, blacksmith shop, distillery, and cooper shop which were active when Washington ran Mount Vernon. (29)

BACON'S CASTLE. In the town of Bacon's Castle is a dwelling by that name, privately owned and not open to the public, which was seized by some of Bacon's followers in 1676 and used as a stronghold. (9)

BROOKNEAL. *Red Hill Shrine*, five miles from Brookneal, 18 miles from Charlotte County Court House, is the last home and burial place of Patrick Henry. (22)

CHARLES CITY. *Berkeley*, seven miles west of Charles City, off Virginia 5, was the home of Benjamin Harrison. (S)

CHARLOTTESVILLE. *Ash Lawn*, five miles southeast of Charlottesville on Virginia 53. Thomas Jefferson designed the house on this estate for his friend James Monroe. (32)
Mitchie Tavern, two miles southeast of Charlottesville on Virginia 53, on the road to Monticello. Here Patrick Henry spent his boyhood, before the building became a tavern. The house

was built by his father. Jefferson often visited this tavern. (22, 32)

Monticello, three miles southeast of Charlottesville on Virginia 53. Jefferson designed this beautiful building, which was his home for much of his adult life. Construction began in 1770. In it he installed many of his own ingenious inventions. His tomb is on the grounds. (32)

University of Virginia, in west end of the city. Thomas Jefferson, who wished to be remembered as "The Father of the University," designed a number of the buildings. (32)

FREDERICKSBURG. *Ferry Farm*. Near here on the Rappahannock River George Washington spent his childhood, and he inherited half this farm when his father died. Not open to the public. (18)

George Washington Birthplace National Monument, 38 miles east of Fredericksburg on Virginia 3. (18, 29)

Hugh Mercer Apothecary Shop, Caroline and Amelia streets. Washington used a small room in this building as an office when he visited Fredericksburg. Dr. Mercer, who operated the shop, became a brigadier general on Washington's staff. (29)

Kenmore, on Washington Street. George Washington often visited here, the home of his sister. (18, 29)

Mary Washington House, Charles and Lewis streets. In 1772 Washington bought this house for his mother. (29)

Rising Sun Tavern, 1306 Caroline Street. Southern patriots, on their way to attend meetings of the Continental Congress, often stopped here. The tavern was built by Charles Washington, the youngest brother of George. (18, 29)

GLENNS. Nearby is the site of *Poplar Spring Church*. After Bacon died, his followers pretended to bury him here in the churchyard. What they buried was a casket full of rocks. Where Bacon is actually buried is not known. (9)

GREEN SPRING. Three and a half miles north of Jamestown on Virginia 31, only foundations remain of a manor house and outbuildings owned by Governor Berkeley. Clearly visible from the road are walls of the jail in which Berkeley kept prisoners who had been prominent in Bacon's Rebellion. Berkeley had them executed. (9)

HANOVER and HANOVER COUNTY are Patrick Henry territory. A marker, 1.5 miles south of Hanover, indicates his birthplace. He was married at Rural Plains, three miles from his birthplace, at the age of 19. He pleaded the Parson's Cause in Hanover Court House (built about 1733). Nearby, at Ashland, was his home Scotchtown. (22)

JAMESTOWN. The site of the original 17th century settlement is part of Colonial National Historical Park, where extensive archeological excavation is carried on by the National Park Service and the Association for the Preservation of Virginia Antiquities. At Jamestown Festival Park, adjacent to the historical park, early Jamestown is re-created, together with full-size reproductions of the ships *Susan Constant*, *Godspeed*, and *Discovery*, in which the first English colonists arrived in 1607. Glassblowers, some from Poland, were among the early settlers in Jamestown. The entire glassblowing operation has been re-created and is conducted just as it was in the 17th century. Archeologists have discovered the foundations of the ·First State House. The Third State House was the one in which Nathaniel Bacon served as a member of the Council of State, then as a burgess. He and his followers burned the building. The Old Church Tower survives from the original Jamestown. The first representative assembly of Europeans in North America was held here. (2, 9)

LOUISA. At Roundabout Plantation, eight miles

southwest of here, Patrick Henry lived from 1765 to 1768. (22)

MECHANICSVILLE. At Newcastle, 11.8 miles northeast of Mechanicsville, Patrick Henry on May 2, 1775, put himself at the head of the Hanover volunteers and marched against Lord Dunmore, the royal governor of Virginia, who had seized the colony's power. (22)

MERCHANT'S HOPE. Near here Nathaniel Bacon was made leader of the rebellion which has been given his name. (9)

MONTROSS. *Old Westmoreland Courthouse*, on Virginia 3. Here Richard Henry Lee, at a public meeting in June 1774, introduced resolutions offering aid to Boston after the port had been closed. (S)

OCCONEECHEE STATE PARK. Near Clarksville, close to the intersection of US 13 and US 58. Occoneechee Island in the Roanoke River was the home of Occoneechi Indians who gave Bacon help in a campaign against Susquehanna Indians. Later he and his followers massacred the Occoneechi when they did not give him supplies he requested. (9)

RICHMOND. *Capitol*. Jefferson helped design this building. In the rotunda is a statue of George Washington by Houdon, the only one of him that was done from life. (29, 32)

St. John's Episcopal Church. East Broad Street between 24th and 25th streets. In this building, Patrick Henry delivered his famous speech which ended, "Give me liberty or give me death." Thomas Jefferson was in attendance, as were other signers: Benjamin Harrison, Carter Braxton, Richard Henry Lee, Thomas Nelson, Jr., and George Wythe. Wythe is buried in the churchyard. (22, 32, S)

Tuckahoe, seven miles west of Richmond on Virginia 650. Thomas Jefferson lived here much of the time until he was nine years old. He went to school in a red brick schoolhouse on the grounds. (Private) (32)

STAFFORD. *Peyton's Ordinary*, 1.8 miles north of Stafford. On several occasions George Washington stayed in this tavern. (29)

TEMPLEMAN. *Grave of Richard Henry Lee*, 8.8 miles southeast of Templeman on Virginia 3, then 1.5 miles north to Lee burying ground. (S)

WESTMORELAND COUNTY. *Stratford Hall*, 40 miles east of Fredericksburg, off Virginia 3. This elegant colonial mansion was the birthplace of both Richard Henry Lee and Francis Lightfoot Lee. The place is actually a working plantation, where visitors can see what 18th century life was like. (S)

WHITE POST. *Greenway Court*, one mile south of White Post on Virginia 277, was the home of a member of the Fairfax family, for whom George Washington worked as a surveyor. (18)

WILLIAMSBURG. Nathaniel Bacon had his headquarters here and proclaimed Governor William Berkeley and several of the governor's supporters to be traitors. (9) Colonial Williamsburg is an area of the old Virginia capital that has been restored to resemble as nearly as possible the 18th century town. A great many of the buildings are associated in one way or another with signers, and various guidebooks are available which detail the historic association of all the structures. Of special interest are:

The Apothecary Shop. George Mason, who suffered from gout, bought medicines here. Patrick Henry traded here, and researchers have found a bill he owed this shop, which he never paid. (22, 28)

The Capitol has been reconstructed according to the original design. Several of the signers sat in the legislature, as did George Washington. Here on May 20, 1765, Patrick Henry spoke against the Stamp Act and introduced resolves that were of great importance in steering the colonies toward independence. George Mason served in the House of Burgesses that met here in 1760, and on May 15, 1776, he offered a Declaration of Rights which greatly influenced

all the colonies and became the basis for the first ten amendments to the Constitution of the United States. Jefferson practiced law in the General Court in the building, and later served as a legislator and as governor. While he was governor, his statute for religious freedom was introduced in the Assembly. (22, 28, 29, 32, S)

College of William and Mary. George Wythe studied and later taught law here. Thomas Jefferson, Benjamin Harrison, and Carter Braxton were also students here. Jefferson enrolled in the college when he was 16 and studied here for two years. (32, S)

The Governor's Palace, north end of Palace Green. Jefferson and Washington often attended social events here. Patrick Henry lived here after he became governor, in 1776. (22, 29, 32)

Peyton Randolph House, Nicholson Street. Here Randolph read aloud to a distinguished gathering Jefferson's *A Summary View of the Rights of British America*. (32)

Raleigh Tavern. Here the Virginia Assembly met on May 27, 1774, under the leadership of Patrick Henry, after the governor had dissolved that body. Later George Washington read to the assembled burgesses the Nonimportation Resolutions that had been drafted by his friend George Mason. (22, 28, 29, 32)

Wythe House, home of signer George Wythe, west side of Palace Green. Jefferson and Washington often visited here. (29, 32)

YORKTOWN. *Nelson House*, also called York Hall, was built by the father and grandfather of Thomas Nelson, Jr., and he lived there when he was young. Now part of Colonial National Historical Park. (S)

Wisconsin

GREEN BAY. When the fort here was the only remaining British fort west of Detroit, the commander, acting on orders, abandoned the place during the war led by Pontiac. (20)

❧ Bibliography

GENERAL READINGS and Readings Related to Features and to Signers

ALLAN, HERBERT S. *John Hancock, Patriot in Purple.* New York: Beechhurst Press, 1953.

ANDREWS, CHARLES M. *The Colonial Period of American History.* Yale University Press, 1936.

———, ed. *Narratives of the Insurrections, 1675–1690.* C. Scribner's Sons, 1915.

APTHEKER, HERBERT. *American Negro Slave Revolts.* Columbia University Press, 1943.

———. *The American Revolution: 1763–1783.* International Publishers, 1960.

———. *The Colonial Era.* International Publishers, 1959.

BAILYN, BERNARD. *The Ideological Origins of the American Revolution.* Belknap Press of Harvard University Press, 1967.

———. *New England Merchants in the Seventeenth Century.* Harper & Row, 1964.

BENSON, MARY S. *Women in Eighteenth Century America.* Columbia University Press, 1935.

BILLINGTON, RAY ALLEN. *Westward Expansion; A History of the American Frontier.* Macmillan, 1967 (1960).

BOLTON, HERBERT E. *Spanish Borderlands.* Yale University Press, 1921.

——— and MARSHALL, THOMAS M. *The Colonization of America.* Macmillan, 1920.

BRADSTREET, ANNE. *The Tenth Muse* (fascsimile reproduction with an introduction by Josephine K. Piercy). Gainesville, Fla.: Scholars' Facsimiles and Reprints, 1965 (1650).

BRIDENBAUGH, CARL. *Cities in Revolt: 1743–1776.* Knopf, 1955.

———. *Cities in the Wilderness: 1625–1742.* Knopf, 1955

———. *The Colonial Craftsman.* Knopf, 1955.

BROWN, WELDON A. *Empire or Independence: A Study in the Failure of Reconciliation, 1774–1783.* Port Washington, N.Y.: Kennikat Press, 1966 (1941).

BURNETT, EDMOND C. *The Continental Congress.* Macmillan, 1941.

COOK, GEORGE ALLEN. *John Wise: Early American Democrat.* New York: Kings Crown Press, 1952.

CRAVEN, WESLEY FRANK. *The Colonies in Transition: 1660–1713.* Harper & Row, 1968.

DAVIDSON, PHILIP. *Propaganda and the American Revolution.* University of North Carolina Press, 1941.

DEXTER, ELISABETH ANTHONY. *Colonial Women of Affairs: A Study of Women in Business and the Professions in America Before 1776.* Houghton Mifflin Co., 1924.

DODD, WILLIAM E. *The Old South: Struggles for Democracy.* Macmillan, 1937.

ERIKSON, KAI T. *Wayward Puritans: A Study in the Sociology of Deviance.* John Wiley, 1966.

FAULKNER, HAROLD UNDERWOOD. *American Economic History.* Harper & Bros., 1954.

FEDERAL WRITERS PROJECT. *Arizona. California. Connecticut. Delaware. Florida. Georgia. Massachusetts. New Jersey. New Mexico. New York. North Carolina. Pennsylvania. Rhode Island. South Carolina. Virginia.* American Guide Series. Works Progress Administration.

FERRIS, ROBERT G., ed. *Signers of the Declaration: Historic Places Commemorating the Signing of the Declaration of Independence.* Natl. Park Service, 1973.

GREENE, EVARTS BOUTELL. *The Revolutionary Generation: 1763–1790.* Macmillan, 1943.

HARRIS, JOHN. *Boston Tea Party: Trigger of Our Revolution.* Boston Globe, 1974.

HARRIS, M. A. *Negro History Tour of Manhattan by Uncle Spike.* New York: Negro History Associates, Inc., 1967.

HAWKE, DAVID FREEMAN. *Benjamin Rush: Revolutionary Gadfly.* Bobbs-Merrill, 1971.

JOHNSON, ALLEN, ed. *Dictionary of American Biography.* Charles Scribner's Sons, 1927–1964.

JONES, RUFUS M. *Quakers in the American Colonies.* W. W. Norton, 1966 (1911).

LABAREE, BENJAMIN WOODS. *The Boston Tea Party.* Oxford University Press, 1964.

LOVEJOY, DAVID S. *The Glorious Revolution in America.* Harper & Row, 1972.

MAIER, PAULINE. *From Resistance to Revolution.* Knopf. 1972.

MALONE, DUMAS. *The Story of the Declaration of Independence.* Oxford University Press, 1954.

MARK, IRVING. *Agrarian Conflicts in Colonial New York, 1711–1775.* Columbia University Press, 1940.

McGEE, DOROTHY HORTON. *Famous Signers of the Declaration of Independence.* Dodd, Mead & Co., 1955.

McLOUGHLIN, WILLIAM G. *New England Dissent, 1630–1833: The Baptists and the Separation of Church and State.* Harvard University Press, 1971.

McMANUS, EDGAR. *A History of Negro Slavery in New York.* Syracuse University Press, 1966.

MENKEN, H. L. *The American Language: An Inquiry into the Development of English in the United States.* 4th ed. Knopf, 1936. Also Supplement I, 1952.

MILLER, HELEN HILL. *The Case for Liberty.* University of North Carolina Press, 1965.

MILLER, JOHN C. *Origins of the American Revolution.* Little, Brown & Co., 1943.

MILLER, P. G. *The New England Mind: From Colony to Province.* Beacon Press, 1968 (1953).

MILLIS, WALTER. *Arms and Men: A Study in American Military History.* Putnam, 1956.

MOTT, FRANK L. *American Journalism, A History of Newspapers in the United States through 260 Years—1690–1950.* Macmillan, 1941.

NOEL HUME, IVOR. *Historical Archaeology.* Knopf, 1969.

———. *Guide to Artifacts of Colonial America.* Knopf, 1970.

OSGOOD, HERBERT L. *The American Colonies in the Eighteenth Century.* Columbia University Press, 1924.

———. *The American Colonies in the Seventeenth Century.* Gloucester, Mass.: P. Smith, 1957.

OSWALD, JOHN CLYDE. *Printing in the Americas.* Gregg Publishing Co., 1937.

PARRINGTON, VERNON LOUIS. *The Colonial Mind: 1620–1800.* Harcourt Brace, 1927.

PECKHAM, HOWARD, and GIBSON, CHARLES, eds. *Attitudes of the Colonial Powers toward the American Indian.* University of Utah Press, 1969.

SANDERSON, JOHN. *Biography of the Signers of the Declaration of Independence.* Philadelphia: W. Brown and C. Peters, 1828.

SARLES, FRANK B., JR., and SHEDD, CHARLES E. *Colonials and Patriots: Historic Places Commemorating Our Forebears: 1700–1783.* Natl. Park Service, 1964.

SCHLESINGER, ARTHUR MEIER. *The Colonial Merchants and the American Revolution, 1763–1776.* New York: F. Ungar Publishing Co., 1964 (1957).

SCOTT, KENNETH. "The Slave Insurrections in New York in 1712." *New York Historical Quarterly,* vol. XLV, 1961.

SMITH, WHITNEY. *The Flag Book of the United States.* William Morrow, 1970.

STOKES, I. N. PHELPS. *The Iconography of Manhattan Island, 1498–1909.* New York: Robert H. Dodd, 1916.

THOMAS, ISAIAH. *The History of Printing in America.* Worcester, Mass.: I. Thomas, 1810.

U.S. DEPT. OF THE INTERIOR. *The National Register of Historic Places.* Natl. Park Service, 1969.

VER STEEG, CLARENCE, and HOFSTADTER, RICHARD, eds. *Great Issues in American History: From Settlement to Revolution, 1564–1776.* Random House, 1969 (1958).

WILLISON, GEORGE F. *Behold Virginia: The Fifth Crown.* Harcourt Brace, 1952.

WINSLOW, O. E. *Meetinghouse Hill: 1630–1783.* Macmillan, 1952.

WINSOR, JUSTIN. *Memorial History of Boston.* James R. Osgood, 1881–1883.

WISE, JOHN. *Churches Quarrel Espoused.* Boston: John Boyles, 1772.

———. *A Vindication of the Government of New England Churches.* 4th ed. Boston: Congregational Board of Publications, 1860.

INTRODUCTION

GIBSON, CHARLES. *Spain in America.* Harper & Row, 1966.
ROCHE, O. I. A. *The Days of the Upright: A History of the Huguenots.* Clarkson N. Potter, 1965.
SMITH, PRESERVED. *The Age of the Reformation.* Henry Holt & Co., 1920.
TAWNEY, R. H. *Religion and the Rise of Capitalism.* Harcourt Brace, 1926.

CHAPTER 1

BENNETT, CHARLES E., compiler. *Settlement of Florida.* University of Florida Press, 1968.
LORANT, STEFAN. *The New World: The First Pictures of America.* Duell, Sloan & Pearce, 1965.
MANUCY, ALBERT C. *Historic Site Survey: Fort Caroline, Florida.* National Park Service (mimeographed), 1940.
PARKMAN, FRANCIS. *Pioneers of France in the New World.* Little, Brown & Co., 1902.
PAYNE, EDWARD JOHN, ed. *Voyages of Hawkins, Frobisher and Drake.* Oxford University Press, 1916.

CHAPTER 2

COTTER, JOHN L. and HUDSON, J. PAUL. *New Discoveries at Jamestown, Site of the First Successful English Settlement in America.* National Park Service, 1957.
HATCH, CHARLES E., JR. *America's Oldest Legislative Assembly and Its Jamestown Statehouses.* National Park Service, 1956.
———. *Jamestown, Virginia, the Townsite and Its Story.* National Park Service and the Assn. for the Preservation of Virginia Antiquities, 1957.

CHAPTER 3

BRADFORD, WILLIAM. *Of Plymouth Plantation, the Pilgrims in America.* Edited with an introduction by Harvey Wish. Capricorn Books, 1962.
BREWSTER, DOROTHY. *William Brewster of the Mayflower: Portrait of a Pilgrim.* New York University Press, 1970.
DEETZ, JAMES. "The Reality of the Pilgrim Fathers." *Natural History,* November 1969.
HARRIS, JAMES RENDEL and JONES, STEPHEN K. *The Pilgrim Press.* Cambridge, England: Heffer, 1922.
WILLISON, GEORGE F. *Saints and Strangers.* Reynal & Hitchcock, 1945.

CHAPTER 4

CHUPACK, HENRY. *Roger Williams.* Twayne Publishers, 1969.
COVEY, CYCLONE. *The Gentle Radical, a Biography of Roger Williams.* Macmillan, 1966.
ERNST, JAMES E. *Roger Williams: New England Firebrand.* Macmillan, 1932.
GARRETT, JOHN. *Roger Williams: Witness Beyond Christendom, 1603–1683.* Macmillan.
MORGAN, EDMUND S. *Roger Williams: The Church and the State.* Harcourt Brace, 1967.
WILLIAMS, ROGER. *The Complete Writings of Roger Williams.* Russell & Russell, 1963.
WINSLOW, OLA ELIZABETH. *Master Roger Williams, a Biography.* Macmillan, 1957.

CHAPTER 5

ADAMS, CHARLES FRANCIS. *Three Episodes of Massachusetts History.* Houghton Mifflin, 1892.
AUGUR, HELEN. *An American Jezebel: The Life of Anne Hutchinson.* Brentano's, 1930.
BATTIS, EMERY. *Saints and Sectaries: Anne Hutchinson and the Antinomian Controversy in the Massachusetts Bay Colony.* University of North Carolina Press, 1962.
BOLTON, REGINALD PELHAM. *A Woman Misunderstood: Anne Hutchinson, Wife of William Hutchinson.* New York: Privately printed, 1931.
HALL, DAVID D., ed. *The Antinomian Controversy, 1636–1638, A Documentary History.* Wesleyan University Press, 1968.
HUFELAND, OTTO. "Anne Hutchinson's Refuge in the Wilderness." *Publications of the Westchester Country Historical Society,* vol. VII. White Plains, 1929.

CHAPTER 6

BIRMINGHAM, STEPHEN. *The Grandees: America's Sephardic Elite.* Herford & Rowe, 1971.
FONER, PHILIP S. *The Jews in American History.* International Publishers, 1945.
FRIEDMAN, LEE M. *Early American Jews.* Harvard University Press, 1934.
MARCUS, JACOB R. *The Colonial American Jew: 1492–1776.* Wayne State University Press, 1970.
SCHAPPES, MORRIS U., ed. *A Documentary History of the Jews in the United States: 1654–1875.* Citadel Press, 1950.

CHAPTER 7

BRAILSFORD, MABEL RICHMOND. *Quaker Women, 1650–1690.* London: Duckworth & Co., 1915.
JONES, RUFUS M. *The Quakers in the American Colonies.* W. W. Norton, 1966 (1911).
See also references for Chapter 5.

CHAPTER 8

ABBOTT, JOHN S. C. *King Philip.* Harper & Bros., 1885 (1857).
CHURCH, BENJAMIN. *The History of Philip's War.* Edited by Thomas Church. Exeter, N. H.: J. & B. Williams, 1837.
ELLIS, GEORGE W., and MORRIS, JOHN E. *King Philip's War.* New York: Grafton Press, 1906.
FOLSOM, FRANKLIN. *Red Power on the Rio Grande: The Native American Revolution of 1680.* Follett, 1973 (juvenile).
FORBES, ALLAN, comp. *Some Indian Events of New England.* Boston: State Street Trust Company, 1934.
HUBBARD, REV. WILLIAM. *The History of the Indian Wars in New England.* Edited by Samuel G. Drake. New York: Burt Franklin, 1971 (1865).
JOSEPHY, ALVIN M., JR. *The Patriot Chiefs.* Viking Press, 1961.
LEACH, DOUGLAS EDWARD. *Flintlock and Tomahawk: New England in King Philip's War.* W. W. Norton & Co., 1958.
———. *The Northern Colonial Frontier 1607–1763.* Holt, Rinehart & Winston, 1966.
LINCOLN, CHARLES H., ed. *Narratives of the Indian Wars.* Charles Scribner's Sons, 1913.
SYLVESTER, HERBERT MILTON. *Indian Wars of New England.* Boston: W. B. Clarke Co., 1910.

CHAPTER 9

HUDSON, J. PAUL. *This Was Green Spring.* The Jamestown Foundation, n.d.
MIDDLEKAUF, ROBERT, ed. *Bacon's Rebellion.* Rand McNally & Co., 1964.
WASHBURN, WILCOMB EDWARD. *The Governor and the Rebel: A History of Bacon's Rebellion in Virginia.* University of North Carolina Press, 1957.
WERTENBAKER, THOMAS J. *Bacon's Rebellion.* The Virginia 350th Anniversary Celebration Corp., 1957.
———. *Torchbearer of Revolution: The Story of Bacon's Rebellion and Its Leader.* Princeton University Press, 1940.

CHAPTER 10

COMFORT, WILLIAM WISTAR. *William Penn: 1644–1718: A Tercentenary Estimate.* University of Pennsylvania Press, 1944.
DAVIDSON, MARSHALL B. "Penn's City: American Athens." *American Heritage,* vol. XII, no. 2, 1961.
JANNEY, SAMUEL M. *The Life of William Penn: With Selections from his Correspondence and Auto-Biography.* Hogan, Perkins & Co., 1852.
JONES, RUFUS. *The Quakers in the American Colonies.* W. W. Norton, 1966 (1911).
TOLLES, FREDERICK B. *Meeting House and Counting House: The Quaker Merchants of Colonial Philadelphia 1682–1783.* W. W. Norton, 1948.
WOOD, RICHARD R. *William Penn: A Twentieth Century Perspective.* Philadelphia Yearly Meeting of the Religious Society of Friends, n.d.

CHAPTER 11

REICH, JEROME R. *Leisler's Rebellion: A Study of Democracy in New York, 1664–1720.* University of Chicago Press, 1953.

CHAPTER 12

McANEAR, BEVERLY, ed. "Mariland's Grevances Why The Have Taken Op Arms." *Journal of Southern History,* vol. VIII, 1942.
McMAHON, JOHN V. L. *An Historical View of the Government of Maryland from Its Colonization to the Present Day.* Baltimore: P. Lucas, Jr., Cushing & Sons, and William and Joseph Neal, 1831.
STEINER, B. C. "The Protestant Revolt in Maryland." *The American Historical Association Annual Report,* 1897.

CHAPTER 13

See Andrews, Charles M.; Craven, Wesley Frank; and Dodd, William E.; in General Readings.

CHAPTER 14

BURR, GEORGE LINCOLN, ed. *Narratives of the Witchcraft Cases, 1648–1706.* Charles Scribner's Sons, 1914.
CALEF, ROBERT. *More Wonders of the Invisible World.* London: N. Hillar & J. Collyer, 1700.
EHRENREICH, BARBARA, and ENGLISH, DEIDRE. *Witches, Midwifes and Nurses, a*

History of Women and Healers. Oyster Bay, N.Y.: Glass Mountain Pamphlets, n.d.

HANSEN, CHADWICK. *Witchcraft at Salem.* George Braziller, 1969.

KITTRIDGE, GEORGE LIMAN. *Witchcraft in Old and New England.* Harvard University Press, 1929.

LEVIN, DAVID. *What Happened in Salem.* Harcourt Brace, 1960.

MATHER, COTTON. *Memorable Providences, Relating to Witchcrafts and Possession.* 1689 (reprinted in Burr, *op. cit.*).

——. *Wonders of the Invisible World.* Boston: Benjamin Harris, 1693.

MATHER, INCREASE. *An Essay for the Recording for the Illustrious Providences* (also called Remarkable Providences). 1684.

MIDDLEKAUFF, ROBERT. *The Mathers.* Oxford University Press, 1971.

NEVINS, WINFIELD S. *Witchcraft in Salem Village in 1692.* Boston: Lee & Shepard, 1892.

PETRY, ANN. *Tituba of Salem Village.* Crowell, 1964 (juvenile).

STARKEY, MARION L. *The Devil in Massachusetts.* Knopf, 1950.

UPHAM, CHARLES W. *Salem Witchcraft; with an Account of Salem Village and a History of Opinions on Witchcraft and Kindred Subjects.* Wiggin and Lunt, 1867 (reprinted 1959 by Frederick Ungar).

Note: The Writers Project of the Works Progress Administration prepared numerous volumes of transcripts of the original documents relating to the Salem witchcraft trials. All these are in the Essex Institute, in Salem.

CHAPTER 15

FRANKLIN, BENJAMIN. *The Autobiography of Benjamin Franklin.* Simon & Schuster, 1955.

MIDDLEKAUFF, ROBERT. *The Mathers.* Oxford University Press, 1971.

VAN DOREN, CARL. *Benjamin Franklin.* Viking Press, 1938.

CHAPTER 16

BONOMI, PATRICIA U. *A Factious People: Politics and Society in Colonial New York.* Columbia University Press, 1971.

BURANELLI, VINCENT. *The Trial of Peter Zenger.* New York University Press, 1957.

EASTERN NATIONAL PARK AND MONUMENT ASSOCIATION. *The Story of Peter Zenger: Defender of Freedom of the Press.* New York City National Park Service Group, National Park Service, 1965.

FRANKO, DR. ALFRED M. *The Place of Mount Vernon's Village Green and St. Paul's Church in American History.* City of Mount Vernon, New York, n.d.

KATZ, STANLEY N. *Introduction to James Alexander's Brief Narrative of the Case and Trial of John Peter Zenger.*

——. *Newcastle's New York: Anglo-American Politics, 1732–1753.* Belknap Press of Harvard University Press, 1968.

LEVY, LEONARD W. *Legacy of Suppression: Freedom of Speech and Press in Early American History.* Belknap Press of Harvard University Press, 1960.

CHAPTER 17

BLACKBURN, JOYCE. *James Edward Oglethorpe.* Lippincott, 1970 (juvenile).

BRUCE, HENRY. *Life of General Oglethorpe.* Dodd, Mead & Co. 1890.

DONNAN, ELIZABETH, ed. *Documents Illustrative of the History of the Slave Trade to America.* Carnegie Institution, 1930–1935.

ETTINGER, AMOS ASCHBACK. *James Edward Oglethorpe, Imperial Idealist.* Clarendon Press, 1936.

Georgia Historical Quarterly, various issues.

HARRIS, THADDEUS MASON. *Biographical Memorials of James Oglethorpe, Founder of the Colony of Georgia in North America.* Boston: Privately printed, 1841.

HÜHNER, LEON. *The Jews of Georgia in Colonial Times.* New York: Gertz Bros., 1902.

REESE, TREVOR R. *Frederica: Colonial Fort and Town.* St. Simons Island, Ga.: Fort Frederica Assn. in cooperation with Fort Frederica National Monument, National Park Service, 1969.

TAILFER et al. *A True and Historical Narrative of the Colony of Georgia.* With comments by the Earl of Egmont. Edited by Clarence Ver Steeg. University of Georgia Press, 1960 (1741).

VAETTI, J. GORDON. *The Man Who Founded Georgia.* Crowell-Collier Press, 1968 (juvenile).

URLSPERGER, SAMUEL, ed. *Detailed Reports on the Salzburger Emigrants who Settled in America.* Edited by George F. Jones. University of Georgia Press, 1968.

WRIGHT, ROBERT. *A Memoir of General James Oglethorpe.* London: Chapman & Hall, 1867.

CHAPTER 18

ABERNATHY, THOMAS P. *Western Lands and the American Revolution.* Appleton-Century, 1937.

AMBLER, CHARLES H. *George Washington and the West.* University of North Carolina Press, 1936.

BILLINGTON, RAY ALLEN. *America's Frontier Heritage.* Holt, Rinehart & Winston, 1966.

——. *Westward Expansion, A History of the American Frontier.* Third ed. Macmillan, 1967.

EVERY, DALE VAN. *Forth to the Wilderness, the First American Frontier.* Morrow, 1961.

FLEXNER, JAMES THOMAS. *George Washington, the Forge of Experience (1732–1775).* Little, Brown & Co., 1965.

NETTELS, CURTIS P. *George Washington and American Independence.* Little, Brown & Co., 1951.

STETSON, CHARLES W. *Washington and His Neighbors.* Richmond, Va.: Garrett and Massie, 1956.

TILBERG, FREDERICK. *Fort Necessity National Battlefield Site, Pennsylvania.* National Park Service, 1961 (1954).

WASHINGTON, GEORGE. *Journal.* Boston: Old South (Church) Leaflets, 1754.

WILSON, WOODROW. *George Washington.* Harper & Bros., 1896.

CHAPTER 19

DICKERSON, OLIVER M. *The Navigation Acts and the American Revolution.* University of Pennsylvania Press, 1951.

FRITZ, JEAN. *Cast for a Revolution: Some American Friends and Enemies, 1728–1814.* Houghton Mifflin, 1972.

MILLER, HELEN HILL. *The Case for Liberty.* University of North Carolina Press, 1965.

MORRIS, RICHARD B. "Then and There the Child Independence was Born." *American Heritage,* vol. XIII, no. 2, February 1962.

TUDOR, WILLIAM. *The Life of James Otis of Massachusetts.* Boston: Wells and Lilly, 1823.

CHAPTER 20

HODGE, FREDERICK WEBB, ed. *Handbook of American Indians North of Mexico.* Smithsonian Institution, Bureau of American Ethnology, 1912.

JOSEPHY, ALVIN M., JR. *The Patriot Chiefs: A Chronicle of American Indian Leadership.* Viking Press, 1961.

PARKMAN, FRANCIS. *The Conspiracy of Pontiac and the Indian War After the Conquest of Canada.* Little, Brown & Co., 1901.

PECKHAM, HOWARD H. *Pontiac and the Indian Uprising.* Princeton University Press, 1947.

CHAPTER 21

BANCROFT, HUBERT HOWE. *History of California.* San Francisco: History Co., 1914–19.

BOLTON, HERBERT EUGENE, ed. *Historical Memoirs of New California by Fray Francisco Palou, O.F.M.* Russell & Russell, 1966.

——. *Anza's California Expeditions.* University of California Press, 1930.

CAUGHEY, JOHN WALTON. *California.* Prentice-Hall, 1953.

CHAPMAN, CHARLES E. *A History of California: The Spanish Period.* Macmillan, 1928.

ENGELHARDT, ZEPHYRIN, O.F.M. *Missions and Missionaries of California.* San Francisco: James H. Barry Co., 1908–1915.

GEIGER, MAYNARD J. *The Life and Times of Fray Junípero Serra, O.F.M.* Washington, D.C.: Academy of American Franciscan History, 1959.

JAYME, LUIS. *Letter of Luís Jayme, O.F.M.* Los Angeles: Davison Bookshop, 1970.

KING, KENNETH M. *Mission to Paradise: The Story of Junípero Serra and the Missions of California.* London: Burns and Oates, 1956.

KENNEALLY, FINBAR, O.F.M., ed. *Writings of Fermin Francisco de Lasuen.* Washington, D.C.: Academy of American Franciscan History, 1965.

POURADE, RICHARD F. *Anza Conquers the Desert: The Anza Expeditions from Mexico to California and the Founding of San Francisco, 1774–1776.* San Diego: The Copley Press, 1971.

TIBESAR, ANTONNE. *Writings of Junípero Serra.* Washington, D.C.: Academy of American Franciscan History, 1955.

WEBB, EDITH BUCKLAND. *Indian Life at the Old Missions.* Los Angeles: Walter F. Lewis, 1952.

CHAPTER 22

DODD, WILLIAM E. "Virginia Takes the Road to Revolution," in *The Spirit of '76 and Other Essays,* by Carl Becker, J. M. Clarke, William E. Dodd. New York: Augustus M. Kelley, 1966 (1927).

MAYO, BERNARD. *Myths and Men, Patrick Henry, George Washington, Thomas Jefferson.* University of Georgia Press, 1959.

MEADE, ROBERT DOUTHAT. *Patrick Henry, Patriot in the Making.* Lippincott, 1957.

MORGAN, GEORGE. *Patrick Henry.* Lippincott, 1929.

TYLER, MOSES COIT. *Patrick Henry.* Houghton Mifflin, 1887.

CHAPTER 23

BOWEN, CATHERINE D. *John Adams and the American Revolution.* Little, Brown & Co., 1950.

BUTTERFIELD, E. H., ed. *The Adams Papers: Diary and Autobiography of John Adams.* Belknap Press of Harvard University Press, 1961.

223

CHAPTER 24

BIGELOW, FRANCIS HILL. *Historic Silver of the Colonies and its Makers.* Macmillan, 1917.

FORBES, ESTHER. *Paul Revere and the World He Lived In.* Houghton Mifflin, 1942.

GOSS, ELBRIDGE H. *The Life of Colonel Paul Revere.* Boston: J. D. Cripples, 1891.

CHAPTER 25

HANLEY, THOMAS O'BRIEN. *Charles Carroll of Carrollton.* Catholic University of American Press, 1970.

ROWLAND, KATE MASON. *The Life of Charles Carroll of Carrollton, 1737–1832.* G. P. Putnam's Sons, 1899.

SMITH, ELLEN HART. *Charles Carroll of Carrollton.* Harvard University Press, 1942.

CHAPTER 26

HARLOW, RALPH VOLNEY. *Samuel Adams, Promoter of the American Revolution: A Study in Psychology and Politics.* Henry Holt & Co., 1923.

HOSMER, JAMES K. *Samuel Adams.* Houghton Mifflin, 1913.

MILLER, JOHN C. *Sam Adams, Pioneer in Propaganda.* Little, Brown & Co., 1936.

CHAPTER 27

COHEN, HENNIG. *The South Carolina Gazette, 1732–1775.* University of South Carolina Press, 1953.

CHAMPAGNE, ROGER JAMES. *The Sons of Liberty and the Aristocracy in New York Politics, 1765–1790.* Unpublished University of Wisconsin Ph.D. dissertation, 1960.

JOHNSON, JOSEPH. *Traditions and Reminiscences of the American Revolution, Chiefly in the South.* Charleston, S.C.: Walker & James, 1851.

McCRADY, EDWARD. *The History of South Carolina under Royal Government.* Macmillan, 1899.

The South Carolina Gazette, various issues, 1765–1776.

STEEDMAN, MARGUERITE. "Charlestown's Forgotten Tea Party." *The Georgia Review,* vol. XXI, no. 2, 1967.

WALSH, RICHARD. *Charleston's Sons of Liberty: A Study of the Artisans, 1763–1789.* University of South Carolina Press, 1959.

———. *The Writing of Christopher Gadsden: 1746–1805.* University of South Carolina Press, 1966.

CHAPTER 28

MILLER, HELEN HILL. *George Mason, Constitutionalist.* Gloucester, Mass.: P. Smith, 1966 (1938).

ROWLAND, KATE MASON. *Life of George Mason, 1725–1792.* G. P. Putnam's Sons, 1892.

RUTLAND, ROBERT A. *George Mason, Reluctant Statesman.* Colonial Williamsburg, Inc., 1961.

CHAPTER 29

FLEXNER, JAMES THOMAS. *George Washington and the American Revolution, (1775–1783).* Little, Brown & Co., 1968.

KETCHUM, RICHARD M., ed. *American Heritage Book of the Revolution.* American Heritage Publ. Co., 1958.

SHY, JOHN. "A New Look at Colonial Militia." *William and Mary Quarterly,* 3rd Ser., vol. XX, 1963.

WARD, CHRISTOPHER. *The War of the Revolution.* Macmillian, 1952.

CHAPTER 30

CLARK, HARRY HAYDEN. "Toward a Reinterpretation of Thomas Paine." *American Literature,* vol. V, 1933.

CONWAY, MONCURE DANIEL. *The Life of Thomas Paine.* G. P. Putnam's Sons, 1892.

DAVIDSON, PHILIP. *Propaganda and the American Revolution.* University of North Carolina Press, 1941.

FONER, PHILIP S., ed. *The Life and Major Writings of Thomas Paine.* Citadel Press, 1945.

PEARSON, HESKETH. *Tom Paine, Friend of Mankind.* Harper & Bros., 1937.

SMITH, FRANK. *Thomas Paine, Liberator.* Frederick A. Stokes Co., 1937.

CHAPTER 31

ALDRIDGE, ALFRED OWEN. *Benjamin Franklin: Philosopher and Man.* Lippincott, 1965.

BURNETT, EDMOND C. *The Continental Congress.* Macmillan, 1941.

JACOBS, WILBUR R. *The Paxton Riots and the Frontier Theory.* Rand McNally & Co., 1967.

LABAREE, LEONARD W., et al, eds. *The Papers of Benjamin Franklin.* Yale University Press, 1959.

VAN DOREN, CARL. *Benjamin Franklin.* Viking Press, 1938.

WROTH, LAWRENCE C. *The Colonial Printer.* University Press of Virginia, 1938.

CHAPTER 32

BECKER, CARL. *The Declaration of Independence.* Harcourt Brace, 1922.

BOYD, JULIAN P. *The Declaration of Independence.* Princeton University Press, 1945.

———. *The Papers of Thomas Jefferson,* vol. I, 1760–1776. Princeton University Press, 1950.

BRODIE, FAWN. *Thomas Jefferson.* Norton, 1974.

MALONE, DUMAS. *Jefferson the Virginian.* Little, Brown & Co., 1948.

MARTIN, EDWIN T. *Thomas Jefferson: Scientist.* Collier Books, 1961.

QUARLES, BENJAMIN. *The Negro in the American Revolution.* University of North Carolina Press, 1961.

RANDALL, HENRY S. *The Life of Thomas Jefferson.* Derby & Jackson, 1958.

Index

Acknowledgments

This book would not have been possible without the suggestions, advice, research, criticism, checking, and nudging of many people. To all I am grateful and to none should go blame for any flaws that have survived their efforts. I alone am responsible.

To Sylvia McNair, my editor at Rand McNally, I must give special thanks for suggesting that I do the book and for showing consistent sympathy and patience as I worked on it.

To Anna Idol, Rachel Oberlander, Todd Sanders, and Rita Stevens, all on the staff of Rand McNally, I am indebted more than I can say for their courteous, creative, and arduous labors that were often performed beyond the call of duty.

I also wish to acknowledge a wide variety of courtesies extended to me by the following:

Frederic S. Baum, New York County Lawyers' Association.

Jacqueline Bearden, St. Augustine Historical Society Library, Florida.

James V. Ciaramitaro, Fort Wayne Military Museum, Detroit.

Colonial Heritage, Bound Brook, N. J.

Hollis Cook, Tubac State Monument, Arizona.

Elsa Dixler, Vassar College.

Hugh De Samper, Colonial Williamsburg, Virginia.

Essex Institute Library, Salem, Mass.

Maynard Geiger, O. F. M., Santa Barbara Mission Library, Calif.

Paul A. Ghioto, Fort Caroline National Memorial, Florida.

Anthony P. Grech, The Association of the Bar of the City of New York.

Cissy Grossman, The Jewish Museum, New York.

Thompson R. Harlow, The Connecticut Historical Society.

Everett L. Hunt, Professor Emeritus, Swarthmore College.

Margaret Davis, Tate Library, Fort Frederica National Monument, Georgia.

Eleanor Mayer, Friends Historical Library of Swarthmore College.

Jon B. Montgomery, New York District, National Park Service.

L. Ross Morrell, State Archeologist, Florida.

People's Bicentennial Commission, Washington, D. C.

Prof. Bert Salwen, New York University.

South Carolina Historical Society.

Nancy Speers, Friends Historical Library, Swarthmore College.

To all the publications listed in the bibliography I am indebted in one way or another, and I feel obliged to note that I relied exclusively on H. L. Mencken's *The American Language* for information about words borrowed from other languages during the colonial period.